JavaScript® and jQuery®
for Data Analysis and Visualization

JavaScript® and jQuery® for Data Analysis and Visualization

Jon J. Raasch
Graham Murray
Vadim Ogievetsky
Joseph Lowery

wrox™
A Wiley Brand

JavaScript® and jQuery® for Data Analysis and Visualization

Published by
John Wiley & Sons, Inc.
10475 Crosspoint Boulevard
Indianapolis, IN 46256
www.wiley.com

To Ally and Kaiya. You brighten all my days.
—GRAHAM MURRAY

For Annie
—VADIM OGIEVETSKY

To Whic, Granger, Charisma, Surley, Two-Gun, FEM,
and especially Rafe. See you soon, guys.
—JOSEPH LOWERY

CREDITS

ABOUT THE AUTHORS

JON J. RAASCH is a freelance web developer specializing in web apps for desktop and mobile devices. A user-experience junkie, he builds HTML5 and JavaScript apps that focus on the users at every touch point.

Jon is the author of several John Wiley & Sons books, including *JavaScript Programming: Pushing the Limits*, *Smashing WebKit*, and *Smashing Mobile Web Development*. A perfectionist when it comes to best practices, you can find him building the modern web in his pajamas.

Follow Jon on Twitter @jonraasch and check out his website http:// jonraasch.com. He's currently based in Portland, OR.

GRAHAM MURRAY is a software architect specializing in building UI development tools. At present, he works at Infragistics, where he builds data visualization UI controls for desktop, web, and mobile. He is passionate about many programming languages, and he builds source-to-source compilers between them. As a kid, he found some BASIC code in the back of a magazine and hasn't stopped programming since.

VADIM OGIEVETSKY is a developer at Metamarkets, where he uses D3 on top of AngularJS to build interactive data-driven applications that scale. Prior to working at Metamarkets, Vadim was part of the Stanford Data Visualization group, where he contributed to Protovis and D3. Vadim is an avid promoter of D3 and web-based data visualization; he has guest lectured on D3 at UC Berkeley, Harvard, and Stanford as well as at other universities, meetups, and corporations.

JOSEPH LOWERY currently builds websites, creates online courses for Lynda.com and other sites, writes fiction, and hangs in Brooklyn. His books about the Web and web-building tools are international bestsellers, having sold more than 400,000 copies worldwide in nine different languages.

ACKNOWLEDGMENTS

I WOULD LIKE TO THANK his co-authors for all their work putting this book together. I'd also like to thank the editors and the rest of the team at Wiley for their support throughout the project. Also, thanks to Martin for the technical proofread.

—JON J. RAASCH

I CAN'T THANK MY WIFE Allison and daughter Kaiya enough for not getting too fed up with me as I was half present while working on this book. It hasn't been an easy time with all the random adversity that cropped up while I was writing. Thanks for always sticking by me and letting me steal a little time for this book, especially when time has been such a precious commodity. My parents, Chris and Tony, provided some very timely babysitting on many occasions, and ignited my love for computers in the first place by letting me use them so much. My in-laws, Diane and Alan were so gracious and put up with us for so long as we were displaced from our house twice while I was writing this book. Thanks to Ambrose Little for the great edits and suggestions, and for encouraging me to do this in the first place, Thanks also to Jason Beres and Bill Hazard for insisting I take this on when I was feeling trepidation. I'd like to thank Robert Elliott and everyone at Wiley. I'd like to give a special thanks to everyone editing the book, especially Charlotte and Nancy, for being so helpful and patient and for helping me turn my esoteric prose into something people might actually enjoy to read. My co-authors Jon, Vadim, and Joe provided some great advice on additional content to cover. Thanks everyone!

—GRAHAM MURRAY

I WOULD LIKE TO THANK Jeffrey Heer, Mike Bostock, and the Stanford Visualization Group for igniting my love of JavaScript and web technologies. Thank you also to my advisor, Terry Winograd, for steering me into the direction of SVG. Special thanks are also in order to Eric Tschetter, Ofir Oss, Sébastien Fragnaud, Young Kim, and Annie Albagli for reading my first drafts and to Charlotte Kughen, Ambrose Little, and the rest of the Wiley team for their editorial support.

—VADIM OGIEVETSKY

SPECIAL THANKS TO Bob Elliott and all the great folks at Wiley for giving me an opportunity to contribute to this book.

—JOSEPH LOWERY

CONTENTS

INTRODUCTION

WHEN IT COMES TO THE WEB, you may have heard the expression "Content is king." Coined by Bill Gates in the 1990s, this oft-repeated mantra stresses the importance of information above all else. Think about it: The average user doesn't visit your site to admire a beautiful design or cool animation—she goes there for content. In that sense, everything we do as web professionals—whether it's design, development, or marketing—has a single goal: conveying information to the user.

And what better source of information is there than raw data? That said, raw data by itself is nothing more than static noise. Data visualization allows us to bridge that gap, turning raw data into meaningful content.

At this point, you've probably gathered that data visualization is a lot more than flashy widgets to impress your boss. Although this book does cover some impressive tools—such as the comprehensive D3 library—the focus at all points is on the information. At a minimum, data visualization conveys this information to the user. But you're going to go deeper than that. That's because data visualization is capable of so much more; in addition to conveying information, data visualization analyzes information to provide meaningful insights.

Good data visualization doesn't just aggregate data into more digestible chunks. Good data visualization leads users to powerful conclusions. It shows rather than tells, and in our experience there is no better way to get your point across. There's just no substitute for leading users to a conclusion they can then draw for themselves.

WHAT'S IN THIS BOOK

JavaScript and jQuery for Data Analysis and Visualization starts off in Part I with a broad discussion of data visualization. It discusses the current state of data visualization and its general goals, and then it covers some of the basic tenets of analysis. Part I closes with an overview of some of the technical foundation that you need to understand the rest of the book, such as the basics of HTML5 canvas and SVG.

Part II takes you into the realm of data analysis and acquisition. It discusses techniques for pulling data from a server and even covers how to combine stored data with form data from the user. Next, it covers data validation as well as techniques for displaying tabular data. Part II wraps up with a discussion of client-side analysis tools, providing a robust statistical analysis toolkit that's based in JavaScript.

Part III explores actual data visualization tools, and in all likelihood it's going to be your favorite part of this book. You'll start off by running through basic charting solutions such as Google Charts. From that point, the book gets into more complex charting options—covering how to build custom solutions with Raphaël as well as how to use the D3 library. Finally, you learn all about more specific data-visualization applications, such as geographic and stock data.

Last but not least, Part IV consolidates everything you learned in Parts I through III with a couple of real-world examples. You first see how to build an interconnected dashboard that renders U.S. Census data using Google Charts and then you see how to use D3 in production to create reusable visualizations.

WHO THIS BOOK IS FOR

This book is geared toward web developers with a basic understanding of front-end development. Although you don't need to have advanced skills in this realm, you should have at least a beginner's level of knowledge of JavaScript and jQuery. Beyond that, we make no assumptions of your skill level. We cover data visualization tools from the ground up, as well as some of their underlying technologies. Whenever possible, we point you to external resources to further support your knowledge in these areas. That way, we can cover the basics quickly and move on to the more and impressive parts of data visualization.

By the end of the book, you'll have advanced knowledge of a variety of data visualization tools and techniques. This book will provide you with a comprehensive toolkit to handle all your visualization needs.

CONVENTIONS

To help you get the most from the text and keep track of what's happening, a number of conventions are used throughout the book.

> **WARNING** *Warnings hold important, not-to-be-forgotten information that is directly relevant to the surrounding text.*

> **NOTE** *Notes indicate notes, tips, hints, tricks, or and asides to the current discussion.*

As for styles in the text:

We *highlight* new terms and important words when we introduce them.

We show filenames, URLs, and code within the text like so: `persistence.properties`.

We present code in two different ways:

```
We use a monofont type with no highlighting for most code examples.
```

We use bold to emphasize code that's particularly important in the present context or to show changes from a previous code snippet.

COMPANION WEBSITE

To complement the content in this book, we've also created a companion website at `www.wrox.com/go/javascriptandjqueryanalysis`. This website provides a variety of useful resources, such as downloads of all the code examples in the book. It's a useful place to turn if you get stuck at any point.

ERRATA

We make every effort to ensure that there are no errors in the text or in the code. However, no one is perfect, and mistakes do occur. If you find an error in one of our books, like a spelling mistake or faulty piece of code, we would be grateful for your feedback. By sending in errata you may save another reader hours of frustration, and at the same time you can help provide even higher quality information.

To find the errata page for this book, go to `http://www.wrox.com` and locate the title using the Search box or one of the title lists. Then, on the book details page, click the Book Errata link. On this page you can view all errata that has been submitted for this book and posted by Wrox editors. A complete book list including links to each book's errata is also available at `www.wrox.com/misc-pages/booklist.shtml`.

If you don't spot "your" error on the Book Errata page, go to `www.wrox.com/contact/techsupport.shtml` and complete the form there to send us the error you have found. We'll check the information and, if appropriate, post a message to the book's errata page and fix the problem in subsequent editions of the book.

P2P.WROX.COM

For author and peer discussion, join the P2P forums at `p2p.wrox.com`. The forums are a web-based system for you to post messages relating to Wrox books and related technologies and interact with other readers and technology users. The forums offer a subscription feature to e-mail you topics of interest of your choosing when new posts are made to the forums. Wrox authors, editors, other industry experts, and your fellow readers are present on these forums.

At `http://p2p.wrox.com` you can find a number of different forums to help you not only as you read this book, but also as you develop your own applications. To join the forums, just follow these steps:

1. Go to `p2p.wrox.com` and click the Register link.

2. Read the terms of use and click Agree.

3. Complete the required information to join and any optional information you want to provide, and click Submit.

4. You will receive an e-mail with information describing how to verify your account and complete the joining process.

> **NOTE** *You can read messages in the forums without joining P2P but to post your own messages, you must join.*

After you join, you can post new messages and respond to messages other users post. You can read messages at any time on the web. If you want to have new messages from a particular forum e-mailed to you, click the Subscribe to this Forum icon by the forum name in the forum listing.

For more information about how to use the Wrox P2P, read the P2P FAQs for answers to questions about how the forum software works as well as many common questions specific to P2P and Wrox books. To read the FAQs, click the FAQ link on any P2P page.

PART I
The Beauty of Numbers Made Visible

1

The World of Data Visualization

WHAT'S IN THIS CHAPTER

➤ Overview of chart design options

➤ Comparison of different business applications for data visualization

➤ Rundown of technological advancements that have made data visualization what it is today

When thinking about data visualization, it's hard to resist the comparison to natural metamorphosis. Consider raw data as the caterpillar: functional, multi-faceted, able to get from here to there, but a little ungainly and really appreciated only by a select few. After data is transformed via visualization, it becomes the butterfly: sleek, agile, and highly recognizable to the point of inspiring and evoking an emotional response. The world of data visualization is an ecosystem unto itself, constantly spawning new nodes of details that—under the proper nourishing conditions—evolve into relatable depictions that consolidate concepts into an understandable, and hopefully compelling, form.

And where does the web professional fit in this metaphor? Why, they are the spinners and caretakers of the cocoon that transforms raw numbers into meaningful representation, of course. Putting the linguistic paraphrasing aside, web designers and developers are a vital component in visualizing data. Naturally, the current and evolving technological landscape has made this role possible—and increasingly efficient.

Overall, *JavaScript and jQuery for Data Analysis and Visualization* serves as a practical field guide to the robust world of data visualization, from the acquisition and nurturing of data to its transfiguration into the optimal visual format. This chapter is intended to provide an overview of the present environment, highlighting its capabilities and limitations and discussing how you, the web professional, are a key player in visualizing data.

BRINGING NUMBERS TO LIFE

Appreciating numeric data can be a challenge. Data visualization with relational graphics and evocative imagery helps make raw data meaningful. But before you can transform the data into a meaningful representation, you have to get it first.

Acquiring the Data

The data sphere is enormous and growing dramatically, if not exponentially, every day. Data is streaming in from everywhere—and when you consider that the Mars Rover, Curiosity, continually sends its data findings back to Earth, you understand that "everywhere" is no exaggeration.

With the tremendous amount of data already available, its acquisition is often just a matter of logistics. If the information is in a non-digital form—that is, written records—it will need to be transcribed into the proper format. Should the desired data be accessible digitally, it may need to be converted from its current structure to one compatible with the display or visualization application.

When your information is in the proper format, you next need to ensure it is exactly the data you need and nothing more. The wealth of data available today makes targeting your data selection, typically through a process known as *filtering*, pretty much a requirement in all situations. Even when organizations fine-tune their data input from the beginning, changes in the sample or desired output over time will force a filtering adjustment.

Why is it so important to restrict your data stream? One clear reason is processing efficiency. Working with an overload of unnecessary information increases application execution time—which corresponds directly to increased bandwidth and, thus, costs. Additionally, filtering makes raw data more meaningful. Focused information is easier to analyze and also more easily digested by end users.

Visualizing the Data

In a sense, the most difficult aspect of data visualization is deciding exactly how the information should be depicted. The web designer must select the optimum representation that communicates the data in the clearest, most desired manner with the highest degree of impact. More importantly, the representation should be a discovery tool that leads the user to meaningful insights. Here's an incomplete list of available formats:

- Area chart
- Bar chart
- Bubble chart
- Candlestick chart
- Column chart
- Donut chart
- Flow chart
- Funnel chart

- ➤ Gauge chart
- ➤ Geographic chart
- ➤ Heat map
- ➤ Hierarchical edge bundling
- ➤ Infographics
- ➤ Line chart
- ➤ Marimekko chart
- ➤ Network node map
- ➤ OLHC (Open-high-low-close) chart

- ➤ Org Chart
- ➤ Pareto chart
- ➤ Pie chart
- ➤ Polar chart
- ➤ Scatter chart
- ➤ Sparkline chart
- ➤ Timelines
- ➤ Tree Maps
- ➤ Word cloud

We've really just scratched the surface with ways data can be presented. Most of these formats can be shown in either 2D or 3D. You can include interactive elements and animation to add dimensions to the data. But be careful to balance these bells and whistles with meaningful data. No amount of eye candy is worth compromising the representation of information.

> **NOTE** *It's important to realize that a key factor in visualization is intent. Raw data on almost every subject can be interpreted in any number of ways. What message is intended to be communicated should be among the first decisions made when beginning the process of representing data visually.*

There are other primary options to consider as well. Do you expose the underlying data or not? If so, are the numbers always visible or are they visible only when some interaction occurs, such as when the viewer's mouse hovers over a data point? Is the initial visualization all there, or does the online version allow the user to drill down for more details? Is animation used to represent a dynamic change? Is there other interactivity available, such as horizontal scrolling along a timeline or zooming into it?

Then, of course, there is styling. With simple bar and pie charts, you'll not only need to decide which colors represent which elements, but also the size, color, style, and font to be applied for labels and legends, if any—yet another choice. Many such selections will be governed by other factors, such as the creating organization's branding or in-house standards; however, just as many will have no such foundation to work from, and the designer's vision will become paramount.

Moving beyond the basics of charting primitives, the visualization designer can choose to include graphics. Not only can background images frame a presentation—both literally and thematically—but symbols can be used as data points, like logos pinned in a map of third-quarter sales. An entire field of data visualization—infographics—is devoted to the combination of information and visual imagery.

The truth is that the web professional's current options for depicting data are a bounty of riches. Although the possibilities may appear to be overwhelming, it's up to the visualization designer to identify the optimum representation and bring it into reality.

Simultaneous Acquisition and Visualization

The world of data visualization doesn't just consume existing data: New data is constantly being added to the stores, even in real time. Information can be collected directly through an HTML form on a website and incorporated into the representation programmatically. One of the most common examples of this is an online poll, such as the one shown in Figure 1-1. After a site visitor has chosen his or her desired response and clicked Vote, the current relative standing of all entries, including the one just entered, is displayed.

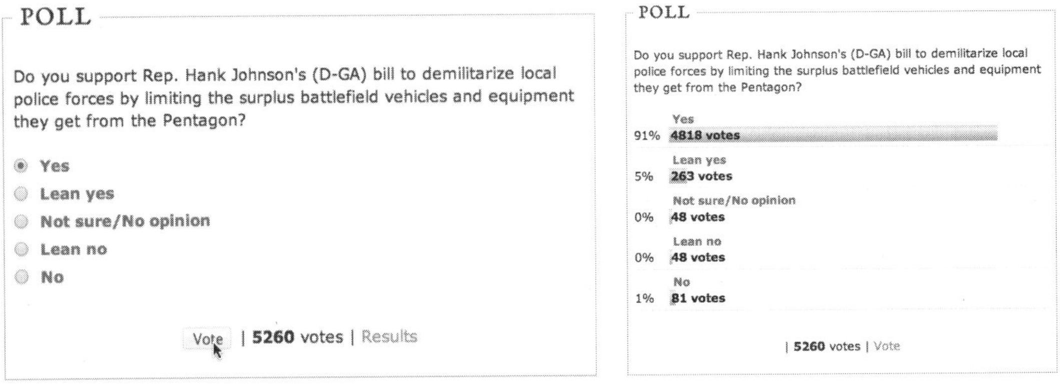

SOURCE: WWW.DAILYKOS.COM/STORY/2014/08/18/1322337/-CHEERS-AND-JEERS-MONDAY

FIGURE 1-1: Some polls allow the user to instantly see the current results.

Collecting live data has a number of challenges, but the recent advances made by the widespread acceptance of HTML5 have ameliorated many of them. When combined with a few key JavaScript libraries, it is now possible to use advanced form elements, such as slider controls, across the full spectrum of modern browsers.

Acquiring the data in real time is just the first step. The web developer is also responsible for validating and standardizing the data. Validation is critical in two ways: first, to ensure that all required information is supplied, and second, to verify that the data is in the proper format. Naturally, if you're trying to find out where your clientele is based, you can't if the requested postal code is left blank. Likewise, if the postal code is in the wrong format, such as a four-digit entry for a U.S. address, the data is worthless. Both of these issues can be corrected by proper validation, whether handled on the client-side with JavaScript, server-side via PHP or another server language, or some combination of the two.

Standardized data is just as important and typically applies to time and date details. There are numerous ways to enter a date: March 10, 2011 could be 03/10/11, 10/03/11, or 11/03/10 depending on whether you're in the United States, Australia, or China, respectively. To make sure the intended date is collected correctly, the entered information will need to be standardized to a format the visualization application recognizes before it is saved. Read Chapter 6 for more information about data validation.

APPLICATIONS OF DATA VISUALIZATION

So there's all this wonderful data out there, just waiting to be brought to life by this almost magical transformative process. But why should it? The question really is *cui bono*? Who benefits? In a sense, the answer is everyone. Whenever information is made clearer and more understandable, it's better for all. But the web professional doesn't get paid by "everyone," so let's narrow the scope and focus on the key groups who stand the most to gain from data visualization.

Uses in the Public Sector

Groups in the public sector include all levels of government (those in it and those trying to get in it), as well as police, military, transportation agencies, and educational and healthcare facilities. Just a few folks, right? Oh, and let's add philanthropy and philanthropic projects, a.k.a. charities, into the mix, just for fun.

All these organizations have a key interest in discovering what is happening (the data) and then conveying that information internally to others in their own group and/or externally to the broader public (the visual). Many such efforts are mandated and essential to the organization's existence. Take, for example, the U.S. census. The data is collected on a massive scale every 10 years—by law—and then impacts multiple facets of American life such as state and regional funding and, of course, congressional representation. The U.S. Census Bureau maintains a treasure trove of the aggregate data, now visually accessible to everyone through its online presence at www.census.gov. Not only are there government-sanctioned representations of the collected census information, like the map in Figure 1-2, but the site also makes APIs available (api.census.gov) for public web developer access.

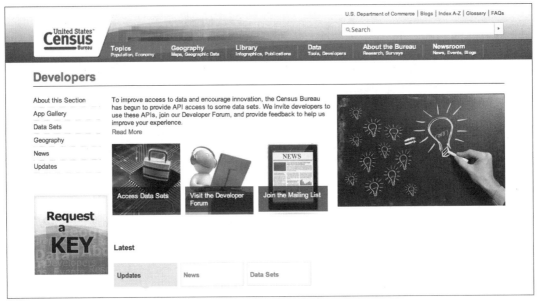

FIGURE 1-2: You'll need to request a no-charge digital key to access the APIs from api.census.gov.

Business-to-Business and Intrabusiness Uses

If the business of business is business, how do you do business? Mostly through marketing, whether you're a vendor targeting another company or one department lobbying internally for increased resources. And the heart of marketing is persuasion—which is often bolstered, if not solely accomplished, by making your case through the compelling presentation of data.

As with the public sector, many such presentations are required. Look through any annual report to see the latest encapsulation of the company's standing, graphically depicted in quickly graspable charts. Today, creating an online report is standard practice. Similar data visualizations are undertaken daily in department and division meetings to plot sales progress, reveal public reaction to products, and adjust business direction.

There are significant data visualization opportunities for the web designer within the business-to-business arena. Most of this type of work, like other website or intranet work, will be handled by an internal team. Cultivating such skills would definitely add value to any web professional's resume.

Additionally, a wide variety of data visualizations are used internally within organizations. These tools help businesses grapple with and understand their own data.

Business-to-Consumer Uses

Obviously, marketing plays as big a role in the business-to-consumer realm as it does in business to business, if not more. Sharp, effective advertising, as well as other forms of marketing, are pretty much required for a company's message to cut through the omnipresent media noise. Often a clearly defined representation of data can make the difference.

Although there are plenty of uses for pie charts, stock charts and other fundamental data representations in business-to-consumer communications, infographics are seen far more frequently. Infographics combine data and information in a visually engaging manner. Sometimes, the data is represented straightforwardly, such as the percentage values shown in the infographic from HealthIT.gov (see Figure 1-3), or more graphically, as shown in the infographic from the CDC (see Figure 1-4).

Infographics is a tremendously rich area with an almost endless range of possibilities; because of the openness of the format, it can be a designer's playground. To learn more about creating this particular type of data visualization, see Chapter 16.

WEB PROFESSIONALS: IN THE THICK OF IT

As noted in this chapter's introduction, web professionals are at the heart of data visualization. Consider that it first takes someone with web savvy to access and translate the data into a usable form. Then, if the data collection is to be ongoing, one or more forms have to be set up correctly online to make sure the needed data is acquired, valid, and—where necessary—standardized. Finally, someone with a working knowledge of browser-compatible languages must create the visual display of the data so that it can be viewed on the Internet.

Control of Presentation

Web professionals—across the spectrum of their functionality—are responsible for this growing sphere of communication. Let's break down the process from their perspective:

➤ A web developer with server-side skills is needed to handle the back-end processing of data to make it accessible.

➤ A JavaScript coder is responsible for filtering, sorting, and manipulating the data to prepare it for representation. This role could also be handled server-side or in combination with client-side technology.

➤ An HTML coder builds any required forms to allow interactive data addition, often with JavaScript libraries for validation.

➤ One or more web designers create the look-and-feel of all data-related pages, including styling the output of the visualized data.

➤ A web coder, leveraging his or her own knowledge of JavaScript, combined with core frameworks and data visualization libraries, displays the data in a representational format.

Although all the described tasks could possibly be fulfilled by a single individual, it's just as likely that these tasks are handled by a group working closely together. Whether it's done by one (very busy) person or a networked team spread around the world, the important take-away is that web professionals own the data visualization process from top to bottom.

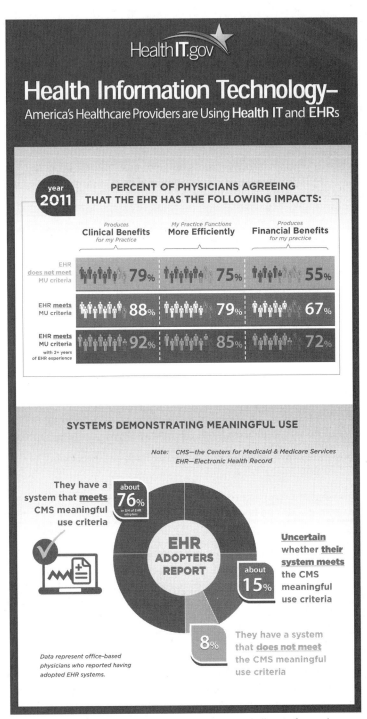

FIGURE 1-3: The icons in this infographic graphically reinforce the numeric percentages.

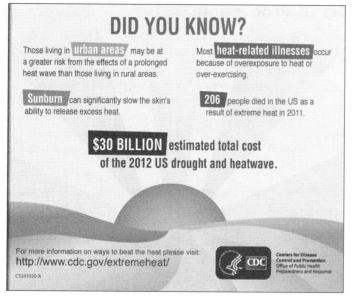

FIGURE 1-4: Infographics are adept at combining highlighted key terms, such as "urban areas" and "heat-related illnesses" with numeric data, as shown in this infographic from the CDC.

> **TIP** *Curious as to what other web professionals have been doing in the field of data visualization? There are a number of sites online that provide a bevy of examples. One of the best that we've found is at* `http://visualizing.org/`, *which not only has compelling galleries but also a robust community dedicated to data and design.*

WHAT TECH BRINGS TO THE TABLE

Web professionals are dependent on robust web software to accomplish any aspect of their work, but the need for power tools is particularly vital to properly handle data visualization. Recent years have witnessed a sea change in online technology that has greatly expanded the possibilities for representing data. Although there are many contributing factors, the following discussion focuses on three key ones:

➤ Faster, more efficient JavaScript engines in browsers

➤ The rapid proliferation of HTML5 compatible browsers

➤ The increased availability of JavaScript frameworks and libraries

Faster and Better JavaScript Processing

For the last several years, browser makers have identified JavaScript processing as a key battle-ground and have pursued faster JavaScript engines with great vigor. The bar graph in Figure 1-5 compares runs of the SunSpider benchmark, created and maintained by WebKit.org, for older browsers (Internet Explorer 7 and Safari 3) against the latest—as of this writing—browsers, Internet Explorer 10 and Safari 6. In this chart, smaller is better, and you can see there has been a radical shift in browser efficiency. The values for the earlier browser versions come from a June 2008 article that appeared on ZDNet (`http://www.zdnet.com/blog/hardware/sunspider-javascript-benchmark-and-acid-3-compatibility-charts-firefox-3-0-rc-3-and-opera-9-50-added/2090`); we ran the benchmarks on the newer browsers ourselves.

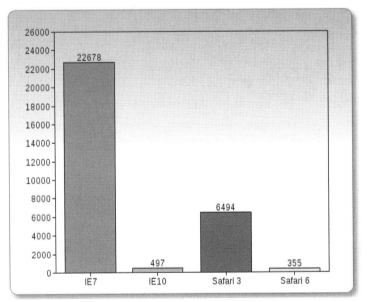

FIGURE 1-5: The lesser values indicate faster and more desirable processing times by JavaScript engines.

The increase in JavaScript processing functionality has had a direct effect on the realm of data visualization, in both the analysis and the rendering phase. The JavaScript engine handles raw numeric computations as well as on-screen drawing, either directly or in conjunction with the hardware renderer. This combination greatly increases the viability of direct browser data visualization, without resorting to a third-party plug-in, like Adobe Flash.

Rise of HTML5

A faster engine isn't much good without fuel to run it—luckily, a load of high-octane HTML5 was delivered just in time. The roots of HTML5 can be traced back to 2004 and the Web Hypertext Application Technology (WHAT) Working Group—but adoption was glacially slow. At one point, the W3C had actually slated the web language for final recommendation status in 2022! The introduction of smartphones, most notably Apple's iPhone, changed all that. The device's embrace of HTML5 in lieu of Flash triggered a feature adoption race among all major browsers, with HTML5 becoming the current standard for mobile devices.

Why is HTML5 so important to data visualization? First, let me clarify that this latest version of the web's primary language brings along two closely knit partners: CSS3 and advanced JavaScript APIs. The enhanced capabilities brought by these three related technologies have truly revolutionized web design and development overall. The following are a few key features that have been especially beneficial for data visualization:

➤ **The <canvas> tag:** Include a seemingly blank <canvas> element on your HTML5 page and suddenly you have access to the full palette of graphics—including primitives (such as circles and rectangles), plotted points with connected lines, gradients, text, imported images, and much more—all drawn by JavaScript, live. What's more, you have the option to make whatever you put on your canvas interactive, capable of being changed by the user (see Figure 1-6).

➤ **SVG:** Although we've had limited SVG support for some time, its usage has greatly expanded with HTML5. This canvas alternative also enables you to create rich graphics on the web.

➤ **Web fonts:** After being limited to a handful of system fonts common to PC and Mac, web designers everywhere were hungry for the possibilities brought by browser support for web fonts. Now, designers can use an ever-growing family of decorative and other font faces to give the impact their infographics and other data visualizations need—while remaining search engine compatible and screen reader friendly.

➤ **Advanced form elements:** Because we were sick and tired of working with the extremely limited set of form elements, this one was pretty high on our personal wish list. HTML5 brings a great number of new input types (such as email, tel, and url) that makes it much easier for users to correctly enter the proper data, especially on mobile devices. In addition, new form controls such as the range slider bring an enhanced user experience into play. Browser support for these elements is not quite at the same level as some of the other HTML5 features, but it does seem to get better with each version release.

> **TIP** *Perhaps the best resource for checking whether HTML5 specifics can be incorporated into a web page is* http://caniuse.com/. *This site tracks each of the HTML5, CSS, and JavaScript API features and their current (as well as past and future) browser version support. We consider Can I Use an essential stop in the planning stage of any new site or application.*

Lowering the Implementation Bar

To complete our car metaphor, let's agree that we have now have a powerful vehicle (our highly efficient JavaScript engine) and a super fuel (widely supported HTML5). Does anyone know how to drive this thing? Thanks to the popularity and ease of use of JavaScript-related libraries, specifically those written in jQuery, the answer for an increasing number of web professionals is a resounding "Yes!"

FIGURE 1-6: HTML5 brings support for advanced functionality such as the <canvas> tag, which opens the door to interactive charting among many other data visualization benefits.

It's true that anyone with sufficient JavaScript know-how could manage the requisite data acquisition, conversion, and rendering required in the data visualization life cycle. However, armed with core jQuery and targeted libraries, such a process becomes much more efficient and successful.

In fact, if there is a single *raison d'etre* for this book, it's the existence and proliferation of these JavaScript libraries that will be leveraged throughout this title. In addition to making it easier to bring the real-world data numbers to life in the first place, most sophisticated JavaScript libraries also make it much more straightforward to modify controlling parameters and even the data itself, all on the fly. This added degree of flexibility strengthens the case for taking advantage of code libraries such as Google Charts, D3, Raphaël and jqPlot to name just a few covered in this book and available right now to be put to work.

SUMMARY

Data visualization is the process of acquiring data, analyzing it, and displaying the resulting information in a graphical fashion. The entire procedure itself can run the gamut from the extremely straightforward, such as creating a pie chart from values in a spreadsheet, to the exceedingly complex, as when building a sophisticated infographic distilling reams of census and geographic data. When thinking about the world of data visualization, keep these key points in mind:

➤ Visualizing data makes it easier for a wider audience to quickly grasp the relative nature of selected data.

➤ There are a tremendous number of options when it comes to deciding which form of representation your information should take. The job of the visualization designer is to realize the optimum choices for communicating the data's message.

➤ Data can be collected and displayed visually in real time through the use of HTML forms and JavaScript coding.

➤ The primary creators of data visualizations are the public sector and the business-to-business, intrabusiness, and business-to-consumer markets.

➤ Advances in browser JavaScript processing, HTML5 browser support, and the proliferation of related JavaScript libraries lay the technological foundation for data visualization.

2

Working with the Essentials of Analysis

WHAT'S IN THIS CHAPTER

➤ Basic analytic concepts

➤ Key mathematical terms commonly applied when evaluating data

➤ Techniques for uncovering patterns within the information

➤ Strategies for forecasting future trends

The current Google definition of *analysis* is a perfect fit when applied to data visualization:

> *Detailed examination of the elements or structure of something, typically as
> a basis for discussion or interpretation.*

You know the expression, "Can't see the forest for the trees"? When you analyze data with visualization in mind, you potentially are looking at both the forest and the trees. The individual data points are, of course, extremely important, but so is the overall pattern they form: the structure referenced in the Google definition. Moreover, the whole purpose of analyzing data for visualization is to discuss, interpret, and understand—to paint a picture *with* the numbers and not *by* the numbers.

This chapter covers the basic tenets of analysis in order to lay a foundation for the material ahead. It starts by defining a few of the key mathematical terms commonly applied when evaluating data. Next, the chapter discusses techniques frequently used to uncover patterns within the information and strategies for forecasting future trends based on the data.

KEY ANALYTIC CONCEPTS

At its heart, most data is number based. For every text-focused explication that starts with "One side feels this way and another side feels that way," the next question is inevitably numeric: "How many are on each side?" Such simplified headcounts are rarely the full scope of a data visualization project and it is often necessary to bring more sophisticated numeric analysis into play. This section explores the more frequently applied concepts.

Mean Versus Median

One of the most common statistical tasks is to determine the average—or *mean*—of a particular set of numbers. The mean is the sum of all the considered values divided by the total number of those values. Let's say you have sales figures for seven different parts of the country, shown in Table 2-1.

TABLE 2-1: Sample Sales by Region

REGION	SALES
Northeast	$100,000
Southeast	$75,000
Midwest	$125,000
Mid-Atlantic	$125,000
Southwest	$75,000
Northwest	$100,000
California	$400,000

All the dollar amounts added together equal $1,000,000. Divide the total by 7—the total number of values—to arrive at the mean: $142,857. Although this is significant in terms of sales as a whole, it doesn't really indicate the more typical figure for most of the regions. The significantly higher amount from California skews the results. Quite often when someone asks for the average, what they are really asking for is the *median*.

The median is the midpoint in a series of values: quite literally, the middle. Let's list regional sales in descending order, from highest to lowest (see Table 2-2).

TABLE 2-2: Sample Sales by Region, Descending Order

REGION	SALES
California	$400,000
Midwest	$125,000

REGION	SALES
Mid-Atlantic	$125,000
Northeast	$100,000
Northwest	$100,000
Southeast	$75,000
Southwest	$75,000

The median sales figure (the Northeast region's $100,000) is actually much closer to what most of the other areas are bringing in. To quantify variance in the data—like that shown in the preceding example—statisticians rely on a concept called *standard deviation*.

Standard Deviation

Standard deviation measures the distribution of numbers from the average or mean of any given sample set. The higher the deviation, the more spread out the data. Knowing the standard deviation allows you to determine, and thus potentially map, which values lie outside the norm.

Following are the steps for calculating the standard deviation:

1. Determine the mean of the values set.
2. Subtract the mean from each value.
3. Square the results. Cleverly, this is called the *squared differences*.
4. Find the mean for all the squared differences.
5. Get the square root of the just-calculated mean. The result is the standard deviation.

Let's run our previous data set through these steps to identify its standard deviation.

1. The mean, as calculated before, is 142,857.
2. Subtract the mean from the values to get the following results:

REGION	SALES	MEAN	DIFFERENCE
Northeast	100,000	142,857	−42,857
Southeast	75,000	142,857	−67,857
Midwest	125,000	142,857	−17,857
Mid-Atlantic	125,000	142,857	−17,857
Southwest	75,000	142,857	−67,857
Northwest	100,000	142,857	−42,857
California	400,000	142,857	257,143

3. To handle the negative values properly, square the results:

REGION	DIFFERENCE	SQUARED DIFFERENCE
Northeast	–42,857	1,836,734,694
Southeast	–67,857	4,604,591,837
Midwest	–17,857	318,877,551
Mid-Atlantic	–17,857	318,877,551
Southwest	–67,857	4,604,591,837
Northwest	–42,857	1,836,734,694
California	257,143	66,122,448,980

4. Add all the squared values together to get 79,642,857,143; divide by 7 (the number of values) and you have 11,377,551,020.

5. Calculate the square root of that value to find that 106,665 is the standard deviation.

When you know the standard deviation from the mean, you can say which figures might be abnormally high or abnormally low. The range runs from 36,191 (the mean minus the standard deviation) to 249,522 (the mean plus the standard deviation). The California sales figure of $400,000 is outside the norm by slightly more than $150,000.

To demonstrate how values can change the standard deviation, try recalculating it after dropping the California sales to $150,000—a figure much more in line with the other regions. With that modification, the standard deviation is 44,031, indicating a much narrower variance range from 98,825 to 186,888.

WORKING WITH SAMPLED DATA

Statisticians aren't always able to access all the data as we were with the regional sales information referenced earlier in this chapter. Polls, for example, almost always reflect the input of just a portion—or sample—of the targeted population. To account for the difference, three separate concepts are applied: a variation on the standard deviation formula, the per capita calculation for taking into account the relative size of the data population, and the margin of error.

Standard Deviation Variation

There's a very simple modification to the standard deviation formula that is incorporated when working with sampled data. Called Bessel's Correction, this change modifies a single value. Rather than divide the sum of the squared differences by the total number of values, the sum is divided by the number of values less one. This seemingly minor change has a significant impact statisticians believe represents the standard deviation more accurately when working with a subset of the entire data set rather than the complete order.

Assume that the previously discussed sales data was from a global sales force and thus the data is only a portion rather than the entirety. In this situation, the sum of the squared differences (79,642,857,143) would be divided by 6 rather than 7, which results in 13,273,809,523 as opposed to 11,377,551,020—a difference of almost 2 trillion. Taking the square root of this value results in a new standard deviation of 115,212 versus 106,665.

Per Capita Calculations

Looking at raw numbers without taking any other factors into consideration can lead to inaccurate conclusions. One enhancement is to bring the size of the population of a sampled region into play. This type of calculation is called *per capita*, Latin for "each head."

To apply the per capita value, you divide the given number attributed to an area by the population of that area. Typically, this results in a very small decimal, which makes it difficult to completely comprehend. To make the result easier to grasp, it is often multiplied by a larger value, such as 100,000, which would then be described as per 100,000 people.

To better understand this concept, compare two of the sales regions that each brought in $75,000: the Southeast and the Southwest. According to the U.S. 2010 census, the population of the Southeast is 78,320,977, whereas the Southwest's population is 38,030,918. If you divide the sales figure for each by their respective population and then multiply that by 100,000, you get the results shown in Table 2-3.

TABLE 2-3: Regional Sales per Capita

REGION	SALES	POPULATION	PER CAPITA	PER 100,000
Southeast	75,000	78,320,977	0.000957598	95.8
Southwest	75,000	38,030,918	0.00197208	197.2

When the per capita calculation is figured in, the perceptive difference is quite significant. Essentially, the Southwest market sales were better than the Southeast by better than 2-to-1. Such framing of the data would be critical information for any organization making decisions about future spending based on current data.

Margin of Error

If you're not sampling the entire population on any given subject, your data is likely to be somewhat imprecise. This impreciseness is known as the *margin of error*. The term is frequently used with political polls where you might encounter a note that it contains a "margin of error of plus or minus 3.5%" or something similar. This percentage value is very easy to calculate and, wondrously, works regardless of the overall population's size.

To find the margin of error, simply divide 1 by the square root of the number of samples. For example, let's say you surveyed a neighborhood about a household cleaning product. If 1,500 people answered your questions, the resulting margin of error would be 2.58 percent. Here's how the math breaks down:

1. Find the square root of your sample size. The square root of 1,500 is close to 38.729.

2. Divide 1 by that square root value. One divided by 38.729 is around 0.0258.

3. Multiply the decimal value by 100 to find the percentage. In this case, the final percentage would be 2.58 percent.

The larger your sample, the smaller the margin of error—stands to reason, right? So if the sample size doubles to 3,000, the margin of error would be 1.82 percent. Note that the percentage value for double the survey size is not half the margin of error for 1,500; the correlation is proportional, but not on a 1-to-1 ratio.

Because this calculation is true regardless of the overall population size—your sampled audience could be in New York or in Montana—it has wide application. Naturally, there are many other factors that could come into play, but the margin of error is unaffected.

DETECTING PATTERNS WITH DATA MINING

Data visualizations are often used in support of illustrating one or more perceived patterns in targeted information. Another term for identifying these patterns and their relationship to each other is *data mining*. The most common data-mining tool is a relational database that contains multiple forms of information, such as transactional data, environmental information, and demographics.

Data mining incorporates a number of techniques for recognizing relationships between various bits of information details. The following are the key techniques:

➤ **Associations:** The Association technique is often applied to transactions, where a consumer purchases two or more items at the same time. The textbook example—albeit a fictional one—is of a supermarket chain discovering that men frequently buy beer when they purchased diapers on Thursdays. This association between the seemingly disparate products enables the retailer to make key decisions, like those involving product placement or pricing. Of course, any association data should be taken with a grain of salt because correlation does not imply causation.

➤ **Classifications:** Classification separates data records into predefined groups or classes according to existing or predictive criteria. For example, let's say you're classifying online customers according to whether they would buy a new car every other year. Using relational, comparative data—identifying other factors that correlated with previous consumers who bought an automobile every two years—you could classify new entries in the database accordingly.

➤ **Decision trees:** A decision tree follows a logic flow dictated by choices and circumstances. In practice, the decision tree resembles a flow chart, like the one shown in Figure 2-1. Decision trees are often used in conjunction with classifications.

➤ **Clusters:** Clustering looks at existing attributes or values and groups entries with similarities. The clustering technique lends itself to more of an exploratory approach than classification because you don't have to predetermine the associated groups. However, this data mining method can also identify members of specific market segments.

➤ **Sequential patterning:** By examining the sequential order in which actions are taken, you can determine the action likely to be taken next. Sequential patterning is a foundation of trend analysis, and timelines are often incorporated for related data visualization.

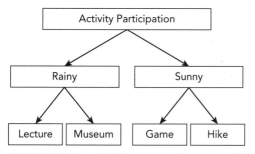

FIGURE 2-1: In a decision tree, environmental factors, such as the weather, along with personal choices, can impact the final decision equally.

These various techniques can be applied separately or in combination with one another.

PROJECTING FUTURE TRENDS

The prediction of future actions based on current behavior is a cornerstone of data visualization. Much projection is based on *regression analysis*. The simplest regression analysis depends on two variables interconnected in a causal relationship. The first variable is considered independent and the second, dependent. Let's say you're looking at how long a dog attends a behavioral school and the number of times the dog chews up the furniture. As you analyze the data, you discover that there is a correlation between the length of the dog's training (the independent variable) and its behavior (the dependent variable): The longer the pet stays in the training, the less furniture destruction. Table 2-4 shows the raw data.

TABLE 2-4: Data for Regression Analysis

DAYS TRAINING	CHEWING INCIDENTS
5	8
10	5
15	6
20	3
25	4
30	2

> **NOTE** *Some statisticians refer to the independent and dependent variables in regression analysis as* exogenous *and* endogenous, *respectively. Exogenous refers to something that was developed from external factors, whereas endogenous is defined as having an internal cause or origin.*

To get a better sense of how regression analysis works, Figure 2-2 shows the basic points plotted on a graph. As you can see, the points are slightly scattered across the grid. Because it involves only two variables, this type of projection is referred to as *simple linear regression.*

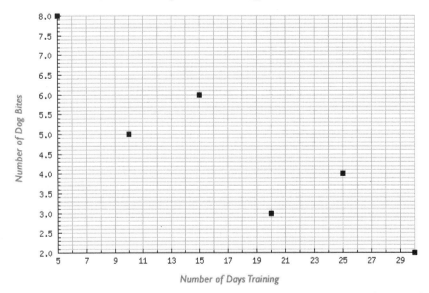

FIGURE 2-2: The number of days training (the independent variable) is shown in the X axis and the number of dog bites (the dependent variable) in the Y.

To clarify the data trend direction, a regression analysis formula is applied that plots a straight line to encapsulate the point distribution (see Figure 2-3). This trend line provides insight to the scattered point distribution—it's a great example of how data visualizations can be used for discovery and understanding.

Of course, there won't always be a one-to-one relationship. It's axiomatic that correlation isn't causation. There are often other factors in the mix. However, narrowing the outside variables—such as limiting the study to one breed—increases the predictive possibilities.

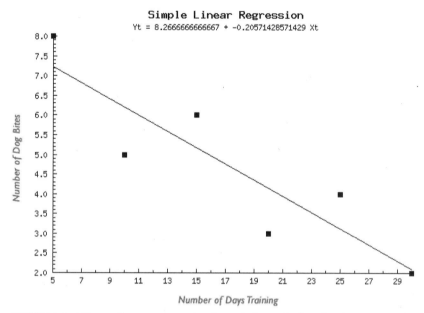

FIGURE 2-3: When a linear progression formula is applied to the data, a straight trend line is indicated.

> **REFERENCE** *The actual mathematics of regression analysis and other concepts covered in this chapter are outside the scope of this book. However, there are numerous online and offline tools to handle the heavy arithmetic lifting. To learn more about these tools and the techniques for using them, see Chapter 8.*

SUMMARY

The analysis of data is an integral aspect of its visualization. A wide range of mathematical and statistical techniques are available to examine both the individual informational components and their overall structure. Here are a few important points regarding the basics of data analysis:

➤ For the most part, data analysis is a numbers game and a core understanding of key mathematical concepts is necessary.

➤ The mean of a series of numbers is found by dividing the sum of the values by their number.

➤ The midpoint in a set of values is referred to as the median.

➤ To find the average distribution of your data, calculate its standard deviation.

➤ Special considerations—including a variation in the standard deviation, per capita calculations, and margin of error—must be kept in mind when analyzing data from a sample of a given population versus the entire population.

➤ Various techniques in data mining can be used to uncover current and predictive patterns. These techniques include associations, classifications, decision trees, clusters, and sequential patterning.

➤ Regression analysis looks at independent and dependent variables to determine trendlines of future behavior.

3

Building a Visualization Foundation

WHAT'S IN THIS CHAPTER

➤ Getting to know charting primitives, including point, bar, and pie charts

➤ Understanding specialized charts, including candlestick, bubble, and surface charts

➤ Examining the underlying technology for these charts, such as HTML5 and SVG

> **CODE DOWNLOAD** *The wrox.com code downloads for this chapter are found at* www.wrox.com/go/javascriptandjqueryanalysis *on the Download Code tab. The code is in the chapter 04 download and individually named according to the names throughout the chapter.*

After you have your data in hand, the big question is how to present it. Before you can make the choice that best communicates your message, you need a thorough grasp of what's possible—in the universe of visualization options as well as in the technology to create them online.

This chapter lays the groundwork for both realms. First, it takes a look at visualizations from the most basic (point, bar, and pie charts among others) to the more specialized (bubble and candlestick charts). Then it examines some of the underlying technology for displaying these visualizations online, primarily HTML5 and SVG.

EXPLORING THE VISUAL DATA SPECTRUM

Trying to choose the right representation for your data is like being a child and walking into a toy store for the first time. There are just so many shiny, attractive options from which to choose. Whether you go with basic building blocks, such as a pie or bar chart, or opt for a more sophisticated conveyance, such as a timeline-based infographic, depends on many factors. To ensure you're making the correct selection, it's important you understand the full range of choices available to you. This section examines a wide range of data visualization possibilities from the simple to the robust.

Charting Primitives

Graphic artists refer to core elements such as lines, rectangles, and ovals as drawing primitives. We borrowed that concept, applied it to data visualizations, and christened it *charting primitives*. Included in this collection are the most familiar members of the visualizations family: plotted points, line charts, bar charts, pie charts, and area charts.

Even though these visualization types are the most basic, there is a thriving set of variations for each one. Although many options are design-oriented—such as 2D versus 3D—others are crucial for representing sophisticated data in a meaningful way.

Data Points

The data point is perhaps the most basic of the charting primitives. A data point is a single element plotted on a graph, typically via the X and Y axes. For this reason, data point charts are also known as XY charts. Moreover, because they can appear as dots scattered across the plane (see Figure 3-1), you may often see them referred to as *scatter charts*.

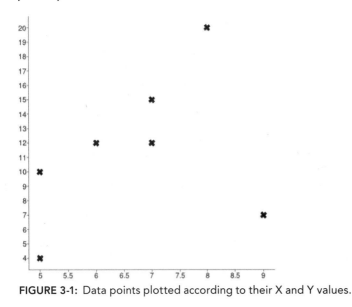

FIGURE 3-1: Data points plotted according to their X and Y values.

Plotted data points are used to illustrate the interconnection between two different sets of data; this interconnection is referred to as the *correlation*. If the data points on the graph appear to be random, without a discernable pattern, there is said to be no correlation. *Positive correlation* occurs when the values generally increase together. The correlation is considered negative when one value goes down while the other goes up. If there is a one-to-one correspondence in either case, the correlation is considered perfect.

Line Charts

When you connect two data points with a continuous line, you create the first segment in a line chart. Line charts are among the most common and form the basis for other types of charts: area, stacked line, and curve fit (also known as smooth line) among others. A single data series is rendered as one line moving from point to point, as shown in Figure 3-2.

FIGURE 3-2: In line charts, markers are often used to highlight the data points on the grid.

Often used to depict data points over time, line charts of sufficient breadth can effectively become trend lines, although they are not necessarily predictive. Stock price charting frequently incorporates line charts, which can be depicted in numerous ways, including a day-to-day change and a percentage change from the median over a set period (see Figure 3-3).

PerfChart: AAPL

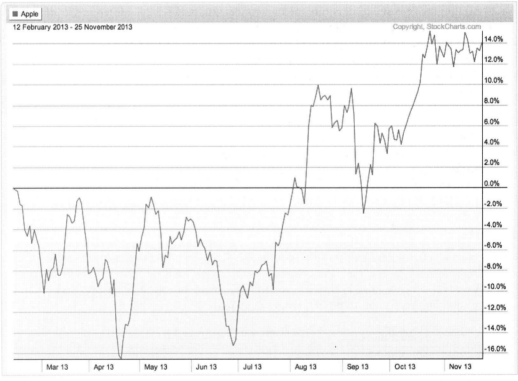

SOURCE: CHART COURTESY OF STOCKCHARTS.COM

FIGURE 3-3: Stock prices, like these percentage variations for Apple, Inc. over a period of 200 days, provide ample material for a line chart.

> **NOTE** *Although it is possible to present line charts in 3D, we don't find the 3D perspective in line charts as effective as in other charting elements, such as a bar or pie chart. That's because the 3D perspective can actually obscure the values. Regardless of your stylistic preferences, you should never compromise the information in your charts.*

Variations in color, weight (or thickness), and type of line—solid, dotted, dashed, and so forth—by themselves or in combination with each other, can be used to depict different data series. Figure 3-4 shows such a line chart with five data series, varied by line color and placement. Another technique is to apply different markers, identifying the data points; markers can be a variety of shapes, such as circles, squares, or diamonds, or even different graphics. (You can see Figure 3-4 in full color in the color insert.)

Seasonality Chart: AMZN,$SPX

Source: Chart courtesy of StockCharts.com

FIGURE 3-4: When comparing data sets with the same unit of measure, as with this seasonality chart of Amazon stock prices over 5 years, line charts can be shown one above the other.

To clarify a data point in a line segment, the exact information can be displayed when the user hovers his or her cursor over a point on the line or taps the point on a mobile device screen.

Stacked line charts, as the term suggests, essentially display one line chart data set above one or more others, but unlike the example shown in Figure 3-4, they typically include the different Y-axis scales. This layout allows for varying units of measure. You could, for example, stack one chart of profit data, another of the percentage of market share, and a third of number of employees over the same time range. All three have different measurement units, yet by offering the visual comparison brought by a stacked line chart, patterns emerge and trends can be identified (see Figure 3-5).

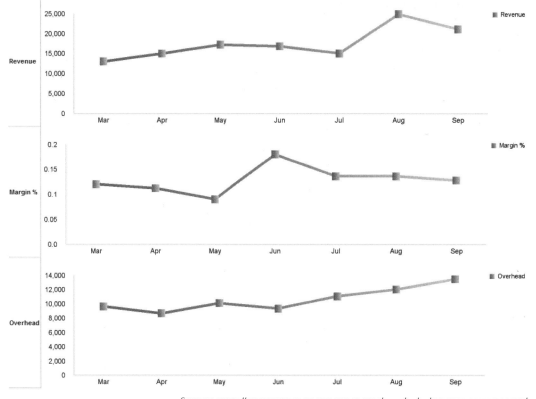

Source: http://www.performance-ideas.com/2012/03/27/stacked-line-charts/

FIGURE 3-5: This example of a stacked line chart by Christoph Papenfuss compares revenue, margin, and overhead over the same timeframe.

Most often, the lines are drawn straight from one point to another. However, some line charts incorporate arcing lines for a more curved, smooth appearance, like those shown in a bell curve. The lines in these types of charts (see Figure 3-6) are said to be *curved* or *spline line charts*.

Polynomial or other mathematical functions—such as quadratic, exponential, or periodic—are applied to the points to smooth the line. A consideration to keep in mind when converting a straight line chart to a curved line chart is that applying any sort of mathematical curving function introduces an approximation of data rather than the precise data itself. However, in some instances, this approximation may be acceptable and even desirable.

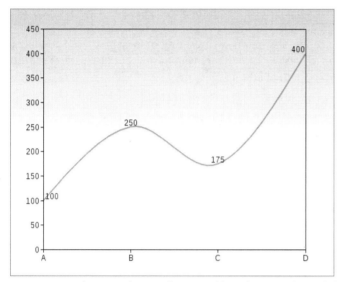

FIGURE 3-6: The smoothness of a curved line chart is achieved through the application of a mathematical function to draw the line.

Bar Charts

Bar charts use one or more proportionately sized rectangular elements to represent specific data values. The rectangles are presented either horizontally or vertically; if the latter, the bars may be referred to as columns. Frequently, multiple bars are placed side-by-side to illustrate relative differences, and the impact of the chart relies on this comparison (see Figure 3-7).

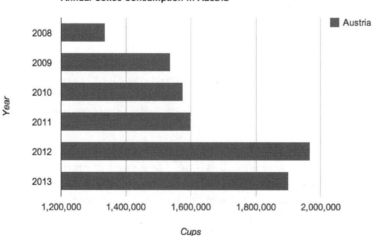

FIGURE 3-7: Bar charts are great for at-a-glance comparisons, such as this one that shows a big spike in Austrian coffee drinking in 2012.

In a bar chart, one axis sets the categories being considered; these categories may be date related, such as a series of months or quarters; locations, such as states or sales offices; or other relevant groupings. The opposing axis shows a series of values in a single unit of measure, most often in an ascending, bottom-to-top, arrangement. The scale of measurement varies, but often starts at zero and extends to a number at or slightly above the highest value entry.

In addition to the simple bar graph, there are two other distinct types of bar charts: grouped and stacked. As the name implies, a grouped bar chart places bars representing related members of a subcategory adjacent to each other—grouped, if you will—beside other similar collections of bars, as shown in Figure 3-8. (You can see Figure 3-8 in full color in the color insert.)

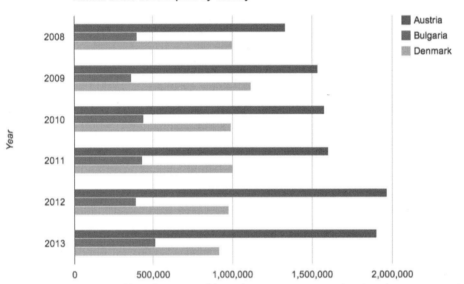
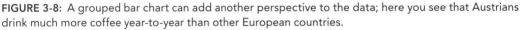

FIGURE 3-8: A grouped bar chart can add another perspective to the data; here you see that Austrians drink much more coffee year-to-year than other European countries.

Stacked bar charts work with subgroups as well, but instead of presenting each cluster as its own individual bar, the subgroups are placed on top of each other to represent a cumulative total value (see Figure 3-9, which is also printed in full color in the color insert). The subgroups are differentiated in some manner, such as varying colors or patterns, each of which is identified with a legend.

All manner of bar charts lend themselves very well to 3D styling. The illusion of depth is heightened by the perspective angle of the viewer relative to the charting elements combined with the rotation, pitch, and yaw of the three-dimensional space itself around the X, Y, and Z axes, respectively. There are so many variations possible when working with 3D bar charts that it can be difficult to decide which one is most fitting. The bar chart shown in Figure 3-10—as simple as it is—went through numerous iterations before being finalized in order to convey the basic information, as well as create the desired impact.

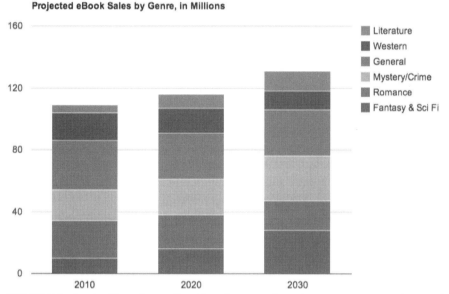

FIGURE 3-9: Stacked bar charts, like this column version, show aggregate totals as well as individual levels.

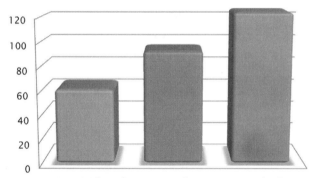

FIGURE 3-10: 3D bar charts typically incorporate shadows and shading to render the three-dimensional imagery in a 2D medium.

NOTE *There are numerous shape variations for bar charts, including cylinders, cones, and pyramids. Some specific constructions, like pyramids, may at first glance appear to work exceedingly well with stacked bar graphs. However, the representation of the data can be misleading because although the height of the element is used to depict the value, the varied volume of the object conveys a different impression. For example, the pyramid chart shown in Figure 3-11 indicates that the top level is 26.76 percent of the total, and the bottom is 23.32 percent. Although the top slice of the pyramid is appropriately a bit taller than the lowest level, volumetrically the bottom is many times larger. For bar charts such as these, labeling is critical.*

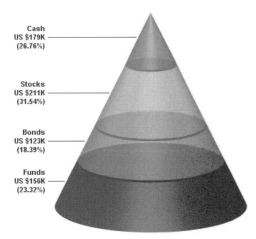

Cash
US $179K
(26.76%)

Stocks
US $211K
(31.54%)

Bonds
US $123K
(18.39%)

Funds
US $156K
(23.32%)

SOURCE: WWW.ADVSOFTENG.COM/GALLERY_PYRAMID.HTML

FIGURE 3-11: Pyramid and other alternative bar chart shapes can be compelling visually but must be labeled properly to avoid data misinterpretation.

Pie Charts

A pie chart is a circular graph composed of separate portions of the circle—a.k.a. *sectors*—to represent relative data sizes of the overall sample, or, in other words, the entire pie. Whereas the data series in a bar chart are open ended and do not need to match any particular total, by their very nature the data series percentages in a pie chart must equal 100 percent. Pie charts like the one shown in Figure 3-12 are great for showing simple relationships between various data segments.

Popular Breeds

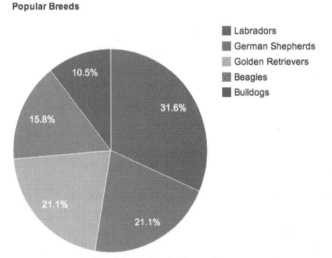

■ Labradors
■ German Shepherds
■ Golden Retrievers
■ Beagles
■ Bulldogs

10.5%

31.6%

15.8%

21.1%

21.1%

FIGURE 3-12: When labeled with data values, a pie chart gives you the hard numbers as well as the visual percentage.

The proportionate size of the sectors or pie slices are determined formulaically where the data value is divided by the total of all values and then multiplied by 100 to find the percentage of the total. That percentage is then multiplied by 360, the number of degrees in a circle, to get the size of the arc for each sector in degrees. For example, consider the following data points.

	NORTH	SOUTH	EAST	WEST	TOTAL
Data	200	125	175	150	650

The total for all values is 650. Dividing the value of each segment by the total provides that segment's percentage (see Table 3-1).

TABLE 3-1: Percentage of Pie Chart Data

	NORTH	SOUTH	EAST	WEST	TOTAL
Data	200	125	175	150	650
Percentage (Data / Total Data)	30.8%	19.2%	27.9%	23.1%	100%

Multiplying the percentages by 360 results in the degrees for each data point, as shown in Table 3-2.

TABLE 3-2: Degrees of Pie Chart Data

	NORTH	SOUTH	EAST	WEST	TOTAL
Data	200	125	175	150	650
Percentage (Data / Total Data)	30.8%	19.2%	27.9%	23.1%	100%
Degree (Percentage × 360)	111°	69°	97°	83°	360°

As you can see, the total for all degrees is equal to 360, a complete circle. Pie charts frequently display both the raw data and the calculated percentages, either all the time or when the user hovers over or taps a particular slice, as shown in Figure 3-13.

To emphasize a particular data point, the associated pie slice is moved slightly from the center or exploded. The exploded pie chart is particularly effective in 3D (see Figure 3-14). As with bar charts, 3D pie charts can be tilted in any orientation and are typically rendered with shading and shadows.

Occasionally, it is helpful to drill down further into a particular pie segment to provide more detail. One technique for accomplishing this is to create a "pie of pie" type chart, where the percentage values of the entire child pie equal the value of the parent slice, as shown in Figure 3-15.

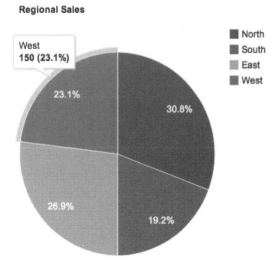

Regional Sales

FIGURE 3-13: The underlying data is available for this pie chart interactively.

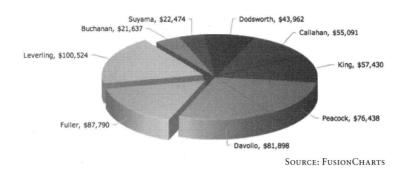

Sales Per Employee

SOURCE: FUSIONCHARTS

FIGURE 3-14: Explode one or more slices of a pie chart—whether 2D or 3D—to highlight them.

Other types of circular charts include donut charts, which can be used to represent multiple series of data. The chart in Figure 3-16, for example, shows a series of countries and their related sales percentages with the total in the middle of the donut.

Another type of circular chart, the polar area diagram, equates the data values to the distance from the center of the circle rather than the percentage degrees of the standard pie chart. Such graphs are often used by meteorologists to chart wind speeds from varying directions in what is referred to as a wind rose like the one shown in Figure 3-17.

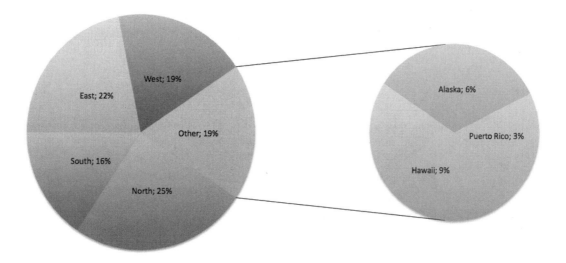

North South East West Hawaii Alaska Puerto Rico

FIGURE 3-15: The pie-of-pie approach breaks a sector out for more detail rather than creating a series of smaller slices.

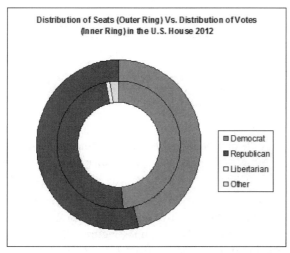

Distribution of Seats (Outer Ring) Vs. Distribution of Votes (Inner Ring) in the U.S. House 2012

Democrat
Republican
Libertarian
Other

HTTP://COMMONS.WIKIMEDIA.ORG/WIKI/FILE:2012_US_HOUSE_DONUT_GRAPH.JPG

FIGURE 3-16: The donut chart uses multiple rings to display a range of related data.

Area Charts

An area chart is, essentially, a line chart where the area between the line and the chart bottom are filled in with a pattern or solid color, as shown in Figure 3-18. Emphasizing the area brings focus to the overall volume indicated by the data.

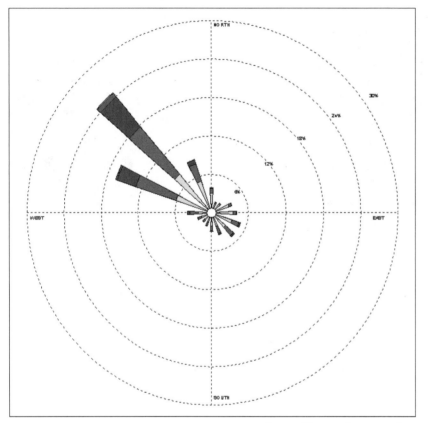

SOURCE: NATURAL RESOURCES CONSERVATION SERVICE, USDA.
FIGURE 3-17: In this polar chart, the wind coming from the northwest is clearly the strongest.

Area charts really come into their own when multiple data series are displayed, either as a side-by-side comparison or overlapping regions. When separate data sets overlap, consider using semi-transparent colors so that all data is visible (see Figure 3-19).

When cumulative data is important, another approach is to stack the area charts, one on top of the other. Similar to stacked bar charts, stacked area charts show relative data values for numerous data sets, typically over a date range as well as displaying the total. For example, Figure 3-20 shows the number of cars, motorcycles, and bicycles involved in traffic incidents from 1999 to 2012. Because of the nature of the stacked area chart, it is immediately apparent that the overall incidents declined, mostly because of the drop in motorcycles accidents, whereas both bicycle and automobiles (after 2001) stayed relatively the same. (See Figure 3-20 in full color in the color insert.)

Exploring Advanced Visualizations

Beyond charting primitives lies a vast and expansive field of visualizations. At first glance, some of these more exotic options may seem like so much eye-candy, but the possibilities covered in this section are purpose driven rather than merely decorative. A candlestick chart, for example, is not just a fancy bar chart with different iconography; the candlestick shapes are typically used to plot the high and low points of specified stock prices as well as their open and closing prices. You'll find similar need-based foundations in all the chart types covered in this section, including candlestick, bubble, surface, map, and infographics.

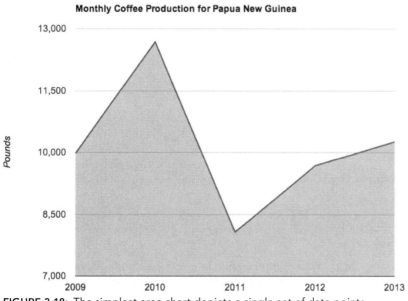

FIGURE 3-18: The simplest area chart depicts a single set of data points.

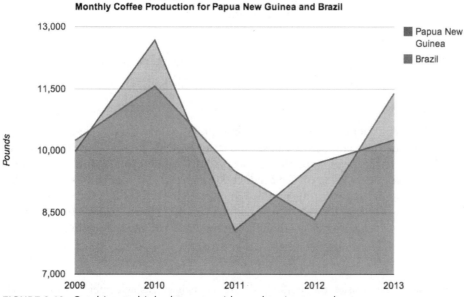

FIGURE 3-19: Combine multiple data sets with overlapping area charts.

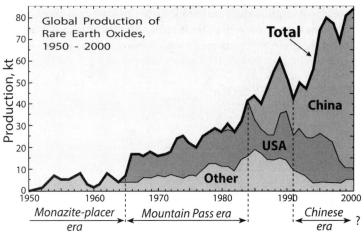

FIGURE 3-20: Stacked area charts enable you to quickly grasp overall trends as well as specific data set changes.

Candlestick Chart

Candlestick charts can convey a great deal of information in a very compact package. A complete candlestick chart combines aspects of both line and bar charts and is generally used in tracking stocks, commodities, and similar exchange items over a range of time.

The primary element is really only a literal candlestick if you consider the old saying "burning the candle at both ends" to be a real possibility. The various elements of the candlestick are derived from four different values, each related to a trading price:

➤ **High:** The top of the upper candlestick wick or *shadow*

➤ **Close:** The bottom of the upper shadow and the top of the candle or body

➤ **Open:** The top of the lower shadow and the bottom of the body

➤ **Low:** The bottom of the lower shadow

Each candlestick displays a data set of values at a specific point in time and complete candlestick charts comprise many such elements as you can see in Figure 3-21. What's really great about candlestick charts is the depth of the information that is conveyed. In addition to tracking the movement of prices over a given period, the length of the candle body indicates the relative pressure in either selling or buying. An additional convention is added to indicate the direction of the pressure: If the body is hollow, the close is greater than the open and buying is more prevalent, whereas if the body is filled with a color, the closing price is less than the opening and selling is predominant.

Bubble Chart

Bubble charts add an extra dimension to the standard data point chart. A single bubble in a bubble chart utilizes three values: one for each axis that determines position on the graph and a third value, indicated by the bubble's size, which could represent any other relevant value. For example, in Figure 3-22 the bubbles are mapped according to life expectancy (X axis) and fertility rate (Y axis) while their size is derived from the population of the countries. Bubble charts like this can help illustrate "apple-to-apple" comparisons; in this example, you can see that although Great Britain and Germany have about the same population size and life expectancy, the fertility rate in the UK is much higher.

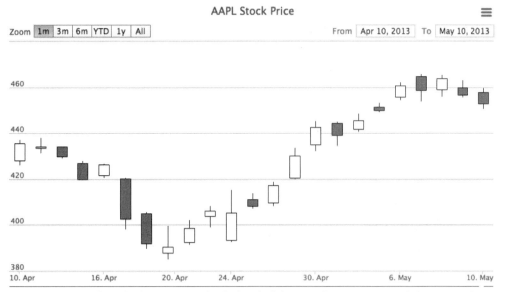

FIGURE 3-21: Candlestick charts convey both detailed data, such as opening and closing stock prices, as well as general trends.

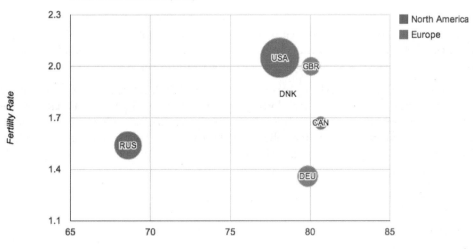

FIGURE 3-22: Bubble charts allow for three data values per element.

The chart shown in Figure 3-22 also demonstrates one of the issues with bubble charts. See the data point below the USA and GBR? Well, maybe you can and maybe you can't. The much smaller circle with the initials DNK is for Denmark. If the third value is relatively too small—as is the case here in Denmark's population—it may not be noticeable. The problem is exacerbated when the third value is zero or negative. Be sure to review all of your data carefully to ensure that all values are fully represented before opting for the bubble chart.

Surface Charts

Whereas many charts use 3D graphics for visual flare, the surface chart is, by its very definition, three dimensional. Similar to bubble charts, surface charts allow you to convey data in three dimensions, for instance Figure 3-23 uses a surface chart to show rainfall distribution across both latitude and longitude.

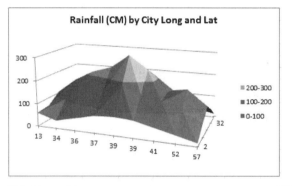

SOURCE: HTTP://DEDICATEDEXCEL.COM/AN-OVERVIEW-OF-CHARTS-IN-EXCEL-2010/

FIGURE 3-23: Surface maps show three dimensions of data.

Another factor that distinguishes surface charts from other chart types is the use of color. Typically, with line and bar graphs, color is used to identify data sets across one or more axes. With a surface chart, separate colors are used to represent a range of data as it maps to the three axes (X, Y, and Z) as shown in Figure 3-24 (which is shown in full color in the color insert).

Instead of 2D and 3D options, the surface chart can be displayed with solid, color-filled regions or as a wireframe. Wireframes are useful when plotting a great deal of data and it's essential to render results quickly and illustrate the data point more clearly. However, because color is such a critical differentiator in surface charts, the lack of a solid colored area in a surface wireframe makes them somewhat difficult to read. A good compromise is to overlay a standard surface map with a grid-like wireframe (see Figure 3-25; you can find it in the color insert).

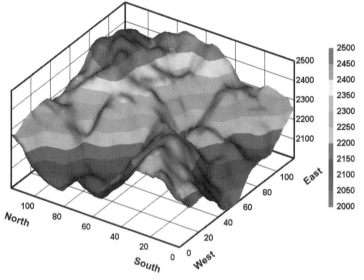

Source: DPlot Graph Software

FIGURE 3-24: Surface maps use color to identify a range of data, as shown by the legend on the right of the figure.

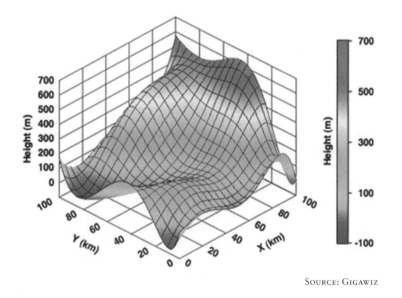

Source: Gigawiz

FIGURE 3-25: Combine solid and wireframe surface charts to get a finer degree of data visualization with the easy readability of color ranges.

Map Charts

Surface charts may appear to be terrain-like, but data visualization offers actual topographic alternatives when needed. In this context, a map chart combines the rendering of a geographic area with selected data, which may be represented as highlighted regions with or without custom markers. The maps themselves can be as detailed as necessary—up to and including being depicted with satellite photography—or they can be rendered as one-color outlines, like the one in Figure 3-26.

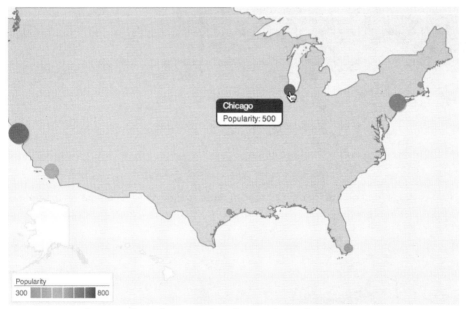

FIGURE 3-26: This map chart shows city locations and populations.

Another type of map chart is the geomap or geochart. Map charts used actual mapping data, which is overlaid with data-driven markers; typically, you can zoom into and scroll around a map chart, just as you could an online map. A geomap, on the other hand, is typically not scrollable and has only limited zoomability. Geomaps also can incorporate bubble-type markers, where the size of the marker is related to a data set. It is possible, however, to include interactivity to reveal data point details on both types of map charts (see Figure 3-27).

Infographics

Like the word itself, an infographic combines information and graphics. In a sense, the term could be applied to any kind of chart, but it has come to encompass a much broader range of conveying knowledge through design. Infographics appeal to the aspect of people that learns visually to both impart relevant information and persuade observers of the inherent message. They range from the simplest *USA Today* front-page graphic on what's happening to densely detailed posters published by the U.S. government (see Figure 3-28) and everything in between—and beyond.

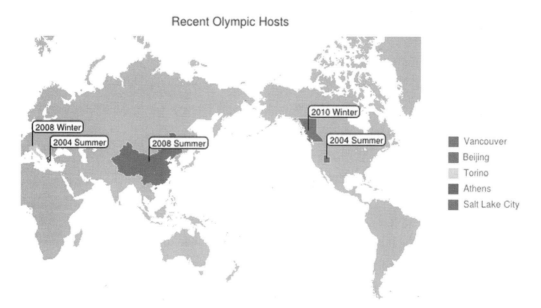

FIGURE 3-27: Map charts can reference the globe while highlighting targeted countries.

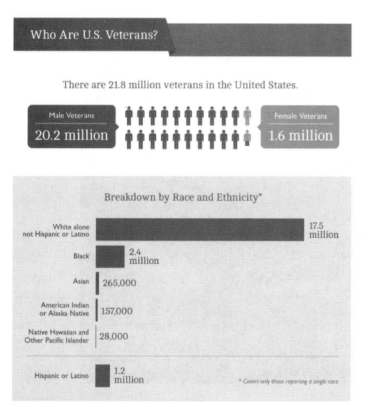

FIGURE 3-28: This excerpt from an infographic on veterans published by the U.S. Census bureau combines iconography, bar charts, and detailed information.

> **NOTE** *Whether imparting serious or frivolous information, infographics are a designer's playground. It's no wonder that there are many online sites that highlight infographics. You can find amazing, inspirational examples at Visual.ly* (`http://visual.ly`)*, Daily Infographic* (`http://dailyinfographic.com`)*, and Cool Infographics* (`http://www.coolinfographics.com`)*.*

Edward Tufte—affectionately known as ET—is one of the champions of infographics in the modern era. In his book *Visual Display of Qualitative Information* (Graphics Press, 2001), he outlines a number of key principles of infographics, including the following:

➤ Show your data. The data itself is critical to an infographic.

➤ Engender thought on the infographic's subject. The goal is to keep the focus on the substance rather than on the prettiness of the graphics or the methodology.

➤ Keep true to your data. Distorting information to make a specific point undercuts the very nature of data.

➤ Encourage comparisons. Numerous data visualizations, such as bar charts, create easy-to-grasp correlations and should be incorporated where possible.

You can see many of these principles in the work of government agencies, such as the infographic from the Jet Propulsion Laboratory shown in Figure 3-29.

Source: NASA

FIGURE 3-29: This infographic from NASA's JPL provides proportional planets with key details about the atmospheres of neighboring planets.

MAKING USE OF THE HTML5 CANVAS

Canvas is one of the most innovative and impactful elements of the HTML5 language, especially in regard to data visualization. With the <canvas> tag, a designer creates a reserved open-ended area on the web page to contain programmatically created graphics at run-time. HTML5 canvas imagery is powered by a robust JavaScript API—the vast majority of which enjoys a healthy degree of cross-browser support currently and can be put to use immediately.

The first step in working with <canvas> is to include the tag in the <body> section of your HTML page. You only need to include three attributes: ID, width, and height. Should this tag not be supported by a browser, you can display an alternative. Any content—whether an alternative image or text message—can be inserted between the opening and closing <canvas> tags. Here's a complete <canvas> tag listing:

```
<canvas id="chart1" width="600" height="400">
  <img src="images/altchart1.jpg">
</canvas>
```

At this stage, nothing would be displayed on the page in this reserved space, assuming the browser supported the HTML5 <canvas> tag. It's quite literally a blank canvas. To draw on the canvas, it needs to be "primed" or initialized with JavaScript. Typically, you do this by placing the necessary JavaScript function in the <head> and calling it when the document is ready. The following are the basic steps for initializing the canvas:

1. Create a variable to hold the canvas object, as identified by its ID.

2. Check to see if the canvas API getContext() method (and thus, the <canvas> tag) is supported.

3. If so, create a variable and apply the getContext() method for the targeted canvas object.

In practice, the code looks like this:

```
<script type="text/javascript">
  function drawCanvas(){
    var theChart = document.getElementById('chart1');
    if (theChart.getContext){
      var theContext = theChart.getContext('2d');
    }
  }
</script>
```

> **NOTE** *In their development of the canvas specification, the W3C indicated that the canvas context value initially defined was two-dimensional or "2d". This action was taken with the thought of possibility extending the specification to include a "3d" context. Although that extension has not really taken hold, a viable replacement, WebGL, has. WebGL libraries specifically for data visualization, such as the one from InCharts3D (http://incharts3d.com/) are beginning to emerge.*

After the context of the canvas is defined, all drawing calls reference this variable with the canvas area treated as coordinate space. The declared width and height attributes of the <canvas> tag determine the number of pixels available in the grid. In this example:

```
<canvas id="chart1" width="600" height="400">
```

There are 600 pixels in the X axis and 400 in the Y. The grid origin (0,0) is, by default, placed in the upper-left corner of the canvas. Armed with this information, a primitive canvas object—a filled rectangle—can be drawn with the fillRect() function. This function takes four arguments: x, y, width, and height. The first two values identify the upper-left corner of the rectangle, whereas the latter two, obviously, supply the dimensions; all values are specified in pixels. For example, to draw a simple filled rectangle 100 pixels wide by 200 tall, where the upper-left corner starts at 50 pixels from the left edge of the canvas and 200 from the top edge, the basic function would look like this:

```
fillRect(50,200,100,200)
```

The output in Figure 3-30 shows the start of a basic bar chart.

FIGURE 3-30: With canvas, you can begin to programmatically create bar charts using the rectangle drawing primitive.

Here's the complete HTML page code for drawing the first rectangle. We've added some basic CSS styling and a tad more HTML to center and outline the canvas.

```
<!doctype html>
<html>
<head>
```

```
<meta charset="UTF-8">
<title>Canvas Example 1</title>
<script type="text/javascript">
  function drawCanvas(){
    var theChart = document.getElementById('chart1');
    if (theChart.getContext){
      var theContext = theChart.getContext('2d');
    theContext.fillRect(50,200,100,200);
    }
  }
</script>
<style>
  #outerWrapper {
    width: 800px;
    margin: 1em auto;
  }
  canvas {
    border: 1px solid #000;
  }
</style>
</head>

<body onload="drawCanvas();">
<div id="outerWrapper">
  <canvas id="chart1" width="600" height="400">
    <img src="images/altchart1.jpg" width="600" height="400">
  </canvas>
</div>
</body>
</html>
```

> **NOTE** *Note that in this simple example, the JavaScript* `onload()` *function is used in the* `<body>` *tag to call the previously defined* `drawCanvas()` *function. In a production scenario, you'd be more likely to use the* `DOMContentLoaded()` *or jQuery* `document.ready()` *function to trigger* `drawCanvas()`.

The canvas API is fairly robust and you can programmatically perform many different illustrating operations. Here's a partial list of what's possible:

➤ Rectangles, both solid and outlined

➤ Points of any dimension

➤ Connected straight lines

➤ Arcs

➤ Circles and ovals, both solid and outlined

➤ Text, with specified font, size, and color

➤ Import images

➤ Complete color control, including alpha transparency

➤ Gradients of any color combination, linear or radial

➤ Shadows of any object or text

➤ Patterns of any object, repeated in a specified direction

In addition to the basic drawing options listed here, canvas objects can be scaled, rotated, and moved (or translated) anywhere on—or off—the canvas. These features can be applied to create animated canvas graphics, such as zooming timelines, all under programmer or user control.

Finally, it's worth noting that canvas typically provides better performance than other drawing alternatives. When you combine that with the plethora of styling options, it's no wonder that many charting plug-ins—such as ChartJS, RGraph, FusionCharts, and Flot—offer `<canvas>` tag–based output.

INTEGRATING SVG

SVG, short for Scalable Vector Graphics, is a useful alternative to HTML5 canvas. Like canvas, SVG enables run-time graphics in a format supported by most modern browsers. Unlike the pixel-based canvas, SVG is, as the name plainly states, vector based. Vectors are resolution independent—which means they do not degrade in quality if rescaled or magnified—and often result in a smaller file size than rasterized graphics.

SVG has been a W3C-approved specification since 2003 and, consequently, enjoys rich tool support, notably Adobe Illustrator and the open-source Inkscape. When a file has been exported as SVG, it can be integrated into a web page with the basic `<img>` tag, like this:

```
<img src="images/chartLogo.svg" width="400" height="150" >
```

> **REFERENCE** *There are some dedicated and enthusiastic supporters of SVG. For a great visual sampler, visit SVG Wow (`http://svg-wow.org`).*

SVG can also be created as an XML file or placed inline in an HTML page. The code requires the use of an XML namespace as well as a particular syntax. Unlike canvas, you don't need JavaScript to create graphics programmatically, although an SVG DOM component is available. Rather, the drawing instructions are detailed in the XML. For example, the following code creates a blue circle in the middle of an area 400 pixels square:

```
<svg height="400" xmlns="http://www.w3.org/2000/svg">
<circle id="circle1" cx="400" cy="200" r="50" fill="blue" />
</svg>
```

After the SVG area is defined (complete with namespace declaration), the `<circle>` tag includes attributes for cx, cy, r, and fill—the center-x, center-y, radius, and fill color, respectively. You can see the result in Figure 3-31.

FIGURE 3-31: This SVG was drawn using XML in the markup.

In addition to offering the same core drawing capabilities as canvas, like rectangles, ovals, lines, polygons, text, gradients, and so forth, SVG also includes a number of filters to provide special effects. Some of the possibilities of SVG effects include the following:

➤ Blend

➤ Offset

➤ Gaussian blur

➤ Color matrix

➤ Composite

➤ Convolve matrix

➤ Diffuse lighting

➤ Specular lighting

➤ Tiling

➤ Turbulence

> **NOTE** *SVG filters are compatible with the latest round of browsers but would not be a good choice if you needed to support older versions.*

SVG filters can be combined. Figure 3-32, for example, shows a combination of blending, offset, and Gaussian blur to add a drop shadow to the previously drawn blue circle.

FIGURE 3-32: Four different filters were combined to create the drop shadow of this SVG drawn circle.

With the scalable vector graphics capability and inherent small size, SVG is an extremely viable medium for data visualization. On the pro side, SVGs are DOM accessible, meaning that you can reference and adjust the values in an SVG, in turn seeing those changes reflected on the screen. On the con side, this DOM accessibility comes at the cost of performance; SVG typically performs worse than canvas.

> **REFERENCE** *Numerous online tools, including the Google Charts API and Raphaël, support SVG. For a closer look at each, see Chapters 9 and 10.*

SUMMARY

When it comes to data visualization, there are a ton of options, both in final rendered output and the underlying technology used to get there. Here are a few things to keep in mind when considering the possibilities:

➤ There are numerous basic charts—or charting primitives—to choose from, most of which include many variations.

➤ Primarily used to chart stock prices, candlestick charts contain a wealth of details, including opening, closing, high, and low prices.

➤ One axis of a bar chart is presented as a single unit of measure, whether numeric, currency, or time-based.

➤ Grouped bar charts compare one collection of bars in related subcategories to other collections; stacked bar charts show a combined value.

➤ To show percentages with multiple data series, use several rings in a donut chart.

➤ When rendering more than one data set in an area chart, be sure to choose semi-transparent colors for the fill color to enable all data to be viewed.

➤ Both bubble and surface charts relay three dimensional data.

➤ Integrated map visualizations can range from photo-realistic to simple outlined regions or borders.

➤ Infographics combine detailed information with related graphics and often incorporate a variety of different charting types.

➤ HTML5 canvas and SVG are two effective tools for drawing graphics in the browser, each with different pros and cons.

Part II: Working with JavaScript for Analysis

4

Integrating Existing Data

WHAT'S IN THIS CHAPTER

➤ The basics of working asynchronously

➤ Techniques for working with different data formats (CSV, XML and JSON)

➤ Shortcuts for styling structured data

➤ Example of rendering external JSON data as a chart

> **CODE DOWNLOAD** *The wrox.com code downloads for this chapter are found at* www.wrox.com/go/javascriptandjqueryanalysis *on the Download Code tab. The code is in the chapter 04 download and individually named according to the names throughout the chapter.*

The lion's share of the data visualist's work involves rendering existing data. Data can be stored in many different formats—plain text, CSV, XML, JSON, and others—but as long as it is in a digital format, chances are there are JavaScript and other server-side routines to access the information for representation. Naturally, some circumstances, such as building a complex infographic, require that you incorporate data manually. However, wherever possible, it's a good idea to keep content (the data) separate from presentation (the charting) as demonstrated throughout this chapter. Not only does this methodology make it a breeze to make updates, but it also opens the door to enhanced accessibility and data transparency.

READING DATA FROM STANDARD TEXT FILES

Data is often stored in a plain text file. To be clear, "plain" or "standard" text refers to files such as
.txt files that contain no extraneous coding or meta information. This section examines techniques
for reading plain text files one line at a time as well as importing and parsing the ubiquitous CSV
format.

Working Asynchronously

There are numerous methods for reading data from a text file, but in the online world it's a good
idea to handle this task asynchronously. Most JavaScript libraries incorporate some form of Ajax
(Asynchronous JavaScript and XML). Using Ajax makes it possible for you to read text files without
refreshing the page. Ajax not only provides performance benefits but also helps you to build single-
page apps (SPAs).

Take a look at a basic text file (which is on the companion website as sample.txt), composed of
several lines of data, like this:

```
Line one
Line two
Line three
Line four
```

After you've included the jQuery library, you can use the get() method to pull in the data.
Following is some basic code that reads the text file and outputs what it finds in a JavaScript alert
(shown in Figure 4-1):

```
jQuery.get('sample.txt', function(theData) {
  alert(theData);
});
```

Get data from text file

Line one
Line two
Line three
Line four

FIGURE 4-1: No additional parsing is needed when outputting the get() method to a console device, such
as an alert dialog box.

The alert_data.html file is on the companion website.

The get() method is shorthand for the jQuery.ajax method and, as such, is fairly robust. Not only
can the get() method pass a URL and a callback, you can also send additional data to the server,
get the status of the request, and more. To learn more about the get() API, visit the jQuery docs:
http://api.jquery.com/jquery.get/.

Reading CSV Files

Although it is possible to store and retrieve basic, unstructured data from a text file, it's far more common to work with CSV files. A CSV file consists of data where each line is a record and each record can contain a number of data columns. The values in each data column are, typically, separated by commas—hence the acronym for Comma Separated Values. The most basic CSV file looks like this:

```
one,two,three
four,five,six
```

The values in a CSV sometimes contain commas themselves, and when that's true, the values must be enclosed or *delimited*, usually with single or double quotes. The separator and delimiter characters are flexible, but must be taken into account when the file is parsed.

> **NOTE** *The standard for CSV files is maintained by the Internet Engineering Task Force (IETF). You can find it online at* `http://tools.ietf.org/html/rfc4180`.

Parsing can be quite challenging, depending on the variables of the particular text file. Luckily, programmer Evan Plaice developed a code library that handles all the heavy lifting. The library, called jquery-csv, is available at `https://code.google.com/p/jquery-csv`.

The jquery-csv library offers a nice range of functionality, including a variety of methods to parse CSVs as well as settings for separators, delimiters, and so on. Using the library's `toObjects()` method you can parse CSV data and quickly present it as an HTML table. First include a reference to the library in your web page:

```
<script src="http://jquery-csv.googlecode.com/git/src/jquery.csv.js"></script>
```

Next, set up your HTML `<body>` with a table, specifying an ID that jQuery can work with:

```
<div class="result">
   <table id="theResult" border="1"></table>
</div>
```

With jquery-csv's help, parsing the data is very straightforward. But before you get started, it's a good idea to establish the groundwork for building the table markup:

```
function createTable(data) {
  var html = '';

  if(data[0].constructor === Object) {
    // build the table header
    html += '<tr>\r\n';
    for(var item in data[0]) {
```

```
      html += '<th>' + item + '</th>\r\n';
    }
    html += '</tr>\r\n';

    // build the table rows
    for(var row in data) {
      html += '<tr>\r\n';
      for(var item in data[row]) {
        html += '<td>' + data[row][item] + '</td>\r\n';
      }
      html += '</tr>\r\n';
    }
  }
  return html;
}
```

This custom `createTable()` function first loops through the first row of data to pull the column names for the CSV and output those in the table. Next it loops through each row, building the rest of the table markup in the process. It uses for-in loops to keep the function flexible enough to work with any number of headers. Pay attention to the use of `data[row][item]`—it drills into the two-dimensional array to grab the current row and item.

With the `createTable()` function complete, you're ready to import and parse the CSV data using the jQuery `get()` method you saw earlier:

```
$( document ).ready(function() {
  $.get('stores.csv', function(theData) {
    var data = $.csv.toObjects(theData);
    var theHtml = createTable(data);
    $('#theResult').html(theHtml);
  });
});
```

Here the `csv.toObjects()` method converts the CSV data to an object named `data`, which is then passed to the `createTable()` function. Then, that markup is injected into the DOM using jQuery's `html()` function. Figure 4-2 shows the unstyled table—with all the data dynamically inserted from a CSV file.

Pull data from CSV file into an object and output as table

Store Name	Address	City	State	Postal Code	Hours
Cindy's Art Gallery	6410 Cindy Lane	Beverly Hills	CA	90212	9:00-5:00 Monday to Friday
Mudgee Art	1001 Mark Ave	San Francisco	CA	94123	9:00-4:30 Monday to Friday
Carpinteria Galleria	6321 Carpinteria Ave	Carpinteria	CA	93013	9:00-5:00 Monday to Friday
Nirvana	153-155 Maitland Street	Ventura	CA	93003	9:00-9:00, 7 days
Cindy's Art Annex	6398 Cindy Lane	Oxnard	CA	93033	09:00-16:30 Monday to Friday
Via Real 3D	6392 Via Real	Carpinteria	CA	93013	08:30 -16:30 Monday to Friday

FIGURE 4-2: Data from CSV files are commonly presented in table format.

The full code for this example is in the `read_csv_into_array.html` file on the companion website.

> **NOTE** *The jquery-csv documentation also includes examples for importing CSV files to use the jQuery plotting library, Flot* (`http://jquery-csv.googlecode.com/git/examples/flot.html`), *and the Google Visualization API* (`http://jquery-csv.googlecode.com/git/examples/google-visualization.html`).

INCORPORATING XML DATA

XML, short for Extensible Markup Language, is often used for storing data of all kinds. This tag-based language is extremely flexible. In fact, there is only one set element, `<?xml?>`, and everything else is custom-fitted to the file needs.

Understanding the XML Format

XML relies on nested tags to create its structure. After the opening `<?xml?>` tag, typically a root node is established that encompasses all the other content. In the following examples, `<sales>` is the root node, followed by data for two regions:

```xml
<?xml version="1.0" encoding="UTF-8"?>
  <sales>
    <region>
      <territory>Northeast</territory>
      <employees>150</employees>
      <year>
        <date>2013</date>
        <amount>115000</amount>
      </year>
    </region>
    <region>
      <territory>Southeast</territory>
      <employees>125</employees>
      <year>
        <date>2013</date>
        <amount>95000</amount>
      </year>
    </region>
  </sales>
```

You can find the `example_data.xml` file on the companion website.

Notice that there's a strong resemblance to HTML. Both have a common ancestor, Standard General Markup Language (SGML), and there have been several XML-based versions for HTML.

In general, XML is much stricter in terms of format, which makes working with the data it contains that much easier because XML follows a very tight set of rules.

XML elements can also contain attributes. For example, you could restructure the preceding example so that the `<year>` tag is an attribute of region:

```xml
<?xml version="1.0" encoding="UTF-8"?>
  <sales>
    <region year="2013">
      <territory>Northeast</territory>
      <employees>150</employees>
      <amount>115,000</amount>
    </region>
    <region year="2013">
      <territory>Southeast</territory>
      <employees>125</employees>
      <amount>95,000</amount>
    </region>
  </sales>
```

Getting XML Data

You can pull data from an XML file into an HTML page in a number of ways, and jQuery's built-in functionality makes the process very straightforward. With the `ajax()` method, you can get any XML file and send the data to a custom parser function:

```javascript
$.ajax({
    type: "GET",
    url: "regional_sales.xml",
    dataType: "xml",
    success: xmlParser
});
```

To understand how to apply the parser function—here called `xmlParser`—you need to know the basic structure of the XML file. The file used in this example follows:

```xml
<?xml version="1.0" encoding="UTF-8"?>
<sales>
  <region year="2013">
    <territory>Northeast</territory>
    <employees>150</employees>
    <amount>115,000</amount>
  </region>
  <region year="2013">
    <territory>Southeast</territory>
    <employees>125</employees>
    <amount>95,000</amount>
  </region>
  <region year="2013">
    <territory>Midwest</territory>
    <employees>225</employees>
    <amount>195,000</amount>
```

```
    </region>
    <region year="2013">
      <territory>West</territory>
      <employees>325</employees>
      <amount>265,000</amount>
    </region>
</sales>
```

Given this data—to extract the territory, the number of employees, and the sales amount values—the custom parser needs to loop through each `<region>` node. First, target these nodes in the XML using jQuery's `find()` function:

```
$(xml).find('region').each(function () {
}
```

Within this `each()` loop, you can assign the values of the XML to variables, and use those variables to build the markup. Then, you can append that markup to the DOM, as shown in the complete `xmlParser()` function here:

```
function xmlParser(xml) {
  $(xml).find('region').each(function () {
    var theTerritory = $(this).find('territory').text();
    var numEmployees = $(this).find('employees').text();
    var theAmount = $(this).find('amount').text();
    $('#sales').append('<tr><td>' + theTerritory + '</td><td>' + numEmployees + '</
td><td>$' + theAmount + '</td></tr>');
  });
}
```

You can find the `import_xml.html` file on the companion website.

After this particular example is executed, it outputs a table (see Figure 4-3).

XML Data Imported

Territory	Employees	Sales
Northeast	150	$115,000
Southeast	125	$95,000
Midwest	225	$195,000
West	325	$265,000

FIGURE 4-3: jQuery includes a built-in XML engine for retrieving and parsing data files.

Styling with XSLT

After you import XML data, it can simply be styled with CSS. However, building up JavaScript strings may not be the most efficient way to incorporate XML, especially if you have a lot of data spread all over the page. One alternative is to use XSLT (Extensible Stylesheet Language

Transformations). As you might suspect from the full name, XSLT does more than style content; it transforms it.

The workflow for incorporating XSLT methodology is somewhat different from what you might be used to:

1. Create an XML data file.
2. Add a link to the XSLT stylesheet in the XML data file.
3. Wrap HTML with XML and XSL tags.
4. Incorporate XSL tags in HTML.
5. Browse the XML file.

In essence, you're mapping the data to an HTML template. An example is provided here so you can see how it works. The example re-creates the table with XML data, but via XSLT.

Starting with a well-formed XML data file, insert an `<?xml-stylesheet?>` tag to link the XSLT file after the opening `<?xml?>` element:

```
<?xml version="1.0" encoding="UTF-8"?>
<?xml-stylesheet type="text/xsl" href="import_xml.xslt"?>
```

Then, open an HTML file that contains the page layout and insert the opening XML declaration:

```
<?xml version="1.0" encoding="UTF-8"?>
```

Wrap the balance of the code in an `<xsl:stylesheet >` tag pair with the proper XSL namespace:

```
<xsl:stylesheet version="1.0" xmlns:xsl="http://www.w3.org/1999/XSL/Transform">
...
</xsl:stylesheet>
```

Insert an `<xsl:output >` element that sets the doctype to HTML, which is all that's needed for an HTML5 document:

```
<xsl:output method="html" encoding="utf-8" indent="yes" />
```

Place an `<xsl:template >` tag pair around the rest of the HTML content and set the `match` attribute to the site root of the data:

```
<xsl:template match="/">
...
</xsl:template>
```

At this stage, the top of the document should look like this:

```
<?xml version="1.0" encoding="UTF-8"?>
<xsl:stylesheet version="1.0" xmlns:xsl="http://www.w3.org/1999/XSL/Transform">
<xsl:output method="html" encoding="utf-8" indent="yes" />
  <xsl:template match="/">
    <html>
```

and the closing should look like this:

```
    </html>
  </xsl:template>
</xsl:stylesheet>
```

Finally, save the file with an `.xslt` extension.

Now, you're ready to insert the necessary code for mapping the XML data to the page. The example scenario has a `<table>` element set up, complete with a header row. All data is contained in the table rows that follow. To loop through this data, use the `<xsl:for-each>` tag that targets the repeating node with the `select` attribute:

```
<xsl:for-each select="sales/region">
  <tr>
  ...
  </tr>
</xsl:for-each>
```

> **NOTE** *Note that the path to the desired node is given, not just the node name itself. This functionality is courtesy of a technology related to XSL called XPath. XPath, like XML and XSLT, is a W3C recommendation and well-supported in all modern browsers.*

Within the `<xsl:for-each>` loop, the XML data values are called with a `<xsl:value-of>` tag, again using the `select` attribute. For example, to get the content of the XML `<territory>` node, the code would be

```
<xsl:value-of select="territory"/>
```

In this scenario, the entire table code, looping through all three XML data values, would be

```
<table id="sales">
  <tr>
    <th>Territory</th>
    <th>Employees</th>
    <th>Sales</th>
  </tr>
  <xsl:for-each select="sales/region">
  <tr>
    <td><xsl:value-of select="territory"/></td>
    <td><xsl:value-of select="employees"/></td>
    <td>$<xsl:value-of select="amount"/></td>
  </tr>
  </xsl:for-each>
</table>
```

You can find the `import_xml_xslt.html` and `ch04_regional_sales_xslt.xml` files on the companion website.

The resulting table, shown in Figure 4-4, is essentially the same as the table developed in the previous example by importing XML data directly via jQuery.

XML Data Imported and Transformed by XSLT

Territory	Employees	Sales
Northeast	150	$115,000
Southeast	125	$95,000
Midwest	225	$195,000
West	325	$265,000

FIGURE 4-4: Use XSLT methodology when developing more complex documents with XML data.

Keep in mind that you need to send the XML file to the browser for viewing, not the XSLT file. It is the transformed XML data that is rendered.

DISPLAYING JSON CONTENT

XML is extremely flexible and quite functional, but it can be a bit heavy syntactically. Fortunately you have another option, JSON, which is designed to improve loading and processing time on the web. JSON is an abbreviation for JavaScript Object Notation and, although it is JavaScript-based, it is actually language- and platform-independent. That said, the JSON format is identical to that of JavaScript objects, which makes it quite easy to work with on the front end.

JSON enjoys widespread browser support and is frequently the primary, if not exclusive, data language option for visualization plug-ins. This section provides an overview of the JSON syntax and techniques for incorporating JSON data into your web pages.

Understanding JSON Syntax

JSON data is built on name/value pairs—a colon separates each key from its value, and commas separate each data pair. For example,

```
{
"region": "Northeast",
"employees":150,
"amount":"115,000"
}
```

Note that all keys and strings are enclosed in double quotes. All the data, which is collectively known as a JSON object, is contained within curly braces. You can also nest arrays and objects within the JSON values using square brackets or curly braces respectively. Here's an example that expresses the previous XML data as JSON:

```
{
  "sales": {
    "region": [
      {
        "territory": "Northeast",
        "employees": "150",
        "amount": "115,000"
      },
      {
        "territory": "Southeast",
        "employees": "125",
        "amount": "95,000"
      },
      {
        "territory": "West",
        "employees": "325",
        "amount": "265,000"
      }
    ]
  }
}
```

You can find the `regional_sales.json` file on the companion website.

> **NOTE** *If you're not sure whether your JSON data is properly structured, you can validate it online at* `http://jsonlint.com`.

Reading JSON Data

Because JSON is formatted similarly to JavaScript, you can read it directly. For example, consider the data put into an object variable, as shown here:

```
var jsonObj = { "sales": [
{"region": "Northeast", "employees":150, "amount":"115,000"},
  {"region": "Southeast", "employees":125, "amount":"95,000"},
  {"region": "West", "employees":325, "amount":"265,000"}
  ]
};
```

You can now drill into any value you need in this object. For example, to display the sales amount of the Southeast in an alert, as shown in Figure 4-5, use the following code:

```
var theAmount = jsonObj.sales[1].amount;
alert(theAmount);
```

You can find the `json_eval.html` file on the companion website.

JSON Object example

FIGURE 4-5: You can access JSON values directly if you know the structure and desired key.

> **NOTE** *jQuery includes a version of* JSON.parse(): *the* parseJSON() *function, which is useful for backwards compatibility. If incorporated into a jQuery script,* parseJSON() *is used only when the browser viewing the page does not support the native function; otherwise, the native* JSON.parse() *is used.*

Another approach is to put the JSON data in a string and then put the parsed string into an object using the JSON.parse() method:

```
var jsonData = '{"regions":[' +
'{"territory":"Northeast","employees":"150","amount":"115,000" },' +
'{"territory":"Southeast","employees":"125","amount":"95,000" },' +
'{"territory":"Midwest","employees":"225","amount":"195,000" },' +
'{"territory":"West","employees":"325","amount":"265,000" }]}';

jsonObj = JSON.parse(jsonData);
```

This code produces the same jsonObj as the previous example.

Asynchronous JSON

Although you can include JSON inline on the page, it is more common to deal with external JSON resources that you access asynchronously. This process is a bit different—you can use jQuery's getJSON() function to automatically parse the data. The getJSON() function takes two parameters: the path to the file and a callback function.

```
$.getJSON("regional_sales.json", function(data) {
});
```

Next, you can use the jQuery `each()` function to loop through the data:

```
$.each(data.sales.region,function (k,v) {
});
```

Here the `each()` loop provides both the key (k) and value (v) from the JSON. To get the value of a key, JavaScript dot notation is applied:

```
var theTerritory = v.territory;
var numEmployees = v.employees;
var theAmount = v.amount;
```

After you have your content, you're ready to build the HTML and insert it in the page with the jQuery `append()` function. Here's the complete code block:

```
$.getJSON("regional_sales.json", function(data) {
  $.each(data.sales.region,function (k,v) {
    var theTerritory = v.territory;
    var numEmployees = v.employees;
    var theAmount = v.amount;
  });
});
```

You can find the `import_json.html` file on the companion website.

This code displays a table of data (see Figure 4-6), but the data could easily be in any other configuration. For example, with a little bit of additional coding, courtesy of the HTML5 `<canvas>` tag, you could create a bar chart from the same data file, as shown in Figure 4-7.

JSON Data Imported

Territory	Employees	Sales
Northeast	150	$115,000
Southeast	125	$95,000
Midwest	225	$195,000
West	325	$265,000

FIGURE 4-6: jQuery's getJSON() function reads JSON data from a file and automatically parses it.

You can find the `ch04_import_json_chart.html` file on the companion website.

The canvas representation of this data starts with a simple `<canvas>` element:

```
<canvas id="chart1" width="600" height="400"></canvas>
```

JSON Data Charted

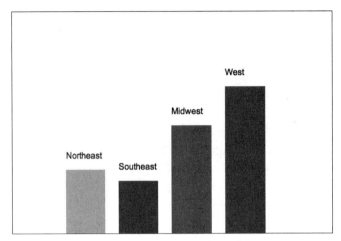

FIGURE 4-7: JSON and the JavaScript-driven graphics of the <canvas> tag are a natural fit.

Next, the following JavaScript imports the data and draws the chart in canvas:

```
$( document ).ready(function() {
  var theChart = document.getElementById('chart1');
  var chartHeight = 400;
  var theWidth = 75;
  var theSpace = 100;
  var theX = 0;
  var theY = 0;
  var theFills = ['orange','blue','red','green'];
  var i = 0;

  if (theChart.getContext){
    var theContext = theChart.getContext('2d');
    $.getJSON("regional_sales.json", function (data) {
      $.each(data.sales.region,function (k,v) {
        var theTerritory = v.territory;
        var theHeight = parseInt(v.amount.replace(/,/g, ''))/1000;
        theY = chartHeight - theHeight;
        theX = theX + theSpace;
        theContext.fillStyle = theFills[i];
        theContext.fillRect(theX,theY,theWidth,theHeight);
        theContext.fillStyle = 'black';
        theContext.font = '12pt Arial';
        theContext.fillText(theTerritory,theX, theY-20);
        ++i;
      });
    });
  }
});
```

Later in the book you dive deeper into canvas and SVG representations, so this chapter doesn't include a detailed discussion of this example. Basically, the script starts by defining a few settings and setting the context for the canvas element. Next it pulls in the JSON data and uses that to construct the visualization in canvas. `theContext.fillStyle` sets the color for each bar, and the bars are then drawn using `theContext.fillRect()`. Finally, a label is applied to each bar in the chart using `theContext.fillText()`.

SUMMARY

After you've collected your data, you need techniques to retrieve it. There are a great many data formats, and the methodology for reading each vary wildly. Here are a few key thoughts to keep in mind when approaching this task:

➤ Ajax is frequently used in modern web apps to load data asynchronously. JavaScript libraries provide useful Ajax APIs—for instance jQuery's `get()`.

➤ The jquery-csv library provides useful tools for parsing CSV files.

➤ XML is a highly structured format, widely used to store data for both online and offline businesses. You can use XSLT to transform the data into an HTML template and browse the data file itself.

➤ JSON is a lightweight format that pairs well with online processing. You can read data retrieved from a JSON file with the jQuery `getJSON()` function.

➤ Because JSON is JavaScript based, it works nicely with a variety of visualization options.

5

Acquiring Data Interactively

WHAT'S IN THIS CHAPTER

➤ Techniques to improve the usability of forms for a better user experience and improved conversion rate

➤ HTML5 form controls—interactive widgets that reduce data segmentation

➤ Mobile form best practices—contextual keyboards, mobile styling, and mobile form widgets.

Most data visualizations leverage existing data on the server or from some external application programming interface (API). However, there are times you want to incorporate data directly from the user into your charts. This chapter explores some best practices for harvesting data from web forms, which can then be used for data visualization. With these techniques, you can create a sustainable data ecosystem, which crowd-sources and displays data autonomously.

USING HTML5 FORM CONTROLS

The widespread adoption of HTML5 forms has revolutionized the way we build forms on the web. Instead of having to rely on plug-ins or user interface (UI) libraries, you can now create rich interactive forms using native HTML5 elements. Skipping the third-party plug-ins does more than improve performance; these native elements are also more reliable. You can count on them to be supported by browsers both today and into the distant future.

Introducing HTML5 Input Types

Back in the days of HTML4, developers had only a handful of input types, such as

```
<input type="text">
<input type="password">
<input type="checkbox">
<input type="radio">
```

HTML5 adds a variety of new types to this list: `email`, `url`, `number`, and `date`, to name a few. These inputs indicate a more specific type of data for the form, which has a variety of important usability and functionality implications:

➤   Input types build special widgets, such as a calendar widget or color picker.

➤   On mobile devices, input types provide a more optimized keyboard, such as a numeric keypad for phone numbers (read more about this later this chapter).

➤   When the user clicks or taps Submit, HTML5 form validation leverages these input types to verify the data types—for instance, testing a properly formed e-mail address (more about this in Chapter 6).

Best of all, you don't have to worry about backward compatibility when it comes to HTML5 input types. Older browsers default to a standard text input if they don't understand the HTML5 input type. Although that might not provide the richer functionality you've intended, it still provides a form that is completely usable across the board.

> **NOTE** *Special input types are also great for future-proofing. Although it's difficult to foresee how browsers will leverage these input types in the future, indicating a specific data type will utilize any enhancements moving forward.*

Form Widgets and Data Formatting

On the surface, HTML5 form widgets create an elegant form experience for the user. But beyond usability, these widgets have important implications for the data in your app. Namely, they ensure that the data the user enters is properly formatted before reaching the logic of your app.

For example, you could allow users to enter dates manually in a standard text input. But this could yield any number of results, such as the following:

➤   February 4, 1986

➤   4 Feb 1986

➤   02-04-86

➤   4/2/86

➤   2 / 4 / 1986

As you can see, open-ended text input can quickly cause data segmentation according to the user's region and preferences (and this is by no means an exhaustive list).

However, if you use the HTML5 calendar widget, it ensures that the data entered by the user remains properly formatted behind the scenes. In these cases, the widget always returns the date in the format 1986-02-04.

That said, support for form widgets can be somewhat limited, even among some A-list browsers. As discussed earlier, if the browser doesn't support the particular form widget, it reverts to a standard text input (with all the data segmentation headaches attached). So make sure to include JavaScript polyfills to fill any gaps in the browser widgets.

Polyfills mimic native browser features for backward compatibility, and there are a variety of options for HTML5 forms. In particular, the html5forms polyfill handles a wide range of HTML5 form features. (You can read more at `http://www.useragentman.com/blog/2010/07/27/creating-cross-browser-html5-forms-now-using-modernizr-webforms2-and-html5widgets-2/`.)

MAXIMIZING MOBILE FORMS

HTML5 also introduces a number of elements that have special implications for mobile devices. Namely, there are a number of input elements that provide a special contextual keyboard depending on the type of data you are requesting. For instance, when asking a user for her e-mail address, you can display a more targeted keyboard that includes default buttons for the @ symbol and dot, as shown in Figure 5-1.

FIGURE 5-1: E-mail inputs on iOS display this unique keyboard.

Although it may seem somewhat trivial, maximizing these contextual keyboards is extremely important for usability. Phone keyboards are notoriously cumbersome, so any improvements to the experience will be met with higher conversion rates.

Using Contextual Keyboards

Fortunately, leveraging contextual keyboards couldn't be easier. Simply set the type attribute of an input element like so:

```
<input type="email" placeholder="Email">
```

Here, the email input type produces the keyboard shown in Figure 5-1 (or a similar keyboard on a non-iOS device).

Besides e-mail inputs, there is also a special keyboard for phone numbers, as shown in Figure 5-2. Similarly, you can leverage this keyboard by setting the input type to tel:

```
<input type="tel" placeholder="Phone number">
```

FIGURE 5-2: A contextual keyboard for phone number inputs on iOS.

> **NOTE** *There are also contextual keyboards for* url *and* number *data types.*

Styling Mobile Forms for Usability

Functionality aside, you can improve the usability of your form by following some simple styling rules. Mainly, it's a good idea to ensure the form is both readable and tappable on the tiny mobile interface.

In general, mobile form designs are "chunkier," using larger input boxes to make it easier to tap in the intended field, even if the user "fat-fingers" it. So make sure to add some extra padding to all your input fields, and also increase the font size a bit so it's not only more legible but also larger on the touchscreen.

When it comes to mobile usability, upping the size of your form fields is one of the lowest hanging fruits. But this is just the tip of the iceberg for mobile form optimization. If you'd like to learn more, try out LukeW's classic book *Web Form Design* (Rosenfeld Media, 2008), as well as his blog, www.lukew.com.

Form Widgets for Mobile

In addition to the native HTML5 form widgets, there are also a number of third-party plug-ins for forms, many of which are geared specifically to mobile devices. Some are designed to bridge the gaps between desktop and mobile browsers whereas others are built to extend existing mobile paradigms. There are a variety of options out there; in particular, jQuery Mobile provides some quality form widgets for mobile (visit http://api.jquerymobile.com/category/widgets/ for more information).

SUMMARY

In this chapter you learned techniques for using forms to acquire data from the user.

First, you learned how to leverage HTML5 form controls to create interactive widgets and reduce data segmentation. You then explored mobile form optimization techniques, using the same HTML5 form controls to call contextual keyboards, which streamline user input on mobile devices. You also learned some basics about mobile form styling and mobile form widgets.

In the next chapter, you dive deeper into HTML5 data types, leveraging them for validation and better data formatting.

6

Validating Your Data

WHAT'S IN THIS CHAPTER

➤ Native HTML5 validation techniques

➤ jQuery Validation Engine

> **CODE DOWNLOAD** *The wrox.com code downloads for this chapter are found at* www.wrox.com/go/javascriptandjqueryanalysis *on the Download Code tab. The code is in the chapter 06 download and individually named according to the names throughout the chapter.*

Form validation is especially important when using that form data for visualization. That's because malformed data can quickly derail a chart or table. For instance, if your chart shows aggregated data across different dates, this data formatting had better be consistent. If one user enters February 4, 1986 and the other enters 2-4-86, you had better figure out some way to align these values before displaying them. In general, the easiest way to do this is to validate the data before you ever store it.

In this chapter you explore the differences between server-side and client-side validation and then discover a variety of client-side techniques. You first look at native HTML5 validation approaches. Those leverage semantic tags to validate fields against various data types and validation rules.

Next, you learn about jQuery Validation Engine, which provides more feature-rich validation. You learn how to use its basic regex validators, as well as more complex rules for numbers and dates. Then you see how to set up intricate relationships between the various fields in your form.

By the end of this chapter, you'll have a robust toolkit for form validation and understand both lightweight and fully featured solutions to suit your needs.

SERVER-SIDE VERSUS CLIENT-SIDE VALIDATION

In the early days of the web, form validation was performed exclusively on the server side. That approach worked well until developers began to focus on how they could improve this flow—it turns out form optimization is extremely important for business goals. For example, an e-commerce company can see substantial returns by improving their checkout forms.

Eventually, client-side validation techniques gained popularity because they allow developers to streamline the error-handling process, providing meaningful cues to the user as he fills out the form.

Whereas server-side validation must be performed after form submission, client-side validation enables you to display errors the moment they occur. This approach typically produces higher conversion rates because it avoids bombarding the user with a number of errors after he submits the form to the server.

Additionally, the user doesn't have to track down the source of an error—it will always be the field she just entered. Finally, it avoids certain nuisances caused by security issues from the back end, for instance when the server makes you re-enter your password rather than injecting it in the markup.

To get an idea of how client-side validation works, take a look at the comparison in Figure 6-1.

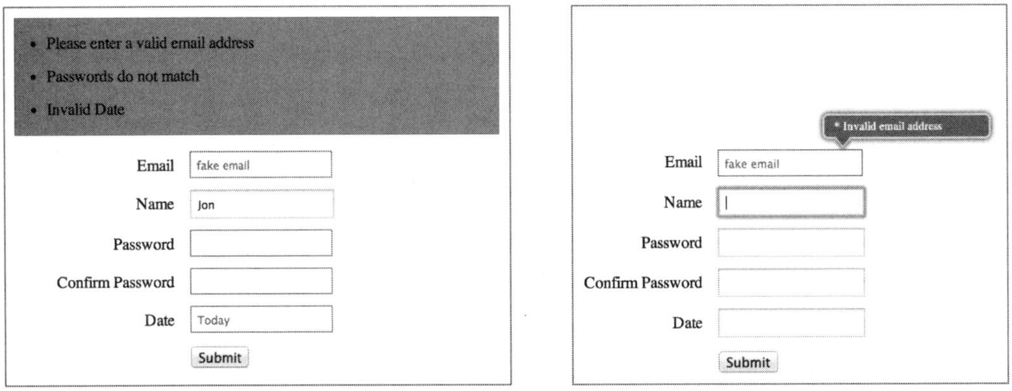

FIGURE 6-1: Compare the grouped error messages from the server (left) with the dynamic inline error messages from the client (right).

Client-side validation provides faster feedback to the user, which in turns allows him to fill out the form faster. Additionally, it provides the user with more confidence that the form is going to go through successfully. Both of these improvements lead to lower abandonment rates, which means more users are buying your product, signing up for your newsletter, or completing whatever action you want them to take.

However, client-side validation comes with some notable drawbacks. Namely, any validation done in the browser is incredibly insecure. A hacker can easily override client-side validation or simply disable JavaScript. So whenever you validate on the client, make sure to double-check any mission-critical fields on the server after the form is submitted.

NATIVE HTML5 VALIDATION

These days, there are a number of approaches to client-side validation. Prior to HTML5, developers relied exclusively on third-party plug-ins and extensions to handle validation. Typically built on top of a library like jQuery, these solutions use JavaScript to validate form content and display inline error messages as needed.

However, in recent years, this validation has gone native with HTML5. Although less customizable than its JavaScript counterparts, native validation provides a variety of advantages such as performance gains and accessibility improvements.

Native Versus JavaScript Validation

In general, it's a good idea to use native tools whenever possible—it just doesn't make sense to reinvent the wheel without a good reason. This wisdom also applies to HTML5 validation, which has certain advantages over alternatives such as jQuery plug-ins:

➤ **Native validation is lightweight.** Because it is implemented at the browser level, the user doesn't have to download external scripts to handle validation. That lightens page load and in turn improves performance.

➤ **Native validation is consistent.** Many sites use HTML5 validation, so the user is undoubtedly already familiar with the visual language of the validation user interface (UI). That's an affordance that allows users to more easily discern validation messages.

➤ **Native validation is localized.** With native validation, the browser automatically translates error messages into the user's language.

As you can see, native HTML5 validation is an attractive alternative to external scripts and plug-ins. However, JavaScript validation provides its own set of advantages:

➤ **JavaScript validation is feature-rich.** Although HTML5 handles the majority of validation situations with ease, it will never be as robust as a validation library. Depending on your needs, you might want something more.

➤ **JavaScript validation is theme-able.** Although HTML5 provides consistently themed messages that the user can recognize immediately, these might or might not work with the visual direction of your site. Styling native validation messages is limited at best, so if you need a distinctly different look and feel, you have to skip HTML5.

➤ **JavaScript validation is compatible with older browsers.** Although HTML5 validation works excellently in all modern browsers, some older browsers are left out, namely IE8 and older versions. If supporting these browsers is a priority, you have to turn to JavaScript solutions, either across the board, or as a polyfill for non-HTML5 browsers.

➤ **JavaScript validation is customizable.** HTML5 provides automated messages for errors that are localized to the user's region, but these messages are more difficult to customize. So if you're not happy with the generic error messages, you might be better off using JavaScript validation.

Getting Started with HTML5 Validation

Chapter 6 covers how to use HTML5 input types to provide richer form controls and a better mobile experience. It turns out that these special input types also have profound implications for form validation.

For example, let's say you have an email input:

```
<input type="email">
```

When the user submits this form, the browser automatically checks against the email data type for proper formatting (@ symbol). Any improperly formatted address triggers an error, as you can see in Figure 6-2.

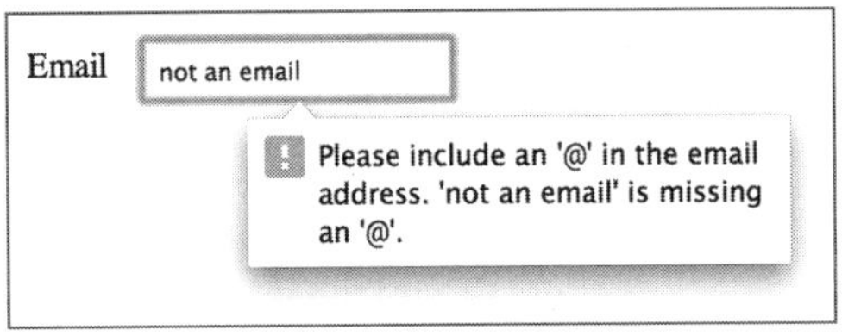

FIGURE 6-2: This email input has triggered an error in Chrome.

HTML5 validates data types other than email, too. For example, if you have a url input, the browser checks for a properly formatted URL.

HTML5 Validation for Numbers

Whereas email and url validation are pretty basic, the number and range inputs provide more intricate control over validation rules. Chapter 5 described how to use these numeric inputs with min, max, and step values:

```
<input type="number" min="0" max="10" step="0.5">
```

Here the number field is restricted between 0 and 10, with 0.5 in between each value. On the surface, these values affect the desktop UI: It starts at zero and then counts up by 0.5 until it hits 10. But HTML5 validation also leverages these attributes, as shown in Figure 6-3.

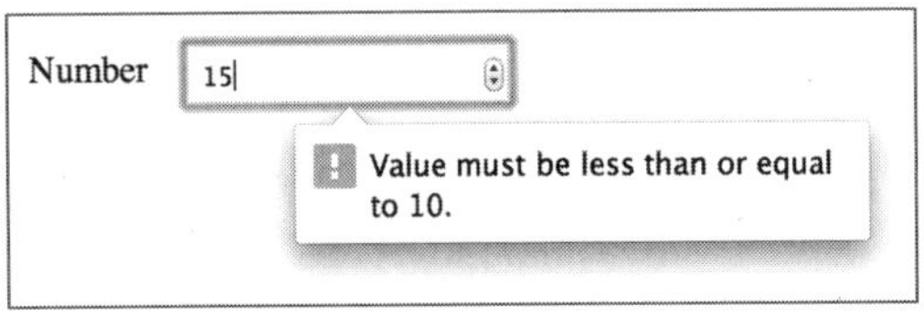

FIGURE 6-3: A value outside of the min and max bounds triggers an error for this number field.

Required Fields and Max Length

Beyond special input types, there are a number of additional validation options you can set directly in the markup. One particularly useful option is the required attribute:

```
<input type="text" required>
```

Here the `required` attribute indicates that the field must be filled. Failing to do so triggers the error shown in Figure 6-4.

FIGURE 6-4: All required fields must be filled in order to submit this form.

> **NOTE** *Keep in mind that basic validation isn't enough to make a field required. For example, if a user leaves an* `email` *input blank, the form will still submit successfully. Blank fields are not matched against the given rule.*

Additionally you can set the max length for any field:

```
<input type="text" maxlength="5">
```

However, with `maxlength`, there isn't even an error message because most browsers don't let you type any extra characters.

Custom HTML5 Validation Rules

You can also set up custom HTML5 validation rules. These rules use regular expressions (regex) to validate content and then display any errors to the user.

To set up custom rules, simply insert regex directly in the markup:

```
<input type="text" pattern="[a-zA-Z]+">
```

When the user submits the form, this field is checked against the regex `[a-zA-Z]+`, which accepts letter values only (no numbers, no spaces, and so on). If the user enters invalid data, a generic error message is triggered, as shown in Figure 6-5.

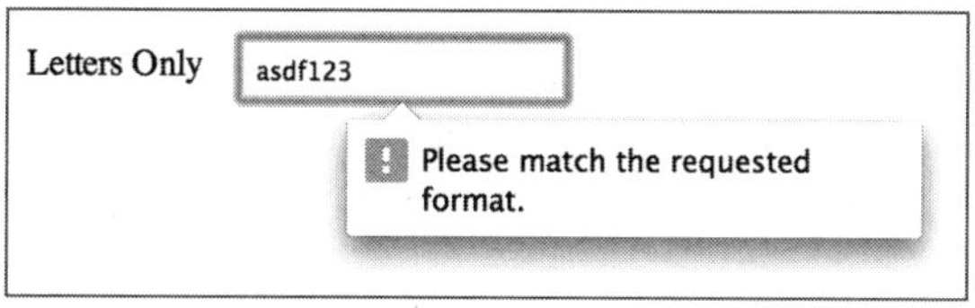

FIGURE 6-5: This generic error message displays if the string fails regex validation.

Custom HTML5 Validation Messages

If you're unhappy with the generic validation messages, either for custom regex rules or the standard fields, you can customize these as well. To do so, you need to leverage JavaScript and the `setCustomValidity()` application programing interface (API):

```
<input type="text" pattern="[a-zA-Z]+"
    oninvalid="setCustomValidity('Please enter only letters.')">
```

On unsuccessful form submission, this field triggers the given error text, as shown in Figure 6-6.

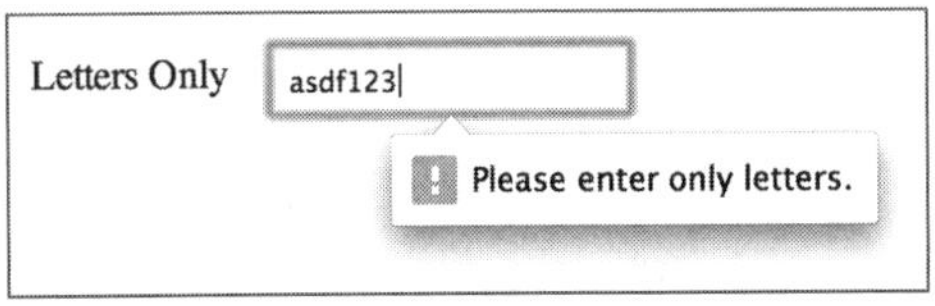

FIGURE 6-6: An error triggers a custom validation message in HTML5.

However, this solution is fairly hacky and leaves a lot to be desired. First off, the same error message displays regardless of the source of the error. For instance, if you use a `pattern` and a `required`, the same message displays for both issues.

Additionally, these hardcoded messages are not localized to the user's language. That might not seem like the biggest problem, but it is if you are mixing hardcoded messages with defaults. As you can see in Figure 6-7, that can lead to a very inconsistent experience. On the left of Figure 6-7, the browser translates the message according to the language setting (in this case Spanish). On the right, a hardcoded message in the same form appears in English.

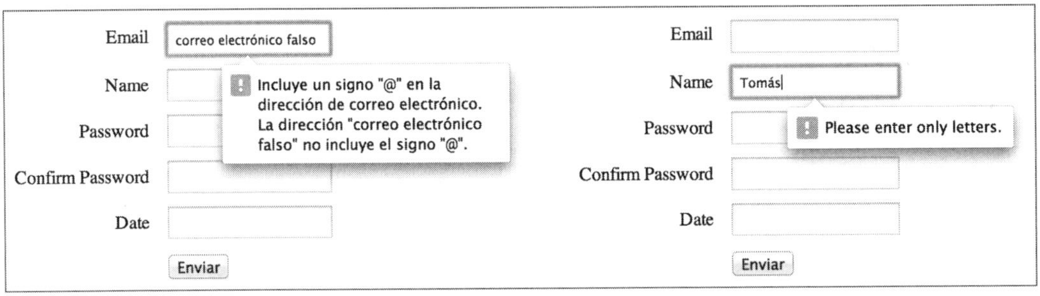

FIGURE 6-7: Custom validation messages don't mix well with localized content.

h5Validate Polyfill

Although HTML5 validation is an excellent option in most browsers, there are still a handful of users working with IE8 and other non-HTML5 browsers. You'll have to decide for yourself whether it's a priority to support client-side validation for these users. Fortunately, if you do decide to provide fallbacks, there are out-of-the-box solutions that bridge the gaps between older browsers and HTML5.

Namely, the h5Validate polyfill provides an easy path to supporting HTML5-style validation in all browsers. This polyfill attempts to mimic native functionality, leveraging the same attributes in the markup as HTML5. That way, you can effortlessly support these features without having to rewrite too much code.

To get started, download the code from github: `https://github.com/dilvie/h5Validate/blob/master/jquery.h5validate.js`. Using the polyfill is a piece of cake; simply include the script at the end of your document.

However, it's not a good idea to use this polyfill across the board. Most browsers support native validation, and there's no sense in reinventing the wheel—or even making these users download the script. You should take steps to ensure that this script loads only where it's needed.

One option is to use feature detection and a JavaScript loader to load the script only when it's needed. Alternatively, you can also use an IE conditional (although it's a bit sloppier):

```
<!--[if lt IE 9]>
<script src="js/jquery.h5validate.js"></script>
<![endif]-->
```

This conditional targets only IE8 and earlier versions, so it misses older versions of other browsers. That isn't a huge concern, though, because market shares for those older browsers are typically very tiny.

JQUERY VALIDATION ENGINE

A quick Internet search turns up a variety of plug-ins for form validation. As with any third-party offerings, these plug-ins can be hit or miss, so it's important to choose the right one. One of the best options available is jQuery Validation Engine, which is available at `https://github.com/posabsolute/jQuery-Validation-Engine`.

jQuery Validation Engine is a robust validation suite that provides a more feature-rich alternative to native HTML5 validation. Depending on your use case, these features may justify the added weight of an extra script.

Getting Started with jQuery Validation Engine

Although it leverages different attributes than HTML5 validation, the jQuery Validation Engine is markup-driven:

```
<input type="text" data-validation-engine="validate[required,custom[email]]">
```

Here, `data-validation-engine` defines the functionality for this field. First, `validate[]` indicates that this field should be validated. Then the validation rules are defined in this array—this particular field is a `required` field that must validate against an `email` regex.

Finally, instantiate the validation engine on your form element:

```
$(".my-form").validationEngine();
```

Now, as you can see in Figure 6-8, malformed data trigger error messages.

> **NOTE** *Although the plug-in supports theming, there is only one official theme at this time.*

FIGURE 6-8: This error message was generated by the jQuery Validation Engine. (If you don't like the appearance, you can retheme the library.)

Validators

The main reason to use jQuery Validation Engine is the variety of validation rules that you can leverage right out of the box. Ranging from simple regex rules to validate an e-mail address to complex date ranges and conditionals, these validators provide more feature-rich controls than native alternatives. And if you need additional rules, the library provides tools to define your own.

Regex Validators

jQuery Validation Engine offers a number of predefined regex rules to cover a variety of common validation use cases. You saw one of these validators in the previous section: `custom[email]`, which checks against an `email` regex. Following the same pattern, you can also set up URL validation:

```
<input type="text" data-validation-engine="validate[custom[url]]">
```

Or establish phone number validation:

```
<input type="text" data-validation-engine="validate[custom[phone]]">
```

Beyond these examples, you can also validate numbers, ISO dates, alphanumeric strings, and more. You can read about all the custom regexes jQuery Validation Engine supports in the documentation: `http://posabsolute.github.io/jQuery-Validation-Engine/#custom-regex`. And if you still need more, you can add your own regex rules to the translation file (for example, `jquery.validationEngine-en.js`).

> **WARNING** *Be careful when validating a phone number because this regex is "relaxed," meaning it allows a variety of phone number formats. That's a pretty wide field with all the international formats, so you might need to add additional validation rules.*

Number Validators

You already learned how to use regex validators such as `custom[number]` and `custom[integer]` to validate the data type of a field. But jQuery Validation Engine provides some additional non-regex validators such as `min[]` and `max[]`:

```
<input type="text"
  data-validation-engine="validate[custom[number],min[0],max[10]]">
```

This example uses both the `min[]` and `max[]` validators, establishing a rule that the number must be between 0 and 10.

> **NOTE** *Beyond* `min[]` *and* `max[]` *there are a handful of tools you can use in more specific cases. For example, the* `creditCard` *validator verifies that an integer could theoretically be a credit card number. Of course, it doesn't verify with the bank that a particular card exists or that it has any available credit.*

Date Validators

jQuery Validation Engine also provides some useful date validation rules. These complement the `custom[date]` regex you learned about earlier, which verifies that the string follows ISO date format: `YYYY-MM-DD`. For example, you can use these additional controls to verify that an ISO date is not only valid, but also in the past:

```
<input type="text" data-validation-engine="validate[custom[date],past[NOW]]">
```

Here the `past[]` validator takes the `NOW` parameter to check this field against the current date (as provided by the browser). As you can see in Figure 6-9, this field triggers an error if the date isn't in the past.

FIGURE 6-9: This field won't validate because the date isn't in the past.

Similarly, you can also check whether a date is in the future:

```
<input type="text" data-validation-engine="validate[custom[date],future[NOW]]">
```

Additionally, you can use your own ISO string with `past[]` and `future[]`. For instance, to check that a user was born before 1995, you could either ask them who MC Hammer is or use the following:

```
<input type="text" data-validation-engine=
   "validate[custom[date],past[1995-01-01]]">
```

Additionally, if you'd like to use a date picker, you can use jQuery Validation Engine in conjunction with the HTML5 form element `<input type="date">`, which you learned about earlier. However, to avoid any collisions between HTML5 and jQuery validation, make sure to add the `novalidate` attribute to your form element:

```
<form novalidate>
<input type="date" data-validation-engine="validate[custom[date],past[NOW]]">
</form>
```

Conditional Validators

One of the most powerful use cases for jQuery Validation Engine is the variety of conditional validation rules. These validators don't just check a single field; rather, they allow you to establish more complex relationships between different fields in your form.

A simple example is validating that the Password and Confirm password fields match:

```
<input type="password" name="my-password">
<input type="password" name="confirm-password"
  data-validation-engine="validate[equals[my-password]]">
```

As you can see, the second field uses the `equals[]` validator to match the field named `my-password`. Now if the two fields don't match, it throws the error message shown in Figure 6-10. (You find out how to customize the text of error messages later in this chapter.)

FIGURE 6-10: These passwords don't match.

Beyond simple matching, you can also compare dates across fields using the `past[]` and `future[]` validators with which you're already familiar. For example, let's say you want to validate the dates for a hotel booking. You want to make sure the end date falls *after* the start date:

```
<input type="text" name="start-date"
  data-validation-engine="validate[future[NOW]]">
<input type="text" name="end-date"
  data-validation-engine="validate[future[start-date]]">
```

Here, the script first checks that the start date is in the future (after all, you wouldn't want to book a hotel for yesterday). Then the end date validates against the start date, producing the error in Figure 6-11 if it isn't in the future.

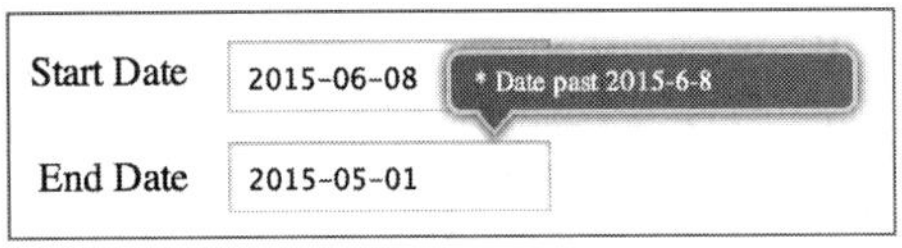

FIGURE 6-11: The end date is before the start date, which triggers an error.

Beyond these examples, there are also validators that set up required relationships between groups of fields, verify the number of checkboxes a user has checked, and more. Take a look at the documentation: `http://posabsolute.github.io/jQuery-Validation-Engine/#validators`.

Writing Custom Rules

You can also define your own validators for jQuery Validation Engine, both on the client side and even on the server.

Client Side

To create a validation rule on the client side, first create a function that returns an error message on failure:

```
function checkFruit(field, rules, i, options){
  var fruits = ["apple", "banana", "pear", "orange"];

  if (fruits.indexOf(field) == -1) {
```

```
        return "Must be a piece of fruit";
    }
}
```

This function checks if the field value is in an array of fruit names, returning an error message if it is not. Next, pass a reference to this function into your validation rules using funcCall[]:

```
<input type="text" data-validation-engine="validate[funcCall[checkFruit]]">
```

Now, if the user enters a value in this field that isn't in the fruit array, it produces the error shown in Figure 6-12.

FIGURE 6-12: Pizza isn't a fruit.

Server Side

With jQuery Validation Engine, you can even establish validation rules that hit a restful API on the server. This ability can be extremely useful in a variety of situations—for example, checking if a username already exists on the system.

First, add an Ajax rule to the translation file (for example, jquery.validationEngine-en.js):

```
"ajaxUsername": {
    "url": "my-api-url",
    "extraDataDynamic": ['#my-username'],
    "alertText": "* This username is already taken",
    "alertTextOk": "All good!",
    "alertTextLoad": "* Validating, please wait"
},
```

This rule defines a few parameters for the Ajax call, such as the URL for the API, the form data to pass in, and various messages. Pay careful attention to extraDataDynamic—that's a list of ID references for the fields you want to pass to your API.

Next, reference this rule as a validator in the markup:

```
<input type="text" id="my-username"
data-validation-engine="validate[ajax[ajaxUsername]]">
```

Now jQuery Validation Engine automatically checks this field against the server. This chapter doesn't get into any server-side code here, but your API should return JSON in the following format:

```
["my-username", false, "No dice"]
```

In this case, these values represent the following:

➤   "my-username" is the ID reference for the given field (which enables you to return a nested array if you are validating multiple fields).

➤   false is a Boolean value for whether the validation passes. In this case it fails.

➤   "No dice" is an optional error message that overwrites the messaging established in the translation file.

To learn more about the `ajax[]` validator, see this tutorial: `www.position-absolute.com/articles/using-form-ajax-validation-with-the-jquery-validation-engine-plugin/`.

> **NOTE** *Even though the* `ajax[]` *validator hits the server-side, that call is originally from the client, and as such you should have similar security concerns as with any client-side validation. Namely, make sure that you double check any crucial validation using traditional server-side techniques to thwart hackers and browser errors.*

Error Messages

jQuery Validation Engine also provides a few ways to customize error messaging, from overwriting default messages to additional language packs. These tools provide significantly more control over error messaging than native HTML5 alternatives.

Modifying Error Messages

You can override the default messaging in jQuery Validation Engine by setting the `data-errormessage` attribute:

```
<input type="text" data-validation-engine="validate[required,custom[email]]"
    data-errormessage="This is a custom error message">
```

You can see this custom message in Figure 6-13.

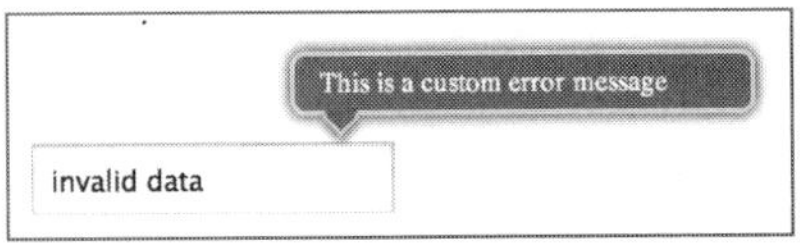

FIGURE 6-13: The default error message for this field has been overwritten.

Earlier, you learned how overwriting native HTML5 validation messages can be problematic because different errors trigger the same messaging. Fortunately, that isn't as much of a problem in jQuery Validation Engine because you can hook into a few additional error message attributes:

```
<input type="email" data-validation-engine="validate[required,custom[email]]"
    data-errormessage-value-missing="Email is required!"
    data-errormessage-custom-error="Let me give you a hint: someone@nowhere.com"
    data-errormessage="This is the fall-back error message.">
```

Here, the script uses `data-errormessage-value-missing` for problems with the `required` validation, and `data-errormessage-custom-error` for problems with any `custom` regexes. Any other errors default to the message in `data-errormessage`.

Localization

HTML5 automatically translates error messages into the user's language for native validation. Fortunately, jQuery Validation Engine also provides some linguistic support—simply include the appropriate locale file on the page. For example, to use English, you'd write the following:

```
<script src="js/jquery.validationEngine-en.js"></script>
<script src="js/jquery.validationEngine.js"></script>
```

The multi-language support in jQuery Validation Engine is useful; however, localization in native validation is still better for two reasons:

➤ jQuery Validation Engine provides support for dozens of languages, but browsers support significantly more (two to three times as many depending on the browser).

➤ While jQuery Validation Engine allows the developer to hard-code a language, native validation localizes to the user's language automatically. However, hard-coding the language can also be a good thing if you're worried about consistency with the other copy on your site.

SUMMARY

In this chapter, you learned a variety of form validation techniques. You first learned how to leverage native HTML5 validation to verify various data types, set the bounds for number values, and define your own regex rules.

Next, you learned how to use jQuery Validation Engine for more robust validation support. You explored the basic regex validators as well as simple validators to constrain number values and dates. Then you leveraged conditional validators to establish more complex relationships between the fields in your form. Finally, you learned how to create your own validators, both on the client and the server, as well as how to customize the messaging.

7

Examining and Sorting Data Tables

➤ Learning the Anatomy of an HTML table

➤ Styling an HTML table with CSS

➤ Learning about semantic markup

➤ Using JavaScript and jQuery to dynamically style and edit tables

➤ Using the DataTables jQuery plug-in to make dynamic tables easy

> **CODE DOWNLOAD** *The wrox.com code downloads for this chapter are found at* www.wrox.com/go/javascriptandjqueryanalysis *on the Download Code tab. The code is in the chapter 07 download and individually named according to the names throughout the chapter.*

Although charts, maps, and other graphically rich representations might be the first things that come to mind when you consider the term *data visualization*, a primary workhorse for displaying and analyzing data has always been the data table. Furthermore, a well-designed chart might represent a concise way to tell a story about your data to most users, but it can present a difficult obstacle to the visually impaired. Thankfully, a properly marked-up data table can carry enough unambiguous meaning that a specially designed piece of software known as a *screen reader* can convert the visual matrix of data into easy-to-digest text-to-speech or Braille content.

Data tables represent an interesting lowest common denominator in terms of in-browser data visualization. Not only can you mark them up for maximum readability and accessibility but every commonly used browser has at least a basic ability to display data tables, even if you intentionally disable extraneous features. Given this, you can apply a design strategy to begin with this base level of support and then to progressively enable more advanced features if the current user agent supports them. In this way, all users have some access to your content, but the users with more capable browsers receive an enhanced view. This strategy is usually referred to as *progressive enhancement*.

OUTPUTTING BASIC TABLE DATA

In Chapter 4, you saw several techniques for using JavaScript to load data asynchronously downloaded from web servers and build HTML tables dynamically on the client. These strategies are useful and powerful, but they have the distinct problem that if the user's browser does not support JavaScript, or if the user has intentionally configured the browser to not execute JavaScript, then you are not able to present them with any data. Meanwhile, if the data table is a static part of the page or is injected into the page by logic on the server side, then it is observable even by base-level user agents or user agents with deliberately constrained capabilities.

Building a Table

In HTML, you use the `<table>` element to render data in tabular format. When you think of a table, visually, you assume that it contains both rows and columns that intersect in a grid, but when you describe a table in HTML markup, it is surprisingly row-oriented. You describe each row contained in the table and all the cells contained in each row, whereas information about the columns contained in the table is mostly inferred (that is, unless you decide to describe information about the columns more explicitly, as discussed later in this chapter). In fact, there is a great deal of inference going on in how browsers interpret a table element, so you must be careful if you want to build a maximally accessible table.

> **NOTE** *The `<table>` element can also be used for layout purposes; it was actually quite often used for this purpose in the early web. This practice has fallen out of favor, for most scenarios, since the introduction of Cascading Style Sheets (CSS). In general, you should check if there is a simpler and cleaner way to achieve your goals using CSS (there generally is) before resorting to using a table for layout purposes.*

Each row of the `<table>` is expressed as a `<tr>` (table row) element, and each cell within the row is indicated by a `<td>` (table data) element.

Repurposing the sales data discussed in Chapter 2 and converting it into an HTML table, you get the markup shown in Listing 7-1.

LISTING 7-1

```html
<!DOCTYPE html>
<html>
<head>
<title>Simple Table</title>
</head>
<body>

<table>
    <tr>
        <td>Region</td>
        <td>Sales</td>
        <td>Mean</td>
    </tr>

    <tr>
        <td>Northeast</td>
        <td>$100,000</td>
        <td>$142,857</td>
    </tr>
    <tr>
        <td>Southeast</td>
        <td>$75,000</td>
        <td>$142,857</td>
    </tr>
    <tr>
        <td>Midwest</td>
        <td>$125,000</td>
        <td>$142,857</td>
    </tr>
    <tr>
        <td>Mid-Atlantic</td>
        <td>$125,000</td>
        <td>$142,857</td>
    </tr>
    <tr>
        <td>Southwest</td>
        <td>$75,000</td>
        <td>$142,857</td>
    </tr>
    <tr>
        <td>Northwest</td>
        <td>$100,000</td>
        <td>$142,857</td>
    </tr>
    <tr>
        <td>California</td>
        <td>$400,000</td>
        <td>$142,857</td>
    </tr>
</table>

</body>
</html>
```

The code in Listing 7-1 results in the table displayed in Figure 7-1. You can find the `MostSimpleTable.html` file on the companion website.

Region	Sales	Mean
Northeast	$100,000	$142,857
Southeast	$75,000	$142,857
Midwest	$125,000	$142,857
Mid-Atlantic	$125,000	$142,857
Southwest	$75,000	$142,857
Northwest	$100,000	$142,857
California	$400,000	$142,857

FIGURE 7-1: This table is very basic.

Notice that the table displayed in Figure 7-1 is not very attractive. This can actually be considered to be "by design." Why? Modern HTML provides good separation of semantic markup from presentation, so, ideally, your markup should describe only the content of your page, and your CSS defines the presentation aspects. Because we have not added any CSS rules that target the elements of the data table in this example, you should not be especially surprised that its presentation is currently a bit lackluster.

> **NOTE** *Early versions of HTML muddied the waters when it came to separation of content and presentation. For example, the* `<font>` *tag enabled you to apply a font of your selection to a section of text. Now, however, you would use CSS to define this sort of presentation property. The* `<font>` *tag and a few other presentation-related element types were deprecated in HTML version 4.01 and removed, finally, in HTML5. This provides additional evidence that HTML should solely define content and semantics, whereas presentation should be delegated to CSS.*

You see how to improve the styling of the table later in this chapter, but first, consider another issue with this table. The semantics of the table content are very unclear. There is an implication that the first (top) row contains cells that represent the headers for the columns below each of them. There is also an implication that the first cell in each row describes the subsequent row content. These are mere inferences, however, and although it may be easy for someone who's looking at this table to draw these inferences, it is not necessarily straightforward for a piece of software (a software agent) or a visually impaired person to do so. Furthermore, when using CSS selectors to style the content of this table, there is no simple way for the styling rules to distinguish between the different types of cells present.

Using Semantic Table Markup

You can solve the problems with the table shown in Figure 7-1 by better defining the semantics, or meaning, of each piece of markup in the table. If the cells in the first row are meant to be the headers of the columns that they top, then you can make this explicit by utilizing the `<th>` element rather than the `<td>` element.

```
<tr>
    <th>Region</th>
    <th>Sales</th>
    <th>Mean</th>
</tr>
```

Now it is clear and unambiguous that you are providing table headers, and not simply another row of data. You can see in Figure 7-2 that changing these cells to be table headers has actually made a small visual difference in the output. Despite the content and presentation separation principles you want to strive for, the browsers do have some presentation defaults associated with some semantic markup elements. In the case of table headers, they default to being bold and centered in their cells, but you can, of course, redefine how table headers are presented using CSS.

You can find the `SimpleTable.html` file on the companion website.

Region	Sales	Mean
Northeast	$100,000	$142,857
Southeast	$75,000	$142,857
Midwest	$125,000	$142,857
Mid-Atlantic	$125,000	$142,857
Southwest	$75,000	$142,857
Northwest	$100,000	$142,857
California	$400,000	$142,857

FIGURE 7-2: Semantic table header elements make a small difference in the output.

Surprisingly, table headers are valid when placed anywhere in the table, but it is important to use them only in places where they make sense contextually and to think about how a screen reader might process a table's content to read it aloud. For example, applying the `<th>` element simply because you want values to be bolded and centered is a poor use of the element.

In the regional sales table from the example, it would actually make sense to treat each region name as a header for the row, which is perfectly valid markup:

```
<tr>
    <th>Northeast</th>
    <td>$100,000</td>
    <td>$142,857</td>
</tr>
```

But now you've constructed a scenario where you have two different sets of headers, and it isn't necessarily obvious which table cells are associated with which headers. It is recommended you resolve these ambiguities by adding `scope` attributes to the header elements. If you amend your header to read

```
<th scope="row">Northeast</th>
```

it will make no difference from the standpoint of default presentation, but you've now made it clear to screen readers (and your CSS selectors, as you see later) that every cell in the same row with that header is owned by that header. Similarly, you can amend the column headers to read

```
<th scope="col">Region</th>
<th scope="col">Sales</th>
<th scope="col">Mean</th>
```

which ensures that every cell in the same column with such a header is owned by that header. So, for example, when you come to the cell in the table that reads $400,000, a screen reader or other software agent would know, unambiguously, that this value is owned by the column header Sales and also the row header California.

> **NOTE** *It's worth noting that it is not only screen readers and CSS selectors that can benefit from enriching the semantic content of a table. A web crawler for a search engine might be able to use the extra meaning provided to improve the indexing of the content, or your browser might be able to more effectively break up a table between pages when printing when given a greater understanding of the table's anatomy.*

There are other pieces of semantic markup that can be applied to parts of the table to clarify the intent of the table designer. Although replacing the <td> elements in the first row with <th> removed a lot of ambiguity from the table layout, you can be much more clear about the different sections of the table by splitting the content into three semantic sub elements—<thead>, <tbody>, and <tfoot>—as shown in Listing 7-2.

LISTING 7-2

```
<!DOCTYPE html>
<html>
<head>
<title>Table With Semantic Markup</title>
</head>
<body>

<table>
    <thead>
        <tr>
            <th scope="col">Region</th>
            <th scope="col">Sales</th>
            <th scope="col">Mean</th>
        </tr>
    </thead>
    <tfoot>
        <tr>
            <th scope="row">Sum</th>
            <td>$1,000,000</td>
            <td></td>
        </tr>
    </tfoot>
    <tbody>
    <tr>
```

```
        <th scope="row">Northeast</th>
        <td>$100,000</td>
        <td>$142,857</td>
    </tr>
    <tr>
        <th scope="row">Southeast</th>
        <td>$75,000</td>
        <td>$142,857</td>
    </tr>
    <tr>
        <th scope="row">Midwest</th>
        <td>$125,000</td>
        <td>$142,857</td>
    </tr>
    <tr>
        <th scope="row">Mid-Atlantic</th>
        <td>$125,000</td>
        <td>$142,857</td>
    </tr>
    <tr>
        <th scope="row">Southwest</th>
        <td>$75,000</td>
        <td>$142,857</td>
    </tr>
    <tr>
        <th scope="row">Northwest</th>
        <td>$100,000</td>
        <td>$142,857</td>
    </tr>
    <tr>
        <th scope="row">California</th>
        <td>$400,000</td>
        <td>$142,857</td>
    </tr>
    </tbody>
</table>

</body>
</html>
```

Now it is as clear as possible that the table is composed of a header section, a body section, and a footer section.

> **NOTE** *Although the footer appears last in presentation order on the page, by default, in the markup it must actually appear before the body of the table. This may have something to do with the fact that if you were spooling a very long table to a printer and want to print the footer at the base of every page, you wouldn't want to have to parse through all the table markup, in advance, to find the footer content.*

When you view the results of our new table in Figure 7-3, you'll notice that the only difference from Figure 7-2 is that the cell contents of the first column, which you've marked as row headers, are now bold and centered. `<thead>`, `<tbody>`, and `<tfoot>` have acted as pure semantic markup, and have not caused any change in the presentation of the table.

You can find the `TableWithSemanticMarkup.html` file on the companion website.

Region	Sales	Mean
Northeast	$100,000	$142,857
Southeast	$75,000	$142,857
Midwest	$125,000	$142,857
Mid-Atlantic	$125,000	$142,857
Southwest	$75,000	$142,857
Northwest	$100,000	$142,857
California	$400,000	$142,857

FIGURE 7-3: This table has both row and column headers.

Although there are no apparent built-in presentation differences, some browsers do utilize the extra context that you've provided in interesting ways. For example, some browsers, when printing, repeat the header section and/or the footer section on each page so that whoever reads the output does not have to refer to the first page to identify the columns. Later in the chapter you see how to apply some rather complex styling to these various sections of the table, but for now, apply some simple CSS rules, if only to clarify the table's anatomy. Add the following code to the `<head>` section of the page:

```
<style type="text/css">
    thead { color: orange; }
    tbody { color: gray; }
    tfoot { color: red; }
</style>
```

As you can see in Figure 7-4, the table looks exactly the same as Figure 7-3 except for the fact that everything in the header area of the table uses an orange text color, everything in the footer area of the table uses a red text color, and all other text is gray.

You can find the `TableWithSemanticMarkupAndCSS.html` file on the companion website.

Region	Sales	Mean
Northeast	$100,000	$142,857
Southeast	$75,000	$142,857
Midwest	$125,000	$142,857
Mid-Atlantic	$125,000	$142,857
Southwest	$75,000	$142,857
Northwest	$100,000	$142,857
California	$400,000	$142,857
Sum	$1,000,000	

FIGURE 7-4: In this table, some CSS styling rules have been used to target the semantic markup of the table.

Labeling Your Table

When providing a table of data to the user, it is important to provide a title or label so the user has sufficient context to understand the data and see how it's related to the rest of the content being provided. In an accessible table, a title is even more important as the user may not have sight cues to relate the table content with surrounding aspects of the page.

To add a title to your table, you can introduce the `<caption>` element to the table:

```
<table>
    <caption>Sales By Region</caption>
    <!-- ... -->
</table>
```

By default the title is presented at the top of the table, although you can configure the placement with CSS (see the `caption-side` property). A title does more than provide an explanation of your table content; most accessibility-oriented user agents specifically look for this caption to better explain the table's context.

If there is anything unusual about the structure of the table, it might be worth trying to provide some extra detail in the caption to attempt to make the content more digestible. However, it is preferable to simply reduce the complexity of the table. If the table is complex enough to need a paragraph describing its content, then it might not be the most effective way to visualize the data.

> **NOTE** *The table element used to have a* summary *attribute. This attribute had no visual presentation on the page, but it provided additional context that was consumable by screen readers. This attribute has been removed in HTML5, however. It's possible that the attribute has been removed because useful information about a table should be accessible to all users, and not just to screen readers.*

You can see a table with a caption displayed in Figure 7-5.

Sales By Region		
Region	Sales	Mean
Northeast	$100,000	$142,857
Southeast	$75,000	$142,857
Midwest	$125,000	$142,857
Mid-Atlantic	$125,000	$142,857
Southwest	$75,000	$142,857
Northwest	$100,000	$142,857
California	$400,000	$142,857
Sum	$1,000,000	

FIGURE 7-5: A descriptive caption has been added to the table.

Configuring the Columns

Thus far, you've created rows and headers, which have only implicitly defined the number of columns that the table contains. Is there anything that can be said more explicitly about the columns, though? The answer is yes, but don't get too excited, yet. There are limitations to the markup that can directly target a table column.

If you catalog the things you might want to do to a column of data in the table, some of the first actions that come to mind are

➤ Setting the font and color of all the cell content in the column

➤ Setting the text alignment of all the cell content in the column

➤ Setting the background color of the entire column

Fortunately there is an element called `<col>` that enables you to describe some styles that target an entire column. Unfortunately, only the third item in the preceding list is directly achievable using `<col>`. Listing 7-3 shows how you would use some `<col>` elements to style the contents of some of the columns in your table.

LISTING 7-3

```
<!DOCTYPE html>
<html>
<head>
<title>Table With Caption and Column Settings</title>

<style type="text/css">
    .col-header { background-color: gray; }
    .col-amount { background-color: orange; }
</style>
</head>
<body>

<table>
    <caption>Sales By Region</caption>
    <colgroup>
        <col class="col-header">
        <col class="col-amount">
        <col class="col-mean">
    </colgroup>
    <thead>
        <tr>
            <th scope="col">Region</th>
            <th scope="col">Sales</th>
            <th scope="col">Mean</th>
        </tr>
    </thead>
    <tfoot>
        <tr>
            <th scope="row">Sum</th>
            <td>$1,000,000</td>
            <td></td>
```

```
        </tr>
    </tfoot>
    <tbody>
    <tr>
        <th scope="row">Northeast</th>
        <td>$100,000</td>
        <td>$142,857</td>
    </tr>
    <tr>
        <th scope="row">Southeast</th>
        <td>$75,000</td>
        <td>$142,857</td>
    </tr>
    <tr>
        <th scope="row">Midwest</th>
        <td>$125,000</td>
        <td>$142,857</td>
    </tr>
    <tr>
        <th scope="row">Mid-Atlantic</th>
        <td>$125,000</td>
        <td>$142,857</td>
    </tr>
    <tr>
        <th scope="row">Southwest</th>
        <td>$75,000</td>
        <td>$142,857</td>
    </tr>
    <tr>
        <th scope="row">Northwest</th>
        <td>$100,000</td>
        <td>$142,857</td>
    </tr>
    <tr>
        <th scope="row">California</th>
        <td>$400,000</td>
        <td>$142,857</td>
    </tr>
    </tbody>

</table>

</body>
</html>
```

In Listing 7-3, you have two new additions to help configure your columns. The first is this:

```
<style type="text/css">
    .col-header { background-color: gray; }
    .col-amount { background-color: orange; }
</style>
```

In that code, there are two CSS classes defined that you assign to the column that contains the row headers and the column that contains the sales amounts, respectively. In both cases they are defining a `background-color`, which happens to be one of the few legal values that you can assign to a column. To assign these classes to their respective columns, the following configuration is used:

```
<colgroup>
    <col class="col-header">
    <col class="col-amount">
    <col class="col-mean">
</colgroup>
```

Here, first, the `<colgroup>` element is used to indicate that you are defining some attributes for a group of columns in the table, and then each individual column's attributes are defined in the child `<col>` elements. In this case, a CSS class is being assigned to each column. The result is that the background of the header column is set to gray, and the background of the amount column is set to orange. You can see the result in Figure 7-6.

You can find the `CaptionAndColumnSettings.html` file on the companion website.

Sales By Region		
Region	**Sales**	**Mean**
Northeast	$100,000	$142,857
Southeast	$75,000	$142,857
Midwest	$125,000	$142,857
Mid-Atlantic	$125,000	$142,857
Southwest	$75,000	$142,857
Northwest	$100,000	$142,857
California	$400,000	$142,857
Sum	$1,000,000	

FIGURE 7-6: In this table, some of the settings of the columns have been explicitly configured.

Your natural inclination after getting the preceding example working would probably be to try to right-align the content of the cells in the number columns like this:

```
<style type="text/css">
    .col-amount { text-align: right; }
    .col-mean { text-align: right; }
</style>
```

However, you will find that this does not actually work. The table cells are not really seen as being Document Object Model (DOM) children of the column, so they don't actually inherit most CSS properties that would normally be inherited in this fashion. In the end, there are only a few valid properties for you to set this way. Nevertheless, right-aligning columns *is* something that you will want to do, so later in this chapter you see a strategy for this that *does* work.

> **NOTE** *If you look at an application programming interface (API) guide for* `<col>`, *you might see lots of interesting properties that can be set at the column level, such as* `align`. *However, some of these were never widely supported, and most of these attributes have been removed in HTML5. Later in the chapter, you find out about some of the recommended alternatives.*

ASSURING MAXIMUM READABILITY

As mentioned in the introduction of this chapter, one of the nice things about data tables is that you can apply the strategy of *progressive enhancement*. In other words, you start with a table that almost all browsers, not to mention screen readers and other software agents, can present, and then you progressively layer on various enhancements that some user agents may support; browsers that don't support the enhancements gracefully react by omitting them. Not every user agent supports every enhancement that you might introduce, but, if you are careful, you should end up with a maximally enhanced table for every scenario.

Most of what you've done so far in this chapter should be presentable to user agents that support HTML4 and later. A few HTML5 attributes have been described that would work on non-HTML5 browsers as long as you provide a polyfill.

> **NOTE** *A polyfill is a piece of code that helps you emulate some functionality that's not natively supported in some of your target browsers. For HTML5, many new elements have been added that don't necessarily have specific presentation defaults, but they help to enhance the semantic content of the page. It's useful to be able to depend on these elements being available regardless of whether the target user agent supports HTML5, hence the prevalence of HTML5 polyfills that are available.*

The current state of your data table as of Figure 7-5 is that it's serviceable but not very good-looking. It's a bit difficult to read, to boot. You can improve these aspects of the table through some judiciously applied CSS and JavaScript. Some of your target platforms will not be able to take advantage of some of these features, but any features you attempt to use that aren't supported should silently be ignored.

Here are some of the issues that it would be good to address in the current table:

➤ There are no visible divisions between the cells.

➤ There are no large visual distinctions other than font weight between the headers and the normal cells.

➤ The numeric columns would look better right aligned.

➤ It can be difficult for the eye to travel along a row of the table without slipping to an adjacent row.

Styling Your Table

Now it's time to pretty things up a bit using the code shown in Listing 7-4.

LISTING 7-4

```html
<!DOCTYPE html>
<html>
<head>
<title>Table With Styled Semantic Markup</title>

<style type="text/css">
/* Remove excess interstitial borders and padding
establish an outer border */
table {
        border-collapse: collapse;
        border: 1px solid #4C4C4C;
}
/* Add a dotted border around both header cells
and normal cells */
th, td {
    border: 1px dotted #707070;
}
/* Add some padding around the header content
removing the cramped spacing. Make the background
color of the headers green. */
th {
    background: #C2F0C2;
    padding: 5px;
}
/* Darken the green background for just the column
headers so that they use a different green than the
row headers. The fact that the column headers are
within a thead element helps to discriminate them
from the row headers. */
thead th {
    background: #9BC09B;
}
/* Set the background behind the caption to a dark
gray and the caption text to white. */
caption {
    background: #4C4C4C;
    padding: 5px;
    color: white;
}
/* This sets a solid bottom border to just the column
headers. This is achieved by using an attribute selector
to select just the th elements with scope set to col. */
th[scope=col] {
    border-bottom: 2px solid #707070;
}
/* This sets a solid right border to just the row headers.
This is achieved by using an attribute selector to
```

```
select just the th elements with scope set to row. It
also left aligns these headers */
th[scope=row] {
    border-right: 2px solid #707070;
    text-align: left;
}
/* This right aligns all the normal cell content and
adds some padding to them */
td {
    text-align: right;
    padding: 5px;
}
/* This sets a different background to just the row
header that resides in the footer row. */
tfoot th {
    background: #BBBBD1;
}
/* This sets a different background to just the
normal cells that reside in the footer row. */
tfoot td {
    background: #CFCFDF;
    color: #8D1919;
}

</style>
</head>
<body>

<table>
    <caption>Sales By Region</caption>
    <colgroup>
        <col class="col-header">
        <col class="col-amount">
        <col class="col-mean">
    </colgroup>
    <thead>
        <tr>
            <th scope="col">Region</th>
            <th scope="col">Sales</th>
            <th scope="col">Mean</th>
        </tr>
    </thead>
    <tfoot>
        <tr>
            <th scope="row">Sum</th>
            <td>$1,000,000</td>
            <td></td>
        </tr>
    </tfoot>
    <tbody>
    <tr>
        <th scope="row">Northeast</th>
        <td>$100,000</td>
        <td>$142,857</td>
    </tr>
```

continues

LISTING 7-4 *(continued)*

```
        <tr>
            <th scope="row">Southeast</th>
            <td>$75,000</td>
            <td>$142,857</td>
        </tr>
        <tr>
            <th scope="row">Midwest</th>
            <td>$125,000</td>
            <td>$142,857</td>
        </tr>
        <tr>
            <th scope="row">Mid-Atlantic</th>
            <td>$125,000</td>
            <td>$142,857</td>
        </tr>
        <tr>
            <th scope="row">Southwest</th>
            <td>$75,000</td>
            <td>$142,857</td>
        </tr>
        <tr>
            <th scope="row">Northwest</th>
            <td>$100,000</td>
            <td>$142,857</td>
        </tr>
        <tr>
            <th scope="row">California</th>
            <td>$400,000</td>
            <td>$142,857</td>
        </tr>
        </tbody>

    </table>

</body>
</html>
```

You can see the result of Listing 7-4 in Figure 7-7.

You can find the `TableStyling.html` file on the companion website.

The table in Figure 7-7 looks much better than earlier versions, doesn't it? The comments in Listing 7-4 explain what each individual styling rule accomplishes. Note how the use of the appropriate semantic HTML elements aided in discriminating between the various types of header rows and normal cells so that they could be styled differently.

Increasing Readability

With the styling in place, you've already improved the readability of the table remarkably, but there is still more that you can do. Most tables are rendered with horizontal lines between the rows. These lines help the eye track between cells in the same row and make it harder for the eye to slip from one row to another. Another trick that is often used to help the eye scan a table row is to use alternating row highlights. For example, a table might have a repeating pattern of a light background followed by a dark background. Conventional wisdom declares that this should make it harder for the eye to slip from one row to an adjacent one due to the visual disparity between them. Here's how you would add some additional styling rules to achieve this:

```
tbody tr:nth-child(odd) {
    background: #DBDBDB;
}
```

Sales By Region		
Region	**Sales**	**Mean**
Northeast	$100,000	$142,857
Southeast	$75,000	$142,857
Midwest	$125,000	$142,857
Mid-Atlantic	$125,000	$142,857
Southwest	$75,000	$142,857
Northwest	$100,000	$142,857
California	$400,000	$142,857
Sum	$1,000,000	

FIGURE 7-7: More comprehensive CSS styling rules have been applied to the table.

This rule is a bit dense, so it helps to break it down; sometimes it helps to deconstruct complicated selectors if you read them from right to left. The `nth-child(odd)` bit is saying to select only odd children (every other child). Then, proceeding a step further to the left, `tr:nth-child(odd)` is the instruction to select all odd children if they are `<tr>` elements. Take a further step to the left, and `tbody tr:nth-child(odd)` is selecting odd children if they are `<tr>` elements and they are contained within a `<tbody>` element. You can see the results of this in Figure 7-8.

You can find the `TableAlternateRowStyling.html` file on the companion website.

Sales By Region		
Region	**Sales**	**Mean**
Northeast	$100,000	$142,857
Southeast	$75,000	$142,857
Midwest	$125,000	$142,857
Mid-Atlantic	$125,000	$142,857
Southwest	$75,000	$142,857
Northwest	$100,000	$142,857
California	$400,000	$142,857
Sum	$1,000,000	

FIGURE 7-8: Now the table has alternating row highlights.

The CSS required to create alternating row highlights actually turns out to be really concise. The downside, however, is that nth-child is actually a CSS level 3 selector, so it is only available in the most modern browsers. Older browsers just ignore the rule, so this rule still safely and gracefully degrades if someone tries to view it on a noncompliant browser.

If you drop some of the concision, you can support alternating highlights on older browsers also. One way of approaching this is to manually add a class to all the odd rows of the table and then select on that class directly in order to highlight the odd rows. If you were generating the table using some code on the server, this method would be relatively straightforward. You could just make sure to emit class="odd" for every other row in the markup generated for the table.

However, there is a distinct downside to approaching this problem in this way. If you were to use some client-side code to change the sorting of the rows, you would also need to reassign all the classes based on the new row order.

Another approach is to use jQuery to manipulate the rows to implement the alternating row highlights, as shown in Listing 7-5. One of the benefits of jQuery is that it can help you emulate some more modern browser features on older browsers.

LISTING 7-5

```
<!DOCTYPE html>
<html>
<head>
<title>Table With Alternating Row Highlight</title>

<script src="jquery/jquery-1.11.1.min.js"></script>

<style type="text/css">
table {
        border-collapse: collapse;
        border: 1px solid #4C4C4C;
}
th, td {
    border: 1px dotted #707070;
}
th {
    background: #C2F0C2;
    padding: 5px;
}
thead th {
    background: #9BC09B;
}
caption {
    background: #4C4C4C;
    padding: 5px;
    color: white;
}
th[scope=col] {
    border-bottom: 2px solid #707070;
}
```

```css
th[scope=row] {
    border-right: 2px solid #707070;
    text-align: left;
}
td {
    padding: 5px;
}
tfoot th {
    background: #BBBBD1;
}
tfoot td {
    background: #CFCFDF;
    color: #8D1919;
}
.row-odd {
    background: #DBDBDB;
}
.row-odd th {
    background: #A2D0A2;
}
.cell-number {
    text-align: right;
}
</style>

<script type="text/javascript">
    function usCurrencyToFloat(currency) {
        currency = currency.replace(/\$/g, '');
        currency = currency.replace(/,/g, '');
        return parseFloat(currency);
    }

    $(function () {
        $("tbody").find("tr:odd").addClass("row-odd");
        $("tbody").find("td").filter(function (index) {
            return !isNaN(usCurrencyToFloat($(this).text()));
        }).addClass("cell-number");
    });
</script>

</head>
<body>

<table>
    <caption>Sales By Region</caption>
    <colgroup>
        <col class="col-header">
        <col class="col-amount">
        <col class="col-mean">
    </colgroup>
    <thead>
        <tr>
            <th scope="col">Region</th>
            <th scope="col">Sales</th>
            <th scope="col">Mean</th>
```

continues

LISTING 7-5 *(continued)*

```
            </tr>
        </thead>
        <tfoot>
            <tr>
                <th scope="row">Sum</th>
                <td>$1,000,000</td>
                <td></td>
            </tr>
        </tfoot>
        <tbody>
        <tr>
            <th scope="row">Northeast</th>
            <td>$100,000</td>
            <td>$142,857</td>
        </tr>
        <tr>
            <th scope="row">Southeast</th>
            <td>$75,000</td>
            <td>$142,857</td>
        </tr>
        <tr>
            <th scope="row">Midwest</th>
            <td>$125,000</td>
            <td>$142,857</td>
        </tr>
        <tr>
            <th scope="row">Mid-Atlantic</th>
            <td>$125,000</td>
            <td>$142,857</td>
        </tr>
        <tr>
            <th scope="row">Southwest</th>
            <td>$75,000</td>
            <td>$142,857</td>
        </tr>
        <tr>
            <th scope="row">Northwest</th>
            <td>$100,000</td>
            <td>$142,857</td>
        </tr>
        <tr>
            <th scope="row">California</th>
            <td>$400,000</td>
            <td>$142,857</td>
        </tr>
        </tbody>

    </table>

</body>
</html>
```

You can see the result of Listing 7-5 in Figure 7-9.

You can find the `TableAlternateRowStylingJQuery.html` file on the companion website.

Sales By Region		
Region	**Sales**	**Mean**
Northeast	$100,000	$142,857
Southeast	$75,000	$142,857
Midwest	$125,000	$142,857
Mid-Atlantic	$125,000	$142,857
Southwest	$75,000	$142,857
Northwest	$100,000	$142,857
California	$400,000	$142,857
Sum	$1,000,000	

FIGURE 7-9: The alternating row highlights in this table were implemented with jQuery.

Review the new aspects of this sample, starting with the following:

```
<script src="jquery/jquery-1.11.1.min.js"></script>
```

This line of code references jQuery, assuming it has been downloaded to a subfolder called `jQuery`, as it is in the code download from the companion site. It could also be loaded through its CDN server. For more information on using the jQuery CDN server see `http://jquery.com /download/`. You should, of course, review jQuery's license terms before use.

The following is the next new bit of CSS:

```
.row-odd {
    background: #DBDBDB;
}
```

This defines a CSS style rule that targets any element that has the class `row-odd`. You use jQuery to make sure that the odd rows have this class assigned. This rule assigns a different background color to the odd rows so that the background color alternates as you achieved earlier through the `nth-child` selector.

Next is the following rule, which targets only `<th>` elements that are in odd rows, coloring their background a darker version of the row header color.

```
.row-odd th {
    background: #A2D0A2;
}
```

And then you have this:

```
.cell-number {
    text-align: right;
}
```

This rule assumes that you'll later use jQuery to assign a class called `cell-number` to any cell that appears to contain a number, in order that they all be right-aligned.

The following is the first actual JavaScript you'll employ to manipulate the table:

```
<script type="text/javascript">
    function usCurrencyToFloat(currency) {
        currency = currency.replace(/\$/g, '');
        currency = currency.replace(/,/g, '');
        return parseFloat(currency);
    }

    $(function () {
        $("tbody").find("tr:odd").addClass("row-odd");
        $("tbody").find("td").filter(function (index) {
            return !isNaN(usCurrencyToFloat($(this).text()));
        }).addClass("cell-number");
    });
</script>
```

It's pretty concise and straightforward, but here's the breakdown. The first bit:

```
function usCurrencyToFloat(currency) {
    currency = currency.replace(/\$/g, '');
    currency = currency.replace(/,/g, '');
    return parseFloat(currency);
}
```

attempts, through pretty brute force means, to convert the currency strings in the table cells into floating point numbers. This is done in order to attempt to identify which cells contain numbers, so that the style defined earlier can right-align only the number cells. This is accomplished through removing any dollar sign characters and commas from the string, and then parsing the result as a floating point number. If the string happens to still not be a valid number then parseFloat returns NaN (Not a number).

Next,

```
$(function () {
    $("tbody").find("tr:odd").addClass("row-odd");
    $("tbody").find("td").filter(function (index) {
        return !isNaN(usCurrencyToFloat($(this).text()));
    }).addClass("cell-number");
});
```

uses jQuery to invoke some code when the DOM is ready. In the ready callback, it invokes:

```
$("tbody").find("tr:odd").addClass("row-odd");
```

which uses jQuery to find just the odd rows from within the body of the table and adds the class row-odd to them. Then it calls

```
$("tbody").find("td").filter(function (index) {
    return !isNaN(usCurrencyToFloat($(this).text()));
}).addClass("cell-number");
```

which finds only cells for which the usCurrencyToFloat function (discussed earlier in this chapter) returns a valid number, and to those cells it adds the class cell-number. As previously discussed, this should ensure that all number columns end up right-aligned.

Adding Dynamic Highlighting

Although the rows are far easier to scan now, there is still more you can do to make this table more readable. You can help the user single out a row and/or a column by coloring it differently than all the others. A good solution for this is to highlight whichever row and/or column is currently under the mouse cursor. You can implement this using jQuery. To achieve this, you would add these styles:

```
td.highlight {
    background: #FF944D;
}

th.highlight {
    background: #B26836;
}
```

This code is anticipating that you'll use jQuery to add a class called `highlight` to any cells and headers that are in the same row or column as the user's mouse cursor.

You would then add the following code to the ready callback from the previous listing:

```
$(document.body).on("mouseover", "td, th", function () {
    var index = $(this).index(),
    row = $(this).parent(),
    trs = $("tr");

    row.children().addClass("highlight");
    for (var i = 0; i < trs.length; i++) {
        trs.eq(i)
            .children()
            .eq(index)
            .addClass("highlight");
    }
});

$(document.body).on("mouseout", "td, th", function () {
    var index = $(this).index(),
    row = $(this).parent(),
    trs = $("tr");

    row.children().removeClass("highlight");
    for (var i = 0; i < trs.length; i++) {
        trs.eq(i)
            .children()
            .eq(index)
            .removeClass("highlight");
    }
});
```

With `$(document.body).on("mouseover", "td, th", function () {` you are listening for the `mouseover` event to fire for any table cell or table header on the page. `var index = $(this).index()` gets the index of the cell, within the table row, that the mouse is directly over. `row = $(this).parent()` gets the row that contains this cell. `trs = $("tr")` gets all table rows. Again, if you have multiple tables on the page, you have to do something a bit more complicated. You'd want to find the closest containing table element for the hovered cell and find only elements within that table.

Given these variables, you can add the `highlight` class to all cells in the current row with `row.children().addClass("highlight")` and then loop through all the rows and highlight all the cells that are in the same column as the hovered cell:

```
for (var i = 0; i < trs.length; i++) {
    trs.eq(i)
        .children()
        .eq(index)
        .addClass("highlight");
}
```

Here, `.eq(index)` is filtering the set of children to just those equaling the current column index.

> **NOTE** *jQuery uses a functional programming style. Most methods operate on the current selection. So when you execute* `trs.eq(i).children().eq(index).addClass("highlight")`, *the selection starts as all the table rows, is filtered down to just the current row, drills to become the children of that row, and is filtered to just the cell from the column with the provided index; then the "highlight" class is applied to the whole selection, which is just the cell from the hovered column, in this case.*

Following this method, the same is done for `mouseout`, except the `highlight` class is being removed from all the previously highlighted cells rather than it being added. Given all this, you end up with something like Figure 7-10, which shows the result of hovering over a cell in the table.

You can find the `TableRowAndColumnHighlights.html` file on the companion website.

Sales By Region		
Region	**Sales**	**Mean**
Northeast	$100,000	$142,857
Southeast	$75,000	$142,857
Midwest	$125,000	$142,857
Mid-Atlantic	$125,000	$142,857
Southwest	$75,000	$142,857
Northwest	$100,000	$142,857
California	$400,000	$142,857
Sum	$1,000,000	

FIGURE 7-10: The hovered row and column are dynamically highlighted.

INCLUDING COMPUTATIONS

Now that you've built a table, made it accessible, and improved its readability with CSS and JavaScript, it's time to see what else can be done to further enhance it with JavaScript. If you think back to when you initially used the data from this table in Chapter 2, you performed some further analysis on the data. This section describes how to perform the same analysis in JavaScript and explains how to automatically add it to the table in the process. Listing 7-6 is the new script block:

LISTING 7-6

```
<script type="text/javascript">
    function usCurrencyToFloat(currency) {
        currency = currency.replace(/\$/g, '');
        currency = currency.replace(/,/g, '');
        return parseFloat(currency);
    }

    function floatToUSCurrency(value) {
        var numString = value.toFixed(2),
        parts = numString.split('.'),
        outParts = [],
        beforeDecimal = "0",
        afterDecimal = "00",
        currSegment;

        beforeDecimal = parts[0];
        afterDecimal = parts[1];

        while (beforeDecimal.length > 3) {
            currSegment = beforeDecimal.substring(
                beforeDecimal.length - 3,
                beforeDecimal.length);
            beforeDecimal = beforeDecimal.substring(
                0,
                beforeDecimal.length - 3);
            outParts.unshift(currSegment);
        }
        if (beforeDecimal.length > 0) {
            outParts.unshift(beforeDecimal);
        }

        return '$' + outParts.join(',') + '.' + afterDecimal;
    }

    function populateCalculatedColumn(
        tableSelector,
        toPopulateIndex,
        toPopulateHeader,
        calculation,
        parse,
        toString) {
        var columns = [],
        rows = $(tableSelector).find("tbody").find("tr"),
        headers, tableInfo = {},
        headerRow = $(tableSelector).find("thead").find("tr"),
        newColumn, header,
        footerRow = $(tableSelector).find("tfoot").find("tr");

        rows.each(function (index, row) {
            $(this).children().each(function (index, cell) {
                var currColumn;
                if ((columns.length - 1) < index) {
```

continues

LISTING 7-6 *(continued)*

```javascript
                    columns.push([]);
                }
                currColumn = columns[index];
                currColumn.push(parse($(this).text()));
            });
        });

        tableInfo.columns = columns;

        headers = headerRow.find("th");
        headers.each(function (index, header) {
            tableInfo[$(this).text()] = columns[index];
        });

        newColumn = calculation(tableInfo);

        rows.each(function (index, row) {
            var thisRow = $(this),
            row;
            while ((thisRow.children().length - 1) < toPopulateIndex) {
                thisRow.append($("<td></td>"));
            }
            cell = thisRow.children().eq(toPopulateIndex);
            cell.text(toString(newColumn[index]));
        });

        while ((headerRow.children().length - 1) < toPopulateIndex) {
            headerRow.append($("<th scope='col'></th>"));
        }
        header = headerRow.children().eq(toPopulateIndex);
        header.text(toPopulateHeader);

        while ((footerRow.children().length - 1) < toPopulateIndex) {
            footerRow.append($("<td></td>"));
        }
        if (newColumn.length > rows.length) {
            footerRow.children.eq(toPopulateIndex).text(
                toString(newColumn[rows.length]));
        }
    }
}

$(function () {
    $(document.body).on("mouseover", "td, th", function () {
        var index = $(this).index(),
        row = $(this).parent(),
        trs = $("tr"), i;

        row.children().addClass("highlight");
        for (var i = 0; i < trs.length; i++) {
            trs.eq(i)
                .children()
                .eq(index)
                .addClass("highlight");
        }
    });
```

```javascript
$(document.body).on("mouseout", "td, th", function () {
    var index = $(this).index(),
    row = $(this).parent(),
    trs = $("tr"), i;

    row.children().removeClass("highlight");
    for (var i = 0; i < trs.length; i++) {
        trs.eq(i)
            .children()
            .eq(index)
            .removeClass("highlight");
    }
});

populateCalculatedColumn(
    "table",
    2,
    "Mean",
    function (tableInfo) {
        var sum = 0, mean, newColumn = [];
        for (var i = 0; i < tableInfo.Sales.length; i++) {
            sum += tableInfo.Sales[i];
        }
        mean = sum / tableInfo.Sales.length;
        for (var i = 0; i < tableInfo.Sales.length; i++) {
            newColumn.push(mean);
        }
        return newColumn;
    },
    usCurrencyToFloat,
    floatToUSCurrency);

populateCalculatedColumn(
    "table",
    3,
    "Difference",
    function (tableInfo) {
        var newColumn = [];
        for (var i = 0; i < tableInfo.Sales.length; i++) {
            newColumn.push(
                tableInfo.Sales[i] - tableInfo.Mean[i]
            );
        }
        return newColumn;
    },
    usCurrencyToFloat,
    floatToUSCurrency);

populateCalculatedColumn(
    "table",
    4,
    "Squared Difference",
    function (tableInfo) {
        var newColumn = [];
```

continues

LISTING 7-6 *(continued)*

```
                    for (var i = 0; i < tableInfo.Sales.length; i++) {
                        newColumn.push(
                            tableInfo.Difference[i] *
                            tableInfo.Difference[i]
                        );
                    }
                    return newColumn;
                },
                usCurrencyToFloat,
                floatToUSCurrency);

            $("tbody").find("tr:odd").addClass("row-odd");
            $("tbody").find("td").filter(function (index) {
                return !isNaN(usCurrencyToFloat($(this).text()));
            }).addClass("cell-number");
        });
    </script>
```

The output is shown in Figure 7-11.

You can find the `TableWithCalculatedColumns.html` file on the companion website.

Sales By Region				
Region	**Sales**	**Mean**	**Difference**	**Squared Difference**
Northeast	$100,000	$142,857.14	$-42,857.14	$1,836,734,448.98
Southeast	$75,000	$142,857.14	$-67,857.14	$4,604,591,448.98
Midwest	$125,000	$142,857.14	$-17,857.14	$318,877,448.98
Mid-Atlantic	$125,000	$142,857.14	$-17,857.14	$318,877,448.98
Southwest	$75,000	$142,857.14	$-67,857.14	$4,604,591,448.98
Northwest	$100,000	$142,857.14	$-42,857.14	$1,836,734,448.98
California	$400,000	$142,857.14	$257,142.86	$66,122,450,448.98
Sum	$1,000,000			

FIGURE 7-11: This table has dynamically calculated columns.

With the new code incorporated, you can now see two additional columns: Difference and Squared Difference. These were calculated by the JavaScript in the preceding code, which you examine shortly. Additionally, since the beginning of this chapter, you've used static values for the Mean column, but now this column is also dynamically calculated.

Using JavaScript for Calculations

Now, it's time to break down how the dynamically calculated columns shown in Figure 7-11 are produced.

```
function usCurrencyToFloat(currency) {
    currency = currency.replace(/\$/g, '');
    currency = currency.replace(/,/g, '');
```

```
        return parseFloat(currency);
    }
```

You might recall that this method was discussed earlier in the chapter. It's being used here to make it possible to manipulate the currency values in the table, and perform calculations based upon them.

```
function floatToUSCurrency(value) {
    var numString = value.toFixed(2),
    parts = numString.split('.'),
    outParts = [],
    beforeDecimal = "0",
    afterDecimal = "00",
    currSegment;

    beforeDecimal = parts[0];
    afterDecimal = parts[1];

    while (beforeDecimal.length > 3) {
        currSegment = beforeDecimal.substring(
            beforeDecimal.length - 3,
            beforeDecimal.length);
        beforeDecimal = beforeDecimal.substring(
            0,
            beforeDecimal.length - 3);
        outParts.unshift(currSegment);
    }
    if (beforeDecimal.length > 0) {
        outParts.unshift(beforeDecimal);
    }

    return '$' + outParts.join(',') + '.' + afterDecimal;
}
```

This, like the conversion from a US currency string to a floating point number, is a rather brute force conversion back to a US currency string from a floating point number. There are more concise ways to achieve this, but this way strives to be pretty straightforward. It basically just adds the comma separators back into the number and then prepends the dollar sign again.

Now turn your attention to the main function that dynamically populates the columns for the table: populateCalculatedColumn. The parameters of the function are the following:

➤ tableSelector is a jQuery selector that you can use to indicate which table should have the column added.

➤ toPopulateIndex indicates the column index at which to add the new column in the table.

➤ toPopulateHeader indicates the desired text of the new header to top the column in the table.

➤ calculation takes a function that allows you to perform a custom calculation to determine the content of each cell in the new table column.

➤ parse takes a function that converts the values in any source columns into values that can be referenced in the calculation.

➤ toString takes a function that renders a floating point value into the final text you expect to see in the column cells.

Now that we've discussed the parameters, let's dive into the body of the method.

```
var columns = [],
rows = $(tableSelector).find("tbody").find("tr"),
headers, tableInfo = {},
headerRow = $(tableSelector).find("thead").find("tr"),
newColumn, header,
footerRow = $(tableSelector).find("tfoot").find("tr");
```

At the top, you are defining some useful variables to use later in the function, including arrays to hold information about the existing columns and headers in the table. Also, the various elements of the table are then located using jQuery selectors. Each of the selectors, such as `$(tableSelector).find("tbody").find("tr")`, first finds the table based on the `tableSelector` parameter and then finds various sub-elements within that table using the jQuery `find` function.

```
rows.each(function (index, row) {
    $(this).children().each(function (index, cell) {
        var currColumn;
        if ((columns.length - 1) < index) {
            columns.push([]); // need to add a new column
        }
        currColumn = columns[index];
        // add the value for this cell to its column
        currColumn.push(parse($(this).text()));
    });
});
```

Here, for each row, the `parse` function (which was passed in as a parameter) is used to collect the value of every cell in each column into a collection of columns for you to reference when calculating column values later.

```
tableInfo.columns = columns;

headers = headerRow.find("th");
headers.each(function (index, header) {
    tableInfo[$(this).text()] = columns[index];
});
```

In this code, the columns, with associated cell values, are stored such that they can be referenced from the `calculation` function. Then, to make it easier to reference various columns from the `calculation` function, it loops through the headers in the header row and stores each column via its header name also.

```
newColumn = calculation(tableInfo);

rows.each(function (index, row) {
    var thisRow = $(this);
    while ((thisRow.children().length - 1) < toPopulateIndex) {
        thisRow.append($("<td></td>"));
    }
    cell = thisRow.children().eq(toPopulateIndex);
    cell.text(toString(newColumn[index]));
});
```

Next, the `calculation` function (which was passed in) is called on the column information that you've collected, which produces a new column (an array of values) that need to be added to the table. To add these to the table, you loop over each of the existing rows in the table and add cells to the current row until there are enough cells to accommodate the new column value. Then the correct cell in the current row is located and the calculated content is added as text content for the cell by means of calling the `toString` function (which was passed in as a parameter).

```
while ((headerRow.children().length - 1) < toPopulateIndex) {
    headerRow.append($("<th scope='col'></th>"));
}
header = headerRow.children().eq(toPopulateIndex);
header.text(toPopulateHeader);
```

This logic should look familiar because it's essentially the same logic that you just used to ensure that there was a cell to hold the new column data and then to populate the cell. In this case, however, you are ensuring that there is a header column to hold the new header value for the dynamically calculated column and then providing the new header text (which was passed in as a parameter) as the text of the header.

```
while ((footerRow.children().length - 1) < toPopulateIndex) {
    footerRow.append($("<td></td>"));
}
if (newColumn.length > rows.length) {
    footerRow.children.eq(toPopulateIndex).text(
        toString(newColumn[rows.length]));
}
```

Finally, this adds a new cell to the footer row, if an appropriate value was returned from the `calculation` function.

Quite a lot of code, huh? Thankfully, there are plenty of libraries out there, both open source and commercial, to accomplish these sorts of things for you. As you can see, however, it isn't too complicated to do it from scratch!

Populating the Table

Now it's time to actually populate the table, so you'll be calling the `populateCalculatedColumn` function a few times. First, you can dynamically create the `Mean` column, which was a static part of the table until this point:

```
populateCalculatedColumn(
    "table",
    2,
    "Mean",
    function (tableInfo) {
        var sum = 0, mean, newColumn = [];
        for (var i = 0; i < tableInfo.Sales.length; i++) {
            sum += tableInfo.Sales[i];
        }
        mean = sum / tableInfo.Sales.length;
        for (var i = 0; i < tableInfo.Sales.length; i++) {
```

```
            newColumn.push(mean);
        }
        return newColumn;
    },
    usCurrencyToFloat,
    floatToUSCurrency);
```

Here, you are targeting all table elements on the page (normally you'd probably use an ID or a class name here; there is only one table on the page, in this instance). This is indicating that the new column should be inserted at index 2 and that it should be headed with the text "Mean". Then, the calculation function is provided, which loops through the Sales column data and divides by the number of entries, which, you might recall from Chapter 2, is how you calculate the mean value. Then, this mean value is returned for every row of the new column. Finally, the functions usCurrencyToFloat and floatToUSCurrency are provided so that values can be read out of the existing columns or rendered into the new column being created.

Next, a column is created that holds the difference between each row's sales value and each row's mean value and is inserted at index 3:

```
populateCalculatedColumn(
    "table",
    3,
    "Difference",
    function (tableInfo) {
        var newColumn = [];
        for (var i = 0; i < tableInfo.Sales.length; i++) {
            newColumn.push(
                tableInfo.Sales[i] - tableInfo.Mean[i]
            );
        }
        return newColumn;
    },
    usCurrencyToFloat,
    floatToUSCurrency);
```

And finally the last column is inserted at column index 4 with a calculation that squares each row's Difference value, again, as discussed in Chapter 2:

```
populateCalculatedColumn(
    "table",
    4,
    "Squared Difference",
    function (tableInfo) {
        var newColumn = [];
        for (var i = 0; i < tableInfo.Sales.length; i++) {
            newColumn.push(
                tableInfo.Difference[i] *
                tableInfo.Difference[i]
            );
        }
        return newColumn;
    },
    usCurrencyToFloat,
    floatToUSCurrency);
```

As a result of your jQuery wizardry, the table has three additional columns that weren't present when the table was delivered from the server.

> **NOTE** *Keep in mind that this sort of operation can lessen the requirement in terms of the upfront analysis that is performed on the data before it is sent to the client, but this sort of strategy can decrease the reach of your table. Any browser that does not have JavaScript enabled will not be able to view these additional columns. This includes many screen reader programs, which can deliberately avoid running scripts. Calculated columns can be extremely useful, however, if you want the user to be able to select extra ad hoc calculations to apply to the data on the client.*

USING THE DATATABLES LIBRARY

You just managed some pretty impressive table manipulation with only jQuery and a bit of elbow grease to assist you, but there are also mature libraries available to do much more elaborate things to help you visualize tabular data. In this section, you use one such library to accomplish some of what you've already accomplished through other means earlier in the chapter. This time, though, there is far less logic for you to write and maintain yourself (which can be a very important thing when working with JavaScript!).

> **NOTE** *JavaScript is a very flexible and fun-to-use language, but it lacks some features that make it an easy language to use for maintaining large code bases. If you need to maintain a lot of JavaScript code, it's best to have a good strategy laid out. One good strategy is to use static analysis tools, such as JSLint or JSHint, to warn you of issues well before your code gets executed. Another valid strategy is to try to minimize the JavaScript code that you have to maintain. Using jQuery helps you a lot in this regard, but there are lots of other libraries that can assist for other scenarios, not to mention lots of plug-ins for jQuery that extend its abilities in various ways.*

The open source library you'll be using in this section is called DataTables (www.datatables.net/). In the code listings and companion code for this chapter, the assumption is that you have downloaded the DataTables plug-in to a subfolder called datatables. This is the arrangement you will find if you download the code from the companion site. As with jQuery you could alternatively load the code from a CDN.

> **NOTE** *There are many advantages to loading JavaScript resources from a CDN, but one of them is that if your users have already visited another site that loaded that resource from the same URL, that resource is already cached on the users' systems, which saves you bandwidth and also saves the user time when loading the page.*

Making Pretty Tables with DataTables

The first thing you can try to do is to use DataTables to perform the same sort of progressive enhancement on the static <table> element that you've been targeting for this whole chapter (see Listing 7-7).

LISTING 7-7

```
<!DOCTYPE html>
<html>
<head>
<title>Table With DataTables</title>

<link rel="stylesheet" type="text/css"
href="datatables/media/css/jquery.dataTables_themeroller.css">
<link rel="stylesheet" type="text/css"
href="jquery-ui-1.11.1/jquery-ui.css">
<script type="text/javascript"
src="jquery/jquery-1.11.1.min.js"></script>
<script type="text/javascript"
src="jquery-ui-1.11.1/jquery-ui.min.js"></script>
<script type="text/javascript"
src="datatables/media/js/jquery.dataTables.min.js">
</script>

<script type="text/javascript">
    $(function () {
        $("#salesByRegion").dataTable({
            bJQueryUI: true
        });
    });
</script>

</head>
<body>

<table id="salesByRegion">
    <caption>Sales By Region</caption>
    <colgroup>
        <col class="col-header">
        <col class="col-amount">
        <col class="col-mean">
    </colgroup>
    <thead>
        <tr>
            <th scope="col">Region</th>
            <th scope="col">Sales</th>
            <th scope="col">Mean</th>
        </tr>
    </thead>
```

```
        <tfoot>
            <tr>
                <th scope="row">Sum</th>
                <td>$1,000,000</td>
                <td></td>
            </tr>
        </tfoot>
        <tbody>
        <tr>
            <th scope="row">Northeast</th>
            <td>$100,000</td>
            <td>$142,857</td>
        </tr>
        <tr>
            <th scope="row">Southeast</th>
            <td>$75,000</td>
            <td>$142,857</td>
        </tr>
        <tr>
            <th scope="row">Midwest</th>
            <td>$125,000</td>
            <td>$142,857</td>
        </tr>
        <tr>
            <th scope="row">Mid-Atlantic</th>
            <td>$125,000</td>
            <td>$142,857</td>
        </tr>
        <tr>
            <th scope="row">Southwest</th>
            <td>$75,000</td>
            <td>$142,857</td>
        </tr>
        <tr>
            <th scope="row">Northwest</th>
            <td>$100,000</td>
            <td>$142,857</td>
        </tr>
        <tr>
            <th scope="row">California</th>
            <td>$400,000</td>
            <td>$142,857</td>
        </tr>
        </tbody>

    </table>

    </body>
    </html>
```

Listing 7-7 produces the output in Figure 7-12.

You can find the `TableUsingDataTables.html` file on the companion website.

Show 10 ⌄ entries		Search:

Sales By Region

Region ▲	Sales ⬍	Mean ⬍
California	$400,000	$142,857
Mid-Atlantic	$125,000	$142,857
Midwest	$125,000	$142,857
Northeast	$100,000	$142,857
Northwest	$100,000	$142,857
Southeast	$75,000	$142,857
Southwest	$75,000	$142,857
Sum	$1,000,000	

Showing 1 to 7 of 7 entries

FIGURE 7-12: The table has been enhanced with the DataTables API.

So, let's take a closer look:

```
$(function () {
    $("#salesByRegion").dataTable({
        bJQueryUI: true
    });
});
```

That's a lot less JavaScript code, huh? So what did it achieve? You get a lot of styling, data paging, dynamic filtering, alternating row highlights, sorting headers, and so on. And all you had to do to achieve this was to target the table by ID and invoke the DataTable library on it. Very cool! Also, you still started with an accessible table that users that don't have the ability to run JavaScript logic can consume.

In the preceding code snippet, `bJQueryUI: true` is indicating that the DataTables library should apply the appropriate classes to the various table elements such that you can style the table with jQuery ThemeRoller themes. The DataTables API, rather curiously, uses some form of Hungarian notation to identify the types of its options, so the lowercase B indicates that `bJQueryUI` is a Boolean option. One of the CSS files loaded at the top of Listing 7-7 is the jQuery UI smoothness theme. By merit of this option, you get some pretty slick styling applied to all the table elements.

> **NOTE** *Notice in Figure 7-12 that the table caption looks rather unstyled. Unfortunately, it doesn't seem like DataTables attempts to mesh this with the other styled elements by default. In order to blend it in better with the other elements, you could experiment with applying the same CSS classes to the `<caption>` as are applied to other parts of the table by DataTables.*

Sorting with DataTables

When running the sample from the preceding section, you'll find that, among other things, you can click the column headers to change the sort order of the rows based on the values in that column, much like you can in software such as Microsoft Excel. With some additional configuration, you can also specify the initial sort order of the rows, using the following code:

```
$(function () {
    $("#salesByRegion").dataTable({
        bJQueryUI: true,
        aaSorting: [ [1, "desc"], [0, "desc"] ]
    });
});
```

Here, the new option you are specifying is `aaSorting`. Again the Hungarian notation is at play here, so `aaSorting` indicates the expected type is an array of arrays. `[ [1, "desc"], [0, "desc"] ]` indicates that you first want the table to be sorted by the column with index 1 descending, and then by the column with index 0 descending. This produces the output shown in Figure 7-13.

You can find the `TableUsingDataTablesSorting.html` file on the companion website.

Show 10 entries		Search:
Sales By Region		
Region	Sales	Mean
Southwest	$75,000	$142,857
Southeast	$75,000	$142,857
California	$400,000	$142,857
Midwest	$125,000	$142,857
Mid-Atlantic	$125,000	$142,857
Northwest	$100,000	$142,857
Northeast	$100,000	$142,857
Sum	$1,000,000	
Showing 1 to 7 of 7 entries		

FIGURE 7-13: DataTables has been used to provide an initial sort for an HTML table.

Something you'll notice, however, when sorting these columns by clicking the headers, or pre-sorting the columns, as in Figure 7-13, is that the numbers aren't quite sorted by value, but rather as strings. DataTables is capable of performing a numeric style sort, but you need to help it parse the numbers from strings to floating points, like so:

```
$(function () {
    function usCurrencyToFloat(currency) {
        currency = currency.replace(/\$/g, '');
        currency = currency.replace(/,/g, '');
        return parseFloat(currency);
    }

    jQuery.fn.dataTableExt.oSort['us-currency-asc']   = function(x,y) {
        var fx = usCurrencyToFloat(x),
        fy = usCurrencyToFloat(y);

        if (fx < fy) {
            return -1;
```

```
        }
        if (fx > fy) {
            return 1;
        }

        return 0;
    };

    jQuery.fn.dataTableExt.oSort['us-currency-desc'] = function(x,y) {
        var fx = usCurrencyToFloat(x),
        fy = usCurrencyToFloat(y);

        if (fx < fy) {
            return 1;
        }
        if (fx > fy) {
            return -1;
        }

        return 0;
    };


    $("#salesByRegion").dataTable({
        bJQueryUI: true,
        aaSorting: [ [1, "desc"], [0, "desc"] ],
        aoColumns: [
            null,
            { sType: "us-currency" },
            { sType: "us-currency" } ]
    });
});
```

Here you are defining how the column type us-currency will be sorted in both an ascending and descending fashion. Then the types of the second and third columns can be changed to us-currency causing them to be sorted based on numeric value rather than by string value (which is the default).

Using Calculated Columns with DataTables

One of the trickier things you accomplished in the previous section was to use jQuery to dynamically add some new columns into the table. DataTables also has some facilities to enable this, but with far less code. You can change the table initialization to read

```
$(function () {
    $("#salesByRegion").dataTable({
        bJQueryUI: true,
        aaSorting: [ [3, "desc"], [1, "desc"] ],
        aoColumnDefs: [
        {
            mRender: function ( data, type, row ) {
                var difference =
                usCurrencyToFloat(row[1]) - usCurrencyToFloat(row[2]);
```

```
                    return floatToUSCurrency(difference);
                },
                aTargets: [ 3 ]
            }]
        });
    });
```

This adds the `aoColumnDefs` option (an array of objects that define some new columns), specifying that your single render function is targeting the column in the table with index 3. The render method calculates the difference between the column at index 2 (the mean value) and the column at index 1 (the sales value) just as you did with the code from the earlier portion of this chapter. This function also uses your two old friends: `usCurrencyToFloat` and `floatToUSCurrency`. Notice, too, that you are leaving an empty column to render these values into:

```html
<table id="salesByRegion">
    <caption>Sales By Region</caption>
    <colgroup>
        <col class="col-header">
        <col class="col-amount">
        <col class="col-mean">
    </colgroup>
    <thead>
        <tr>
            <th scope="col">Region</th>
            <th scope="col">Sales</th>
            <th scope="col">Mean</th>
            <th scope="col">Difference</th>
        </tr>
    </thead>
    <tfoot>
        <tr>
            <th scope="row">Sum</th>
            <td>$1,000,000</td>
            <td></td>
            <td></td>
        </tr>
    </tfoot>
    <tbody>
    <tr>
        <th scope="row">Northeast</th>
        <td>$100,000</td>
        <td>$142,857</td>
        <td></td>
    </tr>
    <tr>
        <th scope="row">Southeast</th>
        <td>$75,000</td>
        <td>$142,857</td>
        <td></td>
    </tr>
    <tr>
```

```
        <th scope="row">Midwest</th>
        <td>$125,000</td>
        <td>$142,857</td>
        <td></td>
    </tr>
    <tr>
        <th scope="row">Mid-Atlantic</th>
        <td>$125,000</td>
        <td>$142,857</td>
        <td></td>
    </tr>
    <tr>
        <th scope="row">Southwest</th>
        <td>$75,000</td>
        <td>$142,857</td>
        <td></td>
    </tr>
    <tr>
        <th scope="row">Northwest</th>
        <td>$100,000</td>
        <td>$142,857</td>
        <td></td>
    </tr>
    <tr>
        <th scope="row">California</th>
        <td>$400,000</td>
        <td>$142,857</td>
        <td></td>
    </tr>
    </tbody>

</table>
```

You can see the result of the column generation in Figure 7-14.

You can find the `TableUsingDataTablesCalculated.html` file on the companion website.

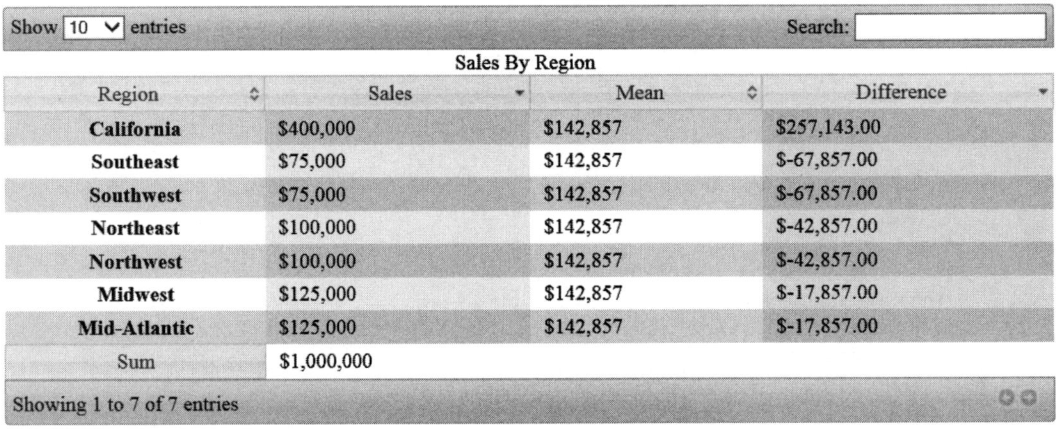

Region	Sales	Mean	Difference
California	$400,000	$142,857	$257,143.00
Southeast	$75,000	$142,857	$-67,857.00
Southwest	$75,000	$142,857	$-67,857.00
Northeast	$100,000	$142,857	$-42,857.00
Northwest	$100,000	$142,857	$-42,857.00
Midwest	$125,000	$142,857	$-17,857.00
Mid-Atlantic	$125,000	$142,857	$-17,857.00
Sum	$1,000,000		

Show 10 entries   Search: _____

Sales By Region

Showing 1 to 7 of 7 entries

FIGURE 7-14: DataTables calculates columns at runtime.

RELATING A DATA TABLE TO A CHART

To wrap up this chapter, you're going to take progressive enhancement to the extreme by taking the same data and presenting an interactive and editable data table with a linked chart displaying the same data. The charting component depends on HTML5 in order to do its sophisticated client-side rendering and represents one additional enhancement that can be made to presenting the data for supporting user agents.

For the last part of this chapter you switch to using the IgniteUI igGrid and igDataChart from Infragistics. These components are not free, but they also reduce some very complex interactive scenarios to simple turnkey configuration. The purpose of this chapter is not to discuss the configuration of chart components, which comes later in this book, so that topic is touched upon only lightly here. The idea, rather, is to focus on how the data tables from this chapter might be correlated with other related visualizations bound to the same data.

First, you should sign up for the trial version of IgniteUI. You can find more information about how to do this at `http://www.igniteui.com`. Additionally, Chapter 14 discusses both IgniteUI and the igDataChart in more detail. For the next code you use the IgniteUI Trial, which you have downloaded or is included with the download for this chapter from the companion website. Information about loading the trial version of IgniteUI can also be found at `http://www.igniteui.com`.

Mashing Visualizations Together

For this example, you are loading the same data as before into both an interactive data table and also an interactive chart. The data table is now editable, additionally, and editing the sales amount for a row causes both the mean column in the table to be updated as well as the linked chart's visuals to react. Selecting a column in the chart causes the appropriate row in the data table to be selected and vice versa.

LISTING 7-8

```html
<!DOCTYPE html>
<html>
<head>
<title>Table Row and Column Highlights</title>
    <script type='text/javascript'
    src='jquery/jquery-1.11.1.min.js'></script>
    <script type="text/javascript"
    src="jquery-ui-1.11.1/jquery-ui.js"></script>
    <script type='text/javascript'
    src="IgniteUI/js/infragistics.core.js"></script>
    <script type='text/javascript'
    src="IgniteUI/js/infragistics.dv.js"></script>
    <link rel="stylesheet"
href="IgniteUI/css/themes/infragistics/infragistics.theme.css">
    <link rel="stylesheet"
href="IgniteUI/css/structure/modules/infragistics.ui.shared.css">
    <link rel="stylesheet"
href="IgniteUI/css/structure/modules/infragistics.ui.chart.css">
```

continues

LISTING 7-8 *(continued)*

```
    <script type='text/javascript'
    src="IgniteUI/js/infragistics.lob.js"></script>
    <link rel="stylesheet" type="text/css"
href="IgniteUI/css/structure/modules/infragistics.ui.grid.css">

    <style>
        #chart1
        {
            margin: 10px;
            float: left;
        }
        #legend1
        {
            margin: 10px;
            float: left;
        }
        #salesByRegion_container
        {
            clear: both;
        }
        #salesByRegion
        {
            margin: 10px;
            max-width: 500px;
        }
    </style>

<script type="text/javascript">
    var data = [{ "Region": "Northeast", "Sales": 100000,
    "Mean": 142857.14 },
    { "Region": "Southeast", "Sales": 75000, "Mean": 142857.14 },
    { "Region": "Midwest", "Sales": 125000, "Mean": 142857.14 },
    { "Region": "Mid-Atlantic", "Sales": 125000, "Mean": 142857.14 },
    { "Region": "Southwest", "Sales": 75000, "Mean": 142857.14 },
    { "Region": "Northwest", "Sales": 100000, "Mean": 142857.14 },
    { "Region": "California", "Sales": 400000, "Mean": 142857.14 }];

    var currSelectedIndex = -1;

    var rowLookup = {};
    data.map(function (item,index) {
        rowLookup[item.Region] = index;
    });

    $(function () {
        $("#chart1").igDataChart({
            width: "500px",
            height: "300px",
            dataSource: data,
            animateSeriesWhenAxisRangeChanges: true,
            axes: [{
                name: "xAxis",
                type: "categoryX",
                label: "Region",
```

```
                    interval: 1,
                    labelAngle: 45
                }, {
                    name: "yAxis",
                    type: "numericY"
                }],
                series: [{
                    name: "Sales",
                    type: "column",
                    xAxis: "xAxis",
                    yAxis: "yAxis",
                    title: "Sales",
                    showTooltip: true,
                    valueMemberPath: "Sales",
                    isTransitionInEnabled: true,
                    isHighlightingEnabled: true,
                    isCustomCategoryStyleAllowed: true,
                    transitionDuration: 1000
                }, {
                    name: "Mean",
                    type: "column",
                    xAxis: "xAxis",
                    yAxis: "yAxis",
                    title: "Mean",
                    showTooltip: true,
                    valueMemberPath: "Mean",
                    isTransitionInEnabled: true,
                    isHighlightingEnabled: true,
                    isCustomCategoryStyleAllowed: true,
                    transitionDuration: 1000
                }],
                legend: { element: "legend1" },
                assigningCategoryStyle: function (evt, ui) {
                    if (currSelectedIndex >= ui.startIndex &&
                        currSelectedIndex <= ui.endIndex) {
                            ui.fill = "#FFB84D";
                    }
                },
                seriesMouseLeftButtonUp: function (evt, ui) {
                    var index = rowLookup[ui.item.Region];
                    currSelectedIndex = index;
                    updateSelectedIndex(true);
                }
            });

            var updateMeans = function () {
                var count = data.length;
                var sum = 0;
                data.map(function (item) { sum += item.Sales });
                var mean = sum / count;
                data.map(function (item) { item.Mean = mean });
                $("#salesByRegion").igGrid("dataBind");
                $("#chart1").igDataChart("notifyClearItems", data);
            };

            var updateSelectedIndex = function (fromChart) {
```

continues

LISTING 7-8 *(continued)*

```
        if (fromChart) {
            var rows = $("#salesByRegion").igGrid("rows");
            var key = data[currSelectedIndex].Region;
            var index = -1;
            $(rows).each(function(i, ele) {
                if ($(ele).attr("data-id") == key) {
                    index = i;
                }
            });
            $('#salesByRegion').igGridSelection(
            'selectRow', index);
        }
        $("#chart1").igDataChart("notifyVisualPropertiesChanged",
        "Sales");
        $("#chart1").igDataChart("notifyVisualPropertiesChanged",
        "Mean");
    }

    $("#salesByRegion").igGrid({
        autoCommit: true,
        dataSource: data,
        autoGenerateColumns: false,
        primaryKey: "Region",
        columns: [
            { headerText: "Region",
            key: "Region",
            dataType: "string" },
            { headerText: "Sales",
            key: "Sales",
            dataType: "number",
            format: "currency" },
            { headerText: "Mean",
            key: "Mean",
            dataType: "number",
            format: "currency" }
        ],
        features: [
            {
                name : 'Sorting',
                type: "local"
            },
            {
                name: "Resizing"
            },
            {
                name: "ColumnMoving",
                columnMovingDialogContainment: "window"
            },
            {
                name: 'Updating',
                enableAddRow: false,
                enableDeleteRow: false,
                editRowEnded: function (evt, ui) {
                    updateMeans();
```

```
                },
                columnSettings: [{
                    columnKey: "Region",
                    editorOptions: {readOnly: true}
                },{
                    columnKey: "Mean",
                    editorOptions: {readOnly: true}
                }]
            },
            {
                name: "Selection",
                mode: 'row',
                rowSelectionChanged: function (evt, ui) {
                    currSelectedIndex = rowLookup[ui.row.id];
                    updateSelectedIndex(false);
                }
            }
        ]
    });

});

</script>

</head>
<body>

<div id="chart1"></div>
<div id="legend1"></div>
<table id="salesByRegion"></table>

</body>
</html>
```

Diving into Listing 7-8, first you have some CSS:

```
<style>
    #chart1
    {
        margin: 10px;
        float: left;
    }
    #legend1
    {
        margin: 10px;
        float: left;
    }
    #salesByRegion_container
    {
        clear: both;
    }
    #salesByRegion
    {
        margin: 10px;
        max-width: 500px;
    }
</style>
```

This ensures that the chart and the legend appear next to each other, and the data table appears beneath. Following that, you have

```
var data = [{ "Region": "Northeast", "Sales": 100000,
"Mean": 142857.14 },
{ "Region": "Southeast", "Sales": 75000, "Mean": 142857.14 },
{ "Region": "Midwest", "Sales": 125000, "Mean": 142857.14 },
{ "Region": "Mid-Atlantic", "Sales": 125000, "Mean": 142857.14 },
{ "Region": "Southwest", "Sales": 75000, "Mean": 142857.14 },
{ "Region": "Northwest", "Sales": 100000, "Mean": 142857.14 },
{ "Region": "California", "Sales": 400000, "Mean": 142857.14 }];

var currSelectedIndex = -1;

var rowLookup = {};
data.map(function (item,index) {
    rowLookup[item.Region] = index;
});
```

Here you are starting with the data in JSON format rather than from a `<table>` to show another mechanism for table creation and to ease binding the data against multiple visualizations. You are also building a hashtable to aid looking up the data indexes based on the region name.

```
$(function () {
    $("#chart1").igDataChart({
        width: "500px",
        height: "300px",
        dataSource: data,
        animateSeriesWhenAxisRangeChanges: true,
        axes: [{
            name: "xAxis",
            type: "categoryX",
            label: "Region",
            interval: 1,
            labelAngle: 45
        }, {
            name: "yAxis",
            type: "numericY"
        }],
        series: [{
            name: "Sales",
            type: "column",
            xAxis: "xAxis",
            yAxis: "yAxis",
            title: "Sales",
            showTooltip: true,
            valueMemberPath: "Sales",
            isTransitionInEnabled: true,
            isHighlightingEnabled: true,
            isCustomCategoryStyleAllowed: true,
            transitionDuration: 1000
        }, {
            name: "Mean",
            type: "column",
            xAxis: "xAxis",
```

```
            yAxis: "yAxis",
            title: "Mean",
            showTooltip: true,
            valueMemberPath: "Mean",
            isTransitionInEnabled: true,
            isHighlightingEnabled: true,
            isCustomCategoryStyleAllowed: true,
            transitionDuration: 1000
        }],
        legend: { element: "legend1" },
        assigningCategoryStyle: function (evt, ui) {
            if (currSelectedIndex >= ui.startIndex &&
                currSelectedIndex <= ui.endIndex) {
                    ui.fill = "#FFB84D";
            }
        },
        seriesMouseLeftButtonUp: function (evt, ui) {
            var index = rowLookup[ui.item.Region];
            currSelectedIndex = index;
            updateSelectedIndex(true);
        }
    });
```

Here you are declaring an `igDataChart` that is bound against the preceding data. It has two column series that are bound to the sales data and the mean data respectively. Those column series are set to transition into view in an animated fashion, and are also set to animate subsequent data changes that will be coming from the `igGrid`. The `assigningCategoryStyle` event has been handled in order that the series can color the currently selected items with an orange color. Finally, the `seriesMouseLeftButtonUp` event is handled so that when items in the series are clicked the selected item in the `igGrid` can also be changed.

Skipping over the update methods for now, you have the declaration of the `igGrid`:

```
$("#salesByRegion").igGrid({
    autoCommit: true,
    dataSource: data,
    autoGenerateColumns: false,
    primaryKey: "Region",
    columns: [
        { headerText: "Region",
          key: "Region",
          dataType: "string" },
        { headerText: "Sales",
          key: "Sales",
          dataType: "number",
          format: "currency" },
        { headerText: "Mean",
          key: "Mean",
          dataType: "number",
          format: "currency" }
    ],
    features: [
        {
            name : 'Sorting',
```

```
                    type: "local"
            },
            {

                name: "Resizing"
            },
            {

                name: "ColumnMoving",
                columnMovingDialogContainment: "window"
            },
            {

                name: 'Updating',
                enableAddRow: false,
                enableDeleteRow: false,
                editRowEnded: function (evt, ui) {
                    updateMeans();
                },
                columnSettings: [{
                    columnKey: "Region",
                    editorOptions: {readOnly: true}
                },{
                    columnKey: "Mean",
                    editorOptions: {readOnly: true}
                }]
            },
            {

                name: "Selection",
                mode: 'row',
                rowSelectionChanged: function (evt, ui) {
                    currSelectedIndex = rowLookup[ui.row.id];
                    updateSelectedIndex(false);
                }
            }
        ]
    });
```

This defines an `igGrid` against the same data as the preceding chart definition. It is set to automatically commit changes because you want the chart to update its content immediately when you finish editing a row in the table. `autoGenerateColumns` is set to `false` so that you can specify the data type and formatting for each of the columns manually, and the primary key for the data items is identified as being the `Region` property. The primary key is important so that rows can be discriminated from each other to support various features of the `igGrid`. Following that, various features are turned on for the `igGrid`:

```
{
    name : 'Sorting',
    type: "local"
},
{
    name: "Resizing"
},
{
    name: "ColumnMoving",
    columnMovingDialogContainment: "window"
},
```

This code enables the sorting feature of the `igGrid` and indicates that the sorting should be performed locally in the browser (rather than remotely). It also turns on the column resizing feature in the `igGrid`, and, finally, it also enables the user to drag the columns to reorder them.

```
{
    name: 'Updating',
    enableAddRow: false,
    enableDeleteRow: false,
    editRowEnded: function (evt, ui) {
        updateMeans();
    },
    columnSettings: [{
        columnKey: "Region",
        editorOptions: {readOnly: true}
    },{
        columnKey: "Mean",
        editorOptions: {readOnly: true}
    }]
},
```

This turns on the updating feature for the `igGrid`. The ability to add and remove rows is hidden because this is not needed for this scenario, and the `Region` and `Mean` columns are marked as being read only. This is because the `Mean` column is auto-calculated based on the `Sales` column, and the `Region` column is the primary key and should remain constant. The `editRowEnded` event is handled in order to call the `updateMeans` method which updates the `Mean` column based on the new `Sales` figures and propagates all the data to the chart.

```
{
    name: "Selection",
    mode: 'row',
    rowSelectionChanged: function (evt, ui) {
        currSelectedIndex = rowLookup[ui.row.id];
        updateSelectedIndex(false);
    }
}
```

This turns on the selection feature for the grid and ensures that entire rows are selected, rather than just cells. The `rowSelectionChanged` event is handled, so that the current selected index can be tracked and the `updateSelectedIndex` function is called to propagate the selection change to the chart.

```
var updateMeans = function () {
    var count = data.length;
    var sum = 0;
    data.map(function (item) { sum += item.Sales });
    var mean = sum / count;
    data.map(function (item) { item.Mean = mean });
    $("#salesByRegion").igGrid("dataBind");
    $("#chart1").igDataChart("notifyClearItems", data);
};
```

The `updateMeans` function calculates the new mean value based on the updated sales data and sets it back into the `data` array. It then rebinds the `igGrid`, and notifies the `igDataChart` that all of the items' values have changed.

```
var updateSelectedIndex = function (fromChart) {
    if (fromChart) {
        var rows = $("#salesByRegion").igGrid("rows");
        var key = data[currSelectedIndex].Region;
        var index = -1;
        $(rows).each(function(i, ele) {
            if ($(ele).attr("data-id") == key) {
                index = i;
            }
        });
        $('#salesByRegion').igGridSelection('selectRow', index);
    }
    $("#chart1").igDataChart("notifyVisualPropertiesChanged", "Sales");
    $("#chart1").igDataChart("notifyVisualPropertiesChanged", "Mean");
}
```

The `updateSelectedIndex` function loops through the visible rows in the `igGrid` and finds the
`index` of the row that matches the primary key for the selected data item and asks the `igGrid` to
select that row. Then it notifies the chart to invalidate the visuals of the two contained series so that
the selection change can be shown. You can see the results of this in Figure 7-15.

FIGURE 7-15: This shows the same data using two separate data visualizations.

Pretty cool, huh? Notice that when you click the columns in the top chart, it selects the appropriate rows in the data table below. Correspondingly, when you select rows in the bottom data table it highlights the appropriate columns in the upper chart. When you click again on the selected row it enters edit mode and you are able to change the sales value for that region. When you select done, or press enter, not only do the values in the mean column update, but the columns in the upper chart also animate to the corresponding new positions. You can see the edit mode experience in Figure 7-16.

FIGURE 7-16: This shows the edit mode experience in the igGrid and the corresponding highlighted column in the igDataChart.

Finally, see how you can click the columns to change the sort order of the data rows in the table, and that you can drag the columns to reorder them. Pretty complex behavior for not a lot of code, huh?

The igGrid component has many other interesting features, such as the ability to filter the displayed data on the fly, or to maintain good performance even with large amounts of data loaded. You can find more information about its available features at http://igniteui.com/grid/overview.

SUMMARY

Data tables provide an important data visualization technique. They can provide data in a very concise format and, with the correct design decisions, can be accessible to a very wide audience. In this chapter you learned how to

➤ Format a basic table using HTML

➤ Enhance the semantic content with markup to aid accessibility and styling

➤ Make a table more accessible to screen readers

➤ Caption a table to provide context for the data

➤ Style a table with CSS

➤ Style a table with JavaScript

➤ Create alternating row highlights for a table using CSS and JavaScript

➤ Highlight the hovered row or column in a table

➤ Generate calculated columns with JavaScript

➤ Use the DataTables library to enhance an HTML table

➤ Use the DataTables library to sort columns

➤ Use the DataTables library to generate calculated columns

➤ Use IgniteUI igGrid and igDataChart to present multiple linked, interactive views of the same data.

8

Statistical Analysis on the Client Side

WHAT'S IN THIS CHAPTER

➤ Basic statistics concepts

➤ Statistical analysis with the jStat library

➤ Charting probability distributions with Flot

> **CODE DOWNLOAD** *The wrox.com code downloads for this chapter are found at* www.wrox.com/go/javascriptandjqueryanalysis *on the Download Code tab. The code is in the chapter 08 download and individually named according to the names throughout the chapter.*

This chapter introduces jStat, a client-side statistical analysis library. With jStat, you learn how to compute basic values, such as the mean and standard deviation, and then how to leverage these values to create probability distributions. This chapter explores some rudimentary statistics but focuses mostly on how to use these tools.

This chapter also introduces the jQuery charting plug-in Flot, which is designed for plotting coordinate data. With Flot, you interface with jStat's probability distributions to render statistical charts like the normal curve.

By the end of this chapter, you'll have a handy toolkit for not only statistical analysis but also for rendering that data on the client side.

STATISTICAL ANALYSIS WITH JSTAT

jStat is a statistical analysis library that you can use on the client side. It isn't as robust as server-side statistics tools such as MATLAB or R, but it does provide similar features. With jStat, you can calculate everything from basic means and standard deviations to more complex probability distributions, such as the normal curve shown in Figure 8-1.

You can download and contribute to the jStat project on Github: `http://jstat.github.io/`.

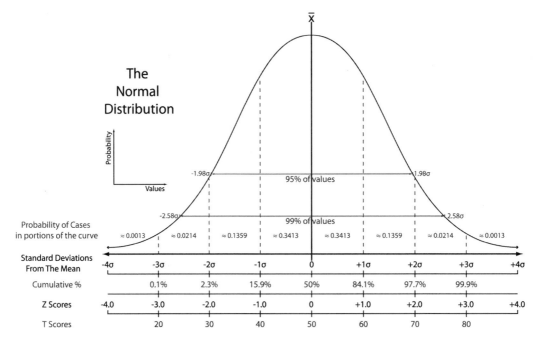

FIGURE 8-1: The normal curve is a useful probability distribution.

Getting Started with jStat

jStat primarily works with vectors and matrices. Vectors are arrays of values—for example, `[1,2,3,4]`—whereas matrices are tables of values—such as `[[1,2],[3,4],[5,6]]`. For example, one student's test scores could be expressed as a vector, and the whole class's test scores could be expressed as a matrix.

To get started, first define a vector:

```
var myVector = [3, 6, 1, 9, 7, 5, 3, 2, 2, 1];
```

You can then use jStat to calculate the sum:

```
jStat( myVector ).sum();
// returns 39
```

or the mean and standard deviation:

```
jStat( myVector ).mean();
// returns 3.9

jStat( myVector ).stdev();
// returns 2.5865034312755126
```

> **NOTE** *The mean is the average of the values. For example, the mean of* [1,2] *is 1.5.*
>
> *The standard deviation indicates the amount of fluctuation in a data set. For instance, the vectors* [4,5,6] *and* [0,5,10] *both have a mean of 5, but the latter has a much higher standard deviation.*

You can also perform similar operations across matrices. For example:

```
var myMatrix = [[2, 5, 8], [6, 1, 4]];

jStat( myMatrix ).sum();
// returns [8, 6, 12]
```

Here, jStat calculates the values using each column in the matrix, for example, the sum of the first values, second values, and third values: [(2+6), (5+1), (8+4)] => [8, 6, 12].

Likewise, you can calculate the mean:

```
jStat( myMatrix ).mean();
// returns [4, 3, 6]
```

or the min and the max:

```
jStat( myMatrix ).min();
// returns [2, 1, 4]

jStat( myMatrix ).max();
// returns [6, 5, 8]
```

You can find this example in the Chapter 08 folder on the companion website. It's named jstat-basics.html.

Stat 101

Although jStat handles a variety of tasks, its primary purpose is statistical analysis. To this end, the library provides a number of tools for computing probability distributions such as beta, gamma, normal, log-normal, and chi-square.

This chapter doesn't talk too much about statistics, but it is useful if you understand simple concepts such as normal distribution, PDF, and CDF.

Normal Distribution Basics

Assuming that the values in your vector are normally distributed (for example, randomly fluctuating around a center point), a normal distribution becomes a useful way to model the system and predict various outcomes. With this particular type of distribution there tend to be a large number of values surrounding the center point, and fewer values as you move further away. Thus the normal distribution produces the classic bell curve shown in Figure 8-2.

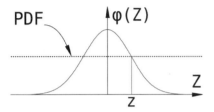

FIGURE 8-2: A normal distribution has the classic bell curve.

This distribution helps predict the likelihood of a given value in the system, which is why the y-values around the center point are higher than those further away. These y-values represent the PDF, or "probability density function," you saw earlier.

It can also be useful to assess the CDF or "cumulative distribution function." Unlike the PDF, which represents the probability of just a single value, the CDF represents the probability of *all* values up to that value. When thinking graphically, the CDF is the area underneath the PDF curve, as shown in Figure 8-3.

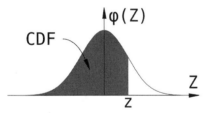

FIGURE 8-3: The shaded area is the CDF of a normal distribution up to point z.

Normal Distributions in Real Life

Normal distributions are all around us; one common example is human heights. The average height of adult males in the United States is 176.3 cm, with a standard deviation of around 7 cm. If you plug these values into jStat, you can get the PDF and CDF for a given height:

```
jStat.normal( 176.3, 7 ).pdf( 178 );
// returns 0.05533561870891004

jStat.normal( 176.3, 7 ).cdf( 178 );
// returns 0.5959419666157191
```

Here, `jStat.normal()` accepts two arguments—the mean and standard deviation. That creates a normal distribution, which is then used to calculate the `pdf()` and `cdf()` for a given value: 178 cm.

Thus, if you're a man from the United States, there's a 5.5 percent probability that you're 178 cm tall (PDF), and a 59.6 percent probability that you're 178 cm tall *or shorter* (CDF). Of course, if you are from the United States, there's also a pretty high probability that you don't know what 178 cm means—it's about 5'10".

RENDERING PROBABILITY DISTRIBUTIONS WITH FLOT

Although computing discrete probabilities for different values is useful, there are also times that you want to render the entire probability distribution graphically. Fortunately, jStat has all the functionality you need to massage the data and export it to a charting tool such as Flot.

Getting Started with Flot

Flot is a simple jQuery charting solution that is particularly good at plotting lines from coordinates. After you've downloaded the plug-in from `http://www.flotcharts.org/`, you need to define a wrapper with dimensions in your document:

```
<div id="flot" style="width: 500px; height: 300px"></div>
```

Next, pass a reference to this wrapper, along with a set of coordinates, into Flot's `plot()` application programming interface (API):

```
$('#flot').plot([ [[0,0], [1,2], [2,6], [3,5], [4,0]] ]);
```

Here, the `plot()` API renders the line graph shown in Figure 8-4.

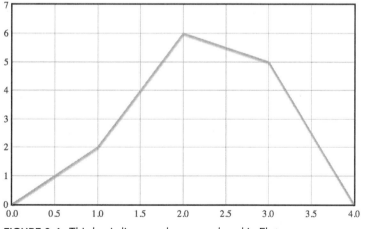

FIGURE 8-4: This basic line graph was rendered in Flot.

You may have noticed that the array of coordinates is itself contained in an array. That allows you to render multiple lines, as shown in Figure 8-5:

```
$('#flot').plot([
  [[0,0], [1,2], [2,6], [3,5], [4,0]],
  [[0,7], [1,6], [2,1], [3,2], [4,6]]
]);
```

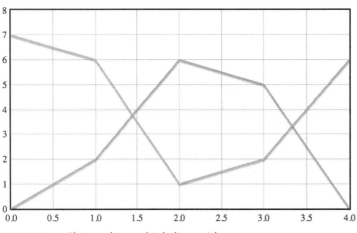

FIGURE 8-5: Flot renders multiple lines with ease.

There are a number of options you can set for Flot. For instance, you can render the bar chart as shown in Figure 8-6:

```
$('#flot').plot([ [[0,7], [1,6], [2,1], [3,2], [4,6]] ], {
  lines: { show: false },
  bars: { show: true }
});
```

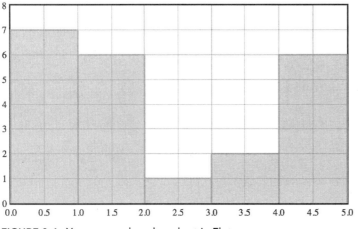

FIGURE 8-6: You can render a bar chart in Flot.

Or you can render a point chart, changing the colors of the dots, as shown in Figure 8-7:

```
$('#flot').plot([ [[0,7], [1,6], [2,1], [3,2], [4,6]] ], {
    lines: { show: false },
    points: { show: true },
    colors: ['#F0F']
});
```

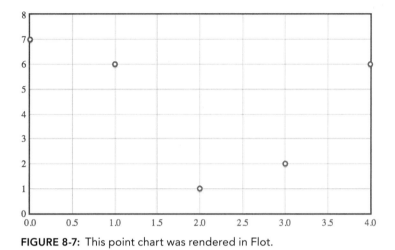

FIGURE 8-7: This point chart was rendered in Flot.

You can find this example in the Chapter 08 folder on the companion website. It's named `flot-basics.html`.

Rendering the Normal Curve

Now that you understand the Flot basics, you can get started with rendering probability distributions. Take another look at the normal distribution for adult male heights in the United States:

```
var myNormal = jStat.normal( 176.3, 7 );
```

Here, jStat creates a normal distribution based on a mean of 176.3 cm and a standard deviation of 7 cm. You already know how to compute a given PDF and CDF using `myNormal.pdf()` and `myNormal.cdf()`. The next step is to create a sequence of these values that can be rendered as a chart. Luckily, jStat has a utility method for this exact purpose—the `seq()` API:

```
var normalPdf = jStat.seq( 160, 192, 100, function(x) {
    // return as coordinates
    return [x, myNormal.pdf(x)];
});
```

As you can see, `seq()` accepts a few arguments:

➤   `160` is the bottom bound for the sequence.

➤   `192` is the top bound.

➤   `100` is the number of values between 160 and 192.

Lastly, the callback massages the data into the format you want to use for the sequence. In this case, a set of coordinates establishes the normal value for each point in the sequence. For instance, the start of this particular sequence is

```
[
    [ 160, 0.00378779534905057 ],
    [ 160.32323232323233, 0.004213283430410283 ],
    [ 160.64646464646464, 0.004676584972725774 ]
    ...
]
```

Now that you've created a sequence, the only thing left is passing those coordinates to Flot:

```
$('#flot').plot([ normalPdf ]);
```

As you can see in Figure 8-8, this code renders the familiar normal curve.

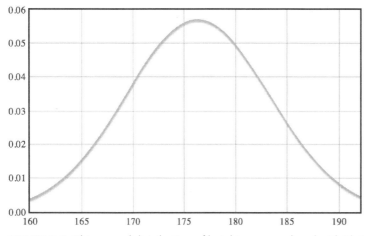

FIGURE 8-8: This normal distribution of heights was rendered with Flot.

Similarly, you can also render a visualization of the CDF for this distribution:

```
// create a coordinate sequence for CDF
var normalCdf = jStat.seq( 160, 192, 100, function(x) {
    return [x, myNormal.cdf(x)];
});

// render it
$('#flot').plot([ normalCdf ]);
```

That renders the CDF chart in Figure 8-9.

You can find this example in the Chapter 08 folder on the companion website. It's named `jstat-and-flot.html`.

The normal distribution is only the tip of the iceberg when it comes to jStat. The library provides a variety of additional analysis tools and probability distributions. To learn more, visit the jStat documentation at `http://jstat.github.io/`.

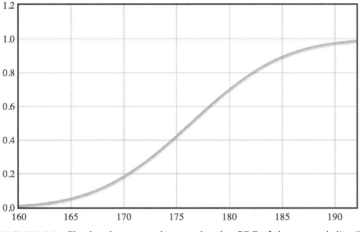

FIGURE 8-9: Flot has been used to render the CDF of the normal distribution.

> **NOTE** *As an exercise, try using Flot to render another probability distribution, such as a beta distribution.*

SUMMARY

In this chapter, you discovered the client-side statistics library jStat. You first figured out how to compute basic values such as mean and standard deviation. Next, you learned about normal distributions and how both the probability density function (PDF) and cumulative distribution function (CDF) relate to the normal curve.

You then explored Flot, the jQuery charting plug-in that builds visualizations from coordinate data. After learning the basics of line, bar, and point charts, you combined Flot with jStat to render the normal curve as well as its CDF.

This chapter is the last that covers data acquisition and manipulation. In the coming chapters, you leverage these data skills to build highly interactive charts. Now that you have a firm foundation in data structures, it's time to dig in and discover fun charting tools you can use to impress your audience.

PART III
Visualizing Data Programmatically

9

Exploring Charting Tools

WHAT'S IN THIS CHAPTER

➤ Building a chart using the HTML5 canvas element from the ground up

➤ Learning the basics of linear interpolation and how it relates to practically everything in charting

➤ Using key frame animation and easing functions to create pleasing transitions in a chart

➤ Using the Google Charts API to make everything easier

➤ Displaying bar, line, and pie visualizations using the Google Charts API.

> **CODE DOWNLOAD** *The wrox.com code downloads for this chapter are found at* www.wrox.com/go/javascriptandjqueryanalysis *on the Download Code tab. The code is in the chapter 09 download and individually named according to the names throughout the chapter.*

Chapter 3, "Building a Visualization Foundation," covers the breadth of charting visualizations, which can be used to tell the desired story with your data. This chapter takes a deep dive into how to actually implement these visualizations.

Building charting visualizations can be a daunting task, even with high-quality charting tools making things as simple as possible. This is because charting application programming interfaces (APIs) need to be quite complex in order to grant you the flexibility to achieve all the scenarios that might be important to you. As with anything complicated, the best strategy for understanding something is to break things down, understand all the smaller moving parts, and then put things together again.

To facilitate this, you start this chapter by building a chart from scratch! Don't worry—it's not quite as scary as it sounds. You will be jumping into the deep end of the pool, but you'll come out a strong swimmer. The custom chart you are building doesn't do everything that a full charting API can accomplish (it would take a full book to lead you through doing that!), but it helps to show how all the parts of a chart interact with each other.

Beyond that, you are building some interesting animation features into your chart that even some fully functional charting APIs don't support, and you are learning how to do some very interesting things with the HTML5 Canvas at the same time.

Later in the chapter, you implement similar scenarios using the Google Charts API, which is a high-level and polished API for creating charting visualizations. You will find that all the scenarios that this chapter investigates take considerably less code and are easier to quickly understand when using the Google Charts API, so if you are looking for "easy mode" you could skip directly to that section of the chapter. However, you might also notice that the Google Chart's versions are less dynamic and don't help you to understand some of the underlying concepts in play.

CREATING HTML5 CANVAS CHARTS

This chapter focuses on the most-used core charting scenarios, including bar, column, line, area, and pie. These visualizations are, far and away, the most used types. First, let's build a basic column chart from scratch! Following that, you can successively layer on features such as axes, animation, and data changes. To render your chart, you use the HTML5 canvas element.

HTML5 Canvas Basics

There is a primer on the HTML5 canvas in the section "Making Use of the HTML5 Canvas" in Chapter 3 of this book. It may be helpful to you to read that section before reading this chapter.

The canvas is a new feature that was added to the HTML standard in HTML5. It provides a basic 2D rendering API, which you can use from JavaScript, for rendering vector graphics and text into a bitmap and displaying that within an HTML page. Prior to the advent of the canvas, it was not so easy to achieve this style of dynamic rendering. Your options were to

➤ Use a plug-in to render the content such as Java, Flash, Silverlight, Scalable Vector Graphics (SVG) (for browsers that did not support it natively), and so on

➤ Render the content as an image on the server and serve as a static file

➤ Try to "fake" the required graphics using Document Object Model (DOM) elements and Cascading Style Sheets (CSS)

Given the prevalence of Flash on desktop machines, that option has been rather popular for charting in the browser. However, given the rejection of the plug-in model from the mobile web, it is no longer a viable option for a website that is designed for extremely broad consumption. Static images are undesirable because they lack any client-side dynamic nature and increase the burden on the server if they need to be generated on demand. Lastly, trying to fake charting graphics using DOM and CSS would be broadly accessible, but is needlessly complicated and rife with limitations to be circumvented.

Luckily, all modern browser versions support both the HTML5 canvas element and the SVG element. Without these, it would be very difficult to create dynamic charting visualizations in browsers while eschewing plug-ins. SVG is discussed in detail in Chapters 10 and 11 whereas the first part of this chapter focuses on the canvas element.

Why would you want to use canvas in preference to SVG? Why would you want to use SVG in preference to canvas? The answer is somewhat complicated, but it boils down to "it depends," or "use a bit of both." SVGs strengths are the following:

➤ It is scalable without losing fidelity. (The S in SVG stands for *scalable*, after all.) This is especially important for the modern web as device screens have increasingly high dots per inch (DPI) metrics. Scalable graphics can, usually, automagically take advantage of a higher DPI screen.

➤ Because SVG is DOM based, you can inspect its layout at runtime in a DOM inspector.

➤ You can apply styling with CSS.

➤ You can attach event handlers to graphical elements.

➤ Most vector graphics editors export to static SVG files.

➤ It performs better than canvas when the size of the element is large.

➤ Interacting with it is declarative. You are interested in defining the outcome, not the low-level means by which it is achieved.

Meanwhile, the strengths of the canvas element are these:

➤ It performs better than SVG when there are lots of graphical elements that need to be rendered or when rendering is progressive/additive.

➤ It is very lightweight in that it does not have required memory and processing overhead associated with each graphical element.

➤ It allows for per-pixel manipulation of the output, allowing for scenarios that would not be practical using the graphics primitives provided to you via SVG.

➤ The API surface is small compared to SVG. It is easy to learn and has implementations with very consistent performance and behavioral semantics across different browser environments.

➤ Interacting with it is very explicit and imperative. You are interested in taking control of the outcome, and the means by which is it is achieved.

Linear Interpolation

Before you dive into writing a chart from scratch, it helps if you're familiar with the style of calculation that you will find all throughout charting (and graphics programming in general). So pervasive is it that many graphics systems provide built-in and optimized functions to perform it (usually named *lerp*). That calculation is called *linear interpolation*. The basic idea of linear interpolation is to connect a line between two points. Let's say you want to connect a line between points x0, y0 and x1, y1. You can vary the value of x between x0 and x1, and calculate the corresponding y value as

```
y = y0 + (y1 - y0) * (x - x0) / (x1 - x2)
```

A useful way to think of $(x - x0) / (x1 - x2)$ is that it resolves to a value between 0 and 1 depending on how far x is between $x0$ and $x1$. It acts as a weighting that you can multiply by the y range $(y1 - y0)$ so that when the weighting is 0 then $y = y0$ and by the time the weighting is 1 then $y = y1$. Linear interpolations are useful for connecting points with line segments, but that's not all you use them for. They are also very useful for blending. If you want a linear animated blend between two values based on a time value that varies between 0 and 1, you can express it with the following equation, where p is the time value, start is the start value to blend from, and end is the end value to blend to:

$$v = start + p * (end - start)$$

How does this relate to the first linear interpolation equation? Well, imagine that the x axis represents time, and the y values represent the in-between values of the blend. The x movement can be simplified to be a parameter p that varies from 0 to 1, as you saw before. These equations are all over this chapter, so it's good to start with a solid grounding in them.

A Simple Column Chart

Column and bar charts let you compare values of discrete categories using either the width or height of a set of rectangles. Figure 9-1 shows a bar chart rendered using the Google Charts API, and Figure 9-2 shows a bar chart using the Google Charts API, for example.

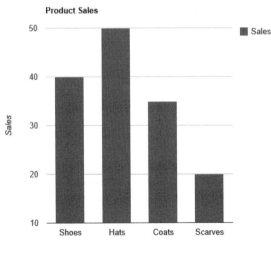

FIGURE 9-1: A column chart rendered with the Google Charts API helps compare values between categories.

Listing 9-1 first shows you how to create a simple column visualization from scratch using the HTML5 canvas.

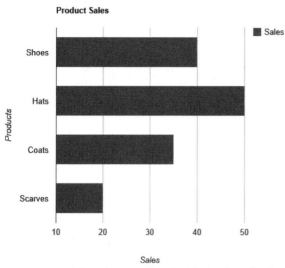

FIGURE 9-2: A bar chart rendered with the Google Charts API displays the same information as the column chart but is oriented differently.

LISTING 9-1

```
var data = [
    { "name": "Shoes", "Q1": 40, "Q2": 25 },
    { "name": "Hats", "Q1": 50, "Q2": 40 },
    { "name": "Coats", "Q1": 35, "Q2": 45 },
    { "name": "Scarves", "Q1": 20, "Q2": 15 }
];

var palette = [
    "rgba(143, 39, 26, 1)",
    "rgba(13, 113, 125, 1)",
    "rgba(72, 176, 19, 1)"
];

var ChartElement = function (chart) {
    this._chart = chart;
    this._color = "rgba(80, 80, 80, 1)";
};
ChartElement.prototype._validate = function () {
    if (this._chart._data === null ||
        isNaN(this._chart._minValue) ||
        isNaN(this._chart._maxValue)) {
        return false;
    }
    return true;
};
```

continues

LISTING 9-1 *(continued)*

```
ChartElement.prototype._update = function () {
    this._chart.update();
}
ChartElement.prototype.color = function (col) {
    this._color = col;
    this._update();
    return this;
};
ChartElement.prototype.chart = function () {
    return this._chart;
};

var ColumnSeries = function (chart) {
    ChartElement.call(this, chart);
    this._valueAccessor = null;
    this._color = "rgba(255, 0, 0, 1)";
};
ColumnSeries.prototype = Object.create(ChartElement.prototype);
ColumnSeries.prototype._validate = function () {
    if (this._valueAccessor === null) {
        return false;
    }
    return ChartElement.prototype._validate.call(this);
};
ColumnSeries.prototype._render = function (ctx) {
    if (!this._validate()) {
        return;
    }

    var currWidth, currHeight,
        currX, currY,
        currColor, i;

    var data = this._chart._data;
    var f = {};
    f.xPositions = [];
    f.yPositions = [];
    f.widths = [];
    f.heights = [];
    currColor = this._color;

    var index = this._index;
    var width = this._chart.seriesWidth();
    var halfWidth = width / 2.0;
    var offset = this._chart.offset(index);
    var zeroPosition = this._chart.scaleY(0);
    var val, scaledX, scaledY;

    for (i = 0; i < data.length; i++) {
        val = this._valueAccessor(data[i]);
        scaledY = this._chart.scaleY(val);
        scaledX = this._chart.scaleX(i);

        f.xPositions.push(scaledX + offset - halfWidth);
```

```
            f.yPositions.push(Math.min(scaledY, zeroPosition));
            f.widths.push(width);
            f.heights.push(Math.abs(scaledY - zeroPosition));
        }

    for (var i = 0; i < f.widths.length; i++) {
        currX = f.xPositions[i];
        currY = f.yPositions[i];
        currWidth = f.widths[i];
        currHeight = f.heights[i];

        ctx.fillStyle = currColor;
        ctx.fillRect(
            currX, currY,
            currWidth, currHeight);
    }
};
ColumnSeries.prototype.valueAccessor = function (accessor) {
    this._valueAccessor = accessor;
    this._update();
    return this;
};

var Chart = function (targetId) {
    this._canvas = document.getElementById(targetId);
    this._ctx = this._canvas.getContext("2d");
    this._ctx.font = "14pt Verdana";

    this._data = null;

    this._totalWidth = this._canvas.width;
    this._totalHeight = this._canvas.height;
    this._leftMargin = 50;
    this._rightMargin = 50;
    this._topMargin = 50;
    this._bottomMargin = 50;

    this._minValue = NaN;
    this._maxValue = NaN;

    this._series = [];

    this._gap = 0.25;

    this._calculatePlotArea();
};
Chart.prototype.column = function () {
    var c = new ColumnSeries(this);
    this._series.push(c);
    c._index = this._series.length - 1;
    this.update();
    return c;
};
Chart.prototype.minValue = function (val) {
    this._minValue = val;
    this.update();
```

continues

LISTING 9-1 *(continued)*

```
        return this;
    };
    Chart.prototype.maxValue = function (val) {
        this._maxValue = val;
        this.update();
        return this;
    };
    Chart.prototype._calculatePlotArea = function () {
        var left = this._leftMargin;
        var top = this._topMargin;
        var width = this._totalWidth -
        (this._leftMargin + this._rightMargin);
        var height = this._totalHeight -
        (this._topMargin + this._bottomMargin);

        this._plotLeft = left;
        this._plotTop = top;
        this._plotWidth = width;
        this._plotHeight = height;
    };
    Chart.prototype._render = function () {
        var ctx = this._ctx;
        ctx.clearRect(0, 0, this._totalWidth, this._totalHeight);
        ctx.fillStyle = "rgba(240,240,240,1)";
        ctx.fillRect(0, 0, this._totalWidth, this._totalHeight);

        for (var i = 0; i < this._series.length; i++) {
            this._series[i]._render(ctx);
        }
    };
    Chart.prototype.update = function () {
        this._render();
        return this;
    };
    Chart.prototype.data = function (data) {
        this._data = data;
        this.update();
        return this;
    };
    Chart.prototype.scaleY = function (val) {
        var p = (val - this._minValue) /
        (this._maxValue - this._minValue);
        p = 1.0 - p;
        return this._plotTop + p * this._plotHeight;
    };
    Chart.prototype.offset = function (seriesIndex) {
        var fullWidth = this._plotWidth / this._data.length;
        var start = this._gap / 2.0 * fullWidth;
        var span = seriesIndex * this.seriesWidth();
        span += this.seriesWidth() / 2.0;
        var offset = start + span;
        return offset;
    };
    Chart.prototype.scaleX = function (val) {
        var p = val / this._data.length;
```

```
        return this._plotLeft + p * this._plotWidth;
    };
    Chart.prototype.seriesWidth = function () {
        var fullWidth = this._plotWidth / this._data.length;
        var actualWidth = fullWidth * (1.0 - this._gap);
        actualWidth /= this._series.length;
        return actualWidth;
    };

    var chart = new Chart("chart")
        .minValue(0)
        .maxValue(60)
        .data(data);

    chart.column()
        .color(palette[0])
        .valueAccessor(function (item) {
            return item.Q1;
        });

    chart.column()
        .color(palette[1])
        .valueAccessor(function (item) {
            return item.Q2;
        });
```

That puts all the JavaScript in place in order to display the visualization. To render that in a web page, though, you need the other bits and pieces. Here is the CSS to use:

```
#chart {
    width: 700px;
    height: 500px;
}
```

And this is the HTML to use:

```
<!DOCTYPE html>
<html>
<head>
    <title>Basic Canvas Chart</title>

    <link rel="stylesheet" href="BasicCanvasChart.css">
</head>
<body>
    <canvas id="chart"
            width="700"
            height="500">
    </canvas>

    <script type="text/javascript" src="BasicCanvasChart.js">
    </script>
</body>
</html>
```

Most of the canvas code in this chapter uses this exact HTML, only with a different CSS and JavaScript reference, so the markup/styling snippets aren't listed for each example. The full files are available on the companion website for this book. Listing 9-1 produces the results displayed in Figure 9-3, and the code is in the file `BasicCanvasChart.js/html/css` on the companion website.

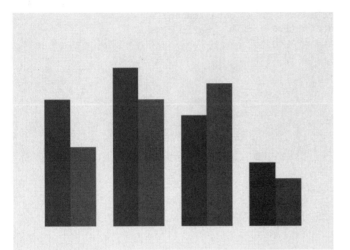

FIGURE 9-3: This shows a column chart built from scratch using the HTML5 canvas.

Okay, let's break down all the components of Listing 9-1 before making things more complicated. The code starts with this:

```
var data = [
    { "name": "Shoes", "Q1": 40, "Q2": 25 },
    { "name": "Hats", "Q1": 50, "Q2": 40 },
    { "name": "Coats", "Q1": 35, "Q2": 45 },
    { "name": "Scarves", "Q1": 20, "Q2": 15 }
];
```

This code just defines the data that is used in the column chart. It contains four categories—Shoes, Hats, Coats, and Scarves—and it contains two values for each of those categories: Q1 and Q2. The goal is to map each of those sets of values to a different column series plotted over the same categories.

A column chart plots data against a continuous numeric axis and a discrete category axis, as opposed to some other chart types—such as scatter charts—that plot the data against two continuous numeric axes.

```
var palette = [
    "rgba(143, 39, 26, 1)",
    "rgba(13, 113, 125, 1)",
    "rgba(72, 176, 19, 1)"
];
```

This code defines a palette to be used to define the colors for the various series added to the chart. The HTML5 canvas supports CSS color strings, so an array of them will suffice to act as a palette.

```
var ChartElement = function (chart) {
    this._chart = chart;
```

```
        this._color = "rgba(80, 80, 80, 1)";
};
ChartElement.prototype._validate = function () {
    if (this._chart._data === null ||
        isNaN(this._chart._minValue) ||
        isNaN(this._chart._maxValue)) {
        return false;
    }
    return true;
};
ChartElement.prototype._update = function () {
    this._chart.update();
}
ChartElement.prototype.color = function (col) {
    this._color = col;
    this._update();
    return this;
};
ChartElement.prototype.chart = function () {
    return this._chart;
};
```

> **NOTE** *The code in this chapter uses JavaScript classical inheritance techniques. The domain concepts in charting are naturally hierarchical, so they lend themselves to representation using inheritance for code reuse.*

The preceding code defines a base class for all of the various elements in the chart. The various series and axis types will inherit from this class. Currently, this supports the ability to store the desired color for the series, holds a reference to the containing chart, and can be asked to validate or update its visual output.

> **NOTE** *Here, I'm using the convention that a property on an object with a preceding underscore character in the name is held to not be part of the public interface of the class. This clues in consumers of the API as to which portions they can safely interact with and which they can't.*

A chart *series* is an element of a chart that is bound to a particular data set. Most charting APIs use the terminology *series* to speak of this element. Figure 9-4 shows a screenshot of the chart with the plot area (which contains two column series) emphasized with a dark background.

```
var ColumnSeries = function (chart) {
    ChartElement.call(this, chart);
    this._valueAccessor = null;
    this._color = "rgba(255, 0, 0, 1)";
};
ColumnSeries.prototype = Object.create(ChartElement.prototype);
```

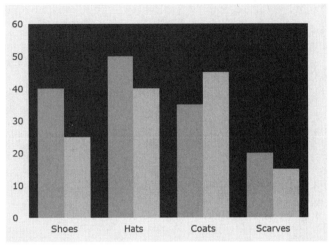

FIGURE 9-4: Here, the plot area portion of the chart is emphasized with a dark background to delineate it from the rest of the chart.

This code defines a constructor for the ColumnSeries class and causes it to inherit from the ChartElement class. The constructor calls the base constructor, initializes the value of the _valueAccessor property to null, and assigns a default color to the series (red).
The _valueAccessor expects to be provided a function that can be used to extract values for the series from each data item.

```
ColumnSeries.prototype._validate = function () {
    if (this._valueAccessor === null) {
        return false;
    }
    return ChartElement.prototype._validate.call(this);
};
```

Next, the _validate function is defined for the ColumnSeries. This should return true when the series has everything that it needs to render. The series must have a _valueAccessor so that it can extract the values that it needs from the data items. Other validation is provided by the base implementation of this function on the ChartElement class.

```
ColumnSeries.prototype._render = function (ctx) {
    if (!this._validate()) {
        return;
    }

    var currWidth, currHeight,
        currX, currY,
        currColor, i;

    var data = this._chart._data;
    var f = {};
    f.xPositions = [];
    f.yPositions = [];
```

```
        f.widths = [];
        f.heights = [];
```

This code begins to define the _render function for the ColumnSeries class. If the series is not currently valid, it will abort. Some useful variables are defined, it fetches the data from the chart and then creates an object called f (this stands for frame, as you will see later) that will hold the calculated values for rendering the columns into the canvas.

```
    currColor = this._color;

    var index = this._index;
    var width = this._chart.seriesWidth();
    var halfWidth = width / 2.0;
    var offset = this._chart.offset(index);
```

Here, you gather the CSS color string which will be used to fill the columns. Following that, the current index of the series within the chart is acquired. This is populated by the chart when the series is created. this._chart.seriesWidth() asks the chart how wide the current series should be. The chart should be able to examine how many series are present to partition the plot space accordingly. The chart is also queried for how much to offset the current series within the grouping of series. Refer to Figure 9-3 to see how each category has a distinct cluster of columns centered around it. The offset indicates how far from the start of that category the center of this series' column should be placed. The chart object knows the total number of series present, so the chart will decide this for you.

To see what is meant by the offset, first examine Figure 9-5, which has a black line at the start of each category along the x axis.

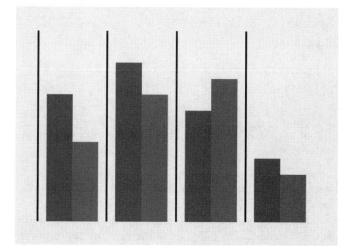

FIGURE 9-5: Some guidelines indicate where the categories on the x axis begin.

Now examine Figure 9-6 to see black lines through the center of all the columns in the first column series contained in the chart. The distance between these black lines and the starts of the categories should all be the same, and they are equal to the offset queried from the chart.

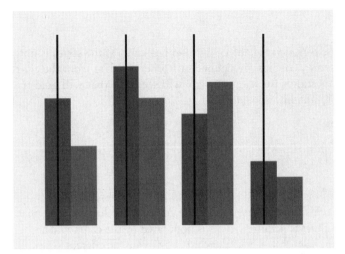

FIGURE 9-6: The guidelines on this chart indicate where the center of each item is for the first series.

```
var zeroPosition = this._chart.scaleY(0);
var val, scaledX, scaledY;
```

This code asks the chart to scale the number 0 into the y-coordinate space of the plot area. Generally, when rendering a column series, the columns move up from 0 if their values are positive and descend down from 0 if their values are negative. Thus, it's important to know the y-coordinate position in the plot area that represents the 0 line of the axis. Following this, some variables are defined to store the current data value, and the x-y coordinates of the top middle of the current column (or bottom middle if its value is negative).

```
for (i = 0; i < data.length; i++) {
    val = this._valueAccessor(data[i]);
    scaledY = this._chart.scaleY(val);
    scaledX = this._chart.scaleX(i);

    f.xPositions.push(scaledX + offset - halfWidth);
    f.yPositions.push(Math.min(scaledY, zeroPosition));
    f.widths.push(width);
    f.heights.push(Math.abs(scaledY - zeroPosition));
}
```

This loop calculates the positions and width and heights of the columns. First it calls the _valueAccessor on the current data item. Then it asks the chart to scale the current value into the y-coordinate system of the plot area and stores that in scaledY. Then it asks the chart for the start of the category at index i and stores that in scaledX. The start of the category is not where the column is located, though, as shown in Figures 9-5 and 9-6. You add the offset to the start of the category to find where the center of the column should be for the current category. You want the position of the top left of the column, however, so next you subtract half of the column width from the value and store that as the x position of the column.

For the y position of the column, the column will either extend up from the 0 line or descend from it, so the minimum of scaledY and zeroPosition should represent the top of the column.

> **NOTE** *Why is the minimum y value at top of the column? In most 2D rendering APIs the coordinate origin is the top left of the screen, and the y coordinates increase as you move down the screen. Because of this, the tops of the columns have lower y values than the bottoms of the columns.*

All the columns have the same `width`, which was provided by the chart at the beginning of the function. The `height` of each column is the distance between the `scaledY` value and the `zeroPosition` value. `Math.abs` is used to ensure that the column `height` is positive regardless of whether the column extends up or down from the `zeroPosition`.

```
ctx.fillStyle = currColor;
for (var i = 0; i < f.widths.length; i++) {
    currX = f.xPositions[i];
    currY = f.yPositions[i];
    currWidth = f.widths[i];
    currHeight = f.heights[i];

    ctx.fillRect(
        currX, currY,
        currWidth, currHeight);
    }
};
```

Finally, provided the values calculated in the previous loop, you can render all the columns as rectangles into the HTML5 canvas 2D context, which was passed into the function. First `ctx.fillStyle = currColor` sets the fill color that will be used for the column to the current color of the series; then `fillRect` is called on the canvas context to render a rectangle into the canvas providing its top, left, width, and height.

```
ColumnSeries.prototype.valueAccessor = function (accessor) {
    this._valueAccessor = accessor;
    this._update();
    return this;
};
```

This function allows for the `_valueAccessor` to be set on the series.

```
var Chart = function (targetId) {
    this._canvas = document.getElementById(targetId);
    this._ctx = this._canvas.getContext("2d");
    this._ctx.font = "14pt Verdana";

    this._data = null;

    this._totalWidth = this._canvas.width;
    this._totalHeight = this._canvas.height;
    this._leftMargin = 50;
    this._rightMargin = 50;
    this._topMargin = 50;
    this._bottomMargin = 50;
```

```
        this._minValue = NaN;
        this._maxValue = NaN;

        this._series = [];

        this._gap = 0.25;

        this._calculatePlotArea();
    };
```

This code block defines a constructor for the `Chart` class. You provide an element ID to the constructor to indicate which canvas element the Chart should inhabit. This element is found in the document, and `getContext("2d")` obtains a 2D rendering context from the located canvas element.

> **NOTE** *What is the significance of* `getContext("2d")`? *Why not just use* `getContext()`? *Well, the canvas element is also used as a container for 3D graphics using WebGL, in which case you call* `getContext("webgl")`.

The constructor also defines initial values for other properties of the chart. Properties defined include

➤ `_totalWidth`: The total width of the chart

➤ `_totalHeight`: The total height of the chart

➤ `_leftMargin`: The left margin around the plot area

➤ `_topMargin`: The top margin around the plot area

➤ `_rightMargin`: The right margin around the plot area

➤ `_bottomMargin`: The bottom margin around the plot area

➤ `_minValue`: The minimum value of the y axis

➤ `_maxValue`: The maximum value of the y axis

➤ `_series`: The series that are added to the chart

➤ `_gap`: The proportion of each category on the x axis that is devoted to white space

Last, `_calculatePlotArea` is called to decide the plot area dimensions.

```
    Chart.prototype.column = function () {
        var c = new ColumnSeries(this);
        this._series.push(c);
        c._index = this._series.length - 1;
        this.update();
        return c;
    };
```

This function causes a new `ColumnSeries` to be created, and adds it to the chart's `_series` array. It also populates the `_index` on the series, and causes it to `update`.

```
Chart.prototype.minValue = function (val) {
    this._minValue = val;
    this.update();
    return this;
};
Chart.prototype.maxValue = function (val) {
    this._maxValue = val;
    this.update();
    return this;
};
```

These functions allow for the minimum and maximum values of the y axis to be set on the chart.

> **NOTE** *This chart implementation delegates most of the range management and scaling logic to the chart because the axes are built-in and not very customizable. In a more complete implementation, scaling and range management is more naturally the concern of the axes.*

```
Chart.prototype._calculatePlotArea = function () {
    var left = this._leftMargin;
    var top = this._topMargin;
    var width = this._totalWidth -
    (this._leftMargin + this._rightMargin);
    var height = this._totalHeight -
    (this._topMargin + this._bottomMargin);

    this._plotLeft = left;
    this._plotTop = top;
    this._plotWidth = width;
    this._plotHeight = height;
};
```

This function determines the viable rectangle for plotting series content within the chart. The goal is that there is sufficient space to render the axis labels within the marginal area.

```
Chart.prototype._render = function () {
    var ctx = this._ctx;
    ctx.clearRect(0, 0, this._totalWidth, this._totalHeight);
    ctx.fillStyle = "rgba(240,240,240,1)";
    ctx.fillRect(0, 0, this._totalWidth, this._totalHeight);

    for (var i = 0; i < this._series.length; i++) {
        this._series[i]._render(ctx);
    }
};
```

This function implements the main render pass for the chart. Here, you perform these steps:

1. Retrieve the canvas 2D context from where it is stored on the chart.

2. Clear any existing content in the canvas.

3. Set the fill color to a gray color.

4. Fill the background of the canvas to the gray color.

5. For each series in the chart, ask the series to render itself into the canvas context. The render code for the `ColumnSeries` was discussed earlier.

> **NOTE** *As opposed to a retained mode system, such as SVG, the canvas element is an immediate mode rendering interface. There is no "undo," and you aren't building a tree of displayed objects. Each time you want to update the content displayed, you will be clearing the content of the canvas and then re-rendering all the content that you want to be displayed. This is in stark contrast to SVG, where you would make some manipulations to the existing SVG DOM tree, and SVG would update the visual to accommodate. As discussed earlier in the chapter, these differences in interaction have various pros and cons.*

```
Chart.prototype.update = function () {
    this._render();
    return this;
};
```

This function is called whenever something has changed that invalidates the current look of the chart. Right now, you are just having it immediately re-render the chart content, but this gets adjusted when animation is introduced later.

```
Chart.prototype.data = function (data) {
    this._data = data;
    this.update();
    return this;
};
```

This function allows for data to be assigned to the chart. It stores the data in a property on the chart and then invalidates the current chart visual.

```
Chart.prototype.scaleY = function (val) {
    var p = (val - this._minValue) /
    (this._maxValue - this._minValue);
    p = 1.0 - p;
    return this._plotTop + p * this._plotHeight;
};
```

This function should have some very familiar-looking math, if you think back to the discussion on linear interpolation at the beginning of the chapter. Here you are using linear interpolation to map from the values along the numeric axis, which range from _minValue to _maxValue, into the y-pixel space of the plot area that ranges from _plotTop to (_plotTop + _plotHeight). p represents how far along the numeric axis val is. Because p is a value between 0 and 1, p = 1.0 - p will invert it. After the inversion, p is used as a weighting to determine the associated position within the plot area. Why the inversion? Conventional screen coordinates (used by the canvas) increase from top to bottom, rather than chart coordinates which should increase from bottom to top (at least, usually).

```
Chart.prototype.scaleX = function (val) {
    var p = val / this._data.length;
    return this._plotLeft + p * this._plotWidth;
};
```

scaleX is a very similar idea to scaleY. It's a linear interpolation that is used to map the index of a category into the pixel space of the plot area. The resulting position should be the start of the category for an index.

```
Chart.prototype.seriesWidth = function () {
    var fullWidth = this._plotWidth / this._data.length;
    var actualWidth = fullWidth * (1.0 - this._gap);
    actualWidth /= this._series.length;
    return actualWidth;
};
```

This function calculates how wide an individual series should be in the chart. This is done by dividing the available plot area width by the number of items, reducing this space by the _gap setting, so some space is left between the clusters for each category and then dividing by the number of series present in the chart.

```
Chart.prototype.offset = function (seriesIndex) {
    var fullWidth = this._plotWidth / this._data.length;
    var start = this._gap / 2.0 * fullWidth;
    var span = seriesIndex * this.seriesWidth();
    span += this.seriesWidth() / 2.0;
    var offset = start + span;
    return offset;
};
```

offset, as you saw before, should calculate how far from the beginning of a category the visual for a series should be placed, based on its index. This is achieved by first finding the start position of the cluster by taking the _gap into account. Then seriesWidth() is added for each series that precedes the series in question, and half of seriesWidth() is added to get an offset that equates to the center of the space reserved for the series.

Provided all this, you can proceed to actually create an instance of the chart:

```
var chart = new Chart("chart")
    .minValue(0)
    .maxValue(60)
    .data(data);

chart.column()
    .color(palette[0])
    .valueAccessor(function (item) {
        return item.Q1;
    });

chart.column()
    .color(palette[1])
    .valueAccessor(function (item) {
        return item.Q2;
    });
```

This code performs the following:

➤ Creates a chart with a y axis that has a minimum value of 0 and a maximum value of 60 and assigns it some data

➤ Adds a column series to the chart that uses the first color in the palette as its color and gets its values from the Q1 property of the items in the data array

➤ Adds a second column series to the chart that uses the second color in the palette as its color and gets its values from the Q2 property of the items in the data array

Implementing Axes

The chart you've built so far performs the work of axes, but does not actually render any labels to tell you what the scales of the axes are! An *axis* is a chart element that displays the values along an edge of a chart. Figure 9-7 emphasizes the axis areas of the chart where the scale labels are displayed.

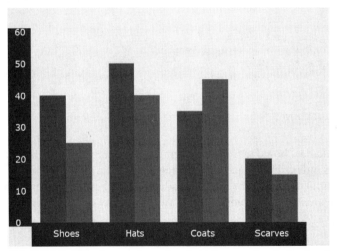

FIGURE 9-7: This shows where the chart axes are by darkening the background behind them.

Also, after the axes are in place, you'll start to make the chart animate, so, to prepare for that, you reorganize a few other things. The style of animation used is called *key frame* animation. Basically, if you can encapsulate everything that represents the render state of a series or axis into a frame class and drive the rendering from this frame, then later you'll be able to display a smooth transition by generating linearly interpolated frames between a starting frame and an ending frame. So, to start:

```
var KeyFrame = function () {
    this.xPositions = [];
    this.yPositions = [];
};
KeyFrame.prototype.clear = function () {
    this.xPositions.length = 0;
    this.yPositions.length = 0;
```

```
    };

    var ColumnsKeyFrame = function () {
        KeyFrame.call(this);
        this.widths = [];
        this.heights = [];
    };
    ColumnsKeyFrame.prototype = Object.create(KeyFrame.prototype);
    ColumnsKeyFrame.prototype.addColumn = function (
        x, y,
        width, height) {

        this.xPositions.push(x);
        this.yPositions.push(y);
        this.widths.push(width);
        this.heights.push(height);

        return this;
    };
    ColumnsKeyFrame.prototype.clear = function () {
        KeyFrame.prototype.clear.call(this);
        this.widths.length = 0;
        this.heights.length = 0;
    };
```

This column's key frame should look familiar to you. Basically, you've moved all the rendering data that was being calculated as local variables in the `ColumnSeries`' `_render` function to this frame class for storage.

```
    var AxisKeyFrame = function () {
        KeyFrame.call(this);
        this.labelTexts = [];
    };
    AxisKeyFrame.prototype = Object.create(KeyFrame.prototype);
    AxisKeyFrame.prototype.addLabel = function (
        x, y,
        text) {

        this.xPositions.push(x);
        this.yPositions.push(y);
        this.labelTexts.push(text);

        return this;
    };
    AxisKeyFrame.prototype.clear = function () {
        KeyFrame.prototype.clear.call(this);
        this.labelTexts.length = 0;
    };
```

Your axis visuals will consist of labels, arranged along the plot area, indicating the scale of the axis. To this effect, the `AxisKeyFrame` class stores much the same data as the `ColumnsKeyFrame`, but stores a text value for the label rather than width and height information.

```
    if (!window.queueFrame) {
        if (window.requestAnimationFrame) {
```

```
            window.queueFrame = window.requestAnimationFrame;
        } else if (window.webkitRequestAnimationFrame) {
            window.queueFrame = window.webkitRequestAnimationFrame;
        } else if (window.mozRequestAnimationFrame) {
            window.queueFrame = window.mozRequestAnimationFrame;
        } else {
            window.queueFrame = function (callback) {
                window.setTimeout(1000.0 / 60.0, callback);
            };
        }
    }
}
```

As part of the change to using key frames for rendering the chart, you switch to using the
`requestAnimationFrame` for scheduling the rendering of the chart. `requestAnimationFrame`, if
available, provides more reliable timer callbacks than `setTimeout` or `setInterval`, making for
smoother animations. `requestAnimationFrame` is not available in some browsers, however, so
the preceding code checks for it and gracefully degrades to using `setTimeout` to animate if it is
unavailable.

```
ChartElement.prototype._update = function () {
    if (!this._validate()) {
        return;
    }
    if (this._chart._data === null) {
        return;
    }
    this._updateFrames();
    this._chart.dirty();
};
ChartElement.prototype._updateFrames = function () {
    this._updateFrame(this._displayFrame);
};
```

Next, you edit some functions on the `ChartElement` class. Before, when a series needed to be
updated, it would just call `update` on the containing chart, causing an immediate re-render.
Now, the _update function calls _updateFrames, which in turn makes sure that the key frame
for the element is updated. Then, it tells the chart that it is dirty, and needs to be re-rendered at
the earliest opportunity. These changes tie into the animation support you'll be adding, but have
another nice side effect. Before, if you changed many different settings, an immediate
re-render was forced after each change. Now, instead, you will mark that a re-render is needed,
but it will happen at some time later, after the current interaction has yielded. In this way,
renders of the chart are batched and deferred. The deferral mechanism is discussed later in
this section.

```
var ColumnSeries = function (chart) {
    ChartElement.call(this, chart);
    this._displayFrame = new ColumnsKeyFrame();
    this._valueAccessor = null;
    this._color = "rgba(255, 0, 0, 1)";
};
```

In the preceding code, the constructor of the `ColumnSeries` is altered to construct an instance of the
`ColumnsKeyFrame` for use later.

```
ColumnSeries.prototype._render = function (ctx) {
    var f = this._displayFrame;
    var currWidth, currHeight,
        currX, currY;
    ctx.fillStyle = this._color;
    for (var i = 0; i < f.widths.length; i++) {
        currX = f.xPositions[i];
        currY = f.yPositions[i];
        currWidth = f.widths[i];
        currHeight = f.heights[i];

        ctx.fillRect(
            currX, currY,
            currWidth, currHeight);
    }
};
```

The _render function, which previously had been deciding what to render and then rendering it, now just renders the information stored in the _displayFrame.

```
ColumnSeries.prototype._updateFrame = function (frame) {
    var data = this._chart._data;
    var index = this._index;

    var width = this._chart.seriesWidth();
    var halfWidth = width / 2.0;
    var offset = this._chart.offset(index);
    var zeroPosition = this._chart.scaleY(0);
    var val, scaledX, scaledY;

    frame.clear();

    for (var i = 0; i < data.length; i++) {
        val = this._valueAccessor(data[i]);

        scaledY = this._chart.scaleY(val);
        scaledX = this._chart.scaleX(i);

        frame.addColumn(
            scaledX + offset - halfWidth,
            Math.min(scaledY, zeroPosition),
            width,
            Math.abs(scaledY - zeroPosition));
    }
};
```

The _updateFrame function contains the logic that used to be in the top half of the _render function, except rather than storing the information about what needs to be rendered in local variables, it populates the key frame that was passed in as a parameter.

```
var CategoryAxis = function (chart) {
    ChartElement.call(this, chart);
    this._displayFrame = new AxisKeyFrame();
    this._labelAccessor = null;
};
```

```
CategoryAxis.prototype = Object.create(ChartElement.prototype);
CategoryAxis.prototype._validate = function () {
    if (this._labelAccessor === null) {
        return false;
    }
    return ChartElement.prototype._validate.call(this);
};
CategoryAxis.prototype._render = function (ctx) {
    var f = this._displayFrame;
    var currText,
        currX, currY;
    ctx.fillStyle = this._color;
    for (var i = 0; i < f.xPositions.length; i++) {
        currX = f.xPositions[i];
        currY = f.yPositions[i];
        currText = f.labelTexts[i];

        var width = ctx.measureText(currText).width;

        ctx.fillText(
            currText,
            currX - width / 2.0,
            currY);
    }
};
CategoryAxis.prototype.labelAccessor = function (accessor) {
    this._labelAccessor = accessor;
    this._update();
    return this;
};
CategoryAxis.prototype._updateFrame = function (frame) {
    var data = this._chart._data;

    var scaledX, nextScaled, label, pos;

    frame.clear();

    for (var i = 0; i < data.length; i++) {
        label = this._labelAccessor(data[i]);

        scaledX = this._chart.scaleX(i);
        nextScaled = this._chart.scaleX(i + 1);

        pos = (scaledX + nextScaled) / 2.0;

        frame.addLabel(
            pos,
            this._chart._totalHeight - 20,
            label);
    }
};
```

The definition of the CategoryAxis follows basically the same pattern as the ColumnSeries, but we've highlighted some of the interesting differences in the preceding code.

```
        var width = ctx.measureText(currText).width;
```

In order to find the left position of some text so that it is centered around a point, you need to know how wide that text is. You can ask the canvas context to measure a string with the current font and tell you how wide that text would be when rendered.

```
    CategoryAxis.prototype.labelAccessor = function (accessor) {
        this._labelAccessor = accessor;
        this._update();
        return this;
    };
```

`labelAccessor` is analogous to `valueAccessor` on the `ColumnSeries`. Here, though, you are allowing for a function to be provided that fetches label text from the items of the `data` array.

```
    label = this._labelAccessor(data[i]);

    scaledX = this._chart.scaleX(i);
    nextScaled = this._chart.scaleX(i + 1);

    pos = (scaledX + nextScaled) / 2.0;
```

As the `CategoryAxis` key frame is being populated, you fetch the label value using the `_labelAccessor` and then determine the x position of the label by finding the midpoint between the start of the current category and the start of the next category.

```
    var NumericAxis = function (chart) {
        ChartElement.call(this, chart);
        this._displayFrame = new AxisKeyFrame();
    };
    NumericAxis.prototype = Object.create(ChartElement.prototype);
    NumericAxis.prototype._render = function (ctx) {
        var f = this._displayFrame;
        var currText,
            currX, currY;
        ctx.fillStyle = this._color;
        for (var i = 0; i < f.xPositions.length; i++) {
            currX = f.xPositions[i];
            currY = f.yPositions[i];
            currText = f.labelTexts[i];

            ctx.textBaseline = "middle";
            ctx.fillText(
                currText,
                currX,
                currY);
        }
    };
    NumericAxis.prototype._updateFrame = function (frame) {
        var min = this._chart._minValue;
        var max = this._chart._maxValue;
        var interval = (max - min) / 6.0;
        var label, scaledY;

        frame.clear();
        for (var i = min; i <= max; i += interval) {
```

```
        label = i.toString();

        scaledY = this._chart.scaleY(i);

        frame.addLabel(
            15,
            scaledY,
            label);
    }
};
```

The `NumericAxis` is roughly the same idea as the `CategoryAxis`. We've again highlighted some of the interesting differences, though.

```
ctx.textBaseline = "middle";
```

When rendering the y-axis labels, you want them to be centered vertically around their location. Thankfully you can tell the canvas to set the text baseline to `"middle"` to achieve this.

```
var min = this._chart._minValue;
var max = this._chart._maxValue;
var interval = (max - min) / 6.0;
```

This calculates a very basic auto interval for the axis. This splits the space into six sections, which results in seven labels being rendered. This is simple, but a bit naïve. It can easily result in lots of decimal points in the labels!

```
for (var i = min; i <= max; i += interval) {
    label = i.toString();
```

Provided a minimum, maximum, and interval, you can loop over the values and convert them into string labels for display.

```
this._xAxis = new CategoryAxis(this);
this._yAxis = new NumericAxis(this);
this._isDirty = false;
```

You add these lines to the `Chart`'s constructor because this chart will be hard coded to use one `CategoryAxis` and one `NumericAxis`, and the chart starts with its dirty flag set to false, indicating it does not need to render yet.

```
Chart.prototype.xAxis = function () {
    return this._xAxis;
};
```

You add the `xAxis` function to the chart so that you can access the chart's x axis to modify its settings.

```
Chart.prototype.dirty = function () {
    if (this._isDirty) {
        return;
    }
    this._isDirty = true;
    var self = this;
    window.queueFrame(function () {
```

```
        self._render();
    });
};
```

This is another new function for the chart that is called by the chart or its elements when they want to indicate that the chart needs to be re-rendered. It calls the `requestAnimationFrame` API to request that the `_render` function of the chart gets called at the earliest opportunity.

```
Chart.prototype._render = function () {
    var ctx = this._ctx;
    ctx.clearRect(0, 0, this._totalWidth, this._totalHeight);
    ctx.fillStyle = "rgba(240,240,240,1)";
    ctx.fillRect(0, 0, this._totalWidth, this._totalHeight);

    this._xAxis._render(ctx);
    this._yAxis._render(ctx);
    for (var i = 0; i < this._series.length; i++) {
        this._series[i]._render(ctx);
    }
};
```

The chart's `_render` function now calls the `_render` functions of the two axes in addition to the series.

```
Chart.prototype.update = function () {
    this._xAxis._update();
    this._yAxis._update();
    for (var i = 0; i < this._series.length; i++) {
        this._series[i]._update();
    }
    return this;
};
```

The chart's `update` function calls the `_update` functions of all the elements.

```
chart.xAxis()
    .labelAccessor(function (item) {
        return item.name;
    });
```

For the final piece, you need to tell the x axis how to retrieve the category labels from the data items when constructing the chart. With the axes incorporated, the chart looks like Figure 9-8, and you can access the files `CanvasChartWithAxes.js/html/css` on the companion website.

Adding Animation

Many of the changes enacted for adding columns to the chart were sneakily preparing you for animating the contents of the chart. You achieve the animation at a high level by having the series and the axes create a new target frame when their settings or data is changed and then perform a linear interpolation (yep, your old friend) between the values of the previous key frame and the next key frame.

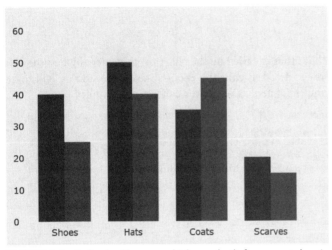

FIGURE 9-8: A chart with axes, which was built from scratch using the HTML5 canvas.

```
KeyFrame.prototype.interpolateThings = function (
    p, target, previous, next, doInterpolate, getFallbackValue) {
    var minCount = Math.min(previous.length, next.length);
    var maxCount = Math.max(previous.length, next.length);
    var i = 0, prevLen = previous.length,
        nextLen = next.length, fallBack = getFallbackValue();
    var lastPrev = prevLen > 0 ? previous[prevLen - 1] : fallBack;
    var lastNext = nextLen > 0 ? next[nextLen - 1] : fallBack;

    for (i = 0; i < maxCount; i++) {
        if (i < minCount) {
            target[i] = doInterpolate(p, previous[i], next[i]);
        }
        else if (i < previous.length) {
            target[i] = doInterpolate(p, previous[i], lastNext);
        }
        else if (i < next.length) {
            target[i] = doInterpolate(p, lastPrev, next[i]);
        }
    }

    target.length = maxCount;
};
KeyFrame.prototype.interpolateNumbers = function (
        p, target, previous, next) {
    this.interpolateThings(p, target, previous, next,
        function (p, prev, next) {
            return prev + p * (next - prev);
        },
        function () {
            return 0;
        });
};
```

```
KeyFrame.prototype.interpolate = function (p, previous, next) {
    this.interpolateNumbers(p,
        this.xPositions,
        previous.xPositions,
        next.xPositions);
    this.interpolateNumbers(p,
        this.yPositions,
        previous.yPositions,
        next.yPositions);
};
```

The preceding code defines the `interpolateThings` function to aid in interpolating arrays of entities that should be interpolated based on the animation progress (which will range from 0 to 1). When one array has fewer items than another, either the last item is used to interpolate with the overflow values, or, if one of the arrays is empty, a default value is used in the interpolation. The `interpolateNumbers` function uses the `interpolateThings` function to define how to interpolate two arrays of numbers. Finally the base `interpolate` function is defined for `KeyFrame`, which interpolates the x positions and the y positions for the `KeyFrame`.

```
ColumnsKeyFrame.prototype.interpolate = function (p, previous, next) {
    KeyFrame.prototype.interpolate.call(this, p, previous, next);
    this.interpolateNumbers(
        p,
        this.widths,
        previous.widths, next.widths);
    this.interpolateNumbers(
        p,
        this.heights,
        previous.heights, next.heights);
};
```

An `interpolate` function is added to the `ColumnsKeyFrame`, which interpolates the widths and heights of the columns.

```
AxisKeyFrame.prototype.interpolate = function (p, previous, next) {
    KeyFrame.prototype.interpolate.call(this, p, previous, next);

    this.interpolateThings(p,
        this.labelTexts,
        previous.labelTexts,
        next.labelTexts,
        function (p, previous, next) {
            return next;
        },
        function () {
            return "";
        });
};
```

As with the `ColumnsKeyFrame`, the main interpolation work is done in the base `interpolate` method, which interpolates the x and y position arrays. This method just ensures that when you interpolate the text of a label it returns the next label value rather than trying to animate the value of the label.

Next there are some changes to `ChartElement`:

```
var ChartElement = function (chart) {
    this._chart = chart;
    this._color = new Color(1, 80, 80, 80);
    this._animationProgress = -1;
    this._animationStartTime = null;
    this._transitionDuration = 1000;
    this._displayFrame = null;
    this._previousFrame = null;
    this._nextFrame = null;
};
```

Some new properties are added:

➤   _animationProgress: Tracks the current progress of the running animation.

➤   _animationStartTime: Tracks the start time of the current animation.

➤   _transitionDuration: The settable duration for the animations that get played in milliseconds.

➤   _displayFrame: The current displaying frame for the chart element. During an animation, this will be an interpolated frame between the _previousFrame and the _nextFrame. This is always the frame that gets rendered.

➤   _previousFrame: The previous key frame that was rendered.

➤   _nextFrame: The next key frame that is the goal of the current animation.

```
ChartElement.prototype.transitionDuration = function (val) {
    this._transitionDuration = val;
    return this;
};
```

This code allows for the duration of the animations to be changed.

```
ChartElement.prototype._startAnimation = function () {
    this._animationProgress = 0;
    this._animationStartTime = window.getHighResTime();
    this._chart.ensureTicking();
};
ChartElement.prototype._isAnimating = function () {
    return this._animationProgress != -1;
};
```

These functions allow for an animation to be started for the chart element and to determine if an animation is currently running for that element. The chart actually manages ensuring that this element's _tickAnimation function gets called as the animation frames are generated, so the element just asks the chart to _ensureTicking and tracks the start time of the current animation.

```
ChartElement.prototype._tickAnimation = function (time) {
    if (!this._isAnimating()) {
        return false;
    }
    var elapsed = time - this._animationStartTime;
```

```
        var finishing = false;

        if (elapsed >= this._transitionDuration) {
            elapsed = this._transitionDuration;
            this._updateFrame(this._previousFrame);
            finishing = true;
        }

        this._animationProgress = elapsed / this._transitionDuration;
        this._animationProgressUpdated();

        if (finishing) {
            this._animationProgress = -1;
            return false;
        }

        return true;
    };
```

_tickAnimation compares the current time to the start time in order to see if the animation is over, or to calculate the current progress based on the desired duration of the animation. In so doing, the _animationProgress property is updated with a value between 0 and 1 that represents the progress of the current animation, which will be the weighting for the blending, and _animationProgressUpdated is called.

```
    ChartElement.prototype._animationProgressUpdated = function () {
        this._displayFrame.interpolate(
            this._animationProgress,
            this._previousFrame,
            this._nextFrame);
    };
```

_animationProgressUpdated is the main driver for the interpolation you've been defining. Each time the animation ticks it will use the current progress to update the _displayFrame to contain values that are an interpolation between the previous key frame and the next key frame. To facilitate this arrangement the _updateFrames method is also modified:

```
    ChartElement.prototype._updateFrames = function () {
        var swap = this._previousFrame;

        this._startAnimation();
        this._previousFrame = this._displayFrame;
        this._displayFrame = swap;

        this._updateFrame(this._nextFrame);
    };
```

_updateFrames is called when a new target frame needs to be generated for the element. To facilitate this, the current _displayFrame becomes the _previousFrame, and a new _nextFrame is generated. When the animation starts ticking, it generates a new _displayFrame that contains the interpolated values between the two. Each successive tick of the animation updates _displayFrame again, shifting it farther away from _previousFrame and closer to _nextFrame.

All of the chart element types need to construct their previous and next frames in their constructors:

```
var CategoryAxis = function (chart) {
    ChartElement.call(this, chart);
    this._displayFrame = new AxisKeyFrame();
    this._previousFrame = new AxisKeyFrame();
    this._nextFrame = new AxisKeyFrame();
    this._labelAccessor = null;
};
var NumericAxis = function (chart) {
    ChartElement.call(this, chart);
    this._displayFrame = new AxisKeyFrame();
    this._previousFrame = new AxisKeyFrame();
    this._nextFrame = new AxisKeyFrame();
};
var ColumnSeries = function (chart) {
    ChartElement.call(this, chart);
    this._displayFrame = new ColumnsKeyFrame();
    this._previousFrame = new ColumnsKeyFrame();
    this._nextFrame = new ColumnsKeyFrame();
    this._valueAccessor = null;
    this._color = new Color(1, 255, 0, 0);
};
```

Finally, the main animation driver is added to the chart:

```
Chart.prototype.ensureTicking = function () {
    var self = this;
    if (this._isTicking) {
        return;
    }
    this._isTicking = true;
    window.queueFrame(function () {
        self.animationTick();
    });
};
Chart.prototype.animationTick = function () {
    var time = window.getHighResTime();
    var self = this;
    var stillAnimating = false;
    if (this._xAxis._tickAnimation(time)) {
        stillAnimating = true;
    }
    if (this._yAxis._tickAnimation(time)) {
        stillAnimating = true;
    }

    for (var i = 0; i < this._series.length; i++) {
        if (this._series[i]._tickAnimation(time)) {
            stillAnimating = true;
        }
    }

    this._render();

    if (stillAnimating) {
        window.queueFrame(function () {
```

```
                self.animationTick();
            });
        } else {
            this._isTicking = false;
        }
    };
```

`ensureTicking` bootstraps things by queuing an animation frame, which calls the `animationTick` method. `animationTick` calls `_tickAnimation` on all of the chart elements, calls the main `_render` method of the chart to render it out to the canvas, and finally, if any of the elements were still in progress, requests a new animation frame that will re-call `animationTick` when the new frame is ready.

With all this in place, you can load the chart and see it animate into place. Figure 9-9 shows the chart in mid animation, and you can find the code in the files `CanvasChartAnimation.js/html /css` on the companion website.

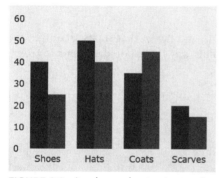

FIGURE 9-9: A column chart animates into view, rendered using the HTML5 canvas.

Why does everything animate in from the corner, though? The first time the chart renders, there is no previous frame state for any of the elements. The interpolation you defined used 0 for any initial numeric state, so everything is animating in from point 0,0. It would be more optimal if the columns were already in position and only their heights were animated. You can achieve that by defining an initial previous frame to use for the chart elements.

```
KeyFrame.prototype._isEmptyFrame = function () {
    return this.xPositions.length === 0;
};
```

First, it helps to be able to detect if you are animating from an unpopulated frame.

```
ChartElement.prototype._animationProgressUpdated = function () {
    var displayFrame = this._displayFrame;
    var previousFrame = this._previousFrame;
    var nextFrame = this._nextFrame;
    var actualProgress = this._easing(this._animationProgress);

    if (previousFrame._isEmptyFrame() &&
        this._populateDefaultFrame) {
        this._populateDefaultFrame(previousFrame, nextFrame);
```

```
        }

        displayFrame.interpolate(
            actualProgress,
            previousFrame,
            nextFrame);
    };
```

Then, if the previous frame is an empty frame, a chart element can generate a default frame rather than animating from the empty frame. You may also notice the addition of the _easing call in this code. You can read more about that later in this chapter.

```
    CategoryAxis.prototype._populateDefaultFrame = function (
            frame, nextFrame) {
        for (var i = 0; i < nextFrame.xPositions.length; i++) {
            frame.xPositions[i] = 0;
            frame.yPositions[i] = this._chart._totalHeight - 20;
        }
    };
```

CategoryAxis provides an implementation of _populateDefaultFrame that starts all of the labels underneath the plot area, but on the left side of the chart. This way they should animate in from the left rather than the top left.

```
    NumericAxis.prototype._populateDefaultFrame = function (
            frame, nextFrame) {
        for (var i = 0; i < nextFrame.xPositions.length; i++) {
            frame.xPositions[i] = nextFrame.xPositions[i];
            frame.yPositions[i] = this._chart._plotTop + this._chart._plotHeight;
        }
    };
```

NumericAxis provides a similar implementation, except it animates the labels in from the bottom of the chart.

```
    ColumnSeries.prototype._populateDefaultFrame = function (
            frame, nextFrame) {
        for (var i = 0; i < nextFrame.xPositions.length; i++) {
            frame.xPositions[i] = nextFrame.xPositions[i];
            frame.yPositions[i] = this._chart._plotTop +
                this._chart._plotHeight;
            frame.widths[i] = nextFrame.widths[i];
            frame.heights[i] = 0;
        }
    };
```

Finally, ColumnSeries provides an implementation that starts the columns in their eventual x-positions, but with a collapsed height and an adjusted top position.

Now, if you run the code you get a much cleaner animation where the columns animate in from the bottom of the chart and the labels slide into place from the bottom left. You can see the results in Figure 9-10, which shows the chart mid animation, and you can find the code in the file CanvasChartAnimationWithStartingFrame.js/html/css on the companion website.

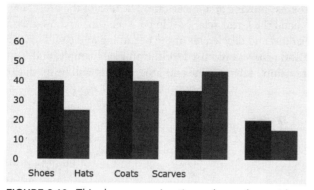

FIGURE 9-10: This shows an animating column chart with starting frames, built from scratch using the HTML5 canvas.

So what was that easing call about?

```
var easing = {};
easing.toIn = function (f, t) {
    return f(t * 2.0) / 2.0;
};
easing.toOut = function (f, t) {
    t = 1 - t;
    return (1.0 - f(t * 2.0)) / 2.0 + 0.5;
};
easing.cubicIn = function (t) {
    return t * t * t;
};
easing.cubicInOut = function (t) {
    if (t < 0.5) {
        return easing.toIn(easing.cubicIn, t);
    } else {
        return easing.toOut(easing.cubicIn, t);
    }
};

var ChartElement = function (chart) {
    this._chart = chart;
    this._color = new Color(1, 80, 80, 80);
    this._animationProgress = -1;
    this._animationStartTime = null;
    this._transitionDuration = 1000;
    this._displayFrame = null;
    this._previousFrame = null;
    this._nextFrame = null;
    this._easing = easing.cubicInOut;
};
```

An easing function adjusts the speed with which an animation progresses. It can make motion look more natural for the beginning and/or the end to play at different speeds compared to the middle portion. Your animation, so far, has left progress moving at a linear rate. The idea of the preceding code is to use a piecewise cubic function to bend the linear relationship between time and progress into a different shape, specifically one that accelerates and decelerates at the beginning and end. Figure 9-11 shows the linear relationship between time and progress you used for the previous sample, and Figure 9-12 shows the piecewise cubic relationship between time and progress that will be used now.

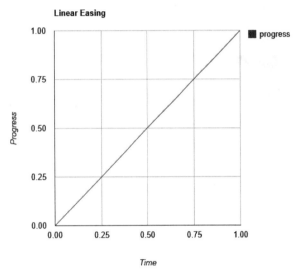

FIGURE 9-11: A linear relation between time and progress creates a steadily progressing animation with no speed changes.

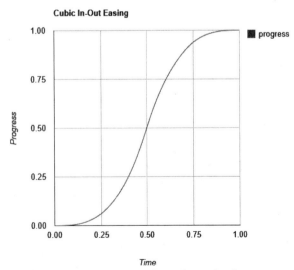

FIGURE 9-12: A piecewise cubic relationship between time and progress creates an animation that speeds up and slows down over time.

Finally, now that all the animation groundwork is in place, you get some really neat effects if you modify the data of the column series with a button on the page.

```
var data2 = [
    { "name": "Shoes", "Q1": 20, "Q2": 35 },
    { "name": "Hats", "Q1": 30, "Q2": 40 },
    { "name": "Coats", "Q1": 45, "Q2": 25 },
    { "name": "Scarves", "Q1": 10, "Q2": 25 }
];
```

First, you need a second set of data.

```
var initialData = true;
var button = document.getElementById("changeData");
button.onclick = function () {
    if (initialData) {
        chart.data(data2);
        initialData = false;
    } else {
        chart.data(data);
        initialData = true;
    }
};
```

Then all you need to do to animate the change is call data to toggle back and forth between the original data and the new data when a button is pressed. You can see the chart mid animation between the two data sets in Figure 9-13, and you can find the code in the files CanvasChartAnimationWithDataUpdate.js/html/css on the companion website.

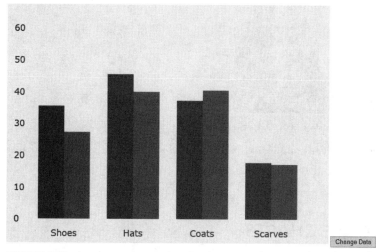

FIGURE 9-13: A column chart animating between data sets, in order to show how the data changes over time.

Things get even more interesting if you have different amounts of data items in the sets you are toggling between:

```
var data = [
    { "name": "Shoes", "Q1": 40, "Q2": 25 },
    { "name": "Hats", "Q1": 50, "Q2": 40 },
    { "name": "Coats", "Q1": 35, "Q2": 45 },
    { "name": "Scarves", "Q1": 20, "Q2": 15 }
];

var data2 = [
    { "name": "Shoes", "Q1": 20, "Q2": 35 },
    { "name": "Hats", "Q1": 30, "Q2": 40 },
    { "name": "Coats", "Q1": 45, "Q2": 25 },
    { "name": "Scarves", "Q1": 10, "Q2": 25 },
    { "name": "Socks", "Q1": 55, "Q2": 15 },
    { "name": "Sweaters", "Q1": 50, "Q2": 35 }
];
```

Figure 9-14 shows the chart in the midst of animating new data items into place, and the code is in the files `CanvasChartAnimationLine.js/html/css` on the companion website. (You can also see this Figure 9-14 in the color insert.) These files also show an implementation of line series.

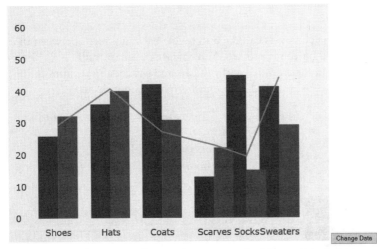

FIGURE 9-14: The custom Canvas chart you are building animates between two data sets to show new data being introduced over time.

STARTING WITH GOOGLE CHARTS

We hope your plunge into the deep-end of building charting tools from scratch has given you a good low-level understanding of how visualizations are put together.

Building your own tools from scratch, or using low-level visualization APIs such as D3, can grant you a great deal of flexibility, but the lack of high-level abstractions and simplifications can truly hamper productivity. Thankfully, the charting API landscape is diverse and there are products to use from all along the complexity spectrum. One constrained and high-level product, which is correspondingly simple to use, is the Google Charts API.

Google Charts API Basics

To use the Google Charts API, you set up a data table instance, with rows corresponding to individual items in a data series and columns corresponding to a set of categories, or some number of data series plotted for those categories. First up, you see how much less code it is to put together a bar chart compared to building your column chart from scratch earlier.

A Basic Bar Chart

All of the following code for the Google Charts API uses this CSS:

```
#chart {
    width: 500px;
    height: 500px;
}
```

This just defines the size of the container for the chart, using CSS. And here's the HTML:

```
<!DOCTYPE html>
<html>
<head>
    <title>Google Charts API Basic Bar Chart</title>

    <script type="text/javascript" src="https://www.google.com/jsapi">
    </script>
    <script type="text/javascript">
        google.load('visualization', '1',
            { packages: ['corechart'] });
    </script>

    <script type="text/javascript"
    src="847060_ch13_GoogleChartsAPIBarChart.js">
    </script>
    <link rel="stylesheet"
    href="847060_ch13_GoogleChartsAPIBarChart.css">
</head>
<body>
    <div id="chart"></div>
</body>
</html>
```

In this code, you are referencing the Google Visualization API scripts and requesting that the corechart package be downloaded. Like many JavaScript APIs, Google Charts is modular so that you can select only the features you want in order to save bandwidth and load pages faster. The <div> is what holds the chart, and that's what you targeted with the CSS rule just before.

```
function renderChart() {
    var data = google.visualization.arrayToDataTable([
        ['product', 'Sales'],
        ['Shoes',  40],
```

```
            ['Hats',   50],
            ['Coats',   35],
            ['Scarves',  20]
        ]);

    var options = {
        title : "Product Sales",
        hAxis: { title: "Sales" },
        vAxis: { title: "Products" }
    };

    var chart = new google.visualization.BarChart(
        document.getElementById("chart"));
    chart.draw(data, options);
}
google.setOnLoadCallback(renderChart);
```

That's not much code, huh? First, you create a data table with two columns. The types of the columns (string and number) are determined automatically. When you request a chart to be rendered, Google Charts tries to do the intelligent thing with them. Next, some options are provided, which basically just assigns some titles to the axes and the chart itself. Last, a `google.visualization.BarChart` is created, targeting the `<div>` with the ID chart, and the chart is drawn, providing the data and the options.

All of that is gathered into a function so that you can call

```
google.setOnLoadCallback(renderChart);
```

This ensures that you don't try to render the chart before the correct JavaScript resources have been downloaded or before the page DOM is ready. You can see the result in Figure 9-15. The `GoogleChartsAPIBarChart.js/html/css` files are on the companion website.

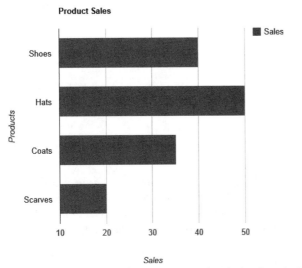

FIGURE 9-15: This bar chart was created with the Google Charts API.

A Basic Pie Chart

Having seen how much the Google Charts API simplifies displaying a bar chart, you can move on to pie charts, which are another popular chart type. Actually, it turns out to be a complete non-issue. Just change the chart initialization line to

```
var chart = new google.visualization.PieChart(
    document.getElementById("chart"));
```

and delete the titles for the axes (you don't have any, anymore):

```
var options = {
    title : "Product Sales"
};
```

You can see the result in Figure 9-16, and you can find the `GoogleChartsAPIPieChart.js/html /css` files on the companion website.

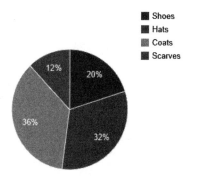

FIGURE 9-16: This pie chart was created with the Google Charts API.

Also, take a moment to notice all the interesting ancillary features that the Google Charts API bundles in for you, for free. When you run the sample, do you notice how you can select slices by clicking them? Do you notice the hover effects when your cursor is over a slice? Okay, now it's time for a neat trick that would be extremely difficult to pull off if you had written this pie chart from scratch. Change the options block to.

```
var options = {
    title : "Product Sales",
    is3D: true
};
```

Now the chart is in faux 3D! Check it out in Figure 9-17. The `GoogleChartsAPIPieChart3D.js` /html/css files are on the companion website. Keep in mind, though, that 3D rarely adds any new information to a visualization you are trying to build, but it can, often, make a visualization harder to interpret. It's a good idea, when considering adding 3D elements to a visualization, to evaluate whether they are actually adding extra information, or whether the addition is purely aesthetic. If the latter, it may be better to use some restraint.

Product Sales

FIGURE 9-17: A simple setting has transformed a pie chart into a faux 3D pie chart.

Working with Chart Animations

Earlier in this chapter, you saw how powerful and flexible animations could be when building them from scratch. But they also take a lot of code and effort to enable. Now check out how you would achieve a similar effect using the Google Charts API:

```
function renderChart() {
    var data = google.visualization.arrayToDataTable([
            ['product', 'Sales', { role: 'annotation' } ],
            ['Shoes',  0, "40"],
            ['Hats',  0, "50"],
            ['Coats',  0, "35"],
            ['Scarves',  0, "20"]
        ]);

    var options = {
        title : "Product Sales",
        hAxis: { title: "Sales", viewWindow: { min: 0, max: 55 } },
        vAxis: { title: "Products" },
        animation: {
            duration: 1000,
            easing: 'inAndOut',
        }
    };
    var button = document.getElementById('changeData');

    var initialAnimationPlayed = false;
    var chart = new google.visualization.BarChart(
        document.getElementById("chart"));
```

```
google.visualization.events.addListener(chart, 'ready',
function() {
    if (!initialAnimationPlayed) {
        initialAnimationPlayed = true;
        data.setValue(0, 1, 40);
        data.setValue(1, 1, 50);
        data.setValue(2, 1, 35);
        data.setValue(3, 1, 20);
        chart.draw(data, options);
    } else {
        button.disabled = false;
    }
});

chart.draw(data, options);

var firstData = true;
button.onclick = function () {
    if (!firstData) {
        firstData = !firstData;
        data.setValue(0, 1, 40);
        data.setValue(1, 1, 50);
        data.setValue(2, 1, 35);
        data.setValue(3, 1, 20);

        data.setValue(0, 2, "40");
        data.setValue(1, 2, "50");
        data.setValue(2, 2, "35");
        data.setValue(3, 2, "20");
    } else {
        firstData = !firstData;
        data.setValue(0, 1, 25);
        data.setValue(1, 1, 40);
        data.setValue(2, 1, 45);
        data.setValue(3, 1, 15);

        data.setValue(0, 2, "25");
        data.setValue(1, 2, "40");
        data.setValue(2, 2, "45");
        data.setValue(3, 2, "15");
    }
    button.disabled = true;
    chart.draw(data, options);
};

}

google.setOnLoadCallback(renderChart);
```

The key differences here are

➤ You start with the data values at 0.

➤ You enable animation for the chart and specify an animation duration and an animation-easing function.

➤ You create a click handler for a button that makes updates to the data table and redraws the chart.

➤ It's important to only make changes to the chart when it is "ready."

This still could have been simpler, actually. Many charting APIs offer a facility to transition in the initial data values without needing to explicitly default the data to 0, but, at the time of this writing, Google Charts API doesn't seem to support this. Also, it's a bit cumbersome to avoid interacting with the chart when it isn't ready to receive commands.

You can see the animated bar chart after the data change has completed in Figure 9-18, which you can find in the `GoogleChartsAPIBarChartAnimated.js/html/css` files on the companion website.

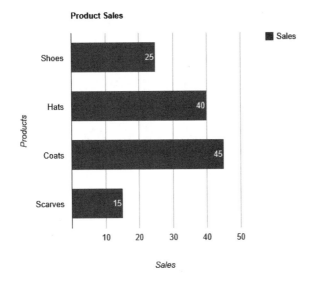

FIGURE 9-18: This animated bar chart was created using the Google Charts API.

You'll find also that if you substitute `LineChart` or `AreaChart` for `BarChart` everything should work fine for those charting types with no additional configuration other than retitling the axes. This is the power of working with a high-level charting API.

The `GoogleChartsAPISelectType.js/html/css` files on the companion website show you how to build a page that easily lets you swap between the main category charting types without animation. You can see the line chart in Figure 9-19.

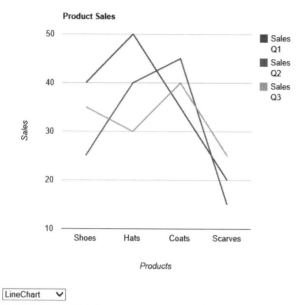

LineChart ⌄

FIGURE 9-19: This line chart was created using Google Charts API.

SUMMARY

You accomplished an awful lot this chapter. You learned:

- ➤ Some of the basics of plotting data in a chart
- ➤ How the HTML5 canvas differs from SVG, Flash, and other graphics tools
- ➤ How to use linear interpolation to map coordinates or blend changes over time
- ➤ How to use the HTML5 canvas and key frames to render and animate data in a page
- ➤ How to use the HTML5 canvas to render dynamic column charts
- ➤ How to use the HTML5 canvas to show changes to data over time
- ➤ How to use the Google Charts API to render a bar chart, a pie chart, and a 3D pie chart
- ➤ How to use the Google Charts API to animate a bar chart

10

Building Custom Charts with Raphaël

WHAT'S IN THIS CHAPTER

➤ The SVG library Raphaël

➤ gRaphaël, a charting plug-in for Raphaël

➤ An example of how to extend Raphaël to create a custom donut chart

> **CODE DOWNLOAD** *The wrox.com code downloads for this chapter are found at www.wrox.com/go/javascriptandjqueryanalysis on the Download Code tab. The code is in the chapter 10 download and individually named according to the names throughout the chapter.*

As developers, we're fortunate to have a variety of excellent charting solutions at our fingertips. Nine times out of ten, these libraries and plug-ins provide all the functionality our apps need.

But what about those times you want something more? In these cases, you have two options: Write something from scratch or extend an existing script. Although reinventing the wheel can be tempting, it's usually best to save time and start with an already-built project.

This chapter first introduces the SVG library Raphaël, which provides an excellent foundation for creating custom graphics. You then explore gRaphaël, a charting plug-in for Raphaël that you can use to create simple visualizations such as pie charts and bar graphs.

Finally, you learn how to extend Raphaël, leveraging its utilities as a starting point for your own custom visuals. You follow a practical example of creating a donut chart plug-in as you pick up concepts you can use to create charts of any type.

INTRODUCING RAPHAËL

Raphaël is a handy JavaScript library for drawing, manipulating, and animating vector graphics. It offers a variety of APIs that standardize and simplify SVG code. This library provides all the building blocks you need to create rich, interactive graphics on the web.

SVG Versus Canvas Charts

Modern web graphics fall into two main categories: SVG and canvas. When you're working with a charting library, this distinction is largely behind the scenes. But there are a few notable differences that are worth considering before you choose a charting solution.

This chapter focuses on SVG charts because they can be easier to customize. Graphics rendered in SVG are easy to manipulate, whereas those rendered in canvas are more static. For example, if you render a circle in SVG, you can resize it, recolor it, move its vertices, add a click handler, and so on. On the other hand, canvas uses static rendering, so if you want to alter the circle, you need to redraw it completely. Although it's not terribly daunting to redraw canvas with the help of a library, it does make it harder to extend an existing library. That's because the logic for rendering canvas is more abstract and obfuscated, whereas SVGs exist plainly in the DOM.

However, this DOM accessibility isn't a free lunch—in general SVG underperforms canvas alternatives. But don't worry, these performance differences are covered in more detail in Chapter 12.

Getting Started with Raphaël

After downloading the library from `http://raphaeljs.com/` and including it on the page, the next step is creating a wrapper element for your SVG:

```
<div id="my-svg"></div>
```

Next, you need to create a drawing canvas that Raphaël can use to add SVGs. In Raphaël, that's called the "paper," which you can assign to your wrapper element:

```
var paper = Raphael(document.getElementById('my-svg'), 500, 300);
```

This code creates a drawing canvas with the wrapper using a width of 500px and a height of 300px. Now you can add any shapes you want:

```
var rect = paper.rect(50, 25, 200, 150);
rect.attr('fill', '#00F');

var circle = paper.circle(300, 200, 100);
circle.attr('fill', '#F00');
circle.attr('stroke-width', 0);
```

Here Raphaël's `rect()` API draws a rectangle that is 200px wide and 150px tall. It places that rectangle at the coordinates (50, 25) within the drawing canvas and then colors it blue (#00F).

Next, the script draws a circle with a radius of 100px that is centered on (300, 200). It colors it red (#F00) and removes the default stroke by setting its width to zero. Because the circle is drawn second, it renders on top of the rectangle, as you can see in Figure 10-1.

FIGURE 10-1: This rectangle and circle are drawn with Raphaël.

You can find this example in the Chapter 10 folder on the companion website. It's named `raphael-basics.html`.

> **NOTE** *If you'd prefer to include Raphaël from a CDN, you can use cdnjs:* `http://cdnjs.com/libraries/raphael`.

Drawing Paths

If you need anything more than simple shapes, you can draw them yourself using coordinates and paths. For example:

```
var triangle = paper.path('M250,50 L100,250 L400,250 L250,50');
```

This line uses the `path()` API to draw a line based on coordinates. Although the path string here might seem daunting, it's actually fairly straightforward:

1. `M250,50` starts the path at coordinates (250,50).
2. `L100,250` draws a line from the starting point to (100,250).
3. `L400,250` draws a line from that vertex to point (400,250).
4. `L250,50` draws a line back to the starting point, closing the shape.

When all these paths are drawn together, it renders the triangle shown in Figure 10-2.

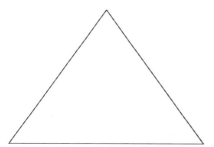

FIGURE 10-2: This triangle was drawn with Raphaël's path() API.

Next, the path string can be simplified a bit:

```
var triangle = paper.path('M250,50 L100,250 L400,250 Z');
```

Here, the last command in the string was replaced with z—a shorthand to close the path at the starting point.

> **NOTE** *To learn more about SVG path strings, visit*
> `https://developer.mozilla.org/en-US/docs/Web/SVG/Tutorial/Paths`.

Importing Custom Shapes into Raphaël

You can also use Raphaël to draw a variety of curves from simple arcs to complex Beziers. However, manually generating the path strings for complex curves can be challenging. Luckily there are tools you can use to generate Raphaël code for curves of any type.

One option is to export an SVG directly from Adobe Illustrator, using SaveDocsAsSVG, a script bundled with Illustrator. Shown in Figure 10-3, this tool allows you to export vectored graphics as SVG code.

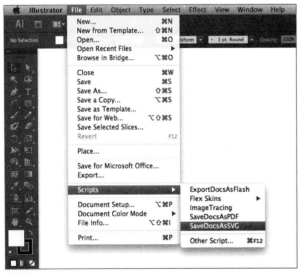

FIGURE 10-3: Adobe Illustrator allows you to export SVGs.

After you save the SVG, simply open it in a text editor and look for the path string. For example, your code might look something like the output for this simple curve:

```
<?xml version="1.0" encoding="iso-8859-1"?>
<!-- Generator: Adobe Illustrator 16.0.4, SVG Export Plug-In . SVG Version: 6.00
  Build 0)  -->
<!DOCTYPE svg PUBLIC "-//W3C//DTD SVG 1.1//EN"
  "http://www.w3.org/Graphics/SVG/1.1/DTD/svg11.dtd">
<svg version="1.1" id="Layer_1" xmlns="http://www.w3.org/2000/svg"
```

```
    xmlns:xlink="http://www.w3.org/1999/xlink" x="0px" y="0px"
    width="600px" height="400px" viewBox="0 0 600 400"
    style="enable-background:new 0 0 600 400;" xml:space="preserve">
<path style="fill:none;stroke:#000000;stroke-width:2.1155;stroke-miterlimit:10;"
    d="M251.742,85.146 C75.453,48.476,100.839,430.671,309.565,250.152"/>
</svg>
```

I've highlighted the important piece here, `M251.742,85.146 C75.453,48.476,100.839,430.671,` `309.565,250.152`. You can now take this string to use with Raphaël's `path()` API:

```
paper.path('M251.742,85.146 C75.453,48.476,100.839,430.671,309.565,250.152');
```

As shown in Figure 10-4, Raphaël now renders the same curve.

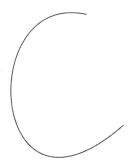

FIGURE 10-4: The SVG from Illustrator is now rendered with Raphaël.

This technique works great when you want to cherry pick a curve or two. But if you need to import a complete graphic, the SVG code can become significantly more complicated. In these cases it's better to turn to a conversion tool like Ready Set Raphael, which is shown in Figure 10-5 and is available at at `www.readysetraphael.com/`. Simply upload the exported SVG to this converter, and it outputs the Raphaël code you need.

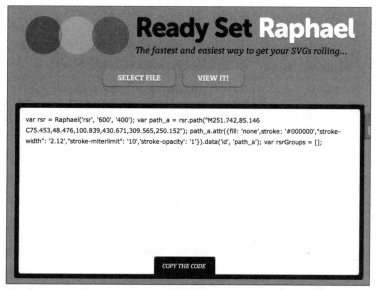

FIGURE 10-5: Ready Set Raphaël converts SVGs to Raphaël code.

Animating Raphaël Graphics

One of the best parts about Raphaël is its robust animation support, which allows you to render a variety of animations with minimal effort. For example, you can animate the triangle you drew earlier:

```
var triangle = paper.path('M250,50 L100,250 L400,250 Z');
triangle.animate({transform: 'r 360'}, 4000, 'bounce');
```

This rotates the triangle 360 degrees (`r 360`), which occurs over a period of `4000` milliseconds, using the `bounce` easing method. If you run this script in the browser then you see the triangle rotate, with a flamboyant bounce effect. If you'd like something a little more subdued, try a different easing method, such as < to ease in, > to ease out, or <> to ease in and out.

You can add any number of transformations to the transform string. For example, to shrink and rotate the triangle, you'd write:

```
triangle.animate({transform: 'r 360 s 0.2'}, 4000, '<>');
```

This uses a scale transformation to shrink the triangle to 20 percent of its original size (while also rotating).

Beyond basic transformations, you can also animate a variety of styling options and even the individual vertices of your shapes. To learn more, visit the Raphaël docs at `http://raphaeljs.com /reference.html#Element.animate`.

Handling Mouse Events with Raphaël

One of the best parts of working with SVG is how easy it is to assign mouse events. Because you can interface directly with the shapes in the SVG, it becomes trivial to assign any event listeners you need:

```
triangle.node.onclick = function() {
  triangle.attr('fill', 'red');
};
```

This script first grabs the DOM reference to the triangle shape in Raphaël and then assigns the `onclick` listener. The example uses the basic `onclick` handler for simplicity, but feel free to use a jQuery event handler or another more robust listener if you'd like.

However, if you run this script in the browser, it might not have the result you expect. Because the triangle is just a thin path, it is extremely difficult to click; SVG mouse events target the shape itself, so in this case you have to click an extremely thin line to trigger the handler. To get around this, simply set a background color for the triangle:

```
triangle.attr('fill', 'white');

triangle.node.onclick = function() {
  triangle.attr('fill', 'red');
};
```

Alternatively, if you need a truly transparent triangle, you can use RGBa:

```
triangle.attr('fill', 'rgba(0,0,0,0)');

triangle.node.onclick = function() {
  triangle.attr('fill', 'rgba(255,0,0,1)');
};
```

Here the triangle starts completely transparent, `rgba(0,0,0,0)`, and then changes to opaque red, `rgba(255,0,0,1)`.

> **TIP** *Don't use transparency unless it's necessary. Opaque colors tend to render and perform better in SVG.*

WORKING WITH gRAPHAËL

There are many charting options for Raphaël, notably gRaphaël, an official release from Sencha Labs, the owners of Raphaël. gRaphaël can render a variety of common visualizations such as pie charts, line graphs, and bar charts.

gRaphaël provides a simple starting point for creating your own custom charts. If you need rich functionality out of the box, you'll be better off with a more robust charting solution such as D3, as covered in chapters 11 and 16 of this book. But if you're looking for something simple and easy to extend, gRaphaël is an excellent choice.

First download the script from `http://g.raphaeljs.com/` and include the core as well as whichever chart modules you need. Next, reference a DOM element to instantiate the SVG paper:

```
var paper = Raphael(document.getElementById('my-chart'), 500, 300);
```

You can find the examples from this section in the Chapter 10 folder on the companion website. It's named `graphael-charts.html`.

> **NOTE** *If you'd prefer to include gRaphaël from a CDN, consider using cdnjs:* `http://cdnjs.com/libraries/graphael`.

Creating Pie Charts

When you've made sure you're including `raphael.js`, `g.raphael.js`, *and* `g.pie.js`, you can render a pie chart with a single line of code:

```
paper.piechart(250, 150, 120, [80, 55, 32, 21, 9, 5, 2]);
```

As shown in Figure 10-6, this creates a pie chart centered at (250,150), with a radius of 120px, and showing the values in the array.

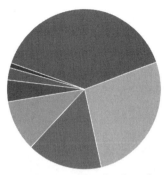

FIGURE 10-6: gRaphaël renders a basic pie chart.

Chances are you'll also want to label the slices of this pie. To do so, you need to dig into the last argument of the `piechart()` API:

```
paper.piechart(250, 150, 120, [80, 55, 32, 21, 9, 5, 2], {
  legend: [
    'croissants',
    'bagels',
    'doughnuts',
    'muffins',
    'danishes',
    'scones',
    'coffee cakes'
  ]
});
```

Passing in the `legend` array creates a labeled legend for the pie chart, as you can see in Figure 10-7.

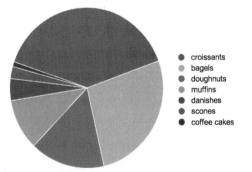

FIGURE 10-7: A legend has been added to the pie chart.

You can use this same option object to tweak the colors of the chart, set up links for the various slices, and more. To learn more about the `piechart()` API, visit `http://g.raphaeljs.com/reference.html#Paper.piechart`.

Creating Line Charts

After you've included `g.line.js`, you can also render line graphs with ease:

```
var xVals = [0, 5, 10, 15, 20, 25, 30, 35, 40, 45, 50],
    yVals = [46, 75, 91, 64, 82, 41, 53, 47, 73, 76, 62];

paper.linechart(0, 0, 500, 300, xVals, yVals);
```

In this code, a line chart is drawn between (0,0) and (500,300) using the provided xVals and yVals. That code renders the line graph shown in Figure 10-8.

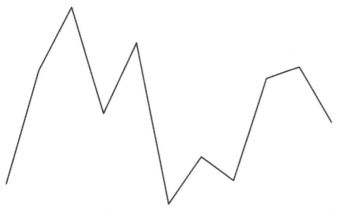

FIGURE 10-8: gRaphaël's basic line chart.

If you need multiple lines, you can pass in additional sets of y values:

```
var xVals = [0, 5, 10, 15, 20, 25, 30, 35, 40, 45, 50],
    yVals = [46, 75, 91, 64, 82, 41, 53, 47, 73, 76, 62],
    yVals2 = [71, 51, 55, 40, 62, 66, 42, 81, 84, 57, 73];

paper.linechart(0, 0, 500, 300, xVals, [yVals, yVals2]);
```

Here, the second set of y values creates a second line that you can see in Figure 10-9.

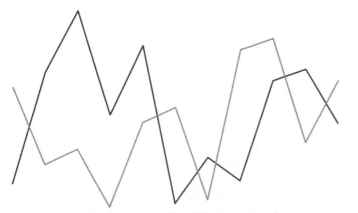

FIGURE 10-9: gRaphaël's line charts allow multiple lines.

You can then establish the x and y axis by passing the axis option:

```
paper.linechart(20, 0, 500, 280, xVals, [yVals, yVals2],
  {axis: '0 0 1 1'});
```

Here the axis array displays axes in TRBL (top right bottom left) order, so in this case the script renders the axes on the bottom and left sides of the chart, as you can see in Figure 10-10.

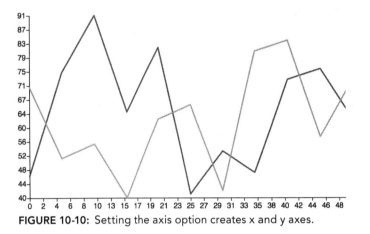

FIGURE 10-10: Setting the axis option creates x and y axes.

However, you may have noticed that the axes are labeled a bit oddly—for instance, look at the number of steps on the x-axis.. Unfortunately, adjusting the labels is a bit complicated—you have to set the axis step value like so:

```
paper.linechart(20, 0, 500, 280, xVals, [yVals, yVals2],
  {axis: '0 0 1 1', axisxstep: 10});
```

Here, axisxstep defines the number of steps to show on the x axis. However, the option is a bit counterintuitive because the value of 10 actually renders 11 steps, as shown in Figure 10-11.

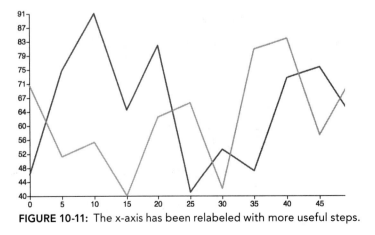

FIGURE 10-11: The x-axis has been relabeled with more useful steps.

Finally, gRaphaël provides a handful of options you can use to alter the visualization. For example, to shade the chart like the area chart in Figure 10-12, simply pass the shade option:

```
paper.linechart(20, 0, 500, 280, xVals, [yVals, yVals2],
    {axis: '0 0 1 1', axisxstep: 10, shade: true});
```

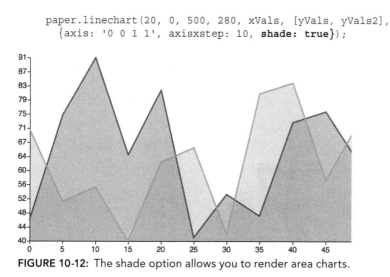

FIGURE 10-12: The shade option allows you to render area charts.

Alternatively, you can create a curved graph like the one in Figure 10-13:

```
paper.linechart(20, 0, 500, 280, xVals, [yVals, yVals2],
    {axis: '0 0 1 1', axisxstep: 10, shade: true,
    smooth: true, symbol: 'circle'});
```

Here, smooth renders the curved lines and symbol renders the points along the line.

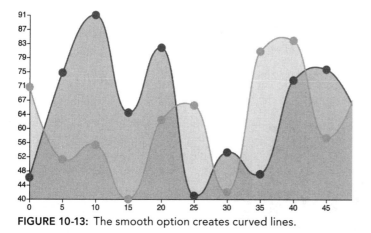

FIGURE 10-13: The smooth option creates curved lines.

These are just a few of the options available to the linechart() API. To learn about more possibilities, visit http://g.raphaeljs.com/reference.html#Paper.linechart.

Creating Bar and Column Charts

gRaphaël also provides some bar chart support, although to be honest the functionality is quite limited. To get started, include the gRaphaël core as well as g.bar.js. The barchart() API works fairly similarly to `linechart()`; the main difference is that you only pass in a single set of values as opposed to (x,y) pairs:

```
var vals = [46, 75, 91, 64, 82, 41, 53, 47, 73, 76, 62];

paper.barchart(0, 0, 500, 300, [vals]);
```

The preceding code renders the column chart shown in Figure 10-14.

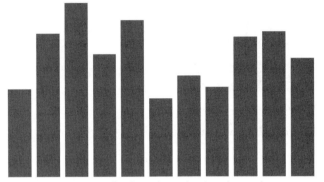

FIGURE 10-14: gRaphaël renders a basic column chart.

Pay careful attention to the values because they are passed as an array contained in an array. That allows you to render multiple sets of bars:

```
var vals = [46, 75, 91, 64, 82, 41, 53, 47, 73, 76, 62],
    vals2 = [71, 51, 55, 40, 62, 66, 42, 81, 84, 57, 73];

paper.barchart(0, 0, 500, 300, [vals, vals2]);
```

As shown in Figure 10-15, this renders the two values side by side.

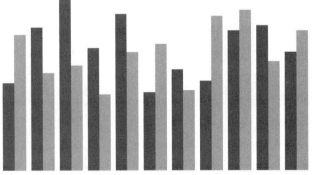

FIGURE 10-15: Adding a second data set creates a clustered column chart.

Unfortunately, labeling gRaphaël's bar chart can be a challenge because there is no native axis support. That said, you can use some of Raphaël's utilities to create your own labels. To get started, take a look at this simple gRaphaël plug-in:

```
Raphael.fn.labelBarChart = function(x_start, y_start, width, labels, textAttr) {
    var paper = this;

    // offset x_start and width for bar chart gutters
    x_start += 10;
    width -= 20;

    var labelWidth = width / labels.length;

    // offset x_start to center under each column
    x_start += labelWidth / 2;

    for ( var i = 0, len = labels.length; i < len; i++ ) {
        paper.text( x_start + ( i * labelWidth ), y_start, labels[i] ).attr
            ( textAttr );
    }
};
```

Don't worry too much about the nuts and bolts of this script. The important piece is the call to `paper.text()`. This API renders text in the SVG according to a variety of parameters.

Next, to use this script, simply pass the labels you want to use:

```
var labels = ['Col 1', 'Col 2', 'Col 3', 'Col 4', 'Col 5', 'Col 6', 'Col 7',
    'Col 8'];

paper.labelBarChart(0, 290, 500, labels, {'font-size': 14});
```

Here, the `labelBarChart()` API creates labels starting at (0, 290), with a width of 290, the result of which you can see in Figure 10-16.

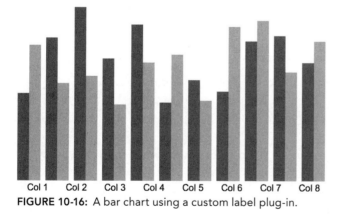

FIGURE 10-16: A bar chart using a custom label plug-in.

That takes care of labeling the different data sets. Labeling the y-axis, on the other hand, is more complex. As an exercise, follow the `labelBarChart()` plug-in example to create a plug-in to label the axis.

EXTENDING RAPHAËL TO CREATE CUSTOM CHARTS

One of the best parts of working with Raphaël and gRaphaël is how lightweight and extensible the libraries are. Each provides an excellent jumping off point for creating your own custom charts.

You've already gotten a glimpse of extending Raphaël with the `labelBarChart()` plug-in earlier in this chapter. In this section, you find out how to use a variety of the utility functions in Raphaël to build the donut chart shown in Figure 10-17.

FIGURE 10-17: This custom donut chart plug-in extends Raphaël.

You create the donut chart as a versatile plug-in with a variety of options. By the end of this example, you'll be able to use these concepts to create any chart you need.

You can find this example in the Chapter 10 folder on the companion website. It's named `custom-donut-chart.html`.

Setting Up with Common Patterns

To get started, extend the Raphaël core and create a new plug-in for donut charts:

```
Raphael.fn.donutChart = function (cx, cy, r, values, options) {
  // ...
}
```

This new function accepts a variety of arguments you need to position and render the chart:

➤ X and Y coordinates of the center point

➤ Radius for the chart

➤ Values to display

➤ Miscellaneous options

Next, store a few variables for later:

```
Raphael.fn.donutChart = function (cx, cy, r, values, options) {
  var paper = this,
      chart = this.set(),
```

```
rad   = Math.PI / 180;

    return chart;
};
```

Here, the script renames `this` to `paper` for easy access to the SVG canvas and then stores a reference to the `set()`, or group of shapes in the SVG. Additionally, it caches the value of a single radian—that'll come in handy later when you do a little trigonometry (don't worry; it isn't too painful). Finally, the script returns the set of shapes in the SVG to allow for easy access and chainability with other APIs.

The next step is setting up a framework for the plug-in options. Besides the main settings for the chart position and values, the plug-in accepts an argument for a general set of options. These secondary options should have smart defaults so that the user can ignore the settings unless they're needed:

```
Raphael.fn.donutChart = function (cx, cy, r, values, options) {
    var paper = this,
        chart = this.set(),
        rad   = Math.PI / 180;

    // define options
    var o = options || {};
    o.width = o.width || r * .15;

    return chart;
};
```

This snippet establishes a basic option for the width of the donut chart (which defaults to 15 percent the size of the radius). As you develop the script, you'll add more options.

Drawing an Arc

Before getting into any data processing, start with the visuals. When it comes to donut charts, the basic graphical building block is an arc, like the one shown in Figure 10-18.

FIGURE 10-18: Donut charts are made up of arcs like this one.

To draw these arcs, you need to create a reusable function that positions and draws each of the curves. Fortunately, you already have all the information you need from the settings; you just have to use some basic math and trigonometry:

```
function draw_arc(startAngle, endAngle) {
  // get the coordinates
  var x1 = cx + r * Math.cos(-startAngle * rad),
      y1 = cy + r * Math.sin(-startAngle * rad),
      x2 = cx + r * Math.cos(-endAngle * rad),
      y2 = cy + r * Math.sin(-endAngle * rad);

  // draw the arc
  return paper.path(
    ["M", x1, y1,
     "A", r, r, 0, +(endAngle - startAngle > 180), 0, x2, y2
    ]
  );
}
```

This function takes the angles for the arc and determines the coordinates for the start and end points of the shape. If you don't understand the trigonometry, don't worry too much. Basically, you need to multiply the radius by the cosine and sine of the angle to get the x and y offsets respectively. Add these to the center coordinates and you have the coordinates for your arc.

> **TIP** *If you'd like to learn more about circle trigonometry, visit* www.mathsisfun.com/sine-cosine-tangent.html. *Despite the URL, we make no promises that math is fun.*

The next step is drawing the arc with the same path() API you used earlier this chapter. Here, the script creates a standard SVG path string from the data. The path starts at (x1,y1) and then draws an arc with radius r to (x2,y2).

If you hardcode values for cx, cy, and r, and pass in a startAngle and endAngle, you should see something like Figure 10-19.

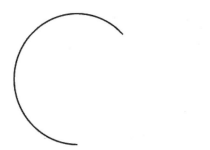

FIGURE 10-19: This arc is drawn using basic trig.

Although you could stop right here and just widen the stroke for each arc, you're going to draw an entire outline. Drawing the whole shape provides more versatility—for example, enabling you to add a stroke to the shape itself. But it also adds some complexity because you need to draw a second arc inside the first, and add that to the original shape:

Seasonality Chart: AMZN,$SPX

| −2009 | −2010 | −2011 | −2012 | −2013 |

Performance of AMZN From 2009 to 2013

Jan Feb Mar Apr May Jun Jul Aug Sep Oct Nov Dec

SOURCE: STOCKCHARTS.COM

WHEN COMPARING DATA SETS WITH THE SAME UNIT OF MEASURE, AS WITH THIS SEASONALITY CHART OF AMAZON STOCK PRICES OVER 5 YEARS, LINE CHARTS CAN BE SHOWN ONE ABOVE THE OTHER. (CHAPTER 3)

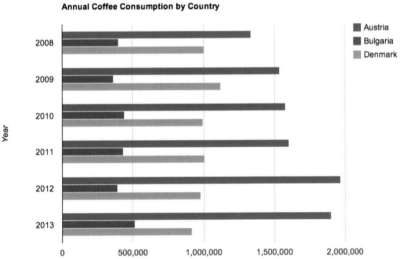

Annual Coffee Consumption by Country

- Austria
- Bulgaria
- Denmark

A GROUPED BAR CHART CAN ADD ANOTHER PERSPECTIVE TO THE DATA; HERE YOU SEE THAT AUSTRIANS DRINK MUCH MORE COFFEE YEAR-TO-YEAR THAN OTHER EUROPEAN COUNTRIES. (CHAPTER 3)

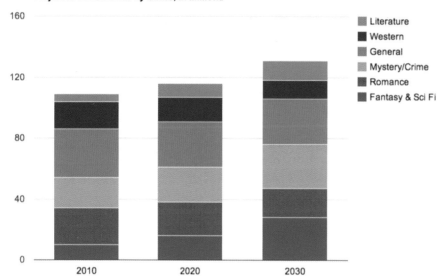

Projected eBook Sales by Genre, in Millions

Legend:
- Literature
- Western
- General
- Mystery/Crime
- Romance
- Fantasy & Sci Fi

STACKED BAR CHARTS, LIKE THIS COLUMN VERSION, SHOW AGGREGATE TOTALS AS WELL AS INDIVIDUAL LEVELS. (CHAPTER 3)

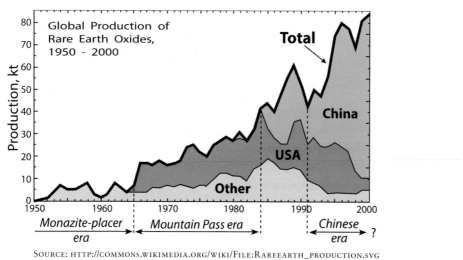

Global Production of Rare Earth Oxides, 1950 - 2000

STACKED AREA CHARTS ENABLE YOU TO QUICKLY GRASP OVERALL TRENDS AS WELL AS SPECIFIC DATA SET CHANGES. (CHAPTER 3)

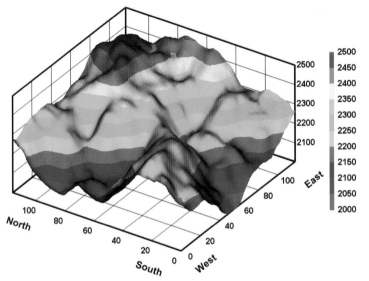

Source: DPlot Graph Software

SURFACE MAPS USE COLOR TO IDENTIFY A RANGE OF DATA, AS SHOWN BY THE LEGEND ON THE RIGHT OF THE FIGURE. (CHAPTER 3)

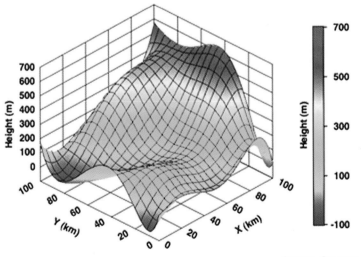

Source: Gigawiz

COMBINE SOLID AND WIREFRAME SURFACE CHARTS TO GET A FINER DEGREE OF DATA VISUALIZATION WITH THE EASY READABILITY OF COLOR RANGES. (CHAPTER 3)

MAP CHARTS CAN REFERENCE THE GLOBE WHILE HIGHLIGHTING TARGETED COUNTRIES. (CHAPTER 3)

Region	Sales	Mean
Northeast	$100,000.00	$142,857.14
Southeast	$75,000.00	$142,857.14
Midwest	$125,000.00	$142,857.14
Mid-Atlantic	$125,000.00	$142,857.14
Southwest	$75,000.00	$142,857.14
Northwest	$100,000.00	$142,857.14
California	$400,000.00	$142,857.14

THIS SHOWS THE SAME DATA USING TWO SEPARATE DATA VISUALIZATIONS. (CHAPTER 7)

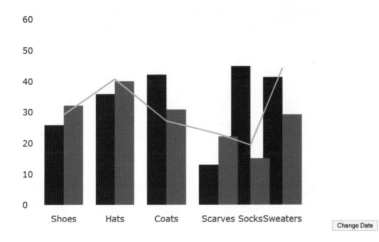

THE CUSTOM CANVAS CHART YOU ARE BUILDING ANIMATES BETWEEN TWO DATA SETS TO SHOW NEW DATA BEING INTRODUCED OVER TIME. (CHAPTER 9)

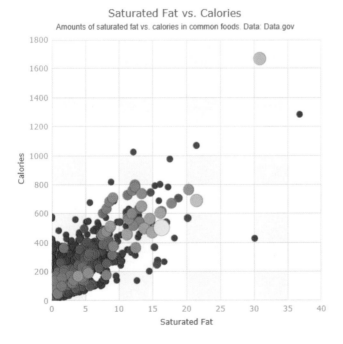

THIS BUBBLE CHART WAS CREATED USING IGDATACHART. (CHAPTER 12)

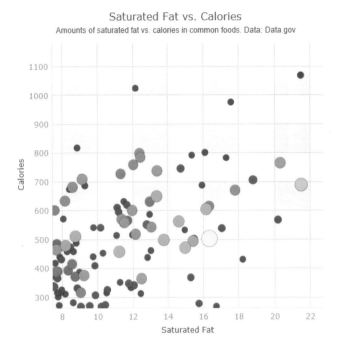

THE BUBBLE CHART HAS BEEN ZOOMED. (CHAPTER 12)

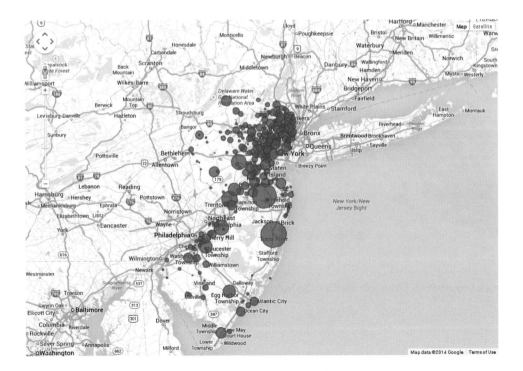

THIS SHOWS GOOGLE MAPS WITH BUBBLE MARKERS DISPLAYING LIBRARY VISITS. (CHAPTER 13)

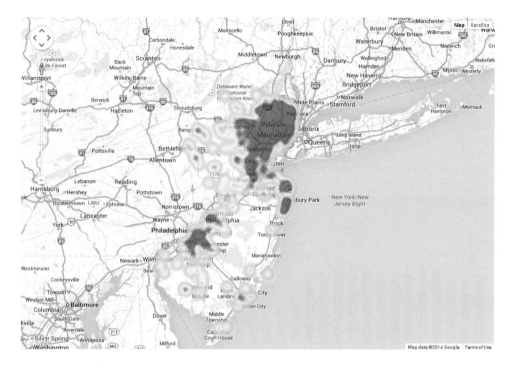

THIS SHOWS A HEAT MAP OF NEW JERSEY LIBRARY DENSITY USING THE GOOGLE MAPS API. (CHAPTER 13)

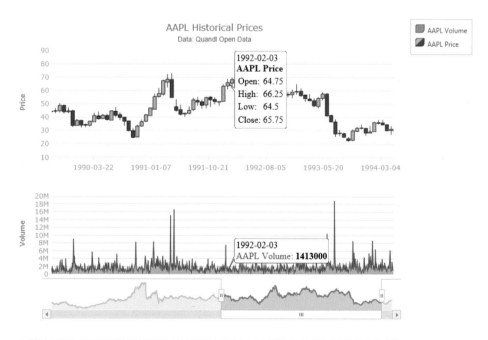

A VOLUME CHART IS SYNCHRONIZED WITH A PRICE CHART. (CHAPTER 14)

Census Data - New York

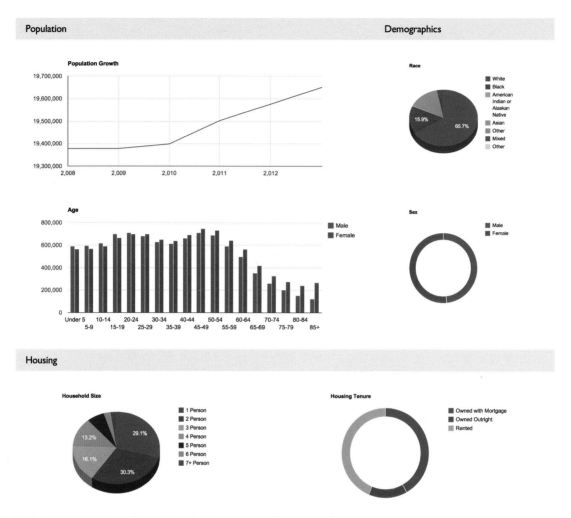

THIS SCREENSHOT SHOWS THE LARGER LAYOUT FOR THE DASHBOARD. (CHAPTER 15)

```
// interior radius
var rin = r - o.width;

// draw arc
function draw_arc(startAngle, endAngle) {
  // get the coordinates
  var x1 = cx + r * Math.cos(-startAngle * rad),
      y1 = cy + r * Math.sin(-startAngle * rad),
      x2 = cx + r * Math.cos(-endAngle * rad),
      y2 = cy + r * Math.sin(-endAngle * rad),

      xin1 = cx + rin * Math.cos(-startAngle * rad),
      yin1 = cy + rin * Math.sin(-startAngle * rad),
      xin2 = cx + rin * Math.cos(-endAngle * rad),
      yin2 = cy + rin * Math.sin(-endAngle * rad);

  // draw the arc
  return paper.path(
    ["M", xin1, yin1,
    "L", x1, y1,
    "A", r, r, 0, +(endAngle - startAngle > 180), 0, x2, y2,
    "L", xin2, yin2,
    "A", rin, rin, 0, +(endAngle - startAngle > 180), 1, xin1, yin1, "z"]
  );
}
```

Here, the script first calculates the interior radius (`rin`) using the radius and the width option you established earlier. Next, it uses the same trigonometry technique to determine the start and end coordinates of the interior arc ((`xin1`,`yin1`) and (`xin2`,`yin2`)).

Then, the path string gets a little more complicated:

1. It starts at the interior start point.
2. It draws a line to the exterior start point.
3. It traces an arc to the exterior end point.
4. It draws a line to the interior end point.
5. It closes the shape by drawing an arc back to the interior start point.

Last but not least, you color these shapes. But rather than hardcode color values, it's better to keep things open ended. A good approach is to add a general style option that you can populate as needed with fill colors, stroke settings, and so on.

```
function draw_arc(startAngle, endAngle, styleOpts) {
  // get the coordinates
  var x1 = cx + r * Math.cos(-startAngle * rad),
      y1 = cy + r * Math.sin(-startAngle * rad),
      x2 = cx + r * Math.cos(-endAngle * rad),
      y2 = cy + r * Math.sin(-endAngle * rad),

      xin1 = cx + rin * Math.cos(-startAngle * rad),
      yin1 = cy + rin * Math.sin(-startAngle * rad),
```

```
      xin2 = cx + rin * Math.cos(-endAngle * rad),
      yin2 = cy + rin * Math.sin(-endAngle * rad);

  // draw the arc
  return paper.path(
    ["M", xin1, yin1,
     "L", x1, y1,
     "A", r, r, 0, +(endAngle - startAngle > 180), 0, x2, y2,
     "L", xin2, yin2,
     "A", rin, rin, 0, +(endAngle - startAngle > 180), 1, xin1, yin1, "z"]
  ).attr(styleOpts);
}
```

Here the function allows you to pass a general `styleOpts` value with any styling information you need. Finally, let's take a look at usage:

```
Raphael.fn.donutChart = function (cx, cy, r, values, options) {
  var paper = this,
      chart = this.set(),
      rad   = Math.PI / 180;

  // define options
  var o = options || {};
  o.width = o.width || r * .15;

  // interior radius
  var rin = r - o.width;

  // draw arc
  function draw_arc(startAngle, endAngle, styleOpts) {
    // get the coordinates
    var x1 = cx + r * Math.cos(-startAngle * rad),
        y1 = cy + r * Math.sin(-startAngle * rad),
        x2 = cx + r * Math.cos(-endAngle * rad),
        y2 = cy + r * Math.sin(-endAngle * rad),

        xin1 = cx + rin * Math.cos(-startAngle * rad),
        yin1 = cy + rin * Math.sin(-startAngle * rad),
        xin2 = cx + rin * Math.cos(-endAngle * rad),
        yin2 = cy + rin * Math.sin(-endAngle * rad);

    // draw the arc
    return paper.path(
      ["M", xin1, yin1,
       "L", x1, y1,
       "A", r, r, 0, +(endAngle - startAngle > 180), 0, x2, y2,
       "L", xin2, yin2,
       "A", rin, rin, 0, +(endAngle - startAngle > 180), 1, xin1, yin1, "z"]
    ).attr(styleOpts);
  }

  draw_arc(0, 240, { fill: '#f0f', stroke: 0 });

  return chart;
};
```

```
var paper = Raphael(document.getElementById('donut-chart'), 250, 250);

paper.donutChart(125, 125, 100, [], { width: 20 });
```

This example renders the arc shown in Figure 10-20, with a pink fill color and no stroke.

FIGURE 10-20: This arc is styled with Raphaël.

Now you've established the basic building blocks for the donut chart graphic. In the coming sections you see how to convert your data into values you can render with this versatile function.

Massaging Data into Usable Values

With the arc function in place, the next step is creating usable values. When it comes to the data in donut charts, they act a lot like pie charts: The only information that matters is percentages. Thus, to render this chart, you have to take a few steps:

1. Fetch the total of all values.

2. Determine the percentage for an individual value.

3. Render that percentage as an angle with the `draw_arc()` function.

4. Start the next arc at the angle where the prior arc stopped.

The first step is really straightforward. Simply loop through the values array you set up earlier to fetch the total:

```
var total = 0;

for (var i = 0, max = values.length; i < max; i++) {
  total += values[i];
}
```

Alternatively, if you aren't worried about backward compatibility for older browsers, you can use the newer `Array.reduce()` method:

```
var total = values.reduce();
```

Next, you need to process and render each individual value. Start with a function that determines what percentage of the donut to render:

```
var angle = 0;

function build_segment(j) {
  var value = values[j],
```

```
        angleplus = 360 * value / total;

    var arc = draw_arc( angle, angle + angleplus );

    angle += angleplus;
}

// build each segment of the chart
for (i = 0; i < max; i++) {
  build_segment(i);
}
```

As you can see, the `build_segment()` function starts by calculating the percentage of the full circle that the segment should occupy. Then it leverages the `draw_arc()` function to render an arc from the starting angle to the ending point. Finally, it increments the angle value to set the starting point for the next segment in the loop.

Next, run the script with a random data set:

```
paper.donutChart(125, 125, 100, [120, 45, 20, 5]);
```

As you can see in Figure 10-21, that script renders the donut chart, but it only renders as outlines. That's because you still need to set the color values.

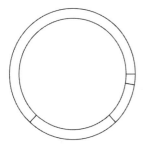

FIGURE 10-21: This screenshot shows the initial donut chart rendering.

Rather than hardcode, you can set the colors up in a way that can be customized:

```
if ( typeof o.colors == 'undefined' ) {
  for (var i = 0, max = values.length; i < max; i++) {
    o.colors.push( Raphael.hsb(i / 10, .75, 1) );
  }
}
```

In the preceding code, the colors are set up using the same options object you used earlier for the chart width. That way, the developer can set the colors if she wants. Alternatively, if the user doesn't set any values, the script uses the Raphaël utility function `hsb()` to create unique colors for each value in the chart. That's a nifty technique that uses the hue to space colors out evenly around the color wheel.

Finally, apply each color in the `build_segment()` loop:

```
function build_segment(j) {
  var value = values[j],
```

```
        angleplus = 360 * value / total,
        styleOpts = {
          fill: o.colors[j]
        };

    var arc = draw_arc( angle, angle + angleplus, styleOpts );

    angle += angleplus;
}
```

Now the script renders the colorful chart shown in Figure 10-22.

FIGURE 10-22: The donut chart has been rendered in color.

Finally, add some customization options for the stroke:

```
o.strokeWidth = o.strokeWidth || 0;
o.strokeColor = o.strokeColor || '#000';
```

and apply them to each segment:

```
function build_segment(j) {
  var value = values[j],
      angleplus = 360 * value / total,
      styleOpts = {
        fill: o.colors[j]
      };

  if ( o.strokeWidth ) {
    styleOpts.stroke = o.strokeColor;
    styleOpts['stroke-width'] = o.strokeWidth;
  }
  else {
    styleOpts.stroke = 'none';
  }

  var arc = draw_arc( angle, angle + angleplus, styleOpts );

  angle += angleplus;
}
```

Here, the stroke is applied if it exists. But as you can see in Figure 10-23, the script now defaults to using no stroke.

FIGURE 10-23: The chart now defaults to strokeless.

Now the plug-in is rendering the chart at its most basic level. Here's the script so far:

```
Raphael.fn.donutChart = function (cx, cy, r, values, options) {
  var paper = this,
      chart = this.set(),
      rad   = Math.PI / 180;

  // define options
  var o = options || {};
  o.width = o.width || r * .15;
  o.strokeWidth = o.strokeWidth || 0;
  o.strokeColor = o.strokeColor || '#000';

  // create colors if not set
  if ( typeof o.colors == 'undefined' ) {
    o.colors = [];

    for (var i = 0, max = values.length; i < max; i++) {
      o.colors.push( Raphael.hsb(i / 10, .75, 1) );
    }
  }

  // interior radius
  var rin = r - o.width;

  // draw arc
  function draw_arc(startAngle, endAngle, styleOpts) {
    // get the coordinates
    var x1 = cx + r * Math.cos(-startAngle * rad),
        y1 = cy + r * Math.sin(-startAngle * rad),
        x2 = cx + r * Math.cos(-endAngle * rad),
        y2 = cy + r * Math.sin(-endAngle * rad),

        xin1 = cx + rin * Math.cos(-startAngle * rad),
        yin1 = cy + rin * Math.sin(-startAngle * rad),
        xin2 = cx + rin * Math.cos(-endAngle * rad),
        yin2 = cy + rin * Math.sin(-endAngle * rad);

    // draw the arc
    return paper.path(
      ["M", xin1, yin1,
```

```
      "L", x1, y1,
      "A", r, r, 0, +(endAngle - startAngle > 180), 0, x2, y2,
      "L", xin2, yin2,
      "A", rin, rin, 0, +(endAngle - startAngle > 180), 1, xin1, yin1, "z"]
    ).attr(styleOpts);
}

// process each segment of the arc and render
function build_segment(j) {
  var value = values[j],
      angleplus = 360 * value / total,
      styleOpts = {
        fill: o.colors[j]
      };

  if ( o.strokeWidth ) {
    styleOpts.stroke = o.strokeColor;
    styleOpts['stroke-width'] = o.strokeWidth;
  }
  else {
    styleOpts.stroke = 'none';
  }

  var arc = draw_arc( angle, angle + angleplus, styleOpts );

  angle += angleplus;
}

var angle = 0,
    total = 0;

// fetch total
for (var i = 0, max = values.length; i < max; i++) {
  total += values[i];
}

// build each segment of the chart
for (i = 0; i < max; i++) {
  build_segment(i);
}

return chart;
};
```

Adding Mouse Interactivity

Now that the script renders the chart, the next step is to add interactivity. Fortunately, setting up a click handler is pretty easy with the SVG event listeners. First, create an option the developer can use for click handlers:

```
o.onclick = o.onclick || function() {};
```

and then apply the handler in the `build_segment()` function:

```
function build_segment(j) {
  var value = values[j],
```

```
        angleplus = 360 * value / total,
        styleOpts = {
          fill: o.colors[j]
        };

  if ( o.strokeWidth ) {
    styleOpts.stroke = o.strokeColor;
    styleOpts['stroke-width'] = o.strokeWidth;
  }
  else {
    styleOpts.stroke = 'none';
  }

  var arc = draw_arc( angle, angle + angleplus, styleOpts );

  arc.click( function() {
    o.onclick(j);
  });

  angle += angleplus;
}
```

As you can see, the script applies a simple click handler to the arc that is returned from the draw_arc() function. Next, add handlers for mouseover and mouseout:

```
o.onmouseover = o.onmouseover || function() {};
o.onmouseout = o.onmouseout || function() {};
```

Now apply the handler:

```
arc.mouseover(function () {
  o.onmouseover(j);
}).mouseout(function () {
  o.onmouseout(j);
});
```

Finally, add some visual flare and animate the segments on mouseover:

```
arc.mouseover(function () {
  arc.stop().animate({transform: 's' + o.animationScale + ' ' + o.animationScale +
  ' ' + cx + " " + cy}, o.animationDuration, o.animationEasing);

  o.onmouseover(j);
}).mouseout(function () {
  arc.stop().animate({transform: ""}, o.animationDuration, o.animationEasing);

  o.onmouseout(j);
});
```

As you can see, the script leverages Raphaël's animate() API to adjust the scale of the segments on mouseover. It starts by stopping any queued animations with stop(), and then goes into a transform animation. Of course, you also need to set up defaults for the animation options:

```
o.animationDuration = o.animationDuration || 300;
o.animationScale = o.animationScale || 1.1;
o.animationEasing = o.animationEasing || 'backOut';
```

Finally, make sure that the plug-in returns the full set of SVG shapes. If you remember, when you first set up the script, you cached a set of SVG shapes:

```
var chart = this.set();
```

Keep this list fresh by pushing each new arc to the set at the end of the `build_segment()` function:

```
chart.push(arc);
```

Labeling the Data

Last but not least, you need to label the chart using Raphaël's `text()` API. First set up some options with smart defaults:

```
o.labels = o.labels || [];
o.labelOffsetX = o.labelOffsetX || 50;
o.labelOffsetY = o.labelOffsetY || 30;
```

Here, the `labels` option allows the user to pass an array of text labels, and `labelOffsetX` and `labelOffsetY` control how far away to render the labels from the chart.

Next, in the `build_segment()` loop, determine which label to include and where:

```
// create labels if they exist
if ( o.labels[j] !== 'undefined' ) {
  var halfAngle = angle + (angleplus / 2),
      label = draw_label( o.labels[j], halfAngle );
}
```

In this snippet, the script first centers the label by calculating the halfway point of the arc. Then it passes this angle along with the text for the label to the `draw_label()` function. That function looks like this:

```
function draw_label( label, angle ) {
    var labelX = cx + ( r + o.labelOffsetX ) * Math.cos( -angle * rad ),
        labelY = cy + ( r + o.labelOffsetY ) * Math.sin( -angle * rad ),
        txt    = paper.text( labelX, labelY, label );

    return txt;
}
```

Here, the script uses more trigonometry to calculate the coordinates for the label. These are adjusted by the values in the offset settings and then passed into Raphaël's `text()` API along with the text for the label. Finally, make sure to pass in your labels:

```
paper.donutChart(200, 200, 100, [120, 45, 20, 5], {
  labels: [
    'tacos',
    'pizzas',
    'burgers',
    'salads'
  ]
});
```

The result is shown in Figure 10-24. As you can see, the styling of these labels leaves something to be desired.

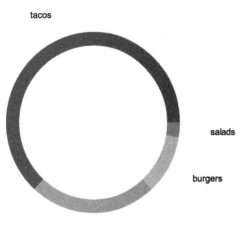

FIGURE 10-24: Custom labels have been added to the donut chart.

Finalize the script by adding some basic styling settings, and make sure to color each label to match its segment:

```
function draw_label( label, angle, styleOpts ) {
  var style = {};

  style.fill = styleOpts.fill || '#000';
  style['font-size'] = styleOpts['font-size'] || 20;

  var labelX = cx + ( r + o.labelOffsetX ) * Math.cos( -angle * rad ),
      labelY = cy + ( r + o.labelOffsetY ) * Math.sin( -angle * rad ),
      txt    = paper.text( labelX, labelY, label ).attr( style );

  return txt;
}
```

That adds a `styleOpts` argument to the script, with some basic defaults for the color and font size. Next, pass the color in the `build_segment()` loop:

```
if ( o.labels[j] !== 'undefined' ) {
  var halfAngle = angle + (angleplus / 2),
      label = draw_label( o.labels[j], halfAngle, {
        fill: o.colors[j]
      });
}
```

Now the labels are looking much better, as you can see in Figure 10-25.

Last but not least, make sure to add this label to the main chart object so the labels get returned along with the other shapes in this SVG:

```
if ( typeof label != 'undefined' ) chart.push( label );
```

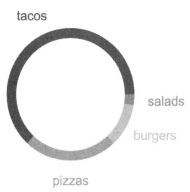

FIGURE 10-25: After styling the labels, the donut chart is complete.

Wrapping Up

Finally, have one last look at the plug-in—this time with the code all put together:

```
Raphael.fn.donutChart = function (cx, cy, r, values, options) {
  var paper = this,
      chart = this.set(),
      rad   = Math.PI / 180;

  // define options
  var o = options || {};
  o.width = o.width || r * .15;
  o.strokeWidth = o.strokeWidth || 0;
  o.strokeColor = o.strokeColor || '#000';

  o.onclick = o.onclick || function() {};
  o.onmouseover = o.onmouseover || function() {};
  o.onmouseout = o.onmouseout || function() {};

  o.animationDuration = o.animationDuration || 300;
  o.animationScale = o.animationScale || 1.1;
  o.animationEasing = o.animationEasing || 'backOut';

  o.labels = o.labels || [];
  o.labelOffsetX = o.labelOffsetX || 50;
  o.labelOffsetY = o.labelOffsetY || 30;

  // create colors if not set
  if ( typeof o.colors == 'undefined' ) {
    o.colors = [];

    for (var i = 0, max = values.length; i < max; i++) {
      o.colors.push( Raphael.hsb(i / 10, .75, 1) );
    }
  }
```

```javascript
// interior radius
var rin = r - o.width;

// draw arc
function draw_arc(startAngle, endAngle, styleOpts) {
  // get the coordinates
  var x1 = cx + r * Math.cos(-startAngle * rad),
      y1 = cy + r * Math.sin(-startAngle * rad),
      x2 = cx + r * Math.cos(-endAngle * rad),
      y2 = cy + r * Math.sin(-endAngle * rad),

      xin1 = cx + rin * Math.cos(-startAngle * rad),
      yin1 = cy + rin * Math.sin(-startAngle * rad),
      xin2 = cx + rin * Math.cos(-endAngle * rad),
      yin2 = cy + rin * Math.sin(-endAngle * rad);

  // draw the arc
  return paper.path(
    ["M", xin1, yin1,
     "L", x1, y1,
     "A", r, r, 0, +(endAngle - startAngle > 180), 0, x2, y2,
     "L", xin2, yin2,
     "A", rin, rin, 0, +(endAngle - startAngle > 180), 1, xin1, yin1, "z"]
  ).attr(styleOpts);
}

// add label at given angle
function draw_label( label, angle, styleOpts ) {
  var style = {};

  style.fill = styleOpts.fill || '#000';
  style['font-size'] = styleOpts['font-size'] || 20;

  var labelX = cx + ( r + o.labelOffsetX ) * Math.cos( -angle * rad ),
      labelY = cy + (r + o.labelOffsetY) * Math.sin( -angle * rad ),
      txt    = paper.text( labelX, labelY, label ).attr( style );

  return txt;
}

// process each segment of the arc and render
function build_segment(j) {
  var value = values[j],
      angleplus = 360 * value / total,
      styleOpts = {
        fill: o.colors[j]
      };

  if ( o.strokeWidth ) {
    styleOpts.stroke = o.strokeColor;
    styleOpts['stroke-width'] = o.strokeWidth;
  }
  else {
    styleOpts.stroke = 'none';
  }
```

```
    // draw the arc
    var arc = draw_arc( angle, angle + angleplus, styleOpts );

    // create labels if they exist
    if ( o.labels[j] !== 'undefined' ) {
      var halfAngle = angle + (angleplus / 2),
          label = draw_label( o.labels[j], halfAngle, {
            fill: o.colors[j]
          });
    }

    // mouse event handlers
    arc.click( function() {
      o.onclick(j);
    });

    arc.mouseover(function () {
      arc.stop().animate({transform: 's' + o.animationScale + ' ' +
      o.animationScale + ' ' + cx + " " + cy}, o.animationDuration,
      o.animationEasing);

      o.onmouseover(j);
    }).mouseout(function () {
      arc.stop().animate({transform: ""}, o.animationDuration, o.animationEasing);

      o.onmouseout(j);
    });

    angle += angleplus;

    chart.push( arc );

    if ( typeof label != 'undefined' ) chart.push( label );
  }

  var angle = 0,
      total = 0;

  // fetch total
  for (var i = 0, max = values.length; i < max; i++) {
    total += values[i];
  }

  // build each segment of the chart
  for (i = 0; i < max; i++) {
    build_segment(i);
  }

  return chart;
};

var paper = Raphael(document.getElementById('donut-chart'), 400, 400);

paper.donutChart(200, 200, 100, [120, 45, 20, 5], {
```

```
    labels: [
      'tacos',
      'pizzas',
      'burgers',
      'salads'
    ]
  });
```

To recap:

1. The script starts by creating an options framework with smart defaults.

2. It defines its first core function, `draw_arc()`, which renders each segment of the donut chart using basic trigonometry and Raphaël's `path()` API.

3. The second core function, `draw_label()`, renders each label at the appropriate location using Raphaël's `text()` API.

4. The third core function, `build_segment()`, first massages the data into a usable format and then passes the refined data to `draw_arc()` and `draw_label()`. Then it applies mouse event listeners, both for a general click event and also to animate the segments on mouseover.

5. The script calculates the total and initiates the `build_segment()` loop to render the chart.

As shown in Figure 10-25, the script is rendering the donut chart nicely, but there's still room for improvement. Mainly you could add more options to make the plug-in more versatile. As an exercise, try adding customizable settings for the following:

➤ Altering the `startAngle` of the chart

➤ Rendering the segments clockwise or counterclockwise

➤ Creating a loading animation that expands the donut when it first appears on the screen

SUMMARY

This chapter explained how to use the SVG library Raphaël to render custom charts. You started by getting familiar with the basics of Raphaël: drawing basic shapes and adding animation and mouse event listeners. You also learned techniques for importing your own vector graphics to use with the library.

Next you were introduced to gRaphaël, a simple charting library for Raphaël. With gRaphaël, you explored rendering a variety of different visualizations, from pie charts to line graphs and bar graphs.

Finally, you followed a practical example to create a donut chart plug-in for Raphaël. In this plug-in, you leveraged your knowledge of Raphaël along with basic trigonometry to render a custom graphic.

In the coming chapters, you discover more charting solutions, including the highly interactive D3, as well as various mapping and time series libraries.

11

Introducing D3

WHAT'S IN THIS CHAPTER

- ➤ Getting started with D3
- ➤ Creating, manipulating, and destroying data-driven elements
- ➤ Working with D3 transitions
- ➤ Dealing with visually complex, nested data structures.
- ➤ Exploring D3's toolkit of functions for simplifying common tasks.
- ➤ Building a file system visualization using a built-in D3 layout.

> **CODE DOWNLOAD** *The wrox.com code downloads for this chapter are found at* www.wrox.com/go/javascriptandjqueryanalysis *on the Download Code tab. The code is in the chapter 11 download and individually named according to the names throughout the chapter.*

D3 is a JavaScript library for general purpose visualization. D3 possesses a powerful selection model for declaratively describing how data should be mapped to the visual elements. It comes bundled with a vast variety of helper functions that can be leveraged when building visualizations and is easily extensible to support custom functionality.

Unlike some other visualization libraries, D3 does not offer any prepackaged "standard" visualizations (bar chart, pie chart, and so on), although you can create your own. If you are only interested in standard quick visualizations then you should check out some of the libraries written on top of D3, such as NVD3 (http://nvd3.org/) and C3.js (http://c3js.org/).

On the surface, D3 appears to be similar to jQuery with regard to selecting and manipulating existing elements on the page. D3 adds a mechanism for adding or removing elements to match a dataset, which makes it particularly apt for data visualization.

The true power (and joy) of using D3 comes from the ability to take a data set and turn it into a fully customized interactive visualization by assigning visual elements to data items and leveraging the vast suite of built-in helper functions.

Imagine looking at a dataset of all U.S. hospitals that list the name, city, state, owner, and location for each facility. See Figure 11-1 for an example of what some rows for the dataset would look like.

(...	name	city	state	lat	lon	owner
0	"Abbeville Area Medical...	"Abbeville"	"SC"	34.160624	-82.382409	"Voluntary Non-Profit – Pr...
1	"Abbeville General Hosp...	"Abbeville"	"LA"	29.972204	-92.106844	"Government – Hospital Dis...
2	"Abbott Northwestern Ho...	"Minneapol...	"MN"	44.952012	-93.262552	"Voluntary Non-Profit – Pr...
3	"Abilene Regional Medic...	"Abilene"	"TX"	32.368408	-99.74275	"Proprietary"
4	"Abington Memorial Hosp...	"Abington"	"PA"	40.118979	-75.11928	"Voluntary Non-Profit – Pr...

FIGURE 11-1: This table shows the first five rows of the hospital data set.

You could be interested in the distribution of hospitals by state visualized as a bar chart, as shown in Figure 11-2. Alternatively you could grab a geo JSON representation of the United States from the census bureau, pick one of D3's geo-projection functions, and plot every hospital on a map. You could then use a Voronoi layout (discussed in Chapter 16) to visualize each hospital's catchment area as shown in Figure 11-3. These examples, with fully annotated source code, can be found in the us-hospitals directory in the Chapter 11 code examples on the companion website.

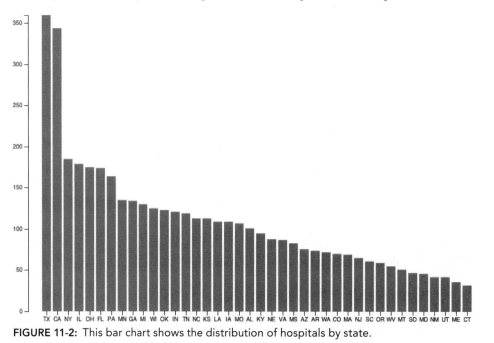

FIGURE 11-2: This bar chart shows the distribution of hospitals by state.

This chapter dives into D3's core concepts: element selections, data joining, and transitions. The D3 community has experienced meteoric growth, and there is no shortage of examples, tutorials, and how-tos online. The aim here is to give you a good framework for understanding any D3 visualization that you might encounter in the wild and give you the ability to remix them or create your own.

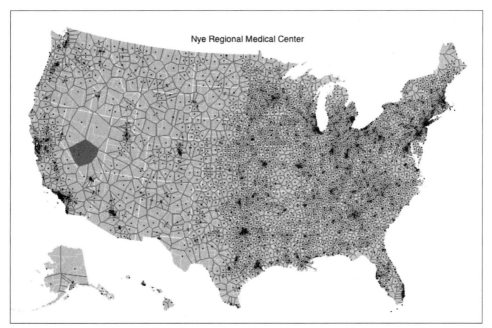

FIGURE 11-3: This geo-visualization shows U.S. hospitals with their areas of influence.

GETTING STARTED

The following is the basic structure of the HTML that would house a D3 visualization. (You can find this file in the `blank/index.html` directory for Chapter 11 on the companion website.)

```html
<!DOCTYPE html>
<html>
  <head>
    <meta charset='utf-8'>
    <script src="../d3/d3.js" charset="utf-8"></script>
    <link rel="stylesheet" href="../common.css">
    <link rel="stylesheet" href="style.css">
    <title>My visualization</title>
  </head>
  <body>
    <script src="script.js"></script>
  </body>
</html>
```

The examples in this chapter use a local copy of D3 so that they may function offline, but a hosted version is also available. To get the latest release in your project, copy this snippet into the `<head>` part of the document:

```html
<script src="http://d3js.org/d3.v3.min.js" charset="utf-8"></script>
```

Alternatively, you can play around with D3 by using an online web development playground such as `http://jsfiddle.net/`. You simply need to select D3 in the sidebar as a library to load and start playing.

DOM and SVG

D3 acts on elements within the page. It can manipulate any element that implements the Document Object Model (DOM) interface. This includes HTML elements (like `<div>` and `<table>`) and SVG elements.

SVG stands for Scalable Vector Graphics, and is a standard that can create visuals out of vector primitives such as lines and circles. SVG is a good choice for visualization because it is based on a DOM, allowing its elements to have events and to be manipulated with D3 selections. SVG can also be scaled to any size without degradation of quality. Figure 11-4 shows a very simple SVG element containing four rectangles.

```
<svg>
  <rect x="0" y="30" width="170" height="20" style="fill: rgb(70, 130, 180);"></rect>
  <rect x="0" y="100" width="20" height="20" style="fill: rgb(70, 130, 180);"></rect>
  <rect x="0" y="170" width="73" height="20" style="fill: rgb(70, 130, 180);"></rect>
  <rect x="200" y="100" width="30" height="30" style="fill: rgb(255, 0, 0);"></rect>
</svg>
```

FIGURE 11-4: Shown here is a representation of an SVG element as presented in the Google Chrome inspector panel.

Because SVG maintains a scene graph of the visual elements displayed, there is some overhead ascribed per element. A visualization that involves hundreds of thousands of elements might be more appropriately implemented using the HTML5 Canvas component. Canvas acts as a simple bitmap container to put you in charge of interpreting the locations of mouse events and coordinate systems.

In this chapter the focus is on applying D3 to create SVG graphics, as it is the most common medium for the task.

Unlike some other visualization tools (such as `http://raphaeljs.com/`) D3 expects you to know and understand the underlying technology into which your visualization is going to be rendered (be it SVG or HTML). As such, it is recommended that you have a reference book at hand to be able to look up the correct usage of different elements. One good SVG reference is *SVG Essentials* by J. David Eisenberg and Amelia Bellamy-Royds (O'Reilly Media, 2014).

It should also be noted that modern browsers come with powerful debugging tools that enable you to see the structure of the document in them. This is a great way to familiarize yourself with SVG (and HTML) as you can always examine the structure of any SVG-based visualization you will find online or in this chapter. Right-click any element and select Inspect Element to see the internal structure of the page. Figure 11-5 shows the Inspect Element menu for the visualization in Figure 11-3.

FIGURE 11-5: The single most useful tool for web development is the inspector console.

.select

The principal data structure in D3 is the *selection*. Selections represent sets of elements and provide operators that can be applied to the selected elements. These operators wrap the element's DOM interface, setting attributes (`attr`), inline styles (`style`), and text content (`text`). Operator values are specified either as constants or functions; the latter are evaluated for each element.

The `selection.select(selector)` function uses a CSS selector string to find the first element within the `selection` that matches the `selector`. It then constructs a new selection containing the found element. Calling `d3.select(selector)` runs over the entire document.

Start with a document containing an SVG with a single rectangle. In reality, you would rarely start from this state, but bear with it for now:

```
<svg>
  <rect x="150" y="100" width="60" height="123"></rect>
</svg>
```

Now perform a simple selection:

```
var svg = d3.select("svg")

svg.select("rect")
  .attr("width", 100)
  .attr("height", 100)
  .style("fill", "steelblue")
  .style("stroke-width", 3)
  .style("stroke", "#FFC000")
```

The result is a square, as shown in Figure 11-6. (You can find this file in the `select/script.js` directory in the Chapter 11 code examples on the companion website.)

The preceding code selects the `<svg>` element in the page and stores it in a variable called `svg`. It then selects the `<rect>` element within `svg` and modifies its attributes and styles. For brevity, the `attr` and `style` operations are chained together because each returns the selection.

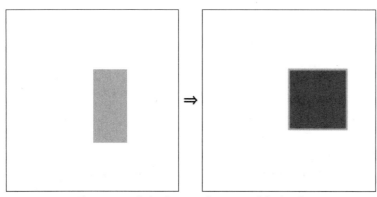

FIGURE 11-6: This rectangle had its attributes modified to become a square.

.selectAll

Although .select is an invaluable tool, your visualization will rarely be composed of a single element. .selectAll works like .select but selects all elements that match. The elements in the selection created by .selectAll can be manipulated concurrently using the attr and style operators.

These operators can receive two types of input:

➤ They can receive a value (.attr("x", 0)) and apply that value to all the elements.

➤ They can receive a function (.attr("y", function(d, i) { return i * 70 + 30 })) that will "run" once per element to compute an element-specific value for the attribute. The first parameter to this function, commonly labeled d, represents the data associated to the element (which is examined in the next section), and the second parameter, commonly labeled i, represents the index of the element in the DOM.

Start with a document containing an SVG with several rectangles:

```
<svg>
  <rect x="150" y="100" width="60" height="123"></rect>
  <rect x="80" y="10" width="20" height="50"></rect>
  <rect x="30" y="130" width="60" height="23"></rect>
</svg>
```

Now perform a simple selectAll (refer to the /selectAll/script.js directory in the Chapter 11 code on the companion website):

```
var svg = d3.select("svg")
svg.selectAll("rect")
  .attr("x", 0)
  .attr("y", function(d, i) { return i * 70 + 30 })
  .attr("width", function(d, i) { return i * 50 + 100 })
  .attr("height", 20)
  .style("fill", "steelblue")
```

As you can see, in Figure 11-7, the three rectangles have been repositioned to resemble a bar chart (albeit a bar chart that is not representing any kind of data).

The `<svg>` is selected like before. After all the `<rect>`s in the SVG are selected, you apply a series of attributes and styles to all of them.

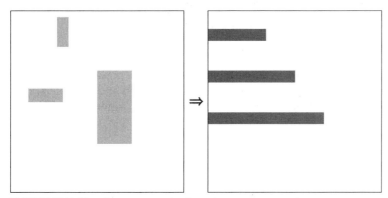

FIGURE 11-7: The three rectangles have been rearranged.

Notice these lines of code:

```
.attr("y", function(d, i) { return i * 70 + 30 })
.attr("width", function(d, i) { return i * 50 + 100 })
```

Instead of a value, you provide the `attr` operator with a function that will be evaluated for every element in the selection. By using the index, you specified different `y` and `width` attributes for every element making the bars appear similar to a bar chart. The actual formulas used to size the bars (`i * 70 + 30`) in this example are arbitrary; soon you find out how to connect this to real data.

D3 always interprets the argument provided to the operands as a function so writing this:

```
.style("fill", "steelblue")
```

is simply shorthand for this:

```
.style("fill", function() {
  return "steelblue"
})
```

.data() (Also Known As Data Joining)

Now that you have seen the basics of how to select elements and assign their attributes declaratively, it's time to dive into the heart of D3: joining data to visual elements.

The `selection.data` operator binds an array of data to the elements of the selection. The first argument is the data to be bound— specified as an array of arbitrary values (such as numbers, strings, or objects). By default the members of the data array are joined to the elements by their index. This behavior can be modified by supplying a key function, which is covered later in the "Key Functions" section.

When data is joined with a selection of elements, three new selections are created:

➤ Elements that already represent data but might need to be updated (update)

➤ Data that has no element representing it yet (enter)

➤ Elements that no longer have data to represent (exit)

The D3 terms "enter" and "exit" originate from the metaphor of directions in theatrical scripts. Metaphorically the datum is an actor, and the elements are costumes. When an actor enters the stage he needs to put on a costume, which is what the audience sees. Similarly, when an actor exits the stage he disappears as far as the audience is concerned.

Let's examine these new selections one-by-one.

Update

The new selection returned by the .data function is the update selection. It represents the elements in the original selection, which were associated with a datum from the provided array. (You can find the following code in the data-update/script.js file for Chapter 11 on the companion website.)

```
var svg = d3.select("svg")

var selection = svg.selectAll("rect")
  .data([170, 20, 73])

selection
  .attr("x", 0)
  .attr("y", function(d, i) { return i * 70 + 30 })
  .attr("width", function(d) { return d })
  .attr("height", 20)
  .style("fill", "steelblue")
```

By adding data to the selection with the .data([170, 20, 73]) call, you are associating the data to the three rectangles that already exist on the page. If there was some data already associated with the elements from a previous data join it would be replaced at this point.

After the data is joined to the elements, you can use the .attr and .style operators to update the visual properties of the elements based on the data. The width of every rectangle in the example represents the number associated with that element because the width attribute is specified as function of the data: .attr("width", function(d) { return d }).

The result of this operation is shown in Figure 11-8

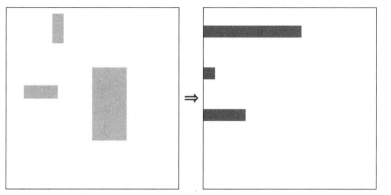

FIGURE 11-8: The three rectangles that were bound to data and sized accordingly.

Enter

In the previous example there were, conveniently, exactly as many data points as rectangles on the screen. Had there been more data points, they would not have found a rectangle to represent them and would have not been visible. Those points need to "enter" the scene by creating new elements to represent them. (The following code is in the `data-enter/script.js` file in the Chapter 11 code download on the companion website.)

```
var svg = d3.select("svg")

var selection = svg.selectAll("rect")
  .data([170, 20, 73, 50])

selection
  .attr("x", 0)
  .attr("y", function(d, i) { return i * 70 + 30 })
  .attr("width", function(d) { return d })
  .attr("height", 20)
  .style("fill", "steelblue")

selection.enter().append("rect")
  .attr("x", 200)
  .attr("y", 100)
  .attr("width", 30)
  .attr("height", 30)
  .style("fill", "red")
```

By adding more data than there are elements you are forcing the unmatched datum (50 in this case) to be placed in the enter selection (accessible with `selection.enter()`).

> **NOTE** *Because selections contain elements, the return value of the* `.enter()` *function is actually a pseudo-selection as it contains placeholders where the elements will be added. It only becomes a selection when* `.append` *is called on it. As a result* `.enter().append(...)` *are always called one after the other. The new elements created by the* `.append` *are attached as children of the element of the parent selection; in this case it is the* `svg` *element.*

As shown in Figure 11-9 the extra datum is now represented by the square off to the side, although it is probably not the final result you want. It would be better if the new element followed the same display rules as the existing elements. To achieve that, you could copy the declarative statements

```
.attr("x", 0)
.attr("y", function(d, i) { return i * 70 + 30 })
.attr("width", function(d) { return d })
.attr("height", 20)
.style("fill", "steelblue")
```

to the enter selection, but because this is such a common use case and repeating code is a bad idea, D3 provides a shortcut:

```
var svg = d3.select("svg")

var selection = svg.selectAll("rect")
  .data([170, 20, 73, 50])

selection.enter().append("rect")

selection
  .attr("x", 0)
  .attr("y", function(d, i) { return i * 70 + 30 })
  .attr("width", function(d) { return d })
  .attr("height", 20)
  .style("fill", "steelblue")
```

Look in the `data-enter-shortcut/script.js` file in the Chapter 11 download for this code.

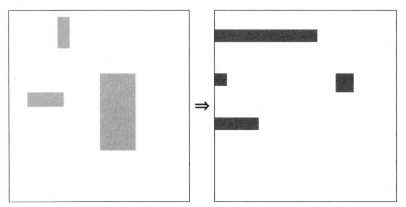

FIGURE 11-9: The extra datum has been added, but it needs to be restyled.

Figure 11-10 shows the new element positioned and styled by the declarations on the update selection.

By calling `.enter().append()` you are telling D3 that you want new data elements to be added to the visualization. Doing this before making any updates ensures that the same changes will be applied to both existing (matched by the initial selection) and new elements (created with `.enter().append()`). If for some reason you wanted to apply some changes to the existing elements and not to the new elements you would have to make your updates before calling `.enter().append()`. This is highly unusual, so make sure you know why you are doing it.

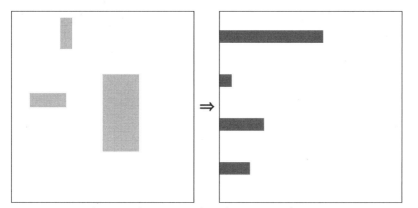

FIGURE 11-10: The new element matches the existing elements.

All previous examples start with an existing svg element within which some number of rectangles are arbitrarily positioned. The purpose of these examples is to showcase selections, and they aren't realistic. In practice, you will likely start from a blank container (probably an HTML <div> within some page. The first step would then be to append an SVG and start creating elements from scratch.

Applying the previously presented logic to an example without an existing SVG, you get the following, which you can find in the data-enter-blank/script.js file on the companion website:

```
var svg = d3.select("body").append("svg")

var selection = svg.selectAll("rect")
  .data([170, 20, 73, 50])

selection.enter().append("rect")

selection
  .attr("x", 0)
  .attr("y", function(d, i) { return i * 70 + 30 })
  .attr("width", function(d) { return d })
  .attr("height", 20)
  .style("fill", "steelblue")
```

Because there is no <svg> to start with, you had to first append it to the visualization container (which in this case is just the <body> element) with d3.select("body").append("svg"). Otherwise, the code is nearly identical to the previous example:

➤ Start off by selecting all the <rect> elements (of which there are none).

➤ Compute the data join.

➤ Put all four data points into the enter selection, which you position and style.

Figure 11-11 shows the bars (and the containing SVG) being created.

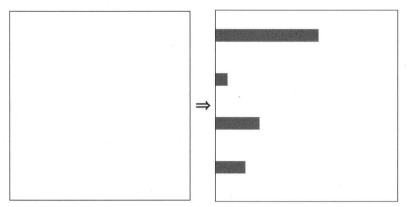

FIGURE 11-11: The bars and the containing SVG are created.

The following is a common pattern that you should be aware of when you browse D3 examples. This code is in the `data-enter-pattern/script.js` file of the Chapter 11 code downloads.

```
var someData = [170, 20, 73, 50]
var svg = d3.select("body").append("svg")

svg.selectAll(".bar").data(someData)
  .enter().append("rect")
    .attr("class", "bar")
    .attr("x", 0)
    .attr("y", function(d, i) { return i * 70 + 30 })
    .attr("width", function(d) { return d })
    .attr("height", 20)
    .style("fill", "steelblue")
```

This code pattern is often used when the elements are added only once to a container that is known to be blank. This pattern would produce the same result as Figure 11-6. There is nothing in this code that you have not seen before, but it tends to trip up people who are new to D3.

Because the `<svg>` element was just created, it must be empty. As a result, calling

```
svg.selectAll(".bar").data(someData)
```

is guaranteed to produce an empty update selection that places all the elements into the enter selection. This allows you to ignore the update selection by not assigning it to a variable; instead, you go straight to `.enter()` to append all of the elements.

Even though the code uses `.selectAll(".bar")`, because there are no elements yet, it will match nothing and create an empty selection. This means you could technically select anything with the same result; in general you should `selectAll` using the same selectors that you apply in the append. It should also be noted that although `.select(".bar")` would also create an empty selection, the data join only works on a selection created with a `selectAll`. The reasons for this are of little consequence.

Exit

The opposite of having more data than visible elements is having too many elements that must then be removed from the screen. The elements that could not be matched to data are placed into the exit selection and can be instantaneously removed by calling `.remove()` on that selection.

If you only ever add elements to an empty container based to data that will not change, you won't encounter a meaningful exit selection. If, however, the displayed data changes from user interaction or with the passage of time then you will likely need to remove the elements that are no longer represented by any data after an update.

Enter/Update/Exit

The following general dynamic example (which is on the companion website as `data-general/script.js`) puts these elements together:

```
var svg = d3.select("body").append("svg")

function updateBars(barData) {
  var selection = svg.selectAll(".bar")
    .data(barData)

  selection.enter().append("rect")
    .attr("class", "bar")
    .attr("x", 0)
    .attr("height", 20)
    .style("fill", "steelblue")

  selection
    .attr("y", function(d, i) { return i * 70 + 30 })
    .attr("width", function(d) { return d })

  selection.exit().remove()
}

updateBars([170, 20, 73]) // step 1

updateBars([34, 100]) // step 2

updateBars([100, 34, 150, 160]) // step 3
```

The example starts with an empty page and appends an `<svg>` element.

The general enter/update/exit code is wrapped in a function `updateBars` that can be called repeatedly to update the bars on the screen with the contents of `barData`.

For clarity and efficiency, you declare all the properties that will never change during the lifetime of the bar on the enter selection and never restate them in the *update*. In the update selection, you restate the data-driven properties for the updating elements as well as for the freshly created elements added from the enter selection.

As shown in Figure 11-12, in Step 1, three bars are created. Step 2 causes the removal of one bar and an update of the two remaining bars. Step 3 tries to represent four data points, causing two bars to be entered.

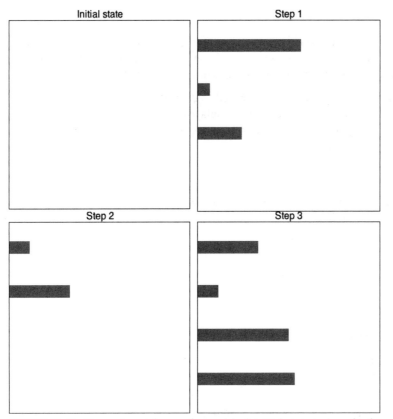

FIGURE 11-12: Three steps take you from a blank initial state to bars for four data points.

It should be noted that, since D3 always leaves the selection in a consistent state, the previous example did not need to create a new selection on every function run. The example could have instead reused the previous selection with the initial selection being the only one that needed to be created:

```
var svg = d3.select("body").append("svg")

var selection = svg.selectAll(".bar")

function updateBars(barData) {
  var selection = selection.data(barData)

  selection.enter().append("rect")
    .attr("class", "bar")
    .attr("x", 0)
    .attr("height", 20)
    .style("fill", "steelblue")

  selection
    .attr("y", function(d, i) { return i * 70 + 30 })
```

```
    .attr("width", function(d) { return d })

  selection.exit().remove()
}
```

The `selection` reference would still need to be updated after every `.data()` call as it creates a new selection. This would be a more efficient than the original example but would only work if the container selection (`svg` in this case) isn't being dynamically updated.

A More Complex Example

This section provides a slightly more complex example to illustrate some more interesting facets of working with enter/update/exit.

The example develops a top trend viewer. Imagine that there is some application programming interface (API) that can provide an updating top ranking for a given trend. The data provided by this API might look something like this:

```
var trends1 = [
  { trend: 'Cats',   score: 1.0 },
  { trend: 'Dogs',   score: 0.8 },
  { trend: 'Fish',   score: 0.4 },
  { trend: 'Ants',   score: 0.3 },
  { trend: 'Koalas', score: 0.2 }
]

var trends2 = [
  { trend: 'Dogs',   score: 1.0 },
  { trend: 'Cats',   score: 0.9 },
  { trend: 'Koalas', score: 0.5 },
  { trend: 'Frogs',  score: 0.3 },
  { trend: 'Bats',   score: 0.2 }
]

// Koalas to the Max!
var trends3 = [
  { trend: 'Koalas', score: 1.0 },
  { trend: 'Dogs',   score: 0.8 },
  { trend: 'Cats',   score: 0.6 },
  { trend: 'Goats',  score: 0.3 },
  { trend: 'Frogs',  score: 0.2 }
]
```

You can find the preceding code and the next code block in the `trends-no-join/data.js` file in the Chapter 11 download.

This data is composed of an array of trends that each have a `trend` and a `score` representing the relative popularity of the trend at a given time. Note that the `score` of the trend can change from update to update.

```
var svg = d3.select("body").append("svg")

function updateTrends(trendData) {
  var selection = svg.selectAll("g.trend")
    .data(trendData)
```

```
// enter
var enterSelection = selection.enter().append("g")
  .attr("class", "trend")

enterSelection.append("text")
  .attr("class", "trend-label")
  .attr("text-anchor", "end")
  .attr("dx", "-0.5em")
  .attr("dy", "1em")
  .attr("x", 100)

enterSelection.append("rect")
  .attr("class", "score")
  .attr("x", 100)
  .attr("height", 20)

// update
selection
  .attr("transform", function(d, i) {
    return "translate(0," + (i * 30 + 20) + ")"
  })

selection.select(".trend-label")
  .text(function(d) { return d.trend })

selection.select(".score")
  .attr("width", function(d) { return d.score * 90 })

// exit
selection.exit().remove()
}

updateTrends(trends1)

updateTrends(trends2)

updateTrends(trends3)
```

This example showcases some important details:

➤ Unlike HTML, where nearly every element can contain other elements in SVG, only the g element (g stands for *group*) can act as a container. Each g element defines its own coordinate system. Finally, g elements cannot be positioned with x, y attributes; they can only be transformed with the transform attribute.

➤ After elements are appended to the pseudo-selection returned by .enter(), you get a regular selection (assigned to enterSelection) to which you can append more elements. enterSelection.append("text") adds a single <text> element to every entered g and returns a selection of those text elements, allowing you to configure them. Note that this example would not work if all the appends were simply chained to each other because every append returns a new selection (it would put the <rect> elements into the <text> elements, which is invalid). The solution is to save a reference to enterSelection and append twice on it.

➤ The text position is fine tuned using `dx` and `dy` attributes. Those are added by the renderer to the x and y attributes respectively and can be specified relative to the text font size (with the em unit). Setting `.attr("dy", "1em")` effectively lowers the text by one line height.

➤ In the update selection, which comprises `g.trend` elements, you can select the trend labels using `selection.select(".trend-label")` to apply the updated trend name to them. The datum bound to the trend labels is inherited from its container by default.

The output of this example is shown in Figure 11-13.

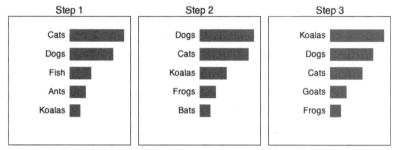

FIGURE 11-13: These steps show the trend bars at three points in time.

Key Functions

The final (and most important) aspect of D3's data join principle is the key function. This section examines how to specify which data points map to which visual elements and why it is so important.

The key function can be provided as the second argument to the `.data()` function and should map a given datum to a string (key) that will be used to identify the element. The key function will be run both on the data bound to the elements in the existing selection and the new data given to the `.data()` function. Any elements whose key matches a data key is placed in the update selection.

You can improve the previous example with a small tweak. The code for the following example is in the `trends-join/script.js` in the Chapter 11 download.

```
var svg = d3.select("body").append("svg")

function updateTrends(trendData) {
  var selection = svg.selectAll("g.trend")
    .data(trendData, function(d) { return d.trend })

// enter
  var enterSelection = selection.enter().append("g")
    .attr("class", "trend")

  enterSelection.append("text")
    .attr("class", "trend-label")
    .attr("text-anchor", "end")
    .attr("dx", "-0.5em")
    .attr("dy", "1em")
```

```
        .attr("x", 100)
        .text(function(d) { return d.trend })

    enterSelection.append("rect")
      .attr("class", "score")
      .attr("x", 100)
      .attr("height", 20)

    // update
    Selection
      .attr("transform", function(d, i) {
        return "translate(0," + (i * 30 + 20) + ")"
      })

    selection.select(".score")
      .attr("width", function(d) { return d.score * 90 })

    // exit
    selection.exit().remove()
  }

updateTrends(trends1)

updateTrends(trends2)

updateTrends(trends3)
```

The changes are very subtle (and invisible, refer to Figure 11-13) but their effect is profound.

By default, the join is done using the index of the datum. Writing `.data(trendData)` is equivalent to writing `.data(trendData, function(d, i) { return String(i) })`. This means that the first `<g>` element would have bound to the Cats trend in Step 1, the Dogs trend in Step 2, and the Koalas trend in Step 3. As a result, the text of the `<text>` element needed to be continuously updated.

In the updated example, the data join is done according to the `trend` property of the data (`function(d) { return d.trend }`). Thus the first `<g>` element stays bound to the Cats trend forever. You utilize this by setting the text of the `<text>` element only once, when creating the elements.

It is very important to define the key function in a way that represents the essence of the data. This is helpful for not having to update labels. Most of all, though, this is critical to getting element transitions to look accurate.

.transition()

The ability to show transitions is a huge advantage of dynamic media—such as the web—over static media.

Transitions are often used in one of the following contexts:

➤ **To visualize data changing over time:** One way to represent time in the data is to vary the visual elements with time. This is typically called *animation*.

➤ **To preserve object constancy within a visualization:** When the positions of the visual elements change based on user interaction, having the elements smoothly transition makes it easier for the viewer to track the change. An example of this would be if, in a bar chart, the user could change the order of the bars.

➤ **To preserve object constancy between visualizations:** When the visualization can trans-morph into a different visualization it is particularly helpful for the individual elements to transition into their new shape.

➤ **To add visual flare to the visualization:** Transitions can add polish to a visualization and, if used with discretion, can make it appear more refined.

For a detailed analysis of the merits of different kinds of transitions, refer to "Animated Transitions in Statistical Data Graphics" by Jeff Heer and George Robertson, which you can find at `http://vis.stanford.edu/papers/animated-transitions`.

D3 is incredibly powerful at expressing transitions with a high degree of customization, which makes it a great choice for dynamic visualizations.

A Basic Transition

Try applying some transitions to a single circle (see the `transition-basic/script.js` file in the code download for Chapter 11):

```
var svg = d3.select("body").append("svg")

svg.append("circle")
    .attr("cx", 20)
    .attr("cy", 20)
    .attr("r", 10)
    .style("fill", "gray")
    .transition()
      .delay(300)
      .duration(700)
      .attr("cx", 150)
      .attr("cy", 100)
      .attr("r", 40)
      .style("fill", "#FFC000")
      .transition()
        .duration(1000)
        .attr("cx", 130)
        .attr("cy", 250)
        .attr("r", 20)
        .style("fill", "red")
        .attr("opacity", 1)
        .transition()
          .duration(1000)
          .attr("opacity", 0)
          .remove()
```

> **NOTE** *The general convention of D3 code is to add indentation every time the return value is a new selection.*

The snapshots of this transition at key points are shown in Figure 11-14. To get the full experience, you should run this example yourself; it's in the `transition-basic/index.html` file.

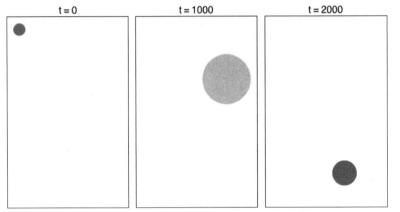

FIGURE 11-14: The circle animation is shown in three snapshots.

There are some important features demonstrated in this example that highlight the immense power and expressibility of the D3 API.

For simplicity, you append a single gray circle like so:

```
svg.append("circle")
    .attr("cx", 20)
    .attr("cy", 20)
    .attr("r", 10)
    .style("fill", "gray")
```

By calling `.transition()` on this single element selection, you create a new type of selection called the *transition selection* (hence the indentation). The transition selection behaves like a regular selection except that the properties defined on it refer to the end state of the transition as opposed to setting the immediate state.

```
.delay(300)
.duration(700)
.attr("cx", 150)
.attr("cy", 100)
.attr("r", 40)
.style("fill", "#6")
```

You can also specify how long the transition will take (700ms in this case) and how long it will delay before starting (300ms). You define the end state and let D3 take care of the rest. Notice that despite using a named color `"gray"` in the starting state and a hex color `"#FFC000"` in the ending state, D3 is able to interpolate between them.

But wait, there's more!

```
.transition()
  .duration(1000)
  .attr("cx", 130)
  .attr("cy", 250)
  .attr("r", 20)
  .style("fill", "red")
  .attr("opacity", 1)
```

Simple transitions can be chained to form complex multistage transitions. Each transition in the chain starts after the previous one is finished.

Notice the tag on an explicit declaration for .attr("opacity", 1) (opacity is 1 by default). This prepares your trusty circle for its grand finale:

```
.transition()
  .duration(1000)
  .attr("opacity", 0)
```

You declare one final transition where you tell the circle to fade out over the course of one second. You needed to set opacity to 1 explicitly first because D3 cannot interpolate an attribute that is not defined (even if there is an implicit default). Finally, you call .remove() on the last transition selection. This tells D3 to remove all the elements in the selection when the transition completes.

This circle existed for a total of three seconds and yet it has taught us so much.

Object Constancy

Now that you have seen how easy it is to transition the elements of a selection, you can revisit the trends example to see how transitions can enhance the visualization. A primary application of transitions is to maintain *object constancy* between the trends, allowing the viewer's eye to easily follow how trends change their rank. You can also add a nice fade in/out effect for arriving and departing trends for a bit of artistic flourish. (Refer to the trends-transition/script.js file.)

```
var svg = d3.select("body").append("svg")

function updateTrends(trendData) {
  var selection = svg.selectAll("g.trend")
    .data(trendData, function(d) { return d.trend })

  // enter
  var enterSelection = selection.enter().append("g")
    .attr("class", "trend")
    .attr("opacity", 0)
    .attr("transform", function(d, i) {
      return "translate(0," + (i * 30 + 20) + ")"
    })

  enterSelection.append("text")
    .attr("class", "trend-label")
    .attr("text-anchor", "end")
    .attr("dx", "-0.5em")
    .attr("dy", "1em")
    .attr("x", 100)
    .text(function(d) { return d.trend })
```

```
enterSelection.append("rect")
  .attr("class", "score")
  .attr("x", 100)
  .attr("height", 20)
  .attr("width", 0)

// update
Selection
  .transition()
    .delay(1200)
    .duration(1200)
    .attr("opacity", 1)
    .attr("transform", function(d, i) {
      return "translate(0," + (i * 30 + 20) + ")"
    })

selection.select(".score")
  .transition()
    .duration(1200)
    .attr("width", function(d) { return d.score * 90 })

// exit
selection.exit()
  .transition()
    .ease("cubic-out")
    .duration(1200)
    .attr("transform", function(d, i) {
      return "translate(200," + (i * 30 + 20) + ")"
    })
    .attr("opacity", 0)
    .remove()
}

updateTrends(trends1)

setTimeout(function() {
  updateTrends(trends2)
}, 4000)

setTimeout(function() {
  updateTrends(trends3)
}, 8000)
```

This example really needs to be seen in action to be fully understood. Please run it yourself using the `trends-transition/step3.html` file.

Examine the enter, update, and exit parts of this transition individually:

➤ The entering `<g>` elements have their `opacity` set to 0, making them invisible. Their initial position is set using the same logical mapping as what they will later transition to when they join the update selection.

➤ The update selection is transitioned over a period of 1200ms (with a 1200ms delay to let the exit transition finish). The end-state `opacity` is set to 1 to get the elements joining in from the enter selection to fade in (this has no effect on the elements that were already on the screen as their opacity was already 1). The `transform` is updated to reflect the new position given the (potentially new) rank of the trend.

➤ The exiting `<g>` elements, whose trends are no longer in the top five, are transitioned 200px to the right and faded out. They use the `cubic-out` easing function to make the transition look more natural. After the transition is finished, they are removed.

This example clearly shows the importance of defining the key function correctly. Without it, these transitions would not look right as the same five elements would simply be recycled to represent the new trends. There would never be a non-empty exit selection and thus no place to specify how the no-longer-top-five trends bid their farewell.

An interesting behavior to note is that because the elements in the exit selection were, by definition, not joined with a new data they end up keeping their (old) bound data value until they are removed. Any operand modification on the exit selection will act on the last data bound to that element.

The key function should never translate two distinct data objects into the same key. Doing so would lead to undefined behavior and strange errors. You need not worry about overlapping keys if you are not defining a key function because the default key function is to key a datum by its index.

Nested Selections

The final point of awesomeness about selections is that they can be nested, allowing you to effectively represent nested data structures that occur so often in data visualization.

Consider the following data structure representing a 4x4 matrix:

```
var matrixData = [
  [9.4, 2.8, 2.3, 6.3],
  [5.3, 6.3, 7.7, 4.7],
  [6.1, 7.3, 7.9, 0.8],
  [1.2, 2.6, 7.3, 2.6]
]
```

It is an array representing the rows where each row is, itself, an array representing the cells of the matrix. Say you wanted to visualize this by rendering the numbers in a grid; you could break down the visualization into two conceptual parts: rendering an array of numbers into a row and rendering the array of rows to form a grid. These two steps can be tackled independently by making use of nested selections. First you can create a selection of rows and associate the data for individual rows with each row element. Because a row element contains other elements in it (for numbers) you must use a group element (`<g>`) because it is the only SVG container element. Next within each row group you create a selection of elements that represent the individual numbers. Because each number will be represented as a circle and some text, those can also be grouped together.

```
var svg = d3.select("body").append("svg")

// First selection (rows)
var rowSelection = svg.selectAll("g.row").data(matrixData)

rowSelection.exit().remove()
```

```
rowSelection.enter().append("g")
  .attr("class", "row")
  .attr("transform", function(d, i) {
    return "translate(0," + (i * 45 + 30) + ")"
  })

// Second selection (cells)
var cellSelection = rowSelection
  .selectAll("g.cell").data(function(d) { return d })

cellSelection.exit().remove()

var enterCellSelection = cellSelection.enter().append("g")
  .attr("class", "cell")
  .attr("transform", function(d, i) {
    return "translate(" + (i * 45 + 30) + ",0)"
  })

// Fill in the cells
enterCellSelection.append("circle")
  .attr("r", function(d) { return Math.sqrt(d * 140 / Math.PI) })

enterCellSelection.append("text")
  .attr("text-anchor", "middle")
  .attr("dy", "0.35em")
  .text(function(d) { return "[" + d + "]" })
```

You can find the preceding code in the `nested-simple/script.js` file in the Chapter 11 download.

You create a selection of `g.row` and associate `matrixData` with it. Because `matrixData` is an array of arrays, the data element being associated with each `g.row` is itself an array. Note that in the example the steps are rearranged, with exit first for better readability.

Next, you use the nested capabilities of D3 selections to create a selection within each `g.row` element. All examples shown previously had only one element (usually the SVG container) in the selection on which you performed a data join. In contrast, the second data join in this example is performed on a selection that already has four elements (`g.row`) in it, each with its own data. In this data join, `.selectAll("g.cell").data(function(d) { return d })`, the first argument to the `data` operator is a function that defines the data to be used in the join within each of the row groups. The trivial function supplied simply returns the row array, causing D3 to create an element for each number in the row (within each row). You use a group (`g.cell`) to represent each number within the row so that both the text and circle elements appear in the same place.

Finally, you fill each `g.cell` with a circle (`circle`) and a label (`text`). At this point the data associated with each `g.cell` element is the corresponding number of the matrix so calling

```
enterCellSelection.append("circle")
  .attr("r", function(d) { return Math.sqrt(d * 140 / Math.PI) })
```

creates a circle and sets its radius in such a way as to make its area equal to d * 140. You can see the resulting bubble matrix in Figure 11-15.

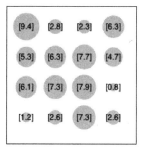

FIGURE 11-15: The result is a bubble matrix.

D3 HELPER FUNCTIONS

The big advantage of D3 is that, after you understand the data join principle and transitions described earlier in this chapter, you are set; other visualization toolkits typically have under-the-covers "magic" that makes is very easy to start using them but hard to understand what is actually going on behind the scenes. In D3 you get the powerful data joins and transitions, the rest you need to provide yourself. Helpfully D3 comes packed with many independent, self-contained function generators that can be of use in a number of scenarios to simplify the task of creating complex visualizations. Most D3 helper functions can be used in contexts completely outside of D3 as they have nothing D3 specific about them.

This section examines some of the most popular helper functions.

Drawing Lines

Line charts are a staple of visualization. Unfortunately, drawing lines in SVG is a pain, as shown here (see the `helper-line-raw/script.js` file in the code downloads):

```
var svg = d3.select("body").append("svg")

svg.append("path")
  .style("fill", "none")
  .style("stroke", "black")
  .style("stroke-width", 2)
  .attr("d", "M10,10L100,100L100,200L150,50L200,75")
```

To draw a line, you need to set the d attribute of a <path> element to a string of M (move) and L (line) commands. D3 has a helper function so that you never have to deal with these crazy strings yourself (see the `helper-line/script.js` file in the Chapter 11 code download):

```
var points = [
  { x: 10,  y: 10  },
  { x: 100, y: 100 },
  { x: 100, y: 200 },
  { x: 150, y: 50  },
  { x: 200, y: 75  }
]
```

```
var lineFn = d3.svg.line()
  .x(function(d) { return d.x })
  .y(function(d) { return d.y })

var svg = d3.select("body").append("svg")

console.log(lineFn(points))
// => "M10,10L100,100L100,200L150,50L200,75"

svg.append("path")
  .style("fill", "none")
  .style("stroke", "black")
  .style("stroke-width", 2)
  .attr("d", lineFn(points))
```

Calling d3.svg.line() returns a function that, when called on an array of data, produces an SVG path string. This function lives within the d3.svg namespace to indicate that it is SVG specific. The results of both of these examples are identical (see Figure 11-16).

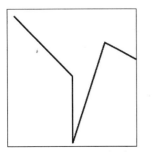

FIGURE 11-16: A path element drawing a polyline

D3's API style makes heavy use of function chaining. The d3.svg.line() helper can be configured to correctly extract the x and y coordinates from the data by using the .x(...) and .y(...) setter methods respectively:

```
.x(function(d) { return d.x })
.y(function(d) { return d.y })
```

The preceding code tells the line helper to use d.x and d.y as the coordinates of the points.

Scales

A scale is a function that maps from an input domain to an output range. Scales find their way into nearly every visualization as you often need to do a transformation to convert data values to pixel sizes.

D3 provides a number of different scales to suit different types of data:

➤ *Quantitative* scales are used for continuous input domains, such as numbers.

➤ *Time* scales are quantitative scales specifically tuned to time data.

➤ *Ordinal* scales work on discrete input domains, such as names or categories.

In the previous bar chart–based examples, the bars were always horizontal. Because of the location of the origin in the SVG coordinate system, horizontal bar charts are simpler to describe compared to the more traditional vertical bar charts.

You can create a vertical bar chart with the help of two scales. You can find the following code in the helper-scales/script.js file.

```
var svg = d3.select("body").append("svg")

function updateGdpBars(gdpData, width, height) {
  var countries = gdpData.map(function(d) { return d.country })
  var xScale = d3.scale.ordinal()
    .domain(countries)
    .rangeBands([0, width], 0.2)

  var maxGdp = d3.max(gdpData, function(d) { return d.gdp })
  var yScale = d3.scale.linear()
    .domain([0, maxGdp])
    .range([height - 20, 20])

  var selection = svg.selectAll(".bar")
    .data(gdpData)

  selection.enter().append("rect")
    .attr("class", "bar")
    .style("fill", "steelblue")

  Selection
    .attr("x", function(d) { return xScale(d.country) })
    .attr("y", function(d) { return yScale(d.gdp) })
    .attr("width", xScale.rangeBand())
    .attr("height", function(d) {
      return Math.abs(yScale(d.gdp) - yScale(0))
    })

  selection.exit().remove()
}

var UN_2012_GDP = [
  { country: "United States",  gdp: 16244600 },
  { country: "China",          gdp:  8358400 },
  { country: "Japan",          gdp:  5960180 },
  { country: "Germany",        gdp:  3425956 },
  { country: "France",         gdp:  2611221 },
  { country: "United Kingdom", gdp:  2471600 }
]

updateGdpBars(UN_2012_GDP, 600, 300)
```

The example shown in Figure 11-17 is much closer to what you might encounter in the wild.

You create two scales, xScale and yScale, for the x and y axes respectively.

```
var countries = gdpData.map(function(d) { return d.country })
var xScale = d3.scale.ordinal()
  .domain(countries)
  .rangeBands([0, width], 0.2)
```

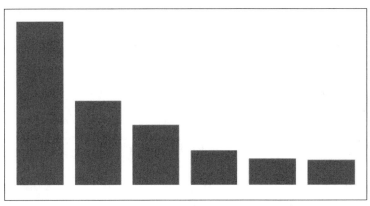

FIGURE 11-17: The bars have been redrawn with a vertical orientation.

The input domain of the xScale is the list of countries (countries). Because this is an ordered list of discrete values, you use the d3.scale.ordinal() scale. You ask the scale to map these values onto a range of [0, width], splitting them into equal bands with 20 percent of the space used as a gap. Later, you will access the width of a single bar using the xScale.rangeBand() method.

```
var maxGdp = d3.max(gdpData, function(d) { return d.gdp })
var yScale = d3.scale.linear()
  .domain([0, maxGdp])
  .range([height - 20, 20])
```

For the y axis you use a d3.scale.linear() scale. This scale creates a simple linear function of the form y = m*x + c for some m and c. You use another helper function, d3.max, to find the maximum gdp within the data.

In many D3 examples, the x and y scales are stored in variables called x and y. This sometimes trips up beginners as people are used to variables x and y being numeric (as opposed to functions).

You position the bars as needed using

```
selection
  .attr("x", function(d) { return xScale(d.country) })
  .attr("y", function(d) { return yScale(d.gdp) })
  .attr("width", xScale.rangeBand())
  .attr("height", function(d) {
    return Math.abs(yScale(d.gdp) - yScale(0))
  })
```

The x and y attributes are determined by using the scales directly. The width is determined from the band size conveniently provided by the ordinal scale. You compute the height by subtracting the value of the scale at the given data value from the scale value at zero.

D3 HELPER LAYOUTS

Another type of helper function provided by D3 is layouts. Unlike the helper functions discussed previously, which help you map data to attribute values, layouts work on the data, augmenting it with more information.

A treemap is a popular visualization that recursively subdivides area into rectangles sized according to some data attribute. You can easily create treemaps with the aid of the `d3.layout.treemap()` layout, which does all the complex computations for you.

Treemaps were introduced by Ben Shneiderman in 1991. You can read more about them at `http://www.cs.umd.edu/hcil/treemap-history/`.

You can see how the treemap layout can be used in practice by applying it to the problem it was originally designed to solve: visualizing the file sizes/hierarchy on a disk drive. You apply the treemap layout to the file structure within the example folder for this chapter.

```
var FILE_DATA = {
  "name": "examples",
  "content": [
    {
      "name": "blank",
      "content": [
        {
          "name": "index.html",
          "size": 320
        }
      ]
    },
    {
      "name": "data-enter",
      "content": [
        {
          "name": "after.html",
          "size": 512
        },
        {
          "name": "before.html",
          "size": 475
        },
        {
          "name": "script.js",
          "size": 404
        }
      ]
    }
    ...lots of data omitted...
  ]
}
```

This is the data to be used in this example. As you can see, it is hierarchical as it describes a file system. (Refer to the `layout-treemap/script.js` file in the code downloads.)

```
var svg = d3.select("body").append("svg")

function updateTreemap(fileData, width, height) {
  var treemap = d3.layout.treemap()
    .size([width, height])
    .children(function(d) { return d.content })
    .value(function(d) { return d.size })

  var nodeData = treemap.nodes(fileData)
```

```
var color = d3.scale.category20c()

var selection = svg.selectAll("g.node")
  .data(nodeData)

// Exit
selection.exit().remove()

// Enter
enterSelection = selection.enter().append("g")
  .attr("class", "node")

enterSelection.append('rect')

enterSelection.append('text')
  .attr('dx', '0.2em')
  .attr('dy', '1em')

// Update
selection
  .attr("transform", function(d) { return "translate(" + d.x + "," + d.y + ")" })

selection.select('rect')
  .attr("width", function(d) { return d.dx })
  .attr("height", function(d) { return d.dy })
  .style("stroke", 'black')
  .style("fill", function(d) { return d.children ? color(d.name) : 'none' })

selection.select('text')
  .text(function(d) {
    if (d.children || d.dx < 50 || d.dy < 10) return null
    return d.name
  })
}

updateTreemap(FILE_DATA, 700, 400)
```

Start off by declaring the layout:

```
var treemap = d3.layout.treemap()
  .size([width, height])
  .children(function(d) { return d.content })
  .value(function(d) { return d.size })
```

You set the container dimensions (`size`), the child node accessor (`children`), and the value function (`value`). These tell the layout how to traverse the hierarchy of the data.

Each layout, by convention, provides a `nodes` and a `links` function for generating the nodes that correspond to the data and the links that represent their interconnections.

```
var nodeData = treemap.nodes(fileData)
```

For the treemap, you are only interested in the nodes. You run the data through the `nodes` function and get back a flat array representing the rectangles of the treemap with lots of useful metadata attached.

Here is what an element of `nodeData` looks like:

```
{
  name: "data-general"
  area: 15716.360529688169
  children: Array[8]
  content: Array[8]
  depth: 1
  x: 174
  y: 202
  dx: 170
  dy: 92
  parent: Object
  value: 1971
}
```

As you can see, all the original values are preserved, but extra metadata for positioning (x, y, dx, and dy) is added.

You now perform the regular data join onto the new `nodeData`.

```
selection
  .attr("transform", function(d) { return "translate(" + d.x + "," + d.y + ")" })

selection.select('rect')
  .attr("width", function(d) { return d.dx })
  .attr("height", function(d) { return d.dy })
```

You position the container group and size the rectangles using the metadata generated by the layout function.

The resulting treemap is shown in Figure 11-18.

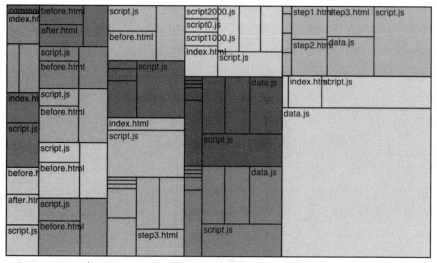

FIGURE 11-18: This treemap visualizes the files in this chapter scaled by file size.

SUMMARY

This chapter introduced D3 and showcased the core principles that make it up:

➤ You saw how to select elements and create new elements using D3.

➤ You found out how to position and style elements using the .attr and .style functions.

➤ You learned D3's core principle of joining data to elements and the resulting enter, update, and exit selections.

➤ You saw how transitions work and how they can be chained together.

➤ You discovered how to fine-tune the joining and maintain constancy by providing a join key function.

➤ You learned about nesting selections within selections as a means of representing nested data structures.

➤ You were introduced to the different types of helper functions provided by D3 that aid in creating visualizations:

  ➤ You learned about scales that help you transform values from the data to pixels.

  ➤ You found out about layouts that reshape your data to make it easier to work with.

12

Incorporating Symbols

WHAT'S IN THIS CHAPTER

➤ Learning how symbols can benefit charting

➤ Leveraging D3 to render symbols using SVG

➤ Making symbols react to the proximity of the mouse

➤ Animating changes to symbols.

➤ Using the Ignite UI igDataChart to automagically plot symbols

➤ Displaying metrics on a symbol with bubble charts

> **CODE DOWNLOAD** *The wrox.com code downloads for this chapter are found at* www.wrox.com/go/javascriptandjqueryanalysis *on the Download Code tab. The code is in the chapter 12 download and individually named according to the names throughout the chapter.*

Chapters 9 through 11 cover some of the mechanics of various chart types using D3, Raphaël, and the Google Charts API. A large focus of these chapters was on charting types where each discrete data value was represented by a separate visual element. This chapter explores charting types, such as line and area, that provide an interpolated shape that connects all the data points. When dealing with such an interpolated shape, it can be useful to use a *symbol*, or *marker*, to indicate exactly where the underlying data values occur in the x-y space of the plot area.

You can use symbols for more than delineating the exact location of data values in an interpolated shape. In fact, some chart types consist only of symbols, such as a scatter chart or a bubble chart. Or, you might want to use a custom symbol to indicate the location of an event on a time series chart, for example.

So, this chapter explains the mechanics of displaying symbols in charts. You start by using D3 to construct and display symbols at a very low level. This not only allows for studying the basics of how a symbol is implemented in visualization application programming interfaces (APIs), but it also gives you the tools to build ad-hoc marker scenarios in Scalable Vector Graphics (SVG) using the D3 API.

> **NOTE** *Although most of this book is designed so that you can digest the chapters individually, and potentially out of sequence, it's highly recommended that you read Chapter 11 before you read this chapter. For brevity, I'll assume you've already absorbed some of the details of D3 because revisiting the basics would be rather redundant and would make this chapter considerably longer.*

Later in the chapter, you see how markers can be represented in a comparatively high-level API that can do a lot of the footwork for you. In Chapter 9, you used the Google Charts API for this purpose, but for variety this chapter investigates a different API. Also, at the time of this writing, the Google Charts API seems to have rather limited facilities to display and customize symbols.

WORKING WITH SVG SYMBOLS WITH D3

Recall from Chapter 11 that D3 is a very powerful tool for creating very dynamic visualizations. It's especially good at helping you to create ad-hoc visualizations that don't quite fit with what most charting APIs anticipated you would want to do with your data. Because of its low-level nature, D3 is also a good instructional tool as you begin to explore a new charting concept. If you aren't so interested in the mechanics of how to implement symbols in a chart, and don't have the need to step outside the bounds of what high-level charting APIs will do for you, feel free to skip ahead to the "Creating a Line Chart with Ignite UI igDataChart" section of this chapter where you find out how to use a much higher-level API that handles all the low-level details automatically.

Creating a D3 Line Chart

In Chapter 11, you created lots of different visualizations using D3, but line charts were only touched upon briefly. Listing 12-1 creates a line chart.

LISTING 12-1

```
var data = [
    { "product": "Shoes", "amount": 40 },
    { "product": "Hats", "amount": 50 },
    { "product": "Coats", "amount": 35 },
    { "product": "Scarves", "amount": 20 }
];
var data2 = [
    { "product": "Shoes", "amount": 25 },
```

```
        { "product": "Hats", "amount": 40 },
        { "product": "Coats", "amount": 45 },
        { "product": "Scarves", "amount": 15 }
];
var currentData = data;

var chartTotalWidth = 500;
var chartTotalHeight = 500;
var margin = {
    left: 100,
    right: 50,
    top : 20,
    bottom: 40
};
var width = chartTotalWidth - margin.left - margin.right;
var height = chartTotalHeight - margin.top - margin.bottom;
var main = d3.select("body").append("svg")
    .attr("width", chartTotalWidth)
    .attr("height", chartTotalHeight)
    .append("g")
    .attr("transform", "translate(" + margin.left + "," + margin.top + ")");

var xScale = d3.scale.ordinal()
    .rangePoints([0, width], 0.4)
    .domain(data.map(function (d) { return d.product; }));

var yScale = d3.scale.linear()
    .range([height, 0])
    .domain([0, d3.max(data, function (d) { return d.amount; })]);

var xAxis = d3.svg.axis()
    .scale(xScale)
    .orient("bottom")
    .outerTickSize(0);

var yAxis = d3.svg.axis()
    .scale(yScale)
    .orient("left");

main.append("g")
    .attr("class", "x axis")
    .attr("transform", "translate(0," + height + ")")
    .call(xAxis);

main.append("g")
    .attr("class", "y axis")
    .call(yAxis);

var updateLine = function () {
    var lineBuilder = d3.svg.line()
        .x(function (d) {
            return xScale(d.product);
        })
        .y(function (d) {
```

continues

LISTING 12-1 *(continued)*

```
                    return yScale(d.amount);
            })
            .interpolate("linear");

        var line = main.selectAll(".line")
            .data([currentData]);

        line
            .enter().append("path")
            .attr("class", "line")
            .attr("d", function (d) {
                return lineBuilder(d);
            });

        line
            .transition()
            .duration(1000)
            .attr("d", function (d) {
                return lineBuilder(d);
            });
    };

    updateLine();

    d3.select("body").append("input")
        .attr("type", "button")
        .attr("value", "click")
        .on("click", function () {
            if (currentData === data) {
                currentData = data2;
            } else {
                currentData = data;
            }
            updateLine();
        });
```

The JavaScript in Listing 12-1 depends on this HTML:

```
<!DOCTYPE html>
<html>
<head>
    <title>Basic Line Chart With Axes</title>

    <script src="d3/d3.min.js" charset="utf-8"></script>

    <link rel="stylesheet" href="D3BasicLineChartWithAxes.css">
</head>
<body>
    <script type="text/javascript" src="D3BasicLineChartWithAxes.js">
    </script>
</body>
</html>
```

And this CSS:

```
.line {
    stroke: #4DDB94;
    fill: transparent;
    stroke-width: 3px;
}
.y.axis path {
    display: none;
}
.axis {
    font: 20px Verdana;
    fill: #444444;
}
.axis path,
.axis line {
    fill: none;
    stroke: #999999;
    shape-rendering: crispEdges;
}
```

The CSS and HTML for the D3 samples in this chapter are all roughly similar, so there's no further discussion of them in this chapter. You can find them on the companion website.

Listing 12-1 produces a line chart like the one shown in Figure 12-1. You can find the D3BasicLineChartWithAxes.js/html/css files on the companion website.

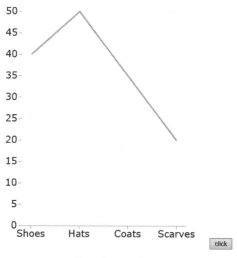

FIGURE 12-1: This shows a line chart using D3.

Most of the preceding code is similar to the examples in Chapter 11 when you were visualizing data using columns. The main difference is that now you are generating a single shape that is a linear interpolation between all the discrete data points rather than a separate shape per data point. Now, let's drill into how that is done:

```
var lineBuilder = d3.svg.line()
    .x(function (d) {
        return xScale(d.product);
    })
    .y(function (d) {
        return yScale(d.amount);
    })
    .interpolate("linear");
```

This code is creating a line builder that will turn a set of x-y positions into some linearly interpolated path geometry (straight lines that connect all the points). Functions declaring how to fetch the x and y values are assigned. These call the x and y scales in order to map the incoming data into the coordinate system of the plot area. Finally, you set the interpolation mode to linear, which declares that the line builder should use straight lines between the data points. There are many other options you can provide here, however, such as basis which will use a B-spline (a smoothed mathematical function over the data points) to connect all the points. When you call this builder on the incoming data, it generates some path data that you can assign to the d attribute on a <path> element.

```
var line = main.selectAll(".line")
    .data([currentData]);

line
    .enter().append("path")
    .attr("class", "line")
    .attr("d", function (d) {
        return lineBuilder(d);
    });
```

In the preceding snippet, a data join is done on a selection containing all the elements that use the line class. This is similar to how you would construct a bar or column chart, however, rather than passing in the array of data points to the join, this is passing in a one-element array where the one element is the subarray with your data. This is because you want there to be just one line produced for the data, but this line needs to refer to the full array of data to be visualized.

Next, a path is appended to represent all the data, and the lineBuilder is called to produce the path geometry for the input data.

To add some neat animations, you are also declaring what should occur when the updateLine method is called successively on new data:

```
line
    .transition()
    .duration(1000)
    .attr("d", function (d) {
        return lineBuilder(d);
    });
```

This code basically regenerates the line geometry and assigns it within the context of a transition animation.

> **NOTE** *You might find it a bit surprising that you don't need to do anything more complicated to animate the shape of the line between different configurations. It is straightforward, here because the line geometry being generated has the same number of control points every time the data is updated, and the sequence of commands in the path geometry remains constant. In this case, every command is a "line to" command. Because this is such a straightforward geometry, it is sufficient that D3 matches by index, then interpolates, all of the floating-point numbers in the two path geometries and produces a "tween" geometry that blends between the two. If the number of control points varied or, worse, the commands used varied, you would probably need to use a custom interpolator.*

Adding Symbols to the Line

Now that you have a line displayed, it's time to move on to marking it up with some symbols. Fortunately, much like the way D3 provides some builders/generators for things like arcs and lines, it also provides a configurable builder for symbol geometry:

```
var symbol = main.selectAll(".symbol")
    .data(currentData);

var symbolBuilder = d3.svg.symbol()
    .type("circle")
    .size(180);
```

When you were rendering the line portion of the chart, you joined the data so as to produce one visual that incorporated all the data points, but in the case of the symbols, the scenario is more like when you were creating the column visuals in Chapter 11. The symbols all have the class `symbol` applied to them, and each is associated with a single data item.

Next, `d3.svg.symbol()` creates a symbol geometry builder. You declare that you want circle shapes for each symbol and provide a desired size. Like most operators in D3, these actions could just as easily be functions that use the contextual data to drive the shape or the size of the symbols.

> **NOTE** *One common charting scenario for which you would probably want to data-drive the size or shape of a marker is a bubble chart. Bubble charts usually map a third value (beyond what is mapped to x and y) to the area of the chart's symbols. Sometimes a fourth value (or the third doubled up) is also mapped to the color selected for the symbols. Mapping four separate values into one chart series can be a bit much to easily digest, however.*

```
symbol
    .enter().append("path")
    .attr("class", "symbol")
    .attr("transform", function (d) {
        return "translate(" + xScale(d.product) +
        "," + yScale(d.amount) + ")";
    })
    .attr("d", function (d) {
        return symbolBuilder(d);
    });
```

This snippet is adding a path for each data item and marking it with the class `symbol`. The symbol builder generates the geometry for each symbol centered around the coordinate origin, so you generate a `translate` transform based on scaling the current category and amount into the plot area's coordinate system. After the coordinate origin has been placed at the center of where you want to render the marker, the symbol geometry builder is called on the data item in order to get the geometry data to assign to the d attribute of the <path>.

```
symbol
    .transition()
    .duration(1000)
    .attr("transform", function (d) {
        return "translate(" + xScale(d.product) +
        "," + yScale(d.amount) + ")";
    });
```

Finally, just as the line was animated, it would be great if the symbols would animate to new positions when new data is introduced. So, for the `update` selection, you start a `transition`, apply a `duration`, and animate a change to the `translate` transform to the new target position for each symbol.

You can see the resulting symbols applied to the line chart in Figure 12-2, and you can find the `D3BasicLineChartWithAxesAndSymbols.html/css/js` files on the companion website.

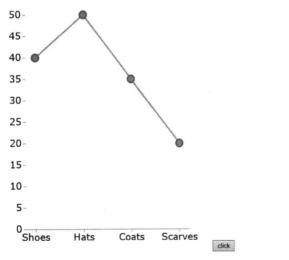

FIGURE 12-2: Symbols have been applied to a line chart using D3.

Making the Symbols Interactive

Another useful aspect of introducing symbols to a line chart is that they give you a way to annotate or highlight individual data values within the line. With no symbols, if you want to highlight a line, the easiest thing to do is to highlight the entire line. After introducing symbols, however, you can highlight an individual symbol to bring a particular data value into focus. The following code shows you how you would highlight the symbol currently under the mouse:

```
symbol
    .enter().append("path")
    .attr("class", "symbol")
    .attr("fill", "#4DDB94")
    .attr("transform", function (d) {
        return "translate(" + xScale(d.product) + "," + yScale(d.amount) + ")";
    })
    .attr("d", function (d) {
        return symbolBuilder(d);
    })
    .on("mouseenter", function() {
        d3.select(this).transition()
            .duration(300)
            .attr("fill", "#f2ed96")
            .attr("transform", function (d) {
                return "translate(" + xScale(d.product) + "," +
                yScale(d.amount) + ")";
            });
    })
    .on("mouseleave", function () {
        d3.select(this).transition()
            .duration(300)
            .attr("fill", "#4DDB94")
            .attr("transform", function (d) {
                return "translate(" + xScale(d.product) + "," +
                yScale(d.amount) + ")";
            });
    });
```

The differences here are that you've pulled the default fill color out of the CSS and are using D3 to apply it, and you've attached a mouse enter and a mouse leave handler to the symbol paths so that you can enact changes as the symbols are hovered over. In each handler, `d3.select(this).transition()` selects the hovered node and starts a transition. The transition either applies the highlight color or sets the color back to the default depending on whether the mouse is entering or leaving the symbol.

You may be wondering why both the transform and the color are being animated in the handler. This is actually to deal with a situation in which you hover over a symbol while a data change transition is being applied. In D3, only one transition can be running at a time for an element (though more than one can be queued). As a result, if you hover over a node during a data transition, it will essentially cancel the translation animation that is occurring. To resolve this, you repeat the target `translate` transform in this transition in addition to the fill color change.

You can see the result of hovering the mouse over one of the symbols in Figure 12-3. You can find the `D3BasicLineChartWithAxesAndSymbolsHover.js/html/css` files on the companion website.

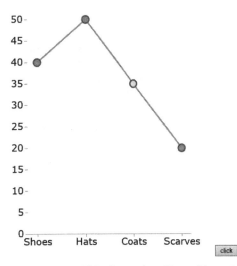

FIGURE 12-3: This shows the effect of hovering over an interactive symbol in your D3 line chart.

There is a discoverability issue here, however. Consumers of the visualization may not even realize that they can hover over the markers to highlight the specific data. You can take it a bit further, and, instead of hovering over a marker to highlight it, you can always highlight the closest symbol to the user's cursor.

The first change is to insert a rectangle into the background of the plot area, like so:

```
var bg = main.append("rect")
    .attr("fill", "#FFFFFF")
    .attr("width", width)
    .attr("height", height);
```

Creating this rectangle is done because your plot area has a transparent backing by default and most SVG implementations seem to not catch mouse events on transparent backgrounds. As a result, you need a background to get constant mouse move updates as the user moves the mouse cursor around the plot area.

```
var getClosestProduct = function (mouse) {
    var minDist = NaN;
    var minIndex = -1;
    for (var i = 0; i < xScale.domain().length; i++) {
        var position = xScale(xScale.domain()[i]);
        var dist = Math.abs(position - mouse[0]);
        if (isNaN(minDist)) {
            minDist = dist;
            minIndex = i;
        } else {
            if (dist < minDist) {
                minDist = dist;
```

```
                minIndex = i;
            }
        }
    }

    return xScale.domain()[minIndex];
};
```

This method helps find the category value that is closest to the current x position of the mouse. It does this by looping through all the categories, mapping each into the coordinate system of the plot area (the range), and measuring the x distance to the mouse cursor. The minimum distance category is found and returned.

```
var previousProduct = null;
main.on("mousemove", function () {
    console.log("here");
    var mouse = d3.mouse(this);
    var closestProduct = getClosestProduct(mouse);

    if (closestProduct != previousProduct) {
        previousProduct = closestProduct;
        var symbol = main.selectAll(".symbol");

        symbol
            .transition()
            .duration(300)
            .attr("fill", function (d) {
            if (d.product == closestProduct) {
                return "#f2ed96";
            }
            return "#4DDB94";
        })
            .attr("transform", function (d) {
                var trans = "translate(" + xScale(d.product) + "," +
                yScale(d.amount) + ")";
                if (d.product == closestProduct) {
                    return trans + " scale(2,2)";
                }
                return trans;
            });
    }
});
```

Given this mousemove handler, you listen to the mouse position changes even on the plot area background. For every move, you determine the current closest category to the cursor. Then, given the category you want to highlight, you apply a transition to all the symbols and modify the color and render scale of just the symbol that has the data value for the closest category.

You can see the result of hovering near to one of the symbols in Figure 12-4. You can find the D3BasicLineChartWithAxesAndSymbolsHoverClosest.js/html/css files on the companion website.

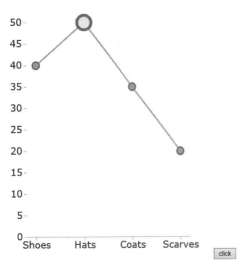

FIGURE 12-4: The closest symbol to the cursor is highlighted.

CANVAS SYMBOLS WITH IGNITE UI IGDATACHART

Now that you've been exposed to some of the basics of adding symbols to charts and making them interactive, it's time to look at a much higher-level charting API to see what more complex built-in (but more constrained) behaviors you can take advantage of.

Chapter 9 focuses on the Google Charts API, but at the time of this writing, that API didn't have very flexible configuration when it came to symbols/markers. Consequently, the latter part of this chapter focuses on the Ignite UI igDataChart by Infragistics (http://www.igniteui.com). The igDataChart is not a free component, but you can find a trial of it at https://igniteui.com/download. After you have signed up, there are also some CDN links for the trial version that are published on the download page, or you can download the trial. This chapter assumes you have extracted Ignite UI into a subfolder called IgniteUI.

The igDataChart is a desktop-grade charting component that focuses on performance, high volumes of data, ease of use, and breadth of features. There are so many features, in fact, that it is split between many different JavaScript files in order to reduce load times.

> **NOTE** *For simplicity, the samples in this chapter will load a combined JavaScript file that contains all the data visualization tools that Ignite UI offers, but for production scenarios it's better to load only the subset of features required. Custom downloads for just the feature sets desired can be obtained from* http://igniteui.com/download.

Creating a Line Chart with Ignite UI igDataChart

A lot less code is required to represent the preceding D3 symbol scenario using the igDataChart. The first code snippet shows the HTML:

```
<!DOCTYPE html>
<html>
<head>
    <title>Area Chart</title>

    <script src="jquery/jquery-1.11.1.min.js"></script>
    <script src="jquery-ui-1.11.1/jquery-ui.min.js"></script>

    <link rel="stylesheet" href="IgniteUI/css/themes/infragistics/~CA
infragistics.theme.css" />
    <link rel="stylesheet"
href="IgniteUI/css/structure/infragistics.css" />
    <link rel="stylesheet" href="IgniteUI/css/structure/modules/~CA
infragistics.ui.chart.css" />
    <script src="IgniteUI/js/infragistics.core.js"></script>
    <script src="IgniteUI/js/infragistics.dv.js"></script>

    <link rel="stylesheet"
        href="IgniteUIChartArea.css" />
</head>
<body>
    <div id="chart"></div>
    <div id="legend"></div>

    <script type="text/javascript" src="IgniteUIChartArea.js">
    </script>

</body>
</html>
```

The preceding code assumes that the Ignite UI trial was extracted into a subfolder called IgniteUI. Also, the download from the companion site contains the trial of Ignite UI in the appropriate location. The HTML content will be roughly the same for the remaining code in the chapter, so this chapter doesn't refer to it again, but the full listings are available in the companion media for the chapter. The same is true for the CSS, which follows:

```
#chart
{
    width: 500px;
    height: 500px;
    float: left;
}
#legend
{
    float: left;
}
```

The CSS classes here apply to the elements that contain the chart and its legend. They define some sizing and layout. The following is the actual code that defines the chart:

```
$(function () {
    var data = [
        { "product": "Shoes", "amount": 40 },
        { "product": "Hats", "amount": 50 },
        { "product": "Coats", "amount": 35 },
        { "product": "Scarves", "amount": 20 }
    ];
    var data2 = [
        { "product": "Shoes", "amount": 25 },
        { "product": "Hats", "amount": 40 },
        { "product": "Coats", "amount": 45 },
        { "product": "Scarves", "amount": 15 }
    ];


    $("#chart").igDataChart({
        dataSource: data,
        title: "Product Sales",
        subtitle: "Sales in various product categories over time",
        rightMargin: 30,
        legend: { element: "legend" },
        axes: [{
            type: "categoryX",
            name: "xAxis",
            label: "product",
            labelExtent: 40
        }, {
            type: "numericY",
            name: "yAxis",
            title: "Sales",
            minimumValue: 0,
            strip: "rgba(230,230,230,.4)",
            maximumValue: 60,
            labelExtent: 40
        }],
        series: [{
            name: "productSales",
            type: "area",
            xAxis: "xAxis",
            yAxis: "yAxis",
            valueMemberPath: "amount",
            showTooltip: true,
            isTransitionInEnabled: true,
            isHighlightingEnabled: true,
            transitionInDuration: 1000,
            title: "Q1"
        }, {
            name: "productSales2",
            dataSource: data2,
            type: "area",
            xAxis: "xAxis",
```

```
        yAxis: "yAxis",
        valueMemberPath: "amount",
        showTooltip: true,
        isTransitionInEnabled: true,
        isHighlightingEnabled: true,
        transitionInDuration: 1000,
        title: "Q2"
    }, {
        name: "itemToolTips",
        type: "itemToolTipLayer",
        transitionDuration: 300
    }]
  });
});
```

This code produces the area chart that's shown in Figure 12-5. (You can find the `IgniteUIChartArea.js/html/css` files on the companion website.) It may not even be appropriate to refer to the preceding as code because it's basically just some JavaScript objects that represent the data to plot in a chart, and some additional JavaScript objects that store the configuration for the chart.

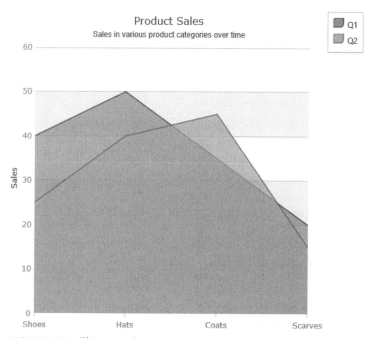

FIGURE 12-5: This area chart was created using the Ignite UI igDataChart.

You'll notice some interesting things if you run the sample in a browser:

➤ The chart has some nice-looking built-in titles for itself and its axes.

➤ The series animate into view in an aesthetically pleasing way.

➤ Some automatically formatted tooltips display when you hover over the data, and the tooltips are shown simultaneously for each data series.

➤ When you hover over a series, you get a glow highlight.

➤ The axes have tick and gridline visuals and alternating color strips.

➤ There is a separate legend component that displays the title for the series and has a color swatch to correlate items with the series in the chart.

It would have taken a rather large amount of code in D3 to build all of these features, and a lot of these behaviors are much more complex and customizable than they appear at first blush. D3's strengths stem from its low-level nature and its ability to tackle out-of-the-box ad-hoc scenarios, but high-level APIs such as igDataChart can massively simplify things if your story fits within their constraints. Luckily, igDataChart is very configurable and flexible so a wide range of scenarios can be represented.

Here's a breakdown of some of the settings used in the configuration for the preceding example:

➤ `dataSource` assigns the data to the chart. All the axes and series in the chart inherit this data source unless they have one specified locally.

➤ `title` assigns the chart-level title or series-level title. The chart title is displayed above the chart, and the series titles are displayed in the legend or in the tooltips.

➤ `subtitle` is a smaller title line that is displayed under the main title for the chart.

➤ `legend` specifies some suboptions for the legend for the chart. Here you point out which element, using a selector, should accept the legend content.

➤ `axes` specifies the axes that you are associating with the chart. These can be positioned on the top, bottom, left, or right of the chart, and you can add as many as you want. When you add a series to the chart, you just need to indicate which axes it uses.

➤ `type` specifies the axis type that is being added. In this case, we are adding a category (ordinal) axis and a numeric axis to map the values into the plot area. There is also a type option for the series that specifies which series type is being added. There are a lot of available series types. You can find some of the available types at http://help.infragistics.com/Doc/ jQuery/2014.1/CLR4.0?page=igDataChart_Series_Types.html, but that page doesn't even touch on all the financial indicators and annotation layers available.

➤ `label` specifies which property holds the label to use for the category labels.

➤ `labelExtent` specifies the amount of space to reserve for the axis labels for an axis. If you leave this unspecified, the chart calculates this automatically, but if you modify the data or zoom level, the label areas update dynamically, so often it's best to fix this value.

➤ `minimumValue`/`maximumValue` specifies the minimum and maximum of the axis range. Otherwise, the axis ranges are also automatically calculated by default.

➤ `strip` specifies alternating color strips for an axis.

➤ `series` specifies the series being added to the chart.

➤ `name` adds identifiers for axes and series.

> ➤ xAxis/yAxis identify which axes a series will use to map its values by name.

> ➤ valueMemberPath indicates which property the series will fetch values from.

> ➤ showTooltip indicates that a tooltip should be shown when the series is hovered.

> ➤ isTransitionInEnabled/isHighlightingEnabled turns on the transition effect and the highlighting effect for a series.

> ➤ transitionInDuration specifies how long, in milliseconds, a transition should take.

All that amounts to is that you are adding a category axis and a numeric axis to the chart, two area series for the two data sets to be displayed, and an item tooltip layer that displays the simultaneous item tooltips. If this layer were omitted, you would get non-simultaneous tooltips depending on which series you were currently over.

That's all okay, but this chapter is about symbols, so where are they?

Adding Symbols to the Chart

Adding symbols to a chart with igDataChart is dead simple. You can either select a symbol shape that you want, or you can select `automatic`, which means that each series that has the automatic setting attempts to select a unique symbol shape (until they run out). Here's how:

```
markerType: "automatic",
```

That's it. You would just add that to the options for each series. If you want to select a particular marker, you use a string such as `circle` or `triangle`. You can see the result in Figure 12-6, and you can find the `IgniteUIChartAreaWithSymbols.js/html/css` files on the companion website.

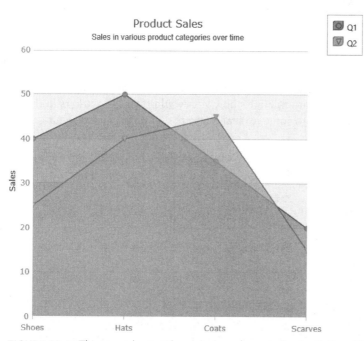

FIGURE 12-6: This area chart with symbols was created using igDataChart.

Notice that there are some other interesting behaviors that have come into play now, too. When you hover over a series, not only is the main series shape highlighted, but the closest data marker is also highlighted, as you achieved earlier with D3.

It's not just line or area charts that support markers; if you change the type of the series to type `column`, you'll see that the columns also have markers. Figure 12-7 shows the result. The `IgniteUIChartColumnWithSymbols.js/html/css` files are on the companion website.

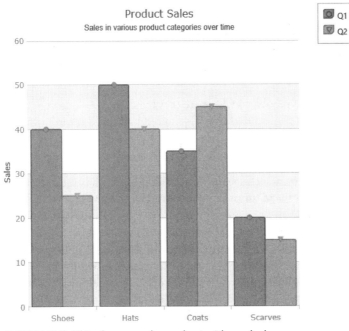

FIGURE 12-7: This shows a column chart with symbols.

Symbols aren't only for delineating where the actual data values are in a chart, though; you can use them as an additional channel for information. Here's how you would turn the markers in the column chart from the preceding example into some textual markers that display each column's value directly above it:

```
var markerFont = "18px Verdana";
    var measureSpan = $("<span>M</span>");
    measureSpan.css("font", markerFont);
    measureSpan.css("visibility", "hidden");
    $("body").append(measureSpan);
    var approxFontHeight = parseFloat(measureSpan.prop("offsetHeight"));
    measureSpan.remove();
    var markerTextMargin = 2.5;

    var textualMarker = {
        measure: function (measureInfo) {
            var cont = measureInfo.context;
```

```
                cont.font = markerFont;
                var data = measureInfo.data;
                var name = "null";
                if (data.item() !== null) {
                    name = data.item().amount.toString();
                }
                var height = approxFontHeight + markerTextMargin * 2.0;
                var width = cont.measureText(name).width + markerTextMargin * 2.0;
                measureInfo.width = width;
                measureInfo.height = height;
            },
        render: function (renderInfo) {
            var ctx = renderInfo.context;
            ctx.font = markerFont;
            if (renderInfo.isHitTestRender) {
                ctx.fillStyle = renderInfo.data.actualItemBrush().fill();
            } else {
                ctx.fillStyle = "black";
            }

            var data = renderInfo.data;
            if (data.item() === null) {
                return;
            }
            var name = data.item().amount.toString();
            var halfWidth = renderInfo.availableWidth / 2.0;
            var halfHeight = renderInfo.availableHeight / 2.0;
            var x = renderInfo.xPosition - halfWidth;

            var y = renderInfo.yPosition - (halfHeight * 2.0);
            if (y < 0) {
                y += (halfHeight * 4.0);
            }

            if (renderInfo.isHitTestRender) {
                ctx.fillRect(x, y, renderInfo.availableWidth,
                renderInfo.availableHeight);
            } else {
                ctx.globalAlpha = 0.5;
                ctx.fillStyle = renderInfo.data.actualItemBrush().fill();
                ctx.fillRect(x, y, renderInfo.availableWidth,
                renderInfo.availableHeight);
                ctx.fillStyle = renderInfo.data.outline().fill();
                ctx.strokeRect(x, y, renderInfo.availableWidth,
                renderInfo.availableHeight);
                ctx.globalAlpha = 1;

                ctx.fillStyle = "black";
                ctx.textBaseline = "top";
                ctx.fillText(name, x + markerTextMargin, y + markerTextMargin);
            }
        }
    }
};
```

You would then assign this `textualMarker` variable to the series using `markerTemplate:`
`textualMarker`. igDataChart uses the HTML5 canvas for rendering (as opposed to SVG like D3).
The preceding code lets you step in and issue commands to the canvas to render some custom
symbol content when required. You have access to the data that would be in context for a symbol,
and the colors that the chart would have used, and you are responsible for rendering content in the
provided context. The code just renders some text in a rectangle to produce the result shown in
Figure 12-8. You can find the `IgniteUIChartColumnWithTextSymbols.js/html/css` files on the
companion website.

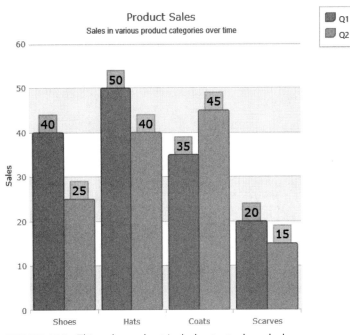

FIGURE 12-8: This column chart includes textual symbols.

Creating a Bubble Chart

Some chart series are entirely composed of symbols, such as the one you can create with the
following code:

```
$(function () {
    $.ajax({
        type: "GET",
        url: "Food_Display_Table.xml",
        dataType: "xml",
        success: loadXml
    });

    var data = [];

    function loadXml(xmlData) {
```

```
$(xmlData).find("Food_Display_Row")
.each(function () {
    var row = $(this);
    var displayName = row.find("Display_Name").text();
    var saturatedFat = parseFloat(row.find("Saturated_Fats").text());
    var calories = parseFloat(row.find("Calories").text());
    var milk = parseFloat(row.find("Milk").text());
    data.push({
        displayName: displayName,
        saturatedFat: saturatedFat,
        calories: calories,
        milk: milk
    });
});

data.sort(function (v1, v2) {
    if (v1.milk < v2.milk) {
        return -1;
    }
    if (v1.milk > v2.milk) {
        return 1;
    }
    return 0;
});
console.log("records loaded: " + data.length);
renderChart();
}

function renderChart() {
    $("#chart").igDataChart({
        dataSource: data,
        title: "Saturated Fat vs. Calories",
        subtitle: "Amounts of saturated fat vs. calories
in common foods. Data: Data.gov",
        horizontalZoomable: true,
        verticalZoomable: true,
        axes: [{
            type: "numericX",
            name: "xAxis",
            title: "Saturated Fat",
            strip: "rgba(230,230,230,.4)"
        }, {
            type: "numericY",
            name: "yAxis",
            title: "Calories",
            strip: "rgba(230,230,230,.4)"
        }],
        series: [{
            name: "saturatedFatVsCalories",
            type: "bubble",
            xAxis: "xAxis",
            yAxis: "yAxis",
            xMemberPath: "saturatedFat",
            yMemberPath: "calories",
            radiusMemberPath: "milk",
```

```
                    fillMemberPath: "milk",
                    labelMemberPath: "displayName",
                    showTooltip: true,
                    tooltipTemplate: "tooltipTemplate",
                    title: "Saturated Fat Vs. Calories",
                    maximumMarkers: 3000,
                    radiusScale: {
                        minimumValue: 10,
                        maximumValue: 25
                    },
                    fillScale: {
                        type: "value",
                        brushes: ["red", "orange", "yellow"]
                    }

                }]
            });
        }

    });
```

For this code, you need to snag some data from the `http://data.gov` website. `http://catalog.data.gov/dataset/mypyramid-food-raw-data-f9ed6` has some data, including calories and saturated fat content, for many different common food types. Using the strategies described in Chapter 4, you can load the file using an AJAX call and put its contents in `data`. Then, provided with two numeric axes, rather than the category and numeric axis combo you were using before, you are able to load a `type: "bubble"` series.

> **NOTE** *When attempting to run the previous sample, if you did not load it via a web server you may have run into some interesting issues. Most browsers block AJAX requests if they are targeted at the local file system. If you are running IIS or Apache on your machine, you can resolve the issue by placing the files from this chapter someplace that you can serve them via IIS/Apache and access them from a* `http://localhost` *address. Alternatively, if you have Python installed, you can navigate to the directory that contains the files for this chapter and run the command* `python -m SimpleHTTPServer`; *then you should be able to access the files via:* `http://localhost:8000/`.

A bubble series enables its symbols to carry more than just x-y position data. Additionally, you can convey at least two additional values by mapping them to the size and color of the symbols. This is done by specifying the `fillMemberPath` and the `radiusMemberPath` to indicate which properties should be used to map to those attributes. `radiusScale` and `fillScale` further customize the look of the symbols so that the chart looks like the one shown in Figure 12-9, which is also shown in the color insert. The `IgniteUIBubbleChart.js/html/css` files are on the companion website.

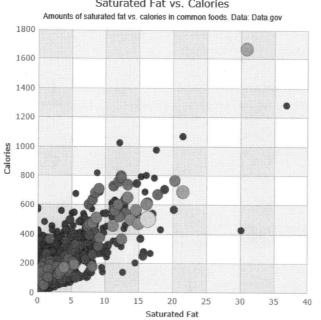

DATA SOURCE: HTTP://CATALOG.DATA.GOV/DATASET/MYPYRAMID-FOOD-RAW-DATA-F9ED6

FIGURE 12-9: This bubble chart was created using igDataChart.

Notice also that zooming has been turned on for the chart:

```
horizontalZoomable: true,
verticalZoomable: true,
```

In Figures 12-10 and 12-11, you can see how you can zoom into the bubble chart to drill down into the dense areas and perceive the fine detail. (You can see Figure 12-11 in full color in the color insert.) Every series in igDataChart supports zooming and panning in this manner. Also note, that it is not just an optical zoom that is occurring here, as the level of detail changes as more data points are revealed or hidden.

Although features such as these are possible, with enough code, using low-level visualization APIs such as D3, they certainly aren't as simple to enable as setting a few properties to true, as with the igDataChart. The strength of products such as Ignite UI is that they can turn very complex scenarios into turnkey solutions.

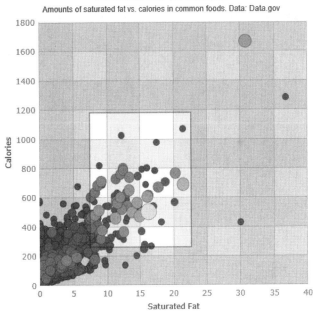

Data source: http://catalog.data.gov/dataset/mypyramid-food-raw-data-f9ed6

FIGURE 12-10: This shows zooming into a bubble chart.

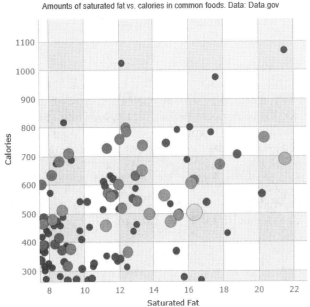

Data source: http://catalog.data.gov/dataset/mypyramid-food-raw-data-f9ed6

FIGURE 12-11: The bubble chart has been zoomed.

SUMMARY

Now you've learned all about adding symbols to charts. Symbols help to annotate individual items in your data and present their location to the consumer of the visualization. Also, as you saw, some charting types consist entirely of symbols. In this chapter, you

➤ Created a line chart using D3 and added symbols to it

➤ Made these symbols more dynamic and made them respond to mouse interaction

➤ Created an area series using the Ignite UI igDataChart charting API.

➤ Added symbols to the igDataChart Area series

➤ Added symbols to a column chart in igDataChart and turned these markers into textual markers

➤ Created a bubble chart using igDataChart

13

Mapping Global, Regional, and Local Data

WHAT'S IN THIS CHAPTER

> ➤ Learning how to plot an interactive map on a web page using the Google Maps API

> ➤ Plotting markers at desired locations on a map

> ➤ Plotting point clouds of data on a map

> ➤ Displaying density information on a map using a heat map

> ➤ Turning publically available vector map geometry into GeoJSON

> ➤ Plotting GeoJSON as SVG using D3 and TopoJSON

> ➤ Using D3 to display animated choropleth maps

> **CODE DOWNLOAD** *The wrox.com code downloads for this chapter are found at* www.wrox.com/go/javascriptandjqueryanalysis *on the Download Code tab. The code is in the chapter 13 download and individually named according to the names throughout the chapter.*

This chapter is all about visualizing data on maps. It starts with visualizing data that has some form of associated geographic position as markers on a map and then moves on to conveying statistical information about geographic regions by varying their color through what is known as *choropleth* mapping.

If you've used the Internet at all in the past decade, chances are you've used the Google Maps web application at some point. It enables you to search for points of interest, find directions between one place and another, and to smoothly zoom and pan around the map to examine things. Fortunately, Google also released an application programming interface (API) that enables you to build web applications that plot various data over the Google Maps tile images and allow this data to be navigable using the same mechanisms as the Google Maps application.

You've already used the D3 JavaScript API in some of the preceding chapters—mostly in the context of charts—but D3 also provides mechanisms for plotting map geometry. In the latter part of this chapter, you use D3 to plot dynamic geometry on a map to convey statistical information about various regions.

The data or geometry you might want to plot on a map can be very large and unwieldy. Furthermore, the APIs you use may have practical limitations in terms of plotting dynamic imagery in an online, interactive fashion (as opposed to doing offline rendering ahead of time). Thus, you have to process the data used in this chapter in various ways to ready it for display on a map. There are countless programming languages you could use to preprocess the data for this purpose, but as this is a book on using JavaScript to present visualizations, here, you also use JavaScript to process the data via the Node.js platform.

WORKING WITH GOOGLE MAPS

At the time of this writing, you can freely use the Google Maps API as long as your website is free to use and is publically accessible, but be sure to review all the terms of use of the Google Maps API before you proceed with using it in a production website. If your website is not free to use, or is not publically accessible, Google also provides a Google Maps for Business products. Your first step, after reviewing the terms of use of the API, should be to sign up for a Google Maps API key. Although not technically required (none of the code samples in this chapter include an API key, and they function without it, as of the time of writing), Google recommends that you use an API key so that you, and they, can track your usage. Thus empowered, you can stay within the quotas they place on the free level of usage for the service. You can obtain an API key here:

```
https://developers.google.com/maps/documentation/javascript/tutorial#api_key
```

After you've obtained your API key, make sure that, when you try to use any of the code in this chapter, you include your API key in the script URL for the Google Maps API scripts:

```
<script type="text/javascript"
src="https://maps.googleapis.com/maps/api/js?key=KEY&sensor=false">
</script>
```

In the preceding code, KEY is the API key that you obtained from Google.

The Basics of Mapping Visualizations

Maps of the earth are an attempt to take the 3D geography of the planet, which is roughly an oblate spheroid, and show it on the 2D Cartesian plane of a sheet of paper. If you want to describe a point on the 3D spheroid of the earth, one popular way is to use latitude, longitude, and elevation values, which represent the angular and radial displacements from the origin point of the spheroid. The origin point is conventionally decided to be the intersection of the equator of the earth and the Prime Meridian, which divides the western and eastern hemispheres of the earth.

Over the years, cartographers have defined various projections, or mathematical formulas, that map from the coordinate system over this spheroid, into a 2D Cartesian coordinate system that you can easily display on a sheet of paper or computer screen.

Your data, when it has a geographic context, will likely be expressed in terms of geographic coordinates (latitude, longitude, and, optionally, elevation) and the mapping tools that you are using will help you take the values and express them in the 2D Cartesian space of the computer screen.

Sometimes you'll be able to select from the many different projections that have been conceived for mapping geometry between these spaces, but sometimes this choice will be dictated for you by the tool in use. The primary use case for the Google Maps API is to plot data over the map tile imagery that Google Maps provides and helps you navigate. These tiles are rendered using a modified version of the Mercator map projection, so when you request that data be plotted over them, you present the data using geographic coordinates, which the Google Maps API applies this projection to in order to map them into 2D Cartesian coordinates over the map.

Thanks to the Google Maps API, you don't often need to think about the fact that your geographic coordinates are not already Cartesian values because the API deals with the transformation into the Cartesian plane, but you will sometimes need to remember that map projections have distorted the actual geometry being plotted. In Figure 13-1 (which you can find in companion files `GoogleMapsProjectionDistortion.html/css/js`), I've asked the Google Maps API to plot a set of randomly placed circles on the map. These circles all have exactly the same radius in geographic coordinates, but you can see how the projection distorts their shape in the Cartesian plane when they are plotted in different places over the map.

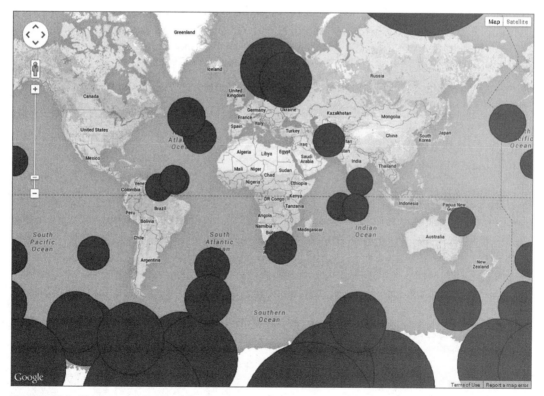

FIGURE 13-1: This is an example of map projection distortion.

The Google Maps API v3

First, you start by getting a basic map to display, using the API, before you try to plot data over it. The following is the HTML markup:

```html
<!DOCTYPE html>
<html>
<head>
    <title>Basic Map</title>

    <script src="https://maps.googleapis.com/maps/api/js?v=3.exp&sensor=false">
</script>

    <link rel="stylesheet" href="GoogleMapsBasic.css">

    <script type="text/javascript" src="GoogleMapsBasic.js">
    </script>
</head>
<body>
    <div id="map"></div>
</body>
</html>
```

The maps script reference is where you would introduce your API key, as previously alluded to. The main content of the page is a `<div>` that will hold the map created by the Google Maps API. Most HTML markup for the Google Maps API code in this chapter looks exactly the same, except it loads different JavaScript, so this is the only time it's covered.

Similarly, all the Google Maps API code for this chapter uses roughly the same CSS, which essentially makes the map take all the available space of the page:

```css
html, body, #map {
    margin: 0;
    padding: 0;
    height: 100%
}
```

Listing 13-1 is the actual code that displays the map.

LISTING 13-1

```javascript
var map;
var statueOfLiberty = new google.maps.LatLng(40.6897445, -74.0451452);

var options = {
    zoom: 12,
    center: statueOfLiberty
};

function createMap() {
```

```
    var mapElement = document.getElementById("map");
    map = new google.maps.Map(mapElement, options);
}


google.maps.event.addDomListener(window, 'load', createMap);
```

The idea here is to center the map view on the Statue of Liberty monument at a specified zoom level. Let's break things down before adding any additional complexity.

```
var map;
var statueOfLiberty = new google.maps.LatLng(40.6897445, -74.0451452);
```

This creates a variable that holds the map, so that it can be interacted with after initial creation and creates a latitude and longitude pair that represents the geographic position of the Statue of Liberty monument. An easy way to discover these coordinates is to search for a point of interest in the Google Maps application. For example, if you search for "Statue of Liberty" in Google Maps and look at the returned Uniform Resource Identifier (URI) in the address box after you select it from the search results, you see:

```
https://www.google.com/maps/place/Statue+of+Liberty+National+Monument/@40.689757,-
74.0451453,17z/data=!3m1!4b1!4m2!3m1!1s0x89c25090129c363d:0x40c6a5770d25022b
```

After the @ sign, you see two coordinates that represent the position of the point of interest. This technique isn't guaranteed to always work, as Google might change the structure of this URI, but, as of the time of this writing, this represents an easy ad hoc way to obtain some coordinates. For a more resilient method, you could look into using the Google Maps Geocoding API for looking up the coordinates of a point of interest or finding the closest point of interest to some geographic coordinates:

```
https://developers.google.com/maps/documentation/geocoding/
 var options = {
     zoom: 12,
     center: statueOfLiberty
 };
```

The preceding code defines the creation options of the map. It declares that the map should start centered around the statue at zoom level 12.

> **NOTE** *The Google Maps image tiles are a tree of tiles. At the top level, you have four tiles, and each level you descend, one tile is subdivided into four sub-tiles. The zoom level represents how deep in this tile tree you are currently displaying images from. Each tile level introduces progressively more resolution to the map imagery. This is actually the same way that most map tile providers work. For example, if you investigate the OpenStreetMap API, you find that the tile level and tile coordinates are a human readable part of the resource path you are requesting from the server. For example,* `http://b.tile.openstreetmap.org/5/7/12.png` *represents a tile from zoom level 5 with x tile coordinate 7 and y tile coordinate 12.*

```
function createMap() {
    var mapElement = document.getElementById("map");
    map = new google.maps.Map(mapElement, options);
}
```

The preceding function creates the map when the DOM is ready to receive it. It locates the DOM element that you want to add the map to and then instantiates the map with the options that indicate it should center on the Statue of Liberty at zoom level 12.

```
google.maps.event.addDomListener(window, 'load', createMap);
```

Finally, this line waits until the window is loaded to call the preceding code and thus creates the map. Not too complicated yet, right? You can see the results in Figure 13-2, and you can find the `GoogleMapsBasic.html/css/js` files on the companion website.

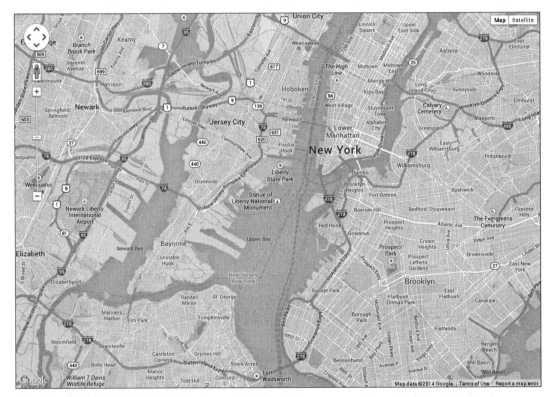

FIGURE 13-2: A basic map is displayed using Google Maps.

The code might have been simple, but the results are very complex. You can zoom and pan and do many things that you can do with the full Google Maps web application, except, with this code, you can embed the experience in your own web application. This book, however, is about visualizing data, so where is the data?

CUSTOMIZING MAPS WITH ICONOGRAPHY

One of the most straightforward ways to visualize data on a map is to position icons (or symbols/markers) over the surface. Google Maps API uses the term markers, so this chapter uses that term to describe how you render point data on your maps.

If you consider most of the maps that you interact with often, one of the most common visualization types that you see is markers. And those markers are usually indicating the locations of various points of interest. When you visit a shopping mall, for instance, and look at a directory, markers indicate the locations of the restrooms and elevators, and textual markers indicate where the various shops are located. When you are looking up the location of the restaurant that you are going to for dinner, using its website, there is a pushpin marker indicating its location on a map. In fact, oftentimes it is the Google Maps API that is used when you use a restaurant's location finder page.

Displaying a Map Marker

So, how do you display a marker using the Google Maps API? It turns out this is extremely simple to do, which is not especially surprising given that it is one of the primary use cases for the API. Given Listing 13-1, you can add the following to the `createMap` function after the map instantiation:

```
statueMarker = new google.maps.Marker({
    position: statueOfLiberty,
    map: map,
    title: "Statue of Liberty"
});
```

Here you instantiate a marker, providing the position of the Statue of Liberty monument, indicate that it should be rendered on the map you just created, and provide it the title "Statue of Liberty." The title will be shown in the tooltip when the user hovers over the marker on the map. Figure 13-3 shows the results of the code; you can find the `GoogleMapsBasicMarker.html/css/js` files on the companion website.

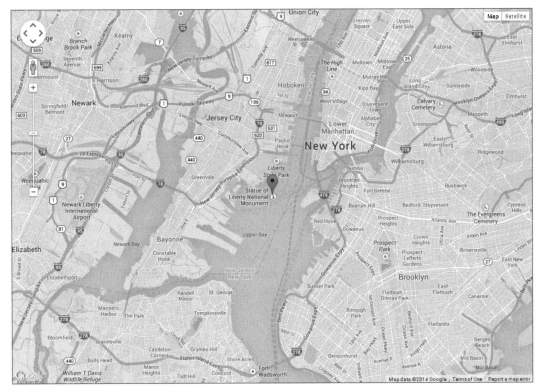

FIGURE 13-3: The Statue of Liberty monument has been called out with a marker.

Notice that the default marker style for Google Maps API is the now-familiar Google Maps stylized pushpin, but there are many ways to customize the look and feel of this marker. For example, you can assign various vector imagery to the marker, rather than using the default look:

```
statueMarker = new google.maps.Marker({
    position: statueOfLiberty,
    map: map,
    icon: {
        path: google.maps.SymbolPath.CIRCLE,
        scale: 12,
        strokeColor: 'red',
        strokeWeight: 5
    },
    title: "Statue of Liberty"
});
```

You see how this looks in Figure 13-4, and the `GoogleMapsBasicMarkerVector.html/css/js` files is on the companion website. This is just a single point of data, though. What if you want to plot a point cloud over the map?

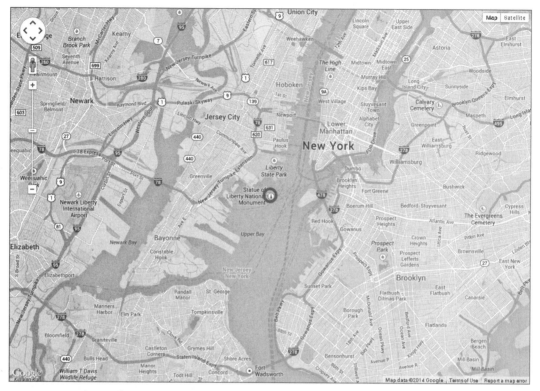

FIGURE 13-4: The marker on this map is a circle icon.

Preparing Data to Plot on a Map

With the markers in the Google Maps API you are dynamically rendering content interactively, and there is an overhead associated with each piece of retained geometry you add to the map. As such, there are practical limits to the number of markers that you can display, especially if you want to target low-power devices such as smartphones and tablets, which generally don't have as much oomph to their CPUs or as much spare memory (graphics or otherwise) to go around as desktop and laptop computers.

There are various strategies you can use to make it easier to render a large point cloud as markers on a map, but the one covered first is culling the number of displayed markers down to a more manageable limit. This helps to avoid overtaxing the system during rendering.

First, however, you need to find an interesting data set to display on the map. A good source of public domain data is the www.data.gov website. Most of the data sets have unrestricted usage, and they are nicely cataloged and searchable by data type. Because the goal is to use JavaScript to display the data over the map, you can make your life much easier by finding a data set that is already expressed as JSON. In fact, there is an extended grammar of JSON called GeoJSON that standard-izes how to convey geographic data and geometry in JSON format.

> **NOTE** *Although it's especially simple to use, GeoJSON can have some down-sides when it comes to sending geographic data over a network connection. If you want high-precision geographic positions, this usually means high-precision floating-point numbers, and when these numbers are serialized as text in a JSON file, they can take up quite a few text characters per number. When this is combined with highly detailed geometry, or large point clouds, the size of a GeoJSON file can grow very quickly. There are mechanisms to avoid this. One solution, which comes up later in this chapter, is to use TopoJSON, which is a modification to the spec that allows for quantized coordinates and topol-ogy sharing, in order to reduce the amount of space all the coordinates take up (among other things). Another strategy is to send binary packed floating points over the wire rather than focusing on human readable string values (which is one of the main attractions to using JSON).*

Browsing around data.gov, I ran into this data set, which was already in GeoJSON format: http://catalog.data.gov/dataset/public-library-survey-pls-2011. This represents all the libraries that responded to the Public Library Survey for 2011. There are more than 9,000 items in this data source, though, so it would be quite a load on the system to render them all, which might result in sluggish performance. To combat this, you create a subset of the data to only the libraries in one state. To do this, as alluded to earlier, you use Node.js.

Node.js is an application platform for running applications written in JavaScript. It leverages Google's V8 JavaScript engine to efficiently run programs at native-like speeds. There are many interesting reasons you might want to leverage Node.js, including writing simple non-blocking web services, but, here, you leverage it simply to not have to use a separate language to cull down the library data. First, use the following steps:

1. Navigate to http://nodejs.org/.

2. Install Node.js for your platform.

3. Create a folder on your computer and unzip the public library data into it.

4. In that same folder, create a text file called process.js, and open it in a text editor.

Then, add the code in Listing 13-2 to the file you created.

LISTING 13-2

```
var fs = require("fs");

fs.readFile("pupld11b.geojson", function (err, data) {
    if (err) {
```

```
        console.log("Error: " + err);
        return;
    }

    var content = JSON.parse(data);

    var features = [];
    var newCollection = {
        "type": "FeatureCollection",
        "features": features
    };
    var currFeature;

    var count = 0;
    if (content.features && content.features.length) {
        for (var i = 0; i < content.features.length; i++) {
            currFeature = content.features[i];
            if (currFeature !== null &&
                currFeature.properties !== null &&
                currFeature.properties.STABR) {
                if (currFeature.properties.STABR === "NJ") {
                    features.push(currFeature);
                    count++;
                }
            }
        }
    }

    var output = JSON.stringify(newCollection);
    fs.writeFile("pupld11b_subset.geojson",
     output, function (err) {
        if (err) {
            console.log("Error: " + err);
            return;
        }

        console.log("done, wrote " + count + " features.");
    });
});
```

Let's break down Listing 13-2. First you have

```
var fs = require("fs");
```

which loads the Node.js file system module so that you can read and write files from disk. Immediately following is this line:

```
fs.readFile("pupld11b.geojson", function (err, data) {
```

Most of the APIs available for the Node.js platform are designed to be fully asynchronous, to avoid blocking the main event loops of the system. As such, input/output (IO) operations, like this one, involve providing a callback that will be invoked when the operation has completed. In the previous code, you are requesting that the GeoJSON file that you downloaded, with the library information, should be read into a string.

```
if (err) {
    console.log("Error: " + err);
    return;
}

var content = JSON.parse(data);

var features = [];
var newCollection = {
    "type": "FeatureCollection",
    "features": features
};
var currFeature;
```

If an error occurs during the file load, the preceding code prints it to the console and then aborts. Otherwise, it parses the GeoJSON into a JavaScript object and then preps a new output array that holds the subset of the data.

```
var count = 0;
if (content.features && content.features.length) {
    for (var i = 0; i < content.features.length; i++) {
        currFeature = content.features[i];
        if (currFeature !== null &&
            currFeature.properties !== null &&
            currFeature.properties.STABR) {
            if (currFeature.properties.STABR === "NJ") {
                features.push(currFeature);
                count++;
            }
        }
    }
}
```

With this code, you loop over the input collection and shift values into the subset if the STABR property is equal to NJ. Thus, features should only contain libraries within the state of New Jersey.

```
var output = JSON.stringify(newCollection);
fs.writeFile("pupld11b_subset.geojson", output, function (err) {
    if (err) {
        console.log("Error: " + err);
        return;
    }

    console.log("done, wrote " + count + " features.");
});
```

Finally, you serialize the subset collection back out to JSON and write it out to a new file called pupld11b_subset.geojson. Alternatively, an error prints out if it's unable to write the new file.

To run the resulting logic, you should start a Node.js command prompt. Because the strategy to achieve this varies depending on the platform on which you are running Node.js, please refer to the Node.js documentation for more information. On Windows, I run a shortcut that was installed along with Node.js that creates a command prompt and ensures that Node.js is accessible to use therein. Given a command prompt, you should navigate to the folder in which you placed `process .js` and the input GeoJSON data. Then you can run the following command:

```
node process.js
```

which should result in the file `pupld11b_subset.geojson` being created. You can see an example of running this command on Windows in Figure 13-5. File `pupld11b.geojson`, `process.js` is on the companion website.

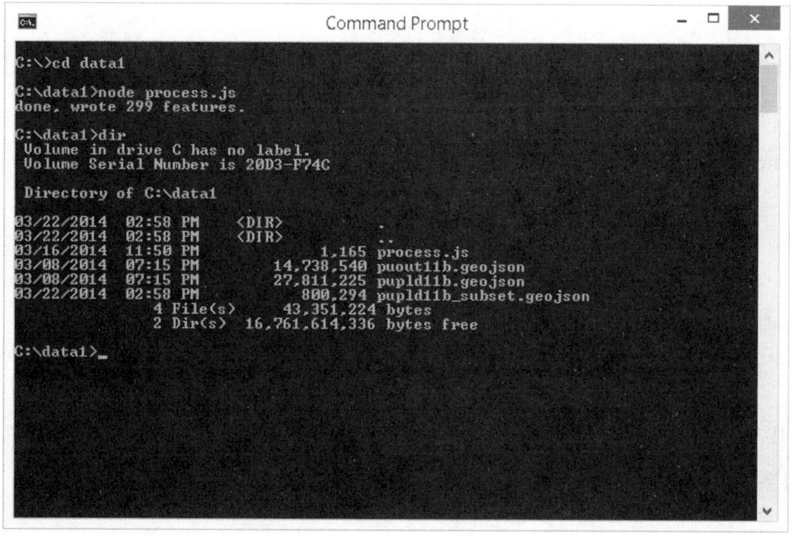

FIGURE 13-5: This shows using Node.js to cull down a GeoJSON file.

Plotting Point Data Using Markers

Given the subset of the GeoJSON file, you can proceed to plot it on the map.

```
$(function () {
    $.ajax({
        type: "GET",
        url: "pupld11b_subset.geojson",
        dataType: "json",
        success: createMap
    });
});
```

As you can see, jQuery is used to get the GeoJSON file and parse it.

> **NOTE** *If you are loading the HTML file off your local disk, rather than running a local web server and using an HTTP URL, some browsers, such as Google Chrome, give you security errors. Chrome is trying to keep malicious websites from accessing files on your local disk with this restriction. Other browsers allow the access as long as you don't try to leave the directory from which the page is loaded. To avoid these issues, you might want to host the pages for the rest of this chapter on a local web server and access them through* http:// localhost; *alternatively, you could use Mozilla Firefox to load them, which, as of the time of writing, does not have the same restriction.*

When the file is successfully parsed, the createMap function is called.

```
var map;
var markers = [];
var njView = new google.maps.LatLng(40.3637892, -74.3553047);

var options = {
    zoom: 8,
    center: njView
};
```

Similar to how you centered the view around the Statue of Liberty earlier, this centers the view over the state of New Jersey.

```
function createMap(data) {
    var mapElement = document.getElementById("map");
    var currentFeature, geometry, libraryName;
    map = new google.maps.Map(mapElement, options);

    for (var i = 0; i < data.features.length; i++) {
        currentFeature = data.features[i];

        if (!currentFeature.geometry) {
            continue;
        }
        geometry = currentFeature.geometry;

        libraryName = "Unknown";
        if (currentFeature.properties) {
            libraryName = currentFeature.properties.LIBNAME;
        }

        markers.push(new google.maps.Marker({
            position: new google.maps.LatLng(
                geometry.coordinates[1],
                geometry.coordinates[0]),
            map: map,
            title: libraryName
        }));
    }
}
```

In the preceding code, the following things happen:

➤ The map is instantiated, as before.

➤ You loop through all the features in the GeoJSON file.

➤ For each feature, the `geometry` of the feature is extracted, which is a latitude and longitude pair, in this case.

➤ For each feature, a marker is added to the map, which is centered on the feature point, and the marker title is set to the associated name of the library.

You can see the result of this in Figure 13-6; `GoogleMapsManyMarkers.html/css/js` are the files on the companion website.

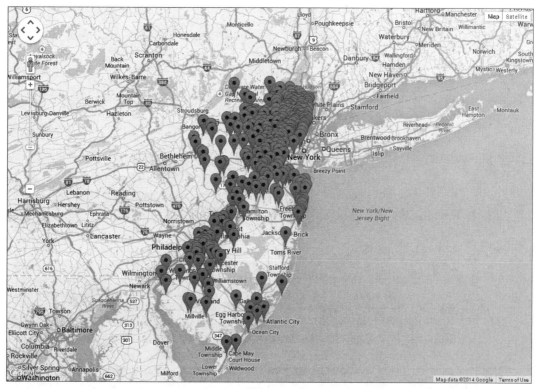

SOURCE FOR LIBRARY DATA: HTTP://CATALOG.DATA.GOV/DATASET/PUBLIC-LIBRARY-SURVEY-PLS-2011

FIGURE 13-6: These markers plot the public libraries in New Jersey.

Also notice that you can hover over the markers with your mouse and (eventually) see a tooltip that contains the name of the library in question. At the initial zoom level, all of the markers are clustered together and occlude each other, but you can zoom in for greater detail and the markers begin to resolve into more dispersed entities. Figure 13-7 shows what the map looks like and an example of a tooltip.

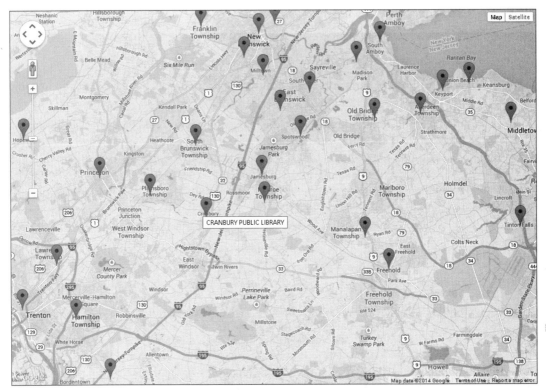

SOURCE FOR LIBRARY DATA: HTTP://CATALOG.DATA.GOV/DATASET/PUBLIC-LIBRARY-SURVEY-PLS-2011

FIGURE 13-7: The map from Figure 13-6 has been zoomed in.

> **NOTE** *Rendering an individual marker for each and every data point is simple to implement, but it is not a very satisfactory strategy as the number of points to visualize increases. As the point count rises, performance issues start to crop up in the tools you are using, and the data simply gets harder to analyze as it increasingly occludes itself. A smarter way of going about rendering larger amounts of point data on a map includes clustering clumps of neighboring markers into a single marker that represents the group, and then splitting apart the grouped marker as the map zooms in further on that area. Another valid strategy would be to switch to using a heat map to visualize the data, which is discussed in the "Displaying Data Density with Heat Maps" section of this chapter.*

So far, you've only dealt with simple icons that delineate a latitude/longitude location on the map, but with a little tweaking, the markers can convey extra channels of data to your user. If you think back to Chapter 12 and bubble charts, you can anticipate the next move.

Plotting an Additional Statistic Using Marker Area

When plotting markers, especially circular ones, you can use the size of the marker to convey another data channel to the consumer of a visualization. If you examine the GeoJSON file you loaded for the previous scenario, you see that there are many extra properties associated with each library that you may choose to visualize above and beyond the library's location.

An interesting statistic that jumps out is the number of visits to each library. Mapping this value to the size of the markers should make their size proportional to the traffic to an individual library, which is a pretty natural usage for relative marker sizes. The following is an altered version of the createMap function, which, instead of creating Marker objects, creates Circle objects and associates them with the map:

```
function createMap(data) {
    var mapElement = document.getElementById("map");
    var currentFeature, geometry, libraryName, visits,
        minVisits, maxVisits, area, radius, i;
    map = new google.maps.Map(mapElement, options);

    for (i = 0; i < data.features.length; i++) {
        currentFeature = data.features[i];
        visits = currentFeature.properties.VISITS;

        if (i === 0) {
            minVisits = visits;
            maxVisits = visits;
        } else {
            minVisits = Math.min(minVisits, visits);
            maxVisits = Math.max(maxVisits, visits);
        }
    }

    for (i = 0; i < data.features.length; i++) {
        currentFeature = data.features[i];

        if (!currentFeature.geometry) {
            continue;
        }
        geometry = currentFeature.geometry;
        visits = currentFeature.properties.VISITS;

        libraryName = "Unknown";
        if (currentFeature.properties) {
            libraryName = currentFeature.properties.LIBNAME;
        }

        area = (visits - minVisits) / (maxVisits - minVisits)
        * 500000000 + 100000;
        radius = Math.sqrt(area / Math.PI);

        circles.push(new google.maps.Circle({
```

```
            center: new google.maps.LatLng(
                geometry.coordinates[1],
                geometry.coordinates[0]),
            map: map,
            radius: radius,
            fillOpacity: .7,
            strokeOpacity: .7,
            strokeWeight: 2,
            title: libraryName,
            visits: currentFeature.properties.VISITS,
            fillColor: '#0066FF',
            strokeColor: '#0047B2'
        }));

        google.maps.event.addListener(circles[i],'mouseover',onMouseOver);


        google.maps.event.addListener(circles[i], 'mouseout', onMouseOut);


    }

    function onMouseOver() {
        map.getDiv().setAttribute('title',this.get('title') + ": " +
        this.get('visits'));
    }

    function onMouseOut() {
        map.getDiv().removeAttribute('title');
    }
}
```

Let's examine the new and interesting parts of the code. First you have

```
for (i = 0; i < data.features.length; i++) {
    currentFeature = data.features[i];
    visits = currentFeature.properties.VISITS;

    if (i === 0) {
        minVisits = visits;
        maxVisits = visits;
    } else {
        minVisits = Math.min(minVisits, visits);
        maxVisits = Math.max(maxVisits, visits);
    }
}
```

which is just trying to gather the minimum and maximum number of visits in order to help establish the domain of the values that you are trying to map onto the size range of the markers.

```
visits = currentFeature.properties.VISITS;
```

In the preceding code, you extract the VISITS property from each item, to reference it in deciding the size of the marker. The Google Maps API is going to expect a radius value (in meters) to define the size of the circles. It's actually much more appropriate to map the VISITS value to area, rather than radius, so you can use a bit of math to convert from the area of a circle to the appropriate radius.

```
area = (visits - minVisits) / (maxVisits - minVisits)
* 500000000 + 100000;
radius = Math.sqrt(area / Math.PI);
```

This maps from the input domain (the visits) to the output range (the area of the circles). If you are wondering why the numbers are so large, this is because the `Circle` object expects radius to be specified in meters, so the area of the circle is in square meters. So if you want the circles to be visible from far away, the area has to be very large. This is also why the circles get larger as you zoom in rather than remaining a constant size. They have a fixed geographical area, rather than a fixed pixel area.

```
circles.push(new google.maps.Circle({
    center: new google.maps.LatLng(
        geometry.coordinates[1],
        geometry.coordinates[0]),
    map: map,
    radius: radius,
    fillOpacity: .7,
    strokeOpacity: .7,
    strokeWeight: 2,
    title: libraryName,
    visits: currentFeature.properties.VISITS,
    fillColor: '#0066FF',
    strokeColor: '#0047B2'
}));
```

This instantiates a `Circle` that

➤   Is centered at the position of the library

➤   Is associated with the map you created

➤   Has the radius you previously calculated

➤   Has 70 percent opacity

➤   Has a two-pixel-wide stroke

➤   Has a title and associated number of visits, which you'll refer to later

➤   Has shades of blue for fill and stroke colors

```
google.maps.event.addListener(circles[i], 'mouseover', onMouseOver);

google.maps.event.addListener(circles[i], 'mouseout', onMouseOut);

function onMouseOver() {
    map.getDiv().setAttribute('title', this.get('title') + ": " +
    this.get('visits'));
}

function onMouseOut() {
    map.getDiv().removeAttribute('title');
}
```

Finally, these event handlers change the `title` attribute of the map container as the `Circle` elements are hovered to approximate a tooltip that displays the name of the library and the number of visits. You can see the result of all this work in Figure 13-8, which is also in the color insert, and you can find the `GoogleMapsManyCircleMarkers.html/css/js` files on the companion website.

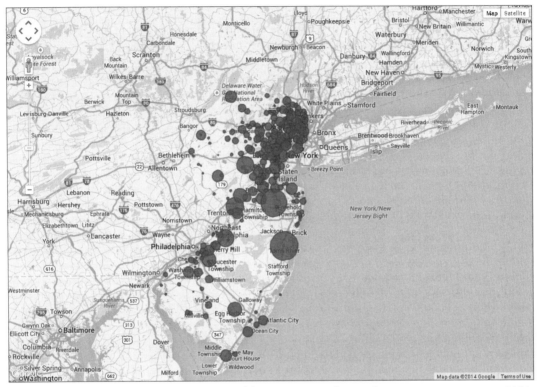

SOURCE FOR LIBRARY DATA: HTTP://CATALOG.DATA.GOV/DATASET/PUBLIC-LIBRARY-SURVEY-PLS-2011

FIGURE 13-8: This shows Google Maps with bubble markers displaying library visits.

Displaying Data Density with Heat Maps

Notice that even though you culled down the number of points displayed when using markers or circles to display the library locations, there was still a lot of occlusion because some regions boast a large number of libraries. The problem with the occlusion is that, even when using semi-transparent circles, it can be difficult for the eye to judge the density of points at various positions without any color differentiation. As a result, 3 or 4 libraries very close together can end up looking identical to 300 libraries very close together.

So, if the density of data points plotted over geographic space is an important part of the story you are trying to tell with the data, it can be desirable to make it as clear as possible what the data density is at each position on the map. One way to achieve this is with a *heat map*, which interpolates between two or more colors so that pixels over the map are colored with a more "hot" color the denser the data points are at that location. A heat map generally renders color around a data point for some configurable radius, and everywhere that the pixels intersect with pixels from other data points, their "heat" is increased, resulting in a hotter color.

Luckily, given what you've built so far, it's actually extremely easy to switch to rendering the library locations using a heat map with the Google Maps API, as shown in Listing 13-3.

LISTING 13-3

```
var map;
var njView = new google.maps.LatLng(40.3637892, -74.3553047);

var options = {
    zoom: 8,
    center: njView
};

function createMap(data) {
    var mapElement = document.getElementById("map");
    var geometry, points, heatmap, heatData;
    map = new google.maps.Map(mapElement, options);

    heatData = [];
    for (var i = 0; i < data.features.length; i++) {
        geometry = data.features[i].geometry;
        heatData.push(new google.maps.LatLng(
                geometry.coordinates[1],
                geometry.coordinates[0]));
    }

    points = new google.maps.MVCArray(heatData);

    heatmap = new google.maps.visualization.HeatmapLayer({
        data: points,
        radius: 20
    });

    heatmap.setMap(map);
}

$(function () {
    $.ajax({
        type: "GET",
        url: "pupld11b_subset.geojson",
        dataType: "json",
        success: createMap
    });
});
```

The new and significant section in Listing 13-3 has been highlighted. If you run the code, you should see the same results as those shown in Figure 13-9 (this figure is in the color insert and the GoogleMapsHeatMap.js/html/css files are on the companion website). The code itself is extremely similar to what you've done already with markers and circles. The main differences are that the `HeatmapLayer` expects an `MVCArray` of point data. Note also that you can configure the radius of the heat map during construction. Some other values you can configure on the heat map include `opacity`, `gradient`, `maxIntensity`, and `dissipating`.

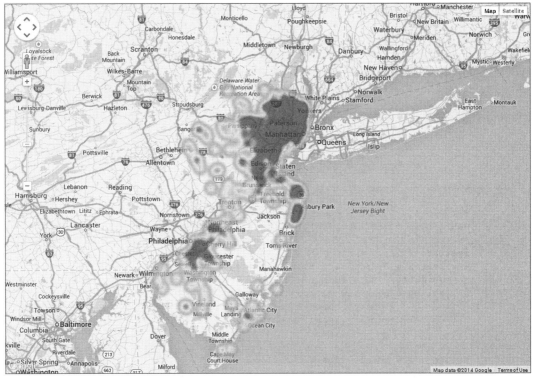

SOURCE FOR LIBRARY DATA: HTTP://CATALOG.DATA.GOV/DATASET/PUBLIC-LIBRARY-SURVEY-PLS-2011

FIGURE 13-9: This shows a heat map of New Jersey library density using the Google Maps API.

This is great, but it's a bit lacking in comparison to the circles example from earlier in the chapter. The circles example was showing more than just the locations of the libraries in that it was also plotting a statistical value associated with each library represented using circle area. Now, with the heat map, you are showing the density of the points in a much clearer fashion, but, data-wise, you've gone back to only conveying the location of the libraries. With a small tweak, however, you can reintroduce a data value into the mix and use it to weight the various points so that they contribute more or less heat to the heat map.

```
heatData = [];
for (var i = 0; i < data.features.length; i++) {
    geometry = data.features[i].geometry;
    weighted = {};
    visits = data.features[i].properties.VISITS;
    weighted.location = new google.maps.LatLng(
```

```
        geometry.coordinates[1],
        geometry.coordinates[0]);
    weighted.weight = visits;
    heatData.push(weighted);
}
```

The preceding code has made the small adjustment to create some objects that contain a `LatLng` position and a weight, which is mapped to `VISITS`, as before. This results in some heat map output where the hottest areas indicate where the most library visits are occurring, as shown in Figure 13-10.

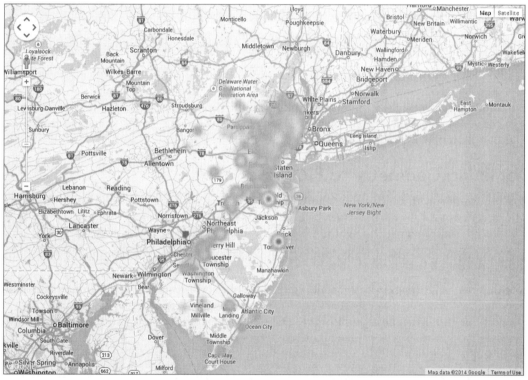

SOURCE FOR LIBRARY DATA: HTTP://CATALOG.DATA.GOV/DATASET/PUBLIC-LIBRARY-SURVEY-PLS-2011

FIGURE 13-10: This weighted heat map shows visits to libraries in New Jersey using the Google Maps API.

A heat map can make it much more possible to render a large point cloud over a map without losing any information due to occlusion, but, as the point count rises, heat maps can be a bit expensive—in terms of both CPU and memory—to render interactively. Because of these performance realities, depending on the speed of your computer, or device, you might notice some slowdown when running either of the preceding examples. A common strategy to mitigate this cost is to do some up-front, server-side processing of the data to make it easier to display the content interactively. In the case of the Google Maps API, if you set up your data in a Google Fusion Table, you can display an optimized heat map with many more points than you can feasibly use with the `HeatmapLayer`. This does, however, require you to define the data you want to pull into the heat map ahead of time.

Switching to showing a density surface rather than individually resolved objects has helped provide a way to show more data on the map, and in a less information-lossy way, than you can easily do with markers. It is not the only strategy that you have available to you, however.

PLOTTING DATA ON CHOROPLETH MAPS

Throughout the previous sections, you saw some of the limitations in visualizing large amounts of point data on a map. Heat maps were discussed as a solution, but there is another strategy for conveying large amounts of data in a map visualization. If your statistics are first aggregated by region, you can color the various regions of a map to convey a channel of information to the visualization consumer. In this section, you see how to build such a visualization.

First, you find out how to acquire some region geometry so that it can be rendered to the screen and dynamically colored. Then you see how to convert this geometry into a format that makes it easier to consume in a browser. Finally, you use D3 to render the regional geometry and create apply a color scale to the result.

Obtaining Geometry to Plot on a Map

When working with the Google Maps API, most geometry you were displaying was in the form of images downloaded from the server. Tile imagery is great in that it requires very little processing power to render on the client, which is especially important on low-power mobile devices, but this isn't really conducive to dynamically coloring the map geometry, or knowing, for example, which piece of geometry the mouse is over.

In order to make things more dynamic, you can acquire some geometry, in the form of vector graphics data, to render on the client. Public government data comes to the rescue again here. The United States Census Bureau, among other government entities, publishes many Esri shapefiles containing geometry for various regional boundaries.

> **NOTE** *An Esri shapefile is a vector graphics file format for storing geospatial vector geometry. It was created by Esri, and has been prevalent for long enough that there is a vast library of shapefiles to choose from when visualizing map data, not to mention many tools for displaying, editing, and managing them. Another benefit of shapefiles is that they are an efficient binary format for transferring vast amounts of geometry without wasted space. Some browser-based mapping products can even load them directly rather than needing to convert to GeoJSON or another JavaScript-based format first:* `www.igniteui.com/map/geo-shapes-series`. *Another interesting aspect of shapefiles is that they actually consist of a set of several different related files and oftentimes there is a paired database file that offers data that can be correlated with each group of displayed geometry.*

At `www.census.gov/geo/maps-data/data/cbf/cbf_state.html`, you can find a set of shape-files that have variously detailed versions of the state boundary geometries for the United States of America. For the purposes of this visualization, only the least-detailed are required: `www2.census.gov/geo/tiger/GENZ2010/gz_2010_us_040_00_20m.zip`. D3 won't directly load the shapefile, so you have to start by converting it to GeoJSON.

Actually, one of the creators of D3 came to the conclusion that GeoJSON had a few inadequacies, so he created a set of extensions to the format called TopoJSON, along with a tool for converting shapefiles to TopoJSON format. The advantage of TopoJSON is that it goes beyond defining geometry and delineates the shared topology of the geometries in the file and helps compress GeoJSON, which is quite a verbose format, by using various quantization tricks.

There is a common problem when dealing with geospatial geometry in that if you are dealing with a file that has too much detail to be efficiently rendered, it can help to reduce the number of points in the polygons or polylines that make it up. Most geospatial file formats would store two separate closed polygons for the states of New Jersey and Pennsylvania, which directly abut each other. As such, their shared border would be contained twice in the two separate polygons, and a straight-forward polygon simplification routine, which would simplify one polygon at a time, would not necessarily simplify the shared border the same way both times. This can, unfortunately, create gaps along the abutting borders.

Converting Geometry for Display Using Topojson

TopoJSON addresses this issue and saves some space by making sure that shared borders are only stored once in the file. Provided a file in TopoJSON format, D3 can convert it back to GeoJSON on the client, and then render it to the page. The tool provided for converting shapefiles to TopoJSON uses Node.js. Good thing you already have it installed, huh?

Before installing TopoJSON, you also need to have Python installed. You can install Python from `www.python.org/`. At the time of this writing, you want the 2.*x* version rather than the 3.*x* version of Python, as the 3.*x* version is not compatible for these purposes. After you have Python installed, if you are using Windows, you might need to add it to your path environment variable. When that is complete, from a node command prompt you should be able to run

```
npm install -g topojson
```

You should see a lot of output stream past, as in Figure 13-11.

If you have errors during the installation, make sure that Python is installed and configured to be in your path, and make sure that node is in context for your command prompt (there is a shortcut for this for Windows, or you could make sure Node.js is in your path environment variable).

After TopoJSON is installed, you should be able to go to the folder where you extracted the shape-file and run this command line:

```
topojson -p STATE -p NAME  -o states.json gz_2010_us_040_00_20m.shp
```

This loads the shapefile and converts it to TopoJSON in an output file called `states.json`. It also makes sure that two properties, STATE and NAME, are extracted from the accompanying database and injected as properties in the TopoJSON for each shape. Given this `states.json` file, you should be able to get a basic map rendered. You should see output similar to Figure 13-12.

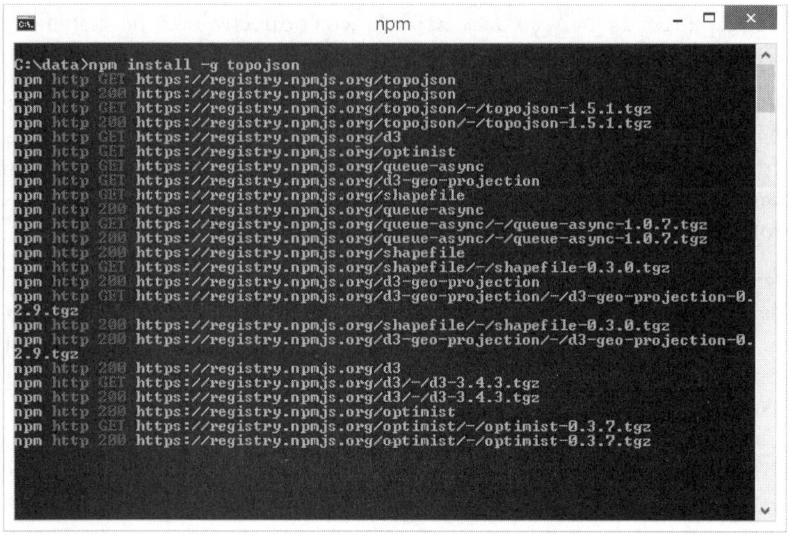

FIGURE 13-11: This shows installing TopoJSON using npm

FIGURE 13-12: A shapefile is converted to TopoJSON.

Rendering Map Geometry Using D3

First of all, much like earlier in this chapter, you are about to load a JavaScript file off the local disk using AJAX, so remember the caveat from earlier in the chapter. As such, unless you are loading the page from a local web server, I'd either recommend using Firefox, which does not, at the time of this writing, block this interaction. Listing 13-4 shows how to load the TopoJSON geometry into D3.

LISTING 13-4

```
var mapWidth = 900;
var mapHeight = 500;

var main = d3
    .select("body")
    .append("svg")
    .attr("width", mapWidth)
    .attr("height", mapHeight);

d3.json("states.json", function (error, states) {
    var statesFeature = topojson.feature(
        states,
        states.objects.gz_2010_us_040_00_20m);

    var path = d3.geo
        .path();

    main
    .selectAll(".state")
    .data(statesFeature.features)
    .enter().append("path")
    .attr("class", "state")
    .attr("d", path);
});
```

This requires the HTML defined as such:

```
<!DOCTYPE html>
<html>
<head>
    <title>D3 Basic Map</title>

    <link rel="stylesheet" href="D3Map.css">
</head>
<body>
    <script src="d3/d3.min.js"></script>
    <script src="topojson/topojson.js"></script>
    <script type="text/javascript" src="D3Map.js"></script>
</body>
</html>
```

The code produces the image in Figure 13-13, which are the D3Map.html/css/js files on the companion website.

GEOMETRY SOURCE: HTTP://WWW.CENSUS.GOV/GEO/MAPS-DATA/DATA/CBF/CBF_STATE.HTML

FIGURE 13-13: This is the result of loading geometry in D3 using TopoJSON.

Listing 13-4 decides a width and height for the map and then creates an `<svg>` element with this size to hold the various map visuals. If you aren't familiar with D3 yet, review Chapter 11 for more detail on some of the mechanics.

Next you have

```
d3.json("states.json", function (error, states) {
```

This causes D3 to load `states.json` as a JSON file, and, when ready, invoke the callback function you are providing with the hydrated JavaScript object. Provided the JavaScript object containing the geometry data:

```
var statesFeature = topojson.feature(
    states,
    states.objects.gz_2010_us_040_00_20m);
```

this code asks TopoJSON to extract the GeoJSON features from the input TopoJSON file. These features are used to generate the path geometry to display the shapes on the map.

```
var path = d3.geo
    .path();
```

This creates a geographic path builder that interprets the GeoJSON feature data and converts it into SVG path data, when you perform the data join, to create the shapes for the states:

```
main
.selectAll(".state")
.data(statesFeature.features)
.enter().append("path")
.attr("class", "state")
.attr("d", path);
```

The previous code performs the data join. You select all elements that have the `state` class. Remember that there are none of these the first time this code executes, but this declaratively lays out the expectation of where those elements should be, which helps D3 to know how to group the data items being joined and identifies to which parent any new elements should be added to.

Next, you operate on the `enter` set and append a `<path>` for each state feature; these paths are then marked with the class `state`, and then the `path` builder is assigned to transform the feature data into SVG `path` geometry. As shown in Figure 13-13, this provides a map of the United States where all the individual state polygons have the same color. That color comes from the CSS file and the rule for the `state` class:

```
.state {
    fill: #5daecc;
    stroke: #225467;
}
```

Displaying Statistics Using a Choropleth Map

Now that you have some polygons displayed for all the separate states, it's time to display an interesting statistic mapped to the polygon color, which is also known as a *choropleth* map.

The U.S. Department of Agriculture provides some Microsoft Excel files that provide various farming statistics broken down by state. I found this by browsing `http://data.gov`, but the actual link to the data's page is `http://www.ers.usda.gov/data-products/agricultural-productivity-in-the-us.aspx`. The file you will use is at

```
http://www.ers.usda.gov/datafiles/Agricultural_Productivity_in_the_US/
StateLevel_Tables_Relative_Level_Indices_and_Growth_19602004Outputs/table03
.xls
```

which has interesting information about the total farm output for each state broken down by year. The easiest thing to do to get this data loaded is to save that `.xls` file as a `.csv` file and then pull out any extraneous rows except for the header row (with the titles for each column) and the actual data for each year. You can see what I mean in Figure 13-14.

```
Year,AL,AR,AZ,CA,CO,CT,DE,FL,GA,IA,ID,IL,IN,KS,KY,LA,MA,MD,ME,MI,MN
1960,0.5668,0.6085,0.4063,3.3565,0.6274,0.1205,0.0889,0.8115,0.7119
1961,0.5765,0.6561,0.4236,3.3836,0.6363,0.1191,0.0867,0.8756,0.7621
1962,0.5604,0.6731,0.4392,3.5495,0.6212,0.1168,0.0865,0.9719,0.7421
1963,0.6288,0.7117,0.4559,3.5883,0.6260,0.1183,0.0916,0.8532,0.8442
1964,0.6314,0.7517,0.4292,3.6871,0.6235,0.1175,0.0902,0.8508,0.8278
1965,0.6643,0.8145,0.4602,3.6855,0.6213,0.1189,0.1002,0.9743,0.8739
1966,0.6244,0.7641,0.4557,3.8480,0.7067,0.1182,0.0939,1.0361,0.8485
1967,0.6010,0.7566,0.4529,3.6392,0.7532,0.1136,0.1106,1.1751,0.9488
1968,0.6202,0.8573,0.4872,3.9624,0.7715,0.1074,0.0962,1.0577,0.8930
1969,0.6550,0.8979,0.5463,4.0376,0.8377,0.1050,0.1143,1.1756,0.9180
1970,0.6513,0.9146,0.5083,3.9649,0.9142,0.1026,0.1111,1.1695,0.9424
1971,0.7248,0.9541,0.5061,4.0235,0.9971,0.1037,0.1076,1.1934,1.0572
1972,0.7187,0.9649,0.5467,4.1421,1.0359,0.0977,0.1121,1.2468,1.0240
1973,0.6937,1.0007,0.5726,4.3713,0.9919,0.0983,0.1205,1.3591,1.0470
```

FIGURE 13-14: This shows the layout of the farm output CSV file.

On the companion website, the file is `farmoutput.csv`. D3 has no problems loading CSV files, but you have a bit of a challenge to overcome here in that the data in this CSV file has abbreviated names for each state, whereas the `STATE` property in your GeoJSON file has only full names. To deal with this, you can construct, or download from the companion website, a CSV file that maps back and forth between the full state names and their abbreviations. This file helps correlate items in the TopoJSON file with items in the farm output CSV file. You can see what this CSV file should look like in Figure 13-15, and you can find it as `stateabbreviations.csv` on the companion website.

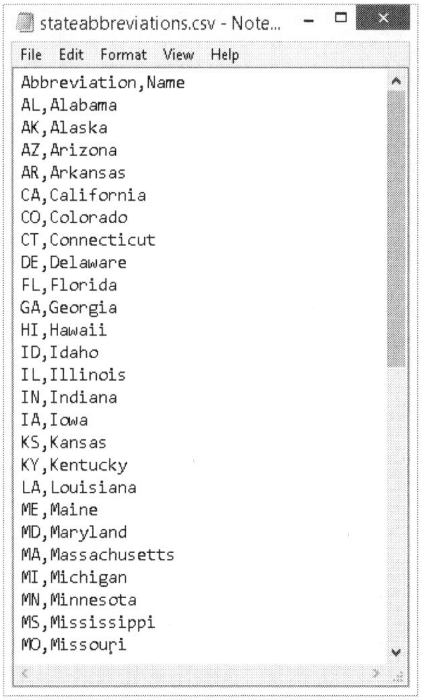
stateabbreviations.csv - Note...

File Edit Format View Help

```
Abbreviation,Name
AL,Alabama
AK,Alaska
AZ,Arizona
AR,Arkansas
CA,California
CO,Colorado
CT,Connecticut
DE,Delaware
FL,Florida
GA,Georgia
HI,Hawaii
ID,Idaho
IL,Illinois
IN,Indiana
IA,Iowa
KS,Kansas
KY,Kentucky
LA,Louisiana
ME,Maine
MD,Maryland
MA,Massachusetts
MI,Michigan
MN,Minnesota
MS,Mississippi
MO,Missouri
```

FIGURE 13-15: This is what the layout of the state abbreviations CSV file looks like.

The following code snippet assumes you have both these CSV files:

```
var mapWidth = 900;
var mapHeight = 500;

var main = d3
    .select("body")
    .append("svg")
    .attr("width", mapWidth)
    .attr("height", mapHeight);
```

First, you have this familiar code, which creates the SVG element

```
var colors = ['#D0E5F2', '#729EBA',
    '#487896', '#2F6180',
    '#143D57', '#08293D'];
```

```
var currentYear = 2004;
var firstYear = 0;
var data = [];
var currentData;
var currentMap;
var statesFeature;
```

In the preceding code, some useful variables are defined for use later. You allow for the current year to be changed with a `<select>` box. So you store both a matrix of all the years' data, and a separate variable holds just the currently selected year's data. `colors` represents an aesthetically pleasing set of colors to use as a color scale with a discrete range of outputs.

```
d3.json("states.json", function (error, states) {
    d3.csv("farmoutput.csv", function (error, farmoutput) {
        d3.csv("stateabbreviations.csv", function (error,
            stateAbbreviations) {
```

The reason for the three-level deep nesting is to chain the callbacks so that you end up with all three files loaded before proceeding to render the map. To refresh, the files are

➤ `states.json`: The TopoJSON file you created by converting the Esri shape file earlier.

➤ `farmoutput.csv`: The CSV file containing all the farm output state per state per year.

➤ `stateabbreviations.csv`: A mapping between the short state abbreviations and the long name of the states. This helps mash up the two data sources.

Now, you can move on to loading the map:

```
statesFeature = topojson.feature(
    states,
    states.objects.gz_2010_us_040_00_20m);
```

This part is unchanged from the previous code, and is, again, converting the TopoJSON input back into GeoJSON features.

```
var i, j, currItem;

var abbreviationsMap = {};

var allAbbrev = [];
for (i = 0; i < stateAbbreviations.length; i++) {
    abbreviationsMap[stateAbbreviations[i].Abbreviation] =
        stateAbbreviations[i].Name;
    allAbbrev.push(stateAbbreviations[i].Abbreviation);
}
```

In the preceding snippet a map (dictionary/hashtable) is built that maps between the abbreviated state names and the full state names, based on the input CSV file. Notice D3 handled parsing the CSV for you, and from within this callback it just looks like a JavaScript object: `stateAbbreviations`.

Next, you transform the farm output data a bit. The input is a CSV where every state has a column, but it is much easier to consume this data from D3 if the values for each state are an array of values where each item in the array has the state name and output value. Also, you need the state names to be the full names because that is what you need to match against in the GeoJSON.

```
for (i = 0; i < farmoutput.length; i++) {
    var year = farmoutput[i];
    var yearNumber = parseInt(year.Year, 10);
    if (i === 0) {
        firstYear = yearNumber;
    }
    currItem = {};
    currItem.year = yearNumber;
    currItem.states = [];
    for (j = 0; j < allAbbrev.length; j++) {
        currItem.states.push({
            name: abbreviationsMap[allAbbrev[j]],
            value: parseFloat(year[allAbbrev[j]])
        });
    }
    data.push(currItem);
}
```

While performing that transformation, the value of the first year in the data (assuming an ascending sort) is captured to help find the index of the current year later on.

Up to this point in your D3 adventures, you've often been using D3 to manipulate SVG elements, but D3 is just as capable at manipulating the HTML Document Object Model (DOM) also. To select the current year's data being displayed, it would help to have an HTML `<select>` element populated with all the valid years that there are data for, and to react to the selection changing. Here's how you would accomplish that using D3:

```
var select = d3.select("select");

select
.selectAll("option")
.data(data)
.enter()
.append("option")
.attr("value", function (d) { return d.year; })
.text(function (d) { return d.year; })
.attr("selected", function (d) {
    if (d.year == currentYear) {
        return "selected";
    }
    return null;
});

select.on("change", function () {
    currentYear = this.value;
    renderMap();
});
```

Following the familiar pattern, you first select the existing `<select>` element by type and then select all the child `<option>` elements (in potentia, as they won't exist the first time), join them with the data (which holds an element for each year), and operate on the `enter` set. For each placeholder in the `enter` set (the first time, there will be one per year), append an `<option>` element and then configure its `value` and `text` based on the current year on the contextual data item. Select the option if and only if its year is equal to the current year. Lastly, this binds a change handler that switches the current year variable and re-renders the map.

Pretty neat, huh? Not a lick of SVG, and you are using the same transformational techniques to concisely operate on DOM objects. To finish up your nested callback you have the following:

```
            renderMap();

            d3.select("body")
              .append("div")
              .text(
"Source: http://www.ers.usda.gov/data-products/~CA
agricultural-productivity-in-the-us.aspx");
            });
        });
});
```

This renders the map for the first time and appends a source line describing where the data came from. So that just leaves rendering the colors on the map. To render the map, use the following:

```
function renderMap() {
    var index = currentYear - firstYear;
    var i;

    currentData = data[index];
    currentMap = {};
    for (i = 0; i < currentData.states.length; i++) {
        currentMap[currentData.states[i].name] =
            currentData.states[i].value;
    }

    var path = d3.geo
        .path();

    var max = d3.max(currentData.states, function (d) {
        return d.value;
    });
    var min = d3.min(currentData.states, function (d) {
        return d.value;
    });
```

In this code, you do the following:

1. Figure out the index into the data collection based on the current selected year and the first year you recorded earlier.

2. Obtain the row for the current year based on the index.

3. Build a hashtable to efficiently retrieve the farm output value from a state name.

4. Create a geographic path builder.

5. Determine the maximum farm output value for the current row.

6. Determine the minimum farm output value for the current row.

Next, you prepare more precursors to rendering the content:

```
var tooltip = d3.select("body")
.append("div")
.attr("class", "tooltip")
.style("position", "absolute")
.style("z-index", 500)
.style("visibility", "hidden");

var colorScale = d3.scale.quantize()
.domain([min, max])
.range(colors);

var states = main
.selectAll(".state")
.data(statesFeature.features);
```

In the preceding code, you do the following:

1. Define an initially hidden tooltip (which is just a styled `<div>` set to be absolutely positioned).

2. Define a color scale as a quantized scale that maps from the linear input domain of the farm output values to a discrete output range.

3. Select all elements in the SVG element with the class `state` and join some data against them, storing the update set in states

Now to render the actual content:

```
states
.enter().append("path")
.attr("class", "state")
.attr("d", path)
.on("mouseenter", function () {
    tooltip.style("visibility", "visible");
})
.on("mouseleave", function () {
    tooltip.style("visibility", "hidden");
})
.on("mousemove", function (d) {
    tooltip.style("top", (d3.event.pageY + 10) + "px")
    .style("left", (d3.event.pageX + 15) + "px")
    .text(d.properties.NAME + ": " + currentMap[d.properties.NAME]);
});
```

For the `enter` set, you append a path for each placeholder. You assign the geographic path builder to operate on the GeoJSON feature and produce SVG path data to get assigned to the `d` attribute on the SVG path. Also, three handlers are bound to toggle the visibility of the tooltip `<div>` and shift it close to the user's mouse cursor. The state name and farm output value are displayed as the tooltip content.

```
states
.transition()
.duration(1000)
.delay(function (d) {
    return (path.bounds(d)[0][0] / mapWidth) * 2000;
})
.style("stroke", "#FF6600")
.style("stroke-width", "2")
.style("fill", function (d) {
    return colorScale(currentMap[d.properties.NAME]);
})
.transition()
.duration(500)
.style("stroke", "#29658A")
.style("stroke-width", "1");
}
```

And last, but certainly not least, you declare how the `update` set is handled, which

1. Starts a `transition` for each element with a 1-second `duration`.

2. Injects a `delay` in the start to each element's `transition` proportional to how far to the right the bounds of the element begin. This helps to create an animation that sweeps across the map from left to right, which is aesthetically pleasing and helps the consumer of the visualization's eye to scan across and notice the changes as they occur.

3. Animates each element's stroke color toward orange during the transition, and temporarily increases the stroke thickness. This has an effect of a glow sweeping across the states during the animation.

4. Animates the fill color toward the color value from the color scale based on the value for the current state for the newly selected year.

5. Chains an additional animation at the end, which returns the stroke color and thickness to normal.

If you run the sample (`D3MapChoropleth.html/css/js`) from the companion website, you see a really pleasant sweeping animation as you change between separate years from the selector. It's quite a complex piece of animation to not be driven by very much code! You can see the results in Figure 13-16, which was snapped while an animation was in progress.

Farm Output by State

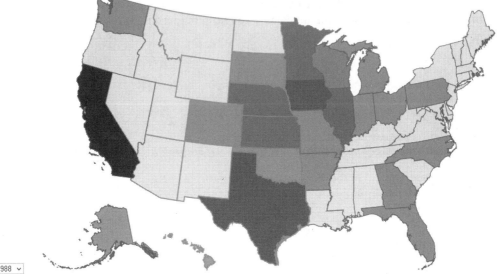

DATA SOURCE: HTTP://WWW.ERS.USDA.GOV/DATA-PRODUCTS/AGRICULTURAL-PRODUCTIVITY-IN-THE-US.ASPX

FIGURE 13-16: This animated choropleth map was created using D3.

SUMMARY

This chapter offered some useful strategies and tools for visualizing data on maps. It also addressed some of the interesting challenges that come up when dealing with the sheer quantity of geometry and data involved when designing map visualizations. In this chapter you

> ➤ Learned how to host components from the Google Maps API in your web applications

> ➤ Controlled the initial focus and zoom level of the map

> ➤ Placed markers on the geographic positions you wanted to visualize

> ➤ Varied the size of markers to convey extra statistics over the map

> ➤ Learned some of the challenges of having too many markers to visualize

> ➤ Learned how to use a heat map to illuminate data density or to convey a statistic

> ➤ Considered using choropleth maps as an alternative to displaying individual data values

> ➤ Learned how to prepare map geometry for display using D3

> ➤ Plotted a choropleth map using D3

> ➤ Animated transitions over your choropleth map

14

Charting Time Series with Ignite UI igDataChart

WHAT'S IN THIS CHAPTER

➤ The basics of working with financial data

➤ Using the Ignite UI igDataChart to visualize stock data

➤ Navigating financial data with a zoom bar

➤ Exploring financial data using overlays and indicators

➤ Updating data in real time in a chart

➤ Using Node.js and Socket.IO to push data to the browser

➤ Plotting extreme amounts of data using the Ignite UI igDataChart

> **CODE DOWNLOAD** *The wrox.com code downloads for this chapter are found at* www.wrox.com/go/javascriptandjqueryanalysis *on the Download Code tab. The code is in the chapter 14 download and individually named according to the names throughout the chapter.*

This chapter introduces you to plotting time series data on a chart. One of the biggest calls for plotting time series data in the software engineering world is to present stock data for analysis. So, the first part of this chapter shows you how to acquire and plot stock data on a chart.

Next, you move on to plotting real-time updates into a time series. Real-time updates in a browser using only JavaScript, you say? Surely impossible. Not at all. Not only are real-time updates possible using pure JavaScript, but they are getting easier and easier to implement as newer browser revisions start to support technologies such as WebSockets.

To plot the stock data and the real-time data for this chapter, you use the Infragistics Ignite UI igDataChart. As shown elsewhere in this book, there are plenty of charting components available for use with JavaScript (including free options) but igDataChart stands apart in terms of the amount of data volume it can display without pre-processing and the frequency of real-time updates it can handle, so it is most appropriate for this chapter. You might remember that igDataChart is discussed briefly in Chapter 12. This chapter retreads a few areas covered there, in case you are reading out of sequence, but you might find it easier to first read and understand the concepts from that chapter before proceeding.

At the end of this chapter, you take charting time series to the limit and plot some massive data on igDataChart. You also discover a strategy for loading massive amounts of data from the server using minimal amounts of bandwidth.

WORKING WITH STOCKS

This isn't a book on how to analyze stock data or how to use technical analysis techniques to make trading decisions, so this chapter focuses solely on the mechanics of how to display stock data in a chart. The examples in this section use some open stock data from Quandl (www.quandl.com/) because it is unencumbered by any usage constraints. Keep in mind that this data was produced in a user-driven wiki environment, but it suits the purposes of this chapter fine because you are simply learning the concepts of plotting this type of content.

The Basics of Stock Data

Data for plotting on stock charts generally consists of five values per data item: Open, High, Low, Close, and Volume. Depending on the visualization you are trying for, you might be using a different subset of these values. Here is the significance of each of these values:

> **Open:** This represents the opening price for a stock over a given period of time.

> **High:** This represents the high price of a stock over a given period of time.

> **Low:** This represents the low price of a stock over a given period of time.

> **Close:** This represents the close price of a stock over a given period of time.

> **Volume:** The volume (amount) of shares of a stock traded over a given period of time.

The main visualizations you implement in this chapter are OHLC and candlestick, which use Open, High, Low, and Close. Volume is optionally incorporated into a visualization if it is very important to show the trade volatility over time. OHLC and candlestick visualizations usually don't attempt to directly convey trade volume (there are some extended versions that do, though) and instead usually depend on a synchronized plot to show volume, if desired. This synchronized plot is usually a second chart aligned under the first chart so that the two charts can be compared time-wise with each other.

Conventionally, a stock time series is displayed from left to right with the earlier prices leftmost and the most recent prices rightmost. You could consider the time axis to be a linear axis (rather than a category axis) because it's representing time, which is a linear scale. But, in practice, most stock data is recorded at a fixed interval, and most stock visualizations contain no data for weekends and should not necessarily display a gap where the data is missing. These aspects add up to it often being more natural to plot stock data on a category axis, where the date value for each item represents the discrete category of that item. If these terms are unfamiliar to you, please review Chapter 9 as they are discussed in more detail there.

A category axis is less appropriate for a time series when your data arrives at a non-fixed interval and you want to show large gaps or large interpolated stretches on the axis where there are no data values present. The data that you'll be visualizing in this chapter does not really fit with those scenarios, though, so this chapter will be focusing exclusively on plotting time series on category axes.

Obtaining Some Stock Data

Before you start plotting stock data on charts, it would help to have some! Quandl is a useful website that provides data, along with application programming interfaces (APIs) that use REST calls to access that data. They also run an initiative called Quandl Open Data that strives to provide user-created and unencumbered open data for use in all manner of applications. You can find the directory of available data at `www.quandl.com/search/*?page=1&source_ids=4922`. The examples in this chapter use some historical Apple Inc. stock data from

```
www.quandl.com/WIKI/AAPL-Apple-Inc-AAPL-Prices-Dividends-Splits-and-Trading-
Volume
```

One of the neat aspects of Quandl is that you can use that page to filter and sort the data and then retrieve a URL that enables you to pull that data as JSON into a web application through an AJAX request to Quandl, or, alternatively, download it and deploy it, as a static file, on your web server. Here, you'll do the latter by downloading this link:

```
www.quandl.com/api/v1/datasets/WIKI/AAPL.json?&trim_start=1984-09-07&trim_
end=1994-09-07&sort_order=asc
```

That link was arrived at by selecting a date filter using the date pickers and then clicking the Download button. This should result in a file called `AAPL.json`, which you should place in the same directory as the examples to follow. This file is also available on the companion website as `AAPL. json`.

Candlesticks and OHLC Visualizations

Before you jump into the implementation of some stock visualizations, it's a good idea to review the anatomy of candlestick and OHLC visualizations. Both visualizations convey roughly the same information, but they are quite different aesthetically. First, examine a candlestick visualization up close in Figure 14-1 (the `IgniteUIFinancialChart.js/html/css` file is on the companion website).

> **NOTE** *When you load some of the code samples in this chapter, you may notice an error, or not see the sample load at all. This is because the data is being loaded via an AJAX request, and if you load the files from your local file system, many browsers reject the request as unsafe. You do not run into this scenario in a production environment because the site and the data will be loaded from the same domain, over HTTP. If you skip ahead to the section "Implementing a Stock Chart Using Ignite UI igDataChart" in this chapter you see a solution discussed for running these samples in a development environment.*

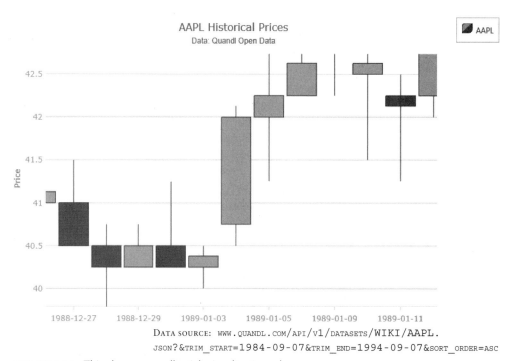

DATA SOURCE: WWW.QUANDL.COM/API/v1/DATASETS/WIKI/AAPL.
JSON?&TRIM_START=1984-09-07&TRIM_END=1994-09-07&SORT_ORDER=ASC

FIGURE 14-1: This shows a candlestick visualization, close up.

A candlestick is made up of a rectangular body and a thin wick (or *shadow*) that extends from its top and bottom. The top and bottom of the rectangular body represent the open and close prices; the top wick position and the bottom wick position represent the high value and the low value, respectively. Now, the high value is always greater than the low value, so the top wick is always mapped to the high value. For open and close, however, open may be higher, or close may be higher, depending on whether prices ended up higher or lower compared to the previous time period.

The simple geometry of the candlestick cannot alone disambiguate whether the price ended higher or lower at the end of the period, so this is usually encoded in the color of the candlestick. One color is used if close is greater than open and another color is used if close is less than open. Alternatively, the candlestick may be filled or left unfilled to represent which direction the prices moved.

OHLC visualizations, on the other hand, can unambiguously indicate which portion of the visual maps to the open price and which portion maps to the close price. You can see a close-up of this visualization in Figure 14-2 (which is on the companion website as `IgniteUIFinancialChartOHLC.js/html/css`). If you load the sample, it starts zoomed out, but you can zoom in by clicking and dragging a rectangle on the area you want to zoom to or by rolling the mouse wheel. If you have a computer with a touchscreen (or a tablet) you can even pinch/spread to zoom in and out.

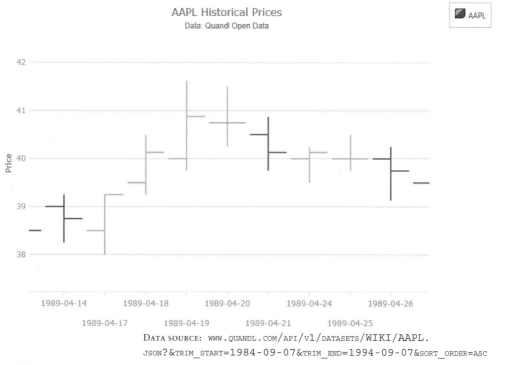

FIGURE 14-2: This shows an OHLC visualization, close up.

The top and bottom of the central line in an OHLC bar means the same thing as in the candlestick visualization, but rather than having a rectangular body that can't unambiguously convey the direction of the price movement over that period, the OHLC bar uses a left-oriented tick for the open price, and a right-oriented tick for the close price over that period. Often, however, the OHLC bar is nevertheless colored to indicate the direction of the movement.

IMPLEMENTING IGNITE UI IGDATACHART

As mentioned earlier, this chapter uses the Infragistics Ignite UI igDataChart component. The essentials of the examples in this chapter may be possible to implement using other components, but these scenarios perform especially well using igDataChart, so you may run into performance issues when using a component that hasn't been designed to express these volumes of data or these frequencies of real-time updates.

The igDataChart component uses the HTML5 `<canvas>` element to do its rendering; it's especially good at pumping out lots of 2D visuals with minimal overhead and high-frequency updates. Furthermore, the chart was designed from the ground up to manage the complexities of displaying millions of data points for you, without requiring you to simplify your data. This makes it possible for you to present large amounts of data to the user and enables them to zoom and pan through it to discover interesting insights at various levels of detail. These capabilities are especially important when you're dealing with time series data. You will often want to be zoomed out so that you can observe the overall shape of the data, but then you'll want to drill down to a specific area to resolve fine detail.

Making complex things simple comes at a cost, however, and thus igDataChart is not a free component, so please see `www.igniteui.com` or `www.infragistics.com` for details and to sign up for the trial version before running the examples in this chapter. The examples in this chapter point at the trial for Ignite UI, extracted in the IgniteUI subfolder; you will notice a watermark that is put in place by the trial version. The watermark is removed if you use a licensed version of the product.

Obtaining Ignite UI

If you visit `www.igniteui.com/download`, you will find information about how to download and install Ignite UI, and also the CDN links that you can alternatively use for the examples for this chapter. After you've downloaded the trial, you can extract the `js` and `css` folders from the Ignite UI install; and copy these to the IgniteUI subfolder where you have put the code for this chapter.

The Ignite UI links used in this chapter load the full Ignite UI trial product, which contains *a lot* of functionality. In a production scenario, you would want to load just the features you need. If you peruse the download section of the Ignite UI site, you see a download tool (`www.igniteui.com/download`) that enables you to select only the features you need, and the site serves up a combined and minified version of the requested features.

Alternatively, you can accomplish specific feature loading via the igLoader from `http://igniteui.com/loader/overview`.

> **NOTE** *When optimizing the load times for JavaScript, there are many important factors, but some of the most important are script size, number of separate files, and the number of different hosts being downloaded from. For production scenarios, loading code for just the features that you need, and loading minified code—which has had all the unnecessary space and characters squeezed out of it—helps a lot. The number of discrete files downloaded, however, can be just as important. There is significant overhead for each round trip to fetch an individual file, so increasing the number of files can negatively affect the load time for your page, whereas decreasing the number of files loaded, conversely, can positively affect load times. So, when possible, it can be very beneficial for JavaScript resources to be packed into a combined file rather than every module being served separately.*

Implementing a Stock Chart Using igDataChart

You have your data, and you have a charting component to use to render it, so now it's time to move on to getting things done. First, Listing 14-1 shows how the HTML would look, and the snippet that follows shows how the CSS would look.

LISTING 14-1

```html
<!DOCTYPE html>
<html>
<head>
    <title>Financial Chart</title>

    <script src="jquery/jquery-1.11.1.min.js"></script>
    <script src="jquery-ui-1.11.1/jquery-ui.min.js"></script>

    <link rel="stylesheet" href="IgniteUI/css/themes/infragistics/↵
infragistics.theme.css" />
    <link rel="stylesheet" href="IgniteUI/css/structure/infragistics.css" />
    <link rel="stylesheet" href="IgniteUI/css/structure/modules/↵
infragistics.ui.chart.css" />
    <script src="IgniteUI/js/infragistics.core.js"></script>
    <script src="IgniteUI/js/infragistics.dv.js"></script>

    <link rel="stylesheet" href="IgniteUIFinancialChart.css" />
</head>
<body>
    <div id="chart"></div>
    <div id="legend"></div>

    <script
    src="IgniteUIFinancialChart.js">
    </script>

</body>
</html>
```

And here's the CSS:

```css
#chart
{
    float: left;
}
#legend
{
    float: left;
}
```

Most of the examples in this chapter use very similar HTML and CSS, so only the deltas from the preceding code will be discussed from here in. Listing 14-1 and the CSS code create a container to store the chart and its legend, and floats them both left so that the legend appears to the right of the chart unless there isn't sufficient space to display it. In that case, the legend gets wrapped below the chart.

> **NOTE** *This is just one example of how to arrange the chart and legend containers. You could, alternatively, float the legend over the chart surface, or put it anywhere else in the Document Object Model (DOM). You could even, for example, put it in a collapsible container. The legend is treated as a separate widget to give you this kind of layout flexibility.*

Given the preceding markup and CSS, Listing 14-2 is the JavaScript to render the financial data into a candlestick chart.

LISTING 14-2

```javascript
$(function () {
    $.ajax({
        type: "GET",
        url: "AAPL.json",
        dataType: "json",
        success: renderChart,
        error: function (xhr, textStatus, errorThrown) {
            console.log(errorThrown +
                ". Loading from a file:// uri won't work in some browsers");
        }
    });

    function renderChart(data) {
        var columnNames = data.column_names;
        var transformed = data.data.map(function (item) {
            var newItem = {};
            for (var i = 0; i < columnNames.length; i++) {
                newItem[columnNames[i]] = item[i];
            }
            return newItem;
        });

        var chartOptions = {
            dataSource: transformed,
            width: "700px",
            height: "500px",
            title: "AAPL Historical Prices",
            subtitle: "Data: Quandl Open Data",
            horizontalZoomable: true,
            verticalZoomable: true,
            rightMargin: 30,
            legend: { element: "legend" },
            axes: [{
```

```
                type: "categoryX",
                name: "xAxis",
                label: "Date",
                labelExtent: 60
            }, {
                type: "numericY",
                name: "yAxis",
                title: "Price"
            }],
            series: [{
                name: "aapl",
                type: "financial",
                xAxis: "xAxis",
                yAxis: "yAxis",
                openMemberPath: "Open",
                highMemberPath: "High",
                lowMemberPath: "Low",
                closeMemberPath: "Close",
                showTooltip: true,
                isTransitionInEnabled: true,
                isHighlightingEnabled: true,
                transitionInDuration: 1000,
                title: "AAPL",
                resolution: 8
            }, {
                name: "itemToolTips",
                type: "itemToolTipLayer",
                useInterpolation: false,
                transitionDuration: 300
            }]
        };

        $("#chart").igDataChart(chartOptions);

    }
});
```

This should give you the result shown in Figure 14-3, and you can find the Ch16_
IgniteUIFinancialChart.js/html/css file on the companion website. Also, you should notice
some really neat interactivity features when you run the sample live:

➤ Hovering over a candlestick highlights it.

➤ A tooltip follows your cursor and displays the prices that are closest to the cursor. This
  punches down to the closest real data value that can't even be easily discerned from the initial
  zoom level.

➤ There is more data in the chart than can readily be seen at the initial zoom level. The time
  periods represented by the candlesticks are dynamically adjusted as you zoom in and out.

➤ You can zoom in and out by rolling your mouse wheel, clicking and dragging a rectangle,
  hitting the Page Up and Page Down keys, or pinching and spreading if you are using a touch
  device. As you zoom in, further extra detail that wasn't initially visible is resolved, and
  though there is lots of data in the chart, everything stays buttery smooth.

➤ When zoomed in, you can hold the Shift button and click and drag over the chart surface to pan around the view.

➤ You can also use the arrow keys to pan when the chart is focused.

➤ When you first load the page, there is a pleasant animation to transition the candlesticks into view.

➤ At zoom levels that would cause the axis labels to collide, they instead automatically stagger their heights to avoid colliding. Pretty neat, huh?

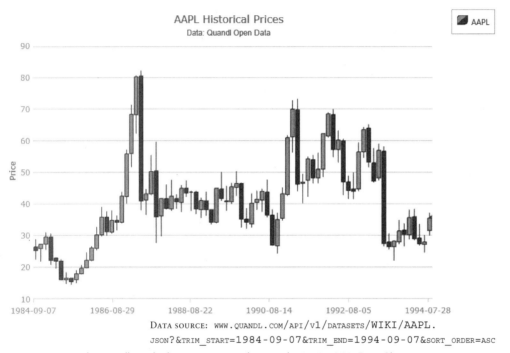

FIGURE 14-3: This candlestick chart was created using the Ignite UI igDataChart.

To break down what's going on in this example, first you have

```
$.ajax({
    type: "GET",
    url: "AAPL.json",
    dataType: "json",
    success: renderChart,
    error: function (xhr, textStatus, errorThrown) {
        console.log(errorThrown +
            ". Loading from a file:// uri won't work in some browsers");
    }
});
```

which is using jQuery to do an AJAX GET of the AAPL.json file that you downloaded earlier from Quandl. type: "GET" indicates that this is an HTTP GET operation, and dataType: "json" warns jQuery to expect the returned data type to be a JSON document.

Did you see an error in the console when you first tried to run the code? Chances are you were trying to load the page from a file:/// URL, and some of the browsers throw a security exception when you try to do this. This isn't a problem in production—when you will be loading the files from a web server—but some of the browsers are trying to make extra sure that rogue websites cannot load files from your local file system in an unauthorized fashion. To work around this, you can often tell your browser, via the command line, to suppress this error while you are debugging the code for your page.

Another way of going about this, however, is to host the files in a local web server when loading them. If you have Apache or IIS installed, you could go that route, but if you came to this chapter directly after reading Chapter 13, then you already have Python and Node installed, and have some quicker methods available to you. For example, if you open a command prompt and change the directory to the one that that holds the files for this chapter, you can run the following command:

```
python -m SimpleHTTPServer 8080
```

This command starts a Python module that serves pages from that directory on port 8080. So, for example, you should be able to load the previous example using this URL:

```
http://localhost:8080/IgniteUIFinancialChart.html
```

And if you were receiving an error before, now it should load properly. Later in this chapter, you see how to do a similar thing with a Node.js module.

> **NOTE** *The Python method in the preceding code is as simple as can possibly be, but it seems to have some stability issues in some scenarios. If you encounter any trouble with pages loading reliably, refer to the Node.js + express method used in the latter stages of this chapter.*

The error handler in the previous code was what rendered an error into the console if you tried to load this page from a file URL. If there is no error with the request, jQuery calls the success handler, where you have provided a function called renderChart, which is the next topic of discussion.

```
function renderChart(data) {
    var columnNames = data.column_names;
    var transformed = data.data.map(function (item) {
        var newItem = {};
        for (var i = 0; i < columnNames.length; i++) {
            newItem[columnNames[i]] = item[i];
        }
        return newItem;
    });
```

The preceding code is the first part of a function that renders the chart based on the contents of the downloaded JSON file. An examination of the JSON file shows that the top-level object has a property called `column_names` and then an array called `data` that has a set of subarrays that represent each row. To ease the loading and binding of this data, it's better that each row had some named properties rather than indexed cells, so the preceding code uses `Array.map` to iterate over the data array and transform each row into an object that contains properties for each named column.

```
var chartOptions = {
    dataSource: transformed,
    width: "700px",
    height: "500px",
    title: "AAPL Historical Prices",
    subtitle: "Data: Quandl Open Data",
    horizontalZoomable: true,
    verticalZoomable: true,
    rightMargin: 30,
```

The preceding code includes the options that are directed at the chart as a whole, rather than its axes or series. This code specifies

- ➤ `dataSource`: This expects an array (among other options) that you set to the transformed data received from `AAPL.json`. Here, the data is set at the chart level, but it is possible to set separate collections of data at the axis and series levels.

- ➤ `width`: The pixel width of the chart. It's also possible to use percent values here to size the chart to its containing elements.

- ➤ `height`: The pixel height of the chart. It's also possible to use percent values here to size the chart to its containing elements. Remember that if you do this, you might need to set the height of the `html` and `body` elements to 100 percent if there is no intervening element with an actual size specified.

- ➤ `title`: The title of the chart will be displayed above the plot area.

- ➤ `subtitle`: The subtitle of the chart will be displayed below the title in a smaller font.

- ➤ `horizontalZoomable`: Indicates that the chart should be zoomable in the horizontal direction.

- ➤ `verticalZoomable`: Indicates that the chart should be zoomable in the vertical direction.

- ➤ `rightMargin`: Leaves some dead area to the right of the chart to make sure there is enough spillover room for the x-axis labels. Some space is left automatically, but when dealing with longer x-axis labels, it can help to provide a larger figure here.

The next line

```
legend: { element: "legend" },
```

indicates that the chart should use an element with ID `"legend"` as the container for its legend. Multiple charts can share the same legend, or individual chart series can split themselves among multiple legends.

```
axes: [{
    type: "categoryX",
    name: "xAxis",
    label: "Date",
    labelExtent: 60
}, {
    type: "numericY",
    name: "yAxis",
    title: "Price"
}],
```

The preceding code snippet defines the two axes for the chart. As discussed earlier, for stock data, it can make more sense to plot the time data on a category axis, rather than a linear axis. A category x axis is defined here, and it displays the Date properties of all the data items as the labels on the axis. labelExtent increases the size of the axis labels area here, so the labels have room to switch to a staggered view if they start colliding. If this step isn't performed, the labels are automatically shortened with the ellipsis character when they begin to collide.

A numeric y axis with standard settings is also created to map the price values into the plot area.

Now it's time to define the series that will display the candlesticks:

```
series: [{
    name: "aapl",
    type: "financial",
    xAxis: "xAxis",
    yAxis: "yAxis",
    openMemberPath: "Open",
    highMemberPath: "High",
    lowMemberPath: "Low",
    closeMemberPath: "Close",
    showTooltip: true,
    isTransitionInEnabled: true,
    isHighlightingEnabled: true,
    transitionInDuration: 1000,
    title: "AAPL",
    resolution: 8
```

This code defines the following:

➤ name: This is a unique identifier that you are required to assign to a series.

➤ type: This indicates the type of series to render. In this case, you want to render a financial series (which can render as candlesticks or OHLC bars).

➤ xAxis: Points to, by name, the x axis to use for this series.

➤ yAxis: Points to, by name, the y axis to use for this series.

➤ openMemberPath: Indicates the property on the data items from which to fetch the opening price.

➤ highMemberPath: Indicates the property on the data items from which to fetch the high price.

➤   `lowMemberPath`: Indicates the property on the data items from which to fetch the low price.

➤   `closeMemberPath`: Indicates the property on the data items from which to fetch the closing price.

➤   `showTooltip`: Indicates that a tooltip should be displayed for this series. If no `tooltipTemplate` is specified, an automatic selection of values is displayed as the tooltip.

➤   `isTransitionInEnabled`: Indicates that the series should be animated into view.

➤   `transitionInDuration`: Specifies the number of milliseconds over which the transition in animation should stretch.

➤   `title`: Provides a value that can be used in the legend and the tooltips to identify the current series.

➤   `resolution`: Controls how aggressively the series coalesces data. The meaning that this has for the financial series, in this instance, is that it coalesces the price data so that no candlesticks thinner than approximately 8 pixels wide are displayed. As you zoom in, more candlesticks are visible until you reach a point where each individual value in the source array has an individual candlestick. You can increase and decrease this value in order to adjust how aggressively this coalescing is performed.

```
    }, {
            name: "itemToolTips",
            type: "itemToolTipLayer",
            useInterpolation: false,
            transitionDuration: 300
        }]
    };
```

Finally, the preceding code creates a layer where floating tooltips annotate the values closest to the mouse cursor, in the x direction. If this weren't specified you would still get tooltips, but only when you were directly over the visuals for the series. The following things are defined:

➤   `name`: Indicates the unique identifier for the tooltip layer

➤   `type`: Specifies that this series is an item tooltip layer

➤   `useInterpolation`: Indicates that the tooltips should snap to the closest values rather than picking an interpolated position between the two closest values

➤   `transitionDuration`: Indicates how long it should take the tooltips to animate from one annotated item to the next

Finally, the container with the ID `chart` is transformed into an igDataChart with the options you defined:

```
    $("#chart").igDataChart(chartOptions);

        }
    });
```

As with the last time you interacted with igDataChart, in Chapter 12, very little code is actually required to achieve the desired effect. Instead, there are lots of declarative options that indicate the precise behaviors you want from all the pieces of the chart. These straightforward options add up to some very complex behaviors when you load the page and interact with the chart.

Now that you have some candlesticks displayed, how would you change to an OHLC bar visualization? The answer is extremely simple. All you need to do is add the highlighted line to the definition of the financial series:

```
series: [{
    name: "aapl",
    type: "financial",
    displayType: "ohlc",
    xAxis: "xAxis",
    yAxis: "yAxis",
    openMemberPath: "Open",
    highMemberPath: "High",
    lowMemberPath: "Low",
    closeMemberPath: "Close",
    showTooltip: true,
    isTransitionInEnabled: true,
    isHighlightingEnabled: true,
    transitionInDuration: 1000,
    title: "AAPL",
    resolution: 8
```

You can see the results in Figure 14-4, and the file is on the companion website as `IgniteUIFinancialChartOHLC.js/html/css`.

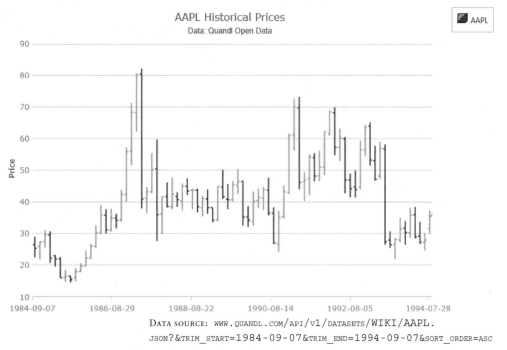

FIGURE 14-4: This shows an OHLC chart using the Ignite UI igDataChart.

Adding a Zoom Bar to the Chart

If you compare the results from Listing 14-2 to what you get if you were to, say, view some stock data on Yahoo! Finance, you have achieved some interesting dynamic effects that aren't represented in Yahoo! Finance, but there are also some things you are missing. Fortunately, these are not especially tricky to add with Ignite UI.

Ignite UI provides a component called igZoombar, which acts as a date range selector that enables you to pan a time series chart as well as change the zoom level. To add it, all you need to do is create it, and make sure it is positioned under the plot area, based on the size you picked for the chart:

```
$("#zoom").igZoombar({
    width: "660px",
    target: "#chart",
    zoomWindowMinWidth: 1.2
});
$("#zoom").css("margin-left", "24px");
```

This code creates the zoom bar, and targets it at the upper stock price chart. This causes the zoom bar to create a clone of the chart visualization, at default zoom level, to act as a thumbnail to guide you around the overall shape of the time series. This code adjusts the width and the left margin to position the zoom bar under the main chart.

By default, the cloned thumbnail chart has most of the visual settings of the main chart, but, in this instance, it would actually be preferable to display a simpler visual in the thumbnail rather than an exact copy. Also, while the zoom bar filters out some aspects of the top chart's settings that you'd likely not want to see in the thumbnail (axis gridlines, for example), it doesn't necessarily adjust the settings exactly as you'd like, so the zoom bar gives you access to the cloned chart in order to tweak additional settings:

```
$("#zoom").igZoombar("clone").igDataChart({
    subtitle: null,
    rightMargin: 0,
    axes: [{ name: "xAxis", interval: NaN }],
    series: [{
        name: "aapl", remove: true
    }, {
        name: "close",
        type: "area",
        xAxis: "xAxis",
        yAxis: "yAxis",
        valueMemberPath: "Close"
    }]
});
```

The preceding code filters out a few properties that the zoom clone currently doesn't automatically filter from the top chart and then removes the financial series and replaces it with a simple area series bound to the close property of the data items.

The closing price is largely considered to be the most important aspect of a stock price to watch. So when displaying a simple thumbnail, mapped to just one value, it makes the most sense as a value to display. Another option is to display the *typical price*, which is generally calculated as the average of the high, low, and close prices for the given period.

The last thing you need to do is to add an element that holds the zoom bar visual to the HTML:

```html
<div id="chart"></div>
<div id="legend"></div>
<div id="zoom"></div>
```

And to amend the CSS such that the zoom bar doesn't try to float left with the chart and legend:

```css
#chart
{
    width: 700px;
    height: 500px;
    float: left;
}
#legend
{
    float: left;
}
#zoom
{
    clear: left;
}
```

The code changes produce the results in Figure 14-5, and you can find the `IgniteUIFinancial ChartZoombar.js/html/css` file on the companion website. Notice how you can drag the range of the zoom bar to pan through time and examine various values. You can also grab the handles on either edge of the range to resize the range and change the zoom level of the chart.

FIGURE 14-5: This financial chart includes a zoom bar to adjust the viewable area.

Adding a Synchronized Chart

Another aspect of Yahoo! Finance that you might want to emulate is the synchronized chart of the trade volume that is plotted underneath the price chart. Ignite UI also makes this exceedingly simple. The basic strategy is to create a second chart underneath the first and then put both the charts in the same syncChannel. When two charts are in the same syncChannel, not only do zoom interactions from one chart get replayed on others in the same syncChannel, but additionally the cursor position is synchronized between the charts so that annotations such as the item tooltips show for all synced charts simultaneously.

```
$("#volumeChart").igDataChart({
    dataSource: transformed,
    width: "700px",
    height: "150px",
    horizontalZoomable: true,
    syncChannel: "channel1",
    rightMargin: 30,
    legend: { element: "legend" },
    axes: [{
```

```
        type: "categoryX",
        name: "xAxis",
        label: "Date",
        labelExtent: 60,
        labelVisibility: "collapsed"
    }, {
        type: "numericY",
        name: "yAxis",
        title: "Volume",
        labelExtent: 60,
        formatLabel: function (v) {
            if (v > 1000000) {
                v /= 1000000;
                return v + "M";
            }
            if (v > 1000) {
                v /= 1000;
                return v + "K";
            }

            return v.toString();
        }
    }],
    series: [{
        name: "aaplVolume",
        type: "area",
        xAxis: "xAxis",
        yAxis: "yAxis",
        brush: "#7C932F",
        outline: "#556420",
        valueMemberPath: "Volume",
        showTooltip: true,
        isTransitionInEnabled: true,
        isHighlightingEnabled: true,
        transitionInDuration: 1000,
        title: "AAPL Volume",
    }, {
        name: "itemToolTips",
        type: "itemToolTipLayer",
        useInterpolation: false,
        transitionDuration: 300
    }]
});
```

The preceding code defines a second chart that sits below the chart you defined before. You also need to add the following line to the top chart:

```
syncChannel: "channel1",
```

In addition, you would need to add an element to hold the second chart to the page:

```
<div id="chart"></div>
<div id="legend"></div>
<div id="volumeChart"></div>
<div id="zoom"></div>
```

and you should move the `clear: left` to the `volumeChart` CSS rule:

```
#volumeChart {
    clear: left;
}
```

In the `volumeChart` options, the settings are mostly the same as the financial chart, but some of the differences have been highlighted and the results are as follows:

➤ The category x-axis labels have been collapsed. This is because they would be the same as the labels in the upper chart, and they really only need to be displayed in one location.

➤ A `formatLabel` function has been added to the y axis for this lower chart. The volume of trades is very high, so in order to reduce the length of the labels, this function shortens and adds a unit specifier if the labels are over certain amounts.

➤ The type of the series used is `area`.

➤ A different brush and outline are set to distinguish this series from the price chart.

➤ The area series is mapped to the `Volume` property of the data items.

➤ An item tooltip layer is also added to the lower chart, so that as the mouse cursor is moved over either chart, you see the item tooltips for the closest data values in both charts.

You can see the result of this in Figure 14-6 (which is also in the color insert), and you can find the `IgniteUIFinancialChartZoombarAndVolume.js/html/css` file on the companion website.

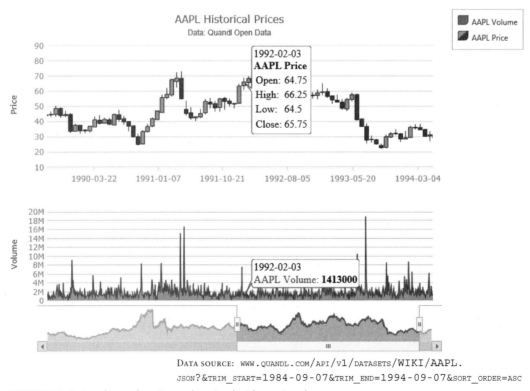

DATA SOURCE: WWW.QUANDL.COM/API/V1/DATASETS/WIKI/AAPL.
JSON?&TRIM_START=1984-09-07&TRIM_END=1994-09-07&SORT_ORDER=ASC

FIGURE 14-6: A volume chart is synchronized with a price chart.

Working with Technical Analysis Tools

As mentioned at the beginning of the chapter, this is not a book on doing technical analysis for stock data, and the chapter doesn't go into this in much detail. It is worth knowing, however, that Ignite UI has a lot of built-in technical indicators and overlays that can help you make sense of stock price plots and try to eke out information that might help with trading decisions.

The following code provides an example of how you would add some price channels to the previous example. Just add this code before the candlestick or OHLC series in the chart:

```
series: [{
    name: "aaplPriceChannel",
    type: "priceChannelOverlay",
    xAxis: "xAxis",
    yAxis: "yAxis",
    openMemberPath: "Open",
    highMemberPath: "High",
    lowMemberPath: "Low",
    closeMemberPath: "Close",
    volumeMemberPath: "Volume",
    isTransitionInEnabled: true,
    isHighlightingEnabled: true,
    transitionInDuration: 1000,
    title: "AAPL Price Channels"
```

Price channels plot the highest of highs and the lowest of lows for a given back period at each given point on the chart. This can give you a good idea when the stock is having some quick up or down movement, because if it moves fast enough it will "break" from the channel. How the prices move within the channel can indicate interesting things to an analyst. You can see the results of adding this price channel series in Figure 14-7. (The file on the companion website is IgniteUIFinancialChartPriceChannels.js/html/css.)

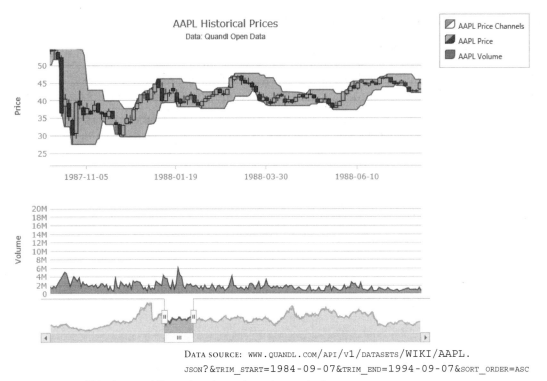

FIGURE 14-7: This shows adding price channels to the stock chart.

> **NOTE** *You can see some of the other technical analysis tools available in Ignite UI at* http://www.igniteui.com/data-chart/financial-indicators.

PLOTTING REAL-TIME DATA

So everything you've seen so far is all very neat, if analyzing financial data is something that interests you. In case it isn't, this section explores another aspect of plotting time series. Everything up to this point in this chapter has been pretty static. The interactions with the chart have been pretty dynamic, but the data itself has not been. So, now it's time for some dynamic data.

For dynamic data, you build a web service that pushes the current CPU and memory usage from the server down to the browser client. In the client, you dynamically update some chart series to display the real-time data streaming down from the server. If you think about it, the following examples have some true real-world applicability because it is often necessary to monitor the performance of a remote machine.

Creating a Node Push Data Service

If you followed along through Chapter 13, then you already have Node.js installed. Otherwise, please follow the instructions in Chapter 13 to install Node.js, and then return here because you use Node.js to create the push data service.

Socket.IO is a really neat client/server JavaScript library that lets you set up a WebSockets connection between the browser and the server. The especially neat part is that, because there are not many browser versions that support WebSockets yet, if they are not available for a particular client, Socket.IO gracefully falls back on another technology, such as Flash or HTTP long polling, in order to emulate the WebSockets behavior. These fallbacks do not necessarily provide a perfect emulation performance-wise, but should be sufficient for you to rely on the basic functionality. If you have ever used SignalR, the idea is roughly the same as with that framework.

> **NOTE** *HTTP is not a full duplex communication channel. The web server cannot send unsolicited information to the client. It can only respond to direct requests for resources from the client. This makes it difficult to push data from the server to the client to, say, implement a notification system. There are various strategies that one can use to try to emulate true bidirectional communication over the HTTP protocol, such as HTTP long polling. These strategies, although very clever, are somewhat inefficient and, unfortunately, introduce latency into the communication channel. WebSockets details how the client and server can agree, using a HTTP-based handshake, to subsequently sidestep HTTP and open a true full duplex (bidirectional simultaneous) communication channel. This is done in order to enable truly efficient low-latency communication and is very important for real-time communication and gaming.*

So, you use Node.js and Socket.IO to open a WebSockets connection, or some approximation thereto, between the server and the client browsers, and on an interval the server broadcasts performance data down to the client. To do this, create a file called `cpuLoadServer.js` or grab the one from the companion website. Fill in the contents of Listing 14-3.

LISTING 14-3

```
var express = require("express");
var application = express();
var server = require("http").createServer(application);
var io = require("socket.io").listen(server);
var os = require("os");
var osUtils = require("os-utils");
var interval = -1;
var currCPU = 0;

application.use(express.static(__dirname));

server.listen(8080);
```

continues

```
io.sockets.on('connection', function () {
    if (interval < 0) {
        interval = setInterval(function () {
            var freeMem = os.freemem();
            var totalMem = os.totalmem();
            io.sockets.emit("cpuUpdate", {
                cpuUsage: currCPU * 100.0,
                freeMem: freeMem,
                totalMem: totalMem,
                usedMem: totalMem - freeMem
            });
        }, 100);
    }
});

function updateCPU() {
    setTimeout(function () {
        osUtils.cpuUsage(function (value) {
            currCPU = value;

            updateCPU();
        });
    }, 0);
}
updateCPU();
```

Not much code huh? Let's dig into it a bit.

```
var express = require("express");
var application = express();
var server = require("http").createServer(application);
var io = require("socket.io").listen(server);
var os = require("os");
var osUtils = require("os-utils");
var interval = -1;
var currCPU = 0;
```

Here you are asking Node.js to load various modules. You are loading the module for express, which builds on the web serving facilities of Node.js and provides some web application middleware behaviors. The main use for it here is to allow for the static HTML, CSS, and JavaScript files to be loaded when you request the client pieces in the browser. Next, the http module is loaded and a server is created. The server delegates to the express application to process its requests.

From there, you load the Socket.IO module and assign it to listen on the HTTP server you created. In this way, you've chained a lot of disparate frameworks together to handle various types of requests. Express handles serving static files down to the client, and Socket.IO handles serving up the client-side script that it needs to function (which you see when you get to the client piece of this) and also responds to the socket handshaking and messages sent back and forth using its protocols.

> **NOTE** *When we refer to handshaking here, we're referring to the process of Socket.IO negotiating between the client and the server over HTTP and discovering which protocol the client and server are able to support. The primary goal is that the connection should be established using WebSockets, which provides a nice low-latency channel for sending two-way information back and forth to the client. If the server or client doesn't support this, however, Socket.IO attempts to fall back on successively distant approximations of this ideal. When the connection has been established, messages can be sent in either direction along the socket channel. In this instance, you are mostly concerned with pushing data down to the client.*

In the previous snippet, you are loading the `os` and `os-utils` modules. The `os` module is distributed with Node.js, whereas `os-utils` represents some neat downloadable utilities that sit on top of the `os` module to normalize and process some of the info for you.

All the pieces you need to set up the server are hooked up, so now you can proceed to making it actually do something:

```
application.use(express.static(__dirname));

server.listen(8080);
```

Here you tell `express` to serve up static content from the current directory so that when you request the client file later, it—and its referenced files—will be downloadable from this directory to the client browser. Normally you would create a subdirectory here, perhaps called `public`, and serve static files from there so that the Node.js code running on the server wouldn't also be downloadable. For simplicity's sake, though, here you keep everything in the same folder.

You also tell the HTTP server to listen on port 8080 for requests. This is why, later on, you provide port 8080 in your requests for the client page.

```
io.sockets.on('connection', function () {
    if (interval < 0) {
        interval = setInterval(function () {
            var freeMem = os.freemem();
            var totalMem = os.totalmem();
            io.sockets.emit("cpuUpdate", {
                cpuUsage: currCPU * 100.0,
                freeMem: freeMem,
                totalMem: totalMem,
                usedMem: totalMem - freeMem
            });
        }, 100);
    }
});
```

The preceding code defines what happens when a Socket.IO connection request is received from a client. When this occurs, unless you are already doing so, you start emitting CPU and memory information, every 100ms, as a JSON object, to all connected sockets.

> **NOTE** *There is no logic anywhere here to tear down this interval later. For production logic, you'd want to listen for connections to be torn down and, when no sockets are left connected, cancel the broadcast interval. This example, however, is more focused on the mechanics of updating the charts than taking a deep dive into Socket.io mechanics. Also note that although a high-frequency broadcast will work well over localhost, it might not scale well to wide area network (WAN) scenarios or having lots of clients connected. But, again, the focus here is on chart updates, not necessarily Socket.io performance semantics and tuning.*

The broadcasting code you just used was relying on a `currCPU` reading to broadcast to the clients. So, finally, this is how that is achieved:

```
function updateCPU() {
    setTimeout(function () {
        osUtils.cpuUsage(function (value) {
            currCPU = value;

            updateCPU();
        });
    }, 0);
}
updateCPU();
console.log("computer performance server running");
```

The `os-utils` module needs to average some values over the space of a second to get a CPU utilization reading. As such, it requires a callback function to call when it has finished determining an average value. This code basically continually runs that method and waits for the callback to be invoked, storing the result where it can be broadcast on the next interval.

To be able to run any of this logic, you have to download some of the Node.js modules that aren't included by default. First navigate to the directory containing `cpuLoadServer.js` and the static files, and then run the following:

```
npm install express
```

Provided you have Node.js installed, and configured in your path, or in context for your command prompt, you should be able to run the preceding command to install the `express` module.

```
npm install socket.io
```

Similarly, this causes the Socket.IO module to be downloaded and installed.

```
npm install os-utils
```

And, finally, after you have run the preceding command and downloaded the os-utils module, you should be able to run the server:

```
node cpuLoadServer.js
```

You can see what it looks like for the server to be running in Figure 14-8; the cpuLoadServer.js file is on the companion website. As a side note, you now have a simple way to serve static files out of the current directory, much like you were achieving with Python earlier in the chapter.

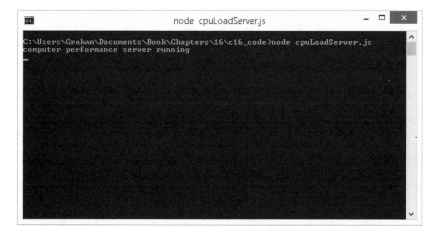

FIGURE 14-8: This shows running the real-time computer performance server.

Receiving Updates in the Client

With some Node.js wrangling you've managed to create a pretty succinct server that broadcasts CPU and memory updates to clients, but how do you display those results? With the power of Socket.IO and the Ignite UI igDataChart this is exceedingly simple, as shown in Listing 14-4.

LISTING 14-4

```
$(function () {
    var cpuData = [];

    function toDisplayCPU(v) {
        return v.toFixed(2);
    }

    function toDisplayMem(v) {
        if (v >= (1024 * 1024 * 1024)) {
            v /= (1024 * 1024 * 1024);
            return v.toFixed(2) + "GB";
        }
```

continues

LISTING 14-4 *(continued)*

```
            if (v >= (1024 * 1024)) {
                v /= (1024 * 1024);
                return v.toFixed(2) + "MB";
            }

            if (v >= (1024)) {
                v /= (1024);
                return v.toFixed(2) + "KB";
            }

            return v;
        }

        function renderChart() {
            var chartOptions = {
                dataSource: cpuData,
                width: "700px",
                height: "500px",
                title: "System Performance",
                subtitle: "CPU utilization over time until present",
                horizontalZoomable: true,
                verticalZoomable: true,
                rightMargin: 30,
                legend: { element: "legend" },
                axes: [{
                    type: "categoryX",
                    name: "xAxis",
                    label: "displayTime",
                    labelAngle: 45
                }, {
                    type: "numericY",
                    name: "yAxis",
                    title: "CPU Utilization",
                    minimumValue: 0,
                    maximumValue: 100,
                    formatLabel: toDisplayCPU
                }, {
                    type: "numericY",
                    name: "yAxisMemory",
                    title: "Memory Utilization",
                    labelLocation: "outsideRight",
                    minimumValue: 0,
                    maximumValue: 8 * 1024 * 1024 * 1024,
                    interval: 1024 * 1024 * 1024,
                    formatLabel: toDisplayMem,
                    majorStroke: "transparent"
                }],
                series: [{
                    name: "cpu",
                    type: "line",
                    xAxis: "xAxis",
```

```
                yAxis: "yAxis",
                valueMemberPath: "cpuUsage",
                showTooltip: true,
                tooltipTemplate:
        "<div><em>CPU:</em> <span>${item.displayCPU}</span></div>",
                title: "CPU Utilization"
            }, {
                name: "mem",
                type: "line",
                xAxis: "xAxis",
                yAxis: "yAxisMemory",
                valueMemberPath: "usedMem",
                showTooltip: true,
                tooltipTemplate:
        "<div><em>Memory:</em> <span>${item.displayMem}</span></div>",
                title: "Memory Utilization"
            }, {
                name: "itemToolTips",
                type: "itemToolTipLayer",
                useInterpolation: false,
                transitionDuration: 300
            }]
        };

        $("#chart").igDataChart(chartOptions);

    }

    renderChart();

    var socket = io.connect("http://localhost:8080");

    socket.on("cpuUpdate", function (update) {
        var currTime = new Date();
        var displayString = currTime.toLocaleTimeString();
        update.displayCPU = toDisplayCPU(update.cpuUsage);
        update.displayMem = toDisplayMem(update.usedMem);
        update.displayTime = displayString;
        cpuData.push(update);
        $("#chart").igDataChart("notifyInsertItem",
            cpuData, cpuData.length - 1, update);
    });
});
```

If you save this as `IgniteUICPULoadChart.js` or grab the file from the companion website, along with the HTML and CSS for this example, and provided the Node.js server is running, you should be able to visit the following site:

```
http://localhost:8080/IgniteUICPULoadChart.html
```

As a result you should see the chart updating in real time. There are two series displayed: one plotting CPU utilization over time and one plotting memory utilization over time. Figure 14-9 shows the result of letting this run for a while (`IgniteUICPULoadChart.js`/html/css is the file on the companion website).

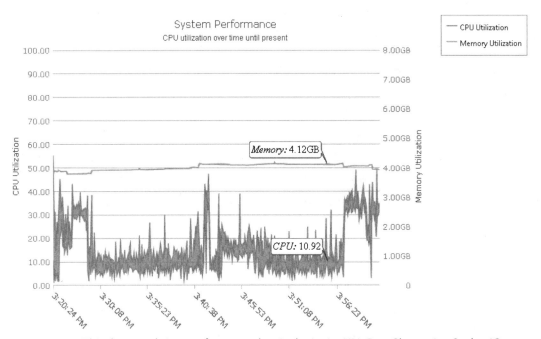

FIGURE 14-9: This shows real-time performance data in the Ignite UI igDataChart using Socket.IO.

But how is this accomplished? You start with the following:

```
var cpuData = [];

function toDisplayCPU(v) {
    return v.toFixed(2);
}

function toDisplayMem(v) {
    if (v >= (1024 * 1024 * 1024)) {
        v /= (1024 * 1024 * 1024);
        return v.toFixed(2) + "GB";
    }

    if (v >= (1024 * 1024)) {
        v /= (1024 * 1024);
        return v.toFixed(2) + "MB";
    }

    if (v >= (1024)) {
        v /= (1024);
        return v.toFixed(2) + "KB";
    }

    return v;
}
```

An empty array, `cpuData`, is defined to hold the real-time data as it is pushed from the server. Two functions are defined that will help to convert the raw numeric values from the server into nice display values for use in the axes of the chart and in the tooltips.

```
function renderChart() {
    var chartOptions = {
        dataSource: cpuData,
        width: "700px",
        height: "500px",
        title: "System Performance",
        subtitle: "CPU utilization over time until present",
        horizontalZoomable: true,
        verticalZoomable: true,
        rightMargin: 30,
        legend: { element: "legend" },
        axes: [{
            type: "categoryX",
            name: "xAxis",
            label: "displayTime",
            labelAngle: 45
        }, {
            type: "numericY",
            name: "yAxis",
            title: "CPU Utilization",
            minimumValue: 0,
            maximumValue: 100,
            formatLabel: toDisplayCPU
        }, {
            type: "numericY",
            name: "yAxisMemory",
            title: "Memory Utilization",
            labelLocation: "outsideRight",
            minimumValue: 0,
            maximumValue: 8 * 1024 * 1024 * 1024,
            interval: 1024 * 1024 * 1024,
            formatLabel: toDisplayMem,
            majorStroke: "transparent"
        }],
        series: [{
            name: "cpu",
            type: "line",
            xAxis: "xAxis",
            yAxis: "yAxis",
            valueMemberPath: "cpuUsage",
            showTooltip: true,
            tooltipTemplate:
    "<div><em>CPU:</em> <span>${item.displayCPU}</span></div>",
            title: "CPU Utilization"
        }, {
            name: "mem",
            type: "line",
            xAxis: "xAxis",
            yAxis: "yAxisMemory",
            valueMemberPath: "usedMem",
```

```
            showTooltip: true,
            tooltipTemplate:
    "<div><em>Memory:</em> <span>${item.displayMem}</span></div>",
            title: "Memory Utilization"
        }, {
            name: "itemToolTips",
            type: "itemToolTipLayer",
            useInterpolation: false,
            transitionDuration: 300
        }]
    };


    $("#chart").igDataChart(chartOptions);

}

renderChart();
```

The `renderChart` function is pretty much the same as when you were dealing with financial data.
The significant differences have been highlighted, though. The differences boil down to a different
strategy for displaying the long x-axis label values, and making sure that some nice looking formatting is used on the large memory utilization numbers to make them more palatable. If you stopped
here, this would provide you a static chart, much like the financial chart before (albeit with no
actual data), but it would not respond to any updates from the server. So let's continue.

```
var socket = io.connect("http://localhost:8080");

socket.on("cpuUpdate", function (update) {
    var currTime = new Date();
    var displayString = currTime.toLocaleTimeString();
    update.displayCPU = toDisplayCPU(update.cpuUsage);
    update.displayMem = toDisplayMem(update.usedMem);
    update.displayTime = displayString;
    cpuData.push(update);
    $("#chart").igDataChart("notifyInsertItem",
        cpuData, cpuData.length - 1, update);
});
```

The preceding snippet is the heart and soul of the real-time update. First you connect to the Socket.IO
server on port 8080. Note, you would use a different value for the URL here for deploying to a production server with a real DNS name.

Next, you define that when a `"cpuUpdate"` message is received on the socket, you would like to

➤   Examine the associated JavaScript object that was received and create some human-readable
    strings for easy use in the tooltips

➤   Create a human-readable time string for use in the axis labels and the tooltips

➤   Add the data to the array being displayed in the chart with `cpuData.push(update);`

➤   Notify the chart that you have modified an associated data array by adding a value to the
    end: `$("#chart").igDataChart("notifyInsertItem", cpuData, cpuData.length -
    1, update);`

JavaScript doesn't have a built-in observable array type for automatically notifying consumers of data changes, so this is why it is necessary to notify the chart that one of its arrays has been modified. Given that notification, igDataChart handles all the necessary update work for you. Alternatively, if you use a framework such as Knockout.js, igDataChart is capable of listening for updates on the observable array types provided and managing these updates for you. Note, however, that some of these frameworks add some additional processing overhead, so the optimal performance scenario might be to invoke the notification methods on the chart directly.

The last thing required is to make sure that the HTML page references the Socket.IO client library. Notice that you don't actually have this file on disk in the directory that Node.js is serving files from; the Socket.IO server is managing serving up this script reference dynamically when asked:

```
<script src="/socket.io/socket.io.js"></script>
```

To see the kind of astonishing update performance you can get out of this combination of Socket.IO and igDataChart, try editing cpuLoadServer.js and changing the broadcast interval from 100ms to 10ms:

```
io.sockets.on('connection', function () {
    if (interval < 0) {
        interval = setInterval(function () {
            var freeMem = os.freemem();
            var totalMem = os.totalmem();
            io.sockets.emit("cpuUpdate", {
                cpuUsage: currCPU * 100.0,
                freeMem: freeMem,
                totalMem: totalMem,
                usedMem: totalMem - freeMem
            });
        }, 10);
    }
});
```

Now, quit your server and restart it. The updates should be coming in really quickly now. Pretty neat, huh?

Exploring Update Rendering Techniques

The previous example continues to add new data points to the end of the series perpetually. Although the igDataChart can gracefully display more than a million points interactively, you still might want to employ some strategies to roll out old data that is no longer interesting. To end this chapter, here's a quick peek at a few strategies:

```
socket.on("cpuUpdate", function (update) {
    var currTime = new Date();
    var displayString = currTime.toLocaleTimeString();
    update.displayCPU = toDisplayCPU(update.cpuUsage);
    update.displayMem = toDisplayMem(update.usedMem);
    update.displayTime = displayString;
    cpuData.push(update);
    $("#chart").igDataChart("notifyInsertItem",
        cpuData, cpuData.length - 1, update);
```

```
    if (cpuData.length > 1000) {
        var oldItem = cpuData.shift();
        $("#chart").igDataChart("notifyRemoveItem",
            cpuData, 0, oldItem);
    }
});
```

This variant on the socket message handler from the previous example achieves a sliding window effect where, after the maximum number of points is displayed, it begins removing the oldest points as new ones are added. The result is that the data appears to slide through the view from right to left. This is achieved by notifying the chart not just of the additions to the data at the end of the array but also of the removals at the beginning of the array. There's no need to worry about the chart rendering twice from the two notifications; it's smart enough to wait until your modification is done before updating the visuals. You can see the result on the companion website in the `IgniteUICPULoadChartSlidingWindow.js/html/css` file.

```
var cpuData = [];
for (var i = 0; i < 1000; i++) {
    cpuData.push({
        displayTime: new Date().toLocaleTimeString(),
        usedMem: NaN,
        cpuUsage: NaN
    });
}
var insertionPoint = 0;
```

Another strategy is to change the definition of the array to look like the preceding code, where you start with 1000 data points defined with no initial values. Then, combine that with this:

```
socket.on("cpuUpdate", function (update) {
        var currTime = new Date();
        var displayString = currTime.toLocaleTimeString();
        update.displayCPU = toDisplayCPU(update.cpuUsage);
        update.displayMem = toDisplayMem(update.usedMem);
        update.displayTime = displayString;
        cpuData[insertionPoint] = update;

        $("#chart").igDataChart("notifySetItem",
            cpuData, insertionPoint, update);

        for (var i = insertionPoint + 1;
            i < Math.min(insertionPoint + 21, 1000);
            i++) {
            cpuData[i] = {
                displayTime: new Date().toLocaleTimeString(),
                usedMem: NaN,
                cpuUsage: NaN
            };
            $("#chart").igDataChart("notifySetItem",
            cpuData, i, cpuData[i]);
        }

        insertionPoint++;
```

```
        if (insertionPoint > 999) {
            insertionPoint = 0;
        }
    });
```

which creates an updating style reminiscent of an EKG machine. The number of points in the series remains static, and when the updates reach the right edge of the chart they wrap back around to the left edge and begin overwriting the oldest content. An extra tweak empties some values ahead of the most recent value to make it more apparent where the most recent values are, at a glance. You can see a snapshot of this behavior in Figure 14-10, and you can find the IgniteUICPULoadChartEKGStyle.js/html/css file on the companion website.

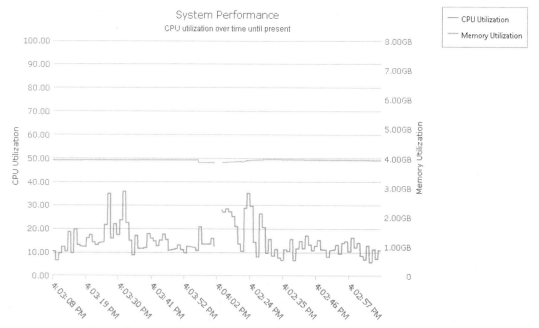

FIGURE 14-10: This real-time updating chart includes EKG-style wrapping.

PLOTTING MASSIVE DATA

To wrap up this chapter, you use the igDataChart to plot massive amounts of data in the browser. Would you believe us if we told you that you could plot one million data points in a JavaScript chart? No? Well, next, you do just that. In fact, plotting that amount of data will prove less of a challenge than transmitting the data, over the wire, to the client.

JSON is pretty wonderful. It's human readable, and there is good support for deserializing it in any decent JavaScript engine, but it does have a bit of a verbosity problem. It is nowhere near as verbose as XML, but is still much more verbose than a packed binary format.

Browsers have not traditionally been very good at processing binary data in JavaScript, but recent versions have begun to improve upon this through the advent of the ArrayBuffer API. Your strategy to load mass amounts of data is to encode a packed binary file containing one million single-precision floating-point numbers, using Node.js. Provided that file, you load it into an `ArrayBuffer` using an `XmlHTTPRequest` and then use a `DataView` to extract the floating-point numbers back into an array on the client side. This data can then be loaded into the chart.

First, you start with the data creation as shown in Listing 14-5.

LISTING 14-5

```
var fs = require("fs");
var numItems = 1000000;
var buf = new Buffer(numItems * 4);

var currValue = 1000.0;

for (var i = 0; i < numItems; i++) {
    currValue += -2.0 + Math.random() * 4.0;
    buf.writeFloatLE(currValue, i * 4);
}

fs.writeFile("data.bin", buf, function (err) {
    if (err) {
        console.log("Error writing file: " + err);
    }
    console.log("file written.");
});
```

This creates a Node.js `Buffer` that is large enough to store one million single-precision floating-point numbers. A single-precision floating-point number is generally encoded using 4 bytes, so the buffer needs to be 4 million bytes long. Provided such a buffer, the code in Listing 14-5 calls `writeFloatLE` for each data point to write each float value, using little endian byte ordering, into the buffer. Given this filled buffer, Node.js's `fs.writeFile` function, which you used earlier in this chapter, can write this buffer to disk as the contents of a file. This produces a file called `data.bin`, which contains the one million data points.

If you create a file called `createMassData.js` and fill it with the contents of Listing 14-5, you should be able to navigate to the directory containing this file and run this command from a Node.js command prompt (on the companion website, the file is `createMassData.js`):

```
node createMassData.js
```

As a result, you should end up with an output file called `data.bin`, which should be 3,907KB in size. This is large, but is nowhere near as large as the data would be if it were encoded as JSON. For comparison, Listing 14-6 contains code that creates the same data but is encoded as a JSON array.

LISTING 14-6

```
var fs = require("fs");
var numItems = 1000000;
```

```
var data = [];
var outputObject = {};

var currValue = 1000.0;
for (var i = 0; i < numItems; i++) {
    currValue += -2.0 + Math.random() * 4.0;
    data.push(currValue);
}
outputObject.data = data;

fs.writeFile("data.json", JSON.stringify(outputObject), function (err) {
    if (err) {
        console.log("Error writing file: " + err);
    }
    console.log("file written.");
});
```

Running that code results in a file called `data.json`, which has the same content as `data.bin` but is encoded as JSON. The resulting size of the file is 18,166KB. That's just over 4.5 times larger than the binary encoded version! If you gzip compress the files, then their sizes are reduced as follows:

➤ `data.bin.gz`: 3,253KB

➤ `data.json.gz`: 7,067KB

The plaintext JSON file, predictably, benefited far more from the compression, but the compressed binary file is still much smaller than the compressed JSON equivalent. You can see, however, that the feasibility of slinging so much JSON around in web applications, as we do today, hangs largely on the fact that it compresses reasonably well, and that web servers and browsers can generally seamlessly gzip compress/decompress files without adding too much additional processing overhead to a request. When you are dealing with mass data, however, every byte counts.

Given the binary file with the one million data points, the remaining challenge is how to pull that down into the browser and load it into a chart. Modern browsers have some APIs to help deal with downloading and processing data at the raw level, but some of it is so new that some of the major high-level JavaScript libraries don't have especially good support for it yet, so you'll be using `XmlHTTPRequest` directly to pull down the data.

Next you define the actual chart as shown in Listing 14-7.

LISTING 14-7

```
$(function () {

    function renderChart(data) {
        $("#chart").igDataChart({
            dataSource: data,
            width: "700px",
            height: "500px",
            horizontalZoomable: true,
            verticalZoomable: true,
```

continues

LISTING 14-7 *(continued)*

```
            axes: [{
                name: "xAxis",
                label: "label",
                type: "categoryX",
                labelAngle: 45
            }, {
                name: "yAxis",
                type: "numericY"
            }],
            series: [{
                name: "line",
                xAxis: "xAxis",
                yAxis: "yAxis",
                type: "line",
                showTooltip: true,
                valueMemberPath: "value",
                isHighlightingEnabled: true,
                isTransitionInEnabled: true
            }],
        });
    };

    var xhr = new XMLHttpRequest();
    xhr.onload = function () {
        if (xhr.status == 200) {
            var arrayBuffer = xhr.response;

            var dataView = new DataView(arrayBuffer);
            var numItems = arrayBuffer.byteLength / 4;

            var data = [];
            for (var i = 0; i < numItems; i++) {
                data.push({
                    label: "Item " + i.toString(),
                    value: dataView.getFloat32(i * 4,  true)
                });
            }

            renderChart(data);
        }
    };

    xhr.open("GET", "data.bin");
    xhr.responseType = "arraybuffer";
    xhr.send(null);
});
```

The actual creation of the chart is nothing new—if you've read the rest of this chapter. No special settings are required to load this quantity of data into an igDataChart series, so let's break down just the highlighted section of Listing 14-7. For starters you have:

```
var xhr = new XMLHttpRequest();
```

This creates a new `XMLHttpRequest`, which is the backbone of every AJAX request. If you are used to using `$.ajax` and its kin in jQuery, they are eventually, under the covers, dealing with this API. Next, you define the callback function that will get invoked when the request completes:

```
var xhr = new XMLHttpRequest();
xhr.onload = function () {
    if (xhr.status == 200) {
        var arrayBuffer = xhr.response;
```

Here, provided that the response is OK (HTTP code 200), you extract it for processing. Provided the response to the request, which should be an `ArrayBuffer`, you extract the data from it:

```
var dataView = new DataView(arrayBuffer);
var numItems = arrayBuffer.byteLength / 4;

var data = [];
for (var i = 0; i < numItems; i++) {
    data.push({
        label: "Item " + i.toString(),
        value: dataView.getFloat32(i * 4,  true)
    });
}
```

First, you create a `DataView` over the `ArrayBuffer`, which will assist in extracting the floating-point values from the binary data response. Because each single-precision floating-point is 4 bytes, and they make up the entire file, you divide by 4 to get the number of items. Then you loop over all of the items and extract each in turn from the array buffer.

```
dataView.getFloat32(i * 4,  true)
```

Here, the first parameter is the byte offset into the buffer, which is determined by multiplying the index times 4 (for the number of bytes in each single-precision floating-point number). The second parameter indicates that the floating points will be encoded in little endian fashion, which you ensured earlier by calling `buf.writeFloatLE(currValue, i * 4)` rather than `buf.writeFloatBE(currValue, i * 4)`, when creating the data file.

```
            renderChart(data);
        }
    };

    xhr.open("GET", "data.bin");
    xhr.responseType = "arraybuffer";
    xhr.send(null);
});
```

Finally, when the data has finished being decoded, you render the chart. Having fully set up the callback that will be called upon successful return of the binary data response, the only thing remaining is to perform an HTTP get for the file `data.bin`, indicate that the response type should be an `ArrayBuffer`, and initiate the asynchronous request. If you run the preceding code, you should see one million data points loaded into the chart as demonstrated in Figure 14-11 (the `IgniteUIMassData.js/html/css` file on the companion website).

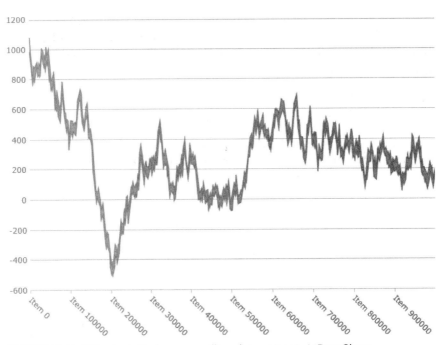

FIGURE 14-11: This chart displays one million data points in igDataChart.

Notice that you can zoom in with your mouse wheel or by clicking and dragging on the chart. After you're zoomed in, you can press Shift and click and drag to pan around. Because igDataChart is good at processing these extreme amounts of data and helping you visualize them, everything stays buttery smooth even under these conditions.

SUMMARY

In this chapter, you learned all about charting time series. One of the most popular time series visualizations is a stock data chart, so you started there, but you ended with some real-time visualizations of computer performance data. You learned:

➤ The anatomy of a candlestick or OHLC chart

➤ How to obtain and load financial data using JavaScript

➤ How to display financial data in the Ignite UI igDataChart

➤ Some of the differences between plotting time series data on a category axis versus a linear axis

➤ How to use a zoom bar to navigate the Ignite UI igDataChart

➤ How to plot a synchronized chart to display trade volatility

➤ How to plot technical indicators against your financial data

➤ How to create a real-time push update server using Node.js

➤ How to render real-time data in the igDataChart

➤ Various strategies for managing real-time data in the igDataChart

➤ Strategies for displaying massive amounts of data in igDataChart

PART IV
Interactive Analysis and Visualization Projects

15

Building an Interconnected Dashboard

➤ Pulling data from the U.S. Census API

➤ Rendering Census data with Google Charts

➤ Styling the chart dashboard responsively

➤ Connecting the components with Backbone

> **CODE DOWNLOAD** *The wrox.com code downloads for this chapter are found at* www.wrox.com/go/javascriptandjqueryanalysis *on the Download Code tab. The code is in the chapter 15 download and individually named according to the names throughout the chapter.*

With this chapter, you create an interactive dashboard that charts U.S. census data. You start by exploring the Census API and learn how to overcome its many challenges. Next you render static charts from this data using Google Charts. You create visualizations for a variety of data:

➤ Demographic data for sex and race

➤ Housing data

➤ Population growth and age breakdowns

After creating the charts, you then integrate them into an interconnected dashboard. You start by styling the dashboard responsively and then integrate form controls to translate user input into rendered changes on the screen. In the end, you'll have created a simple Backbone app that renders complex data.

THE U.S. CENSUS API

In recent years, the U.S. government has been releasing a variety of public APIs for governmental data. Collected at www.data.gov, these APIs provide a variety of useful data sets. Notably, the Census API offers a wealth of intricate demographic information about U.S. residents.

To get started with the API, register for an API key at www.census.gov/developers/. After you're in the site, you see that there are a variety of different data sets available. For now, take a look at the Decennial Census Data:

```
http://www.census.gov/data/developers/data-sets/decennial-census-data.html
```

A quick word of warning: Working with the Census API can be cumbersome. Rather than using an intuitive data structure, you have to dig through mountains of XML to figure out how to access the desired data.

For example, say you want to figure out simple gender information. The first step is to look in http://api.census.gov/data/2010/sf1/variables.xml for the key for the data you want. In this case, you need P0120002 and P0120026, which are aggregated values for the "sex by age" data for men and women respectively.

Next, include these keys along with your API key in a call to the API:

```
http://api.census.gov/data/2010/sf1?get=
P0120002,P0120026&for=state:*&key=[your_api_key]
```

For now, just paste this link in your browser. If your API key is working, you should see this data:

```
[["P0120002","P0120026","state"],
["2320188","2459548","01"],
["369628","340603","02"],
["3175823","3216194","04"],
["1431637","1484281","05"],
...
["287437","276189","56"],
["1785171","1940618","72"]]
```

That's 2010 census data for men and women broken down by state. For instance, the second line, ["2320188","2459548","01"] represents:

➤ "2320188": The number of men (P0120002)

➤ "2459548": The number of women (P0120026)

➤ "01": In Alabama

The final value, 01, is the FIPS (Federal Information Processing Standards) state code for Alabama. Unfortunately, you can't query the Census API using intuitive strings such as men, women, and Alabama; instead, you have to use random government codes such as P0120002, P0120026, and 01.

> **TIP** *For a list of FIPS state codes, visit* http://en.wikipedia.org/wiki/ Federal_Information_Processing_Standard_state_code.

The previous example pulls a list for all states, but you can also specify a given state using the FIPS state code. For example, to pull the information for only Alabama, you'd call

```
http://api.census.gov/data/2010/sf1?get=P0120002,P0120026&for=state:01
   &key=[your_api_key].
```

That returns a much smaller data set:

```
[["P0120002","P0120026","state"],
["2320188","2459548","01"]]
```

> **TIP** USA Today *provides a more intuitive API for census data at* http://developer.usatoday.com/docs/read/Census. *It's handy for simple data, but not nearly as powerful as the API from* www.census.gov.

RENDERING CHARTS

Now that you have data from the census API, rendering it in a chart will be a piece of cake. To keep things simple, you're going use Google Charts and just hardcode the charts for a specific state (New York). Then, later in this chapter you integrate these components into an interactive Backbone app that works for all 50 states in the United States.

Sex Chart

First, let's create a chart using the male versus female demographic information you accessed earlier. To get started, grab the data using jQuery's ajax() API:

```
$.ajax({
  url: "http://api.census.gov/data/2010/sf1",
      data: {
    get: "P0120002,P0120026",
    for: "state:36",
    key: "[your API key]"
  },
  success: function(data) {
    console.log(data);
  }
});
```

This snippet reformats the query to `api.census.gov`, breaking out the query variables into the `data` object. After you've entered your API key, you should see the console outputting the sex data you accessed earlier.

Next, display this data in a chart. First include a wrapper for the chart, the Google JS API, and load the chart's API:

```
<div id="sex-chart"></div>

<script src="https://www.google.com/jsapi"></script>
<script>
google.load("visualization", "1", {packages:["corechart"]});
google.setOnLoadCallback(renderCharts);
</script>
```

Now, the API calls `renderCharts()` whenever the chart scripts load. Add the Ajax call to `api.census.gov` to this callback, and render the chart:

```
function renderCharts() {
  $.ajax({
    url: "http://api.census.gov/data/2010/sf1",
    data: {
      get: "P0120002,P0120026",
      for: "state:36",
      key: "[your API key]"
    },
    success: function(data) {
      var processed = [
        ["Sex", "Population"],
        ["Male", ~~data[1][0]],
        ["Female", ~~data[1][1]]
      ];

      var chartData = google.visualization.arrayToDataTable(processed);

      var options = {
        title: "Sex",
        pieHole: 0.8,
        pieSliceText: "none"
      };

      var chart = new google.visualization.PieChart(
        document.getElementById("sex-chart")
      );

      chart.draw(chartData, options);
    }
  });
}
```

In the success callback, you see a bit of data massaging to convert the raw census data to the format Google Charts expects. In defining the `processed` variable, you first include an array to name the columns of the chart and then pass in each row of data. For each row, you simply pull the relevant value from the Census API data and then convert it to an integer using the `~~` literal.

> **NOTE** *The ~~ literal is similar to Math.floor, except with better performance.*

The script next creates an `options` object for Google Charts, setting some basic options, along with `pieHole` to render the donut chart in Figure 15-1. (Check out the color insert for the full dashboard that's being built in this chapter.)

Sex

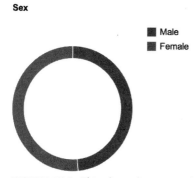

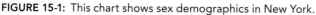

FIGURE 15-1: This chart shows sex demographics in New York.

You can find this example in the Chapter 15 folder on the companion website. It's named `sex-chart.html`.

Race Chart

You can now take a similar approach to create a chart for race demographics. When working with the Census API, the first step is hunting down just what keys you want to pull from the data set. In this case, you need to look at the `P8. RACE` section, in particular `P0080003` through `P0080009`.

Next, you can follow the patterns in the sex chart to render this new chart in the `renderCharts()` callback:

```
$.ajax({
  url: "http://api.census.gov/data/2010/sf1",
  data: {
    get: "P0080003,P0080004,P0080005,P0080006,P0080007,P0080008,P0080009",
    for: "state:36",
    key: "[your API key]"
  },
  success: function(data) {
    var races = [
      "White",
      "Black",
      "American Indian or Alaskan Native",
      "Asian",
      "Native Hawaiian or Pacific Islander",
      "Other",
      "Mixed"
    ],
```

```
processed = [
  ["Race", "Population"]
];

// lose the last value (state ID)
data[1].pop();

for ( i in data[1] ) {
  processed.push([
    races[i],
    ~~data[1][i]
  ]);
}

var chartData = google.visualization.arrayToDataTable(processed);

var options = {
  title: "Race",
  is3D: true
};

var chart = new google.visualization.PieChart(
  document.getElementById("race-chart")
);

chart.draw(chartData, options);
  }
});
```

Here the code follows the sex chart example for the most part except that it's dealing with more values, so it's a bit easier to loop through these values to create the `processed` variable. Finally, instead of a donut chart, this data makes more sense to display as a pie chart, so the `pieHole` in the options has been replaced with `is3D` to render the 3D pie chart in Figure 15-2.

Race

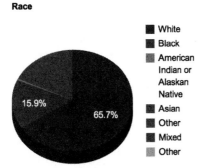

■	White
■	Black
■	American Indian or Alaskan Native
■	Asian
■	Other
■	Mixed
■	Other

FIGURE 15-2: Race demographics in New York have been charted.

TIP *Make sure to include a wrapper for each chart in the markup, as shown in the example in the Chapter 10 folder on the companion website. It's named* race-chart.html. *Note that it might render differently based on the size of your screen; Google Charts adds information depending on the size of the chart wrapper.*

Household Size Chart

Next let's create a visualization for the information in H13. Household Size, in particular H0130002 through H0130008:

```javascript
$.ajax({
  url: "http://api.census.gov/data/2010/sf1",
  data: {
    get: "H0130002,H0130003,H0130004,H0130005,H0130006,H0130007,H0130008",
    for: "state:36",
    key: "[your API key]"
  },
  success: function(data) {
    var processed = [
      ["Household Size", "Households"]
    ];

    // lose the last value (state ID)
    data[1].pop();

    for ( i in data[1] ) {
      processed.push([
        (~~i+1) + ( i == 6 ? "+" : "" ) + " Person",
        ~~data[1][i]
      ]);
    }

    var chartData = google.visualization.arrayToDataTable(processed);

    var options = {
      title: "Household Size",
      is3D: true
    };

    var chart = new google.visualization.PieChart(
      document.getElementById("household-chart")
    );

    chart.draw(chartData, options);
  }
});
```

Here, the script follows the patterns from the race chart almost exactly, with one exception. Rather than hardcoding the name for each key, it generates them dynamically using the loop index to create keys like "1 Person," "2 Person," and "7+ Person." That renders the chart in Figure 15-3.

You can find this example in the Chapter 15 folder on the companion website. It's named household-chart.html.

Household Size

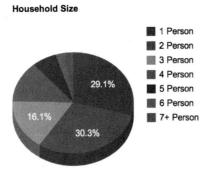

FIGURE 15-3: This chart shows household sizes in New York.

Household Tenure Chart

Next you create a chart for household tenure data—that is, the percentage of homes that are owned versus rented. This chart is again very simple; this time it follows the basic sex chart example, except with the data in H11. TOTAL POPULATION IN OCCUPIED HOUSING UNITS BY TENURE.

```
$.ajax({
  url: "http://api.census.gov/data/2010/sf1",
  data: {
    get: "H0110002,H0110003,H0110004",
    for: "state:36",
    key: "[your API key]"
  },
  success: function(data) {
    var processed = [
      ["Tenure", "Housing Units"],
      ["Owned with Mortgage", ~~data[1][0]],
      ["Owned Outright", ~~data[1][1]],
      ["Rented", ~~data[1][2]]
    ];

    var chartData = google.visualization.arrayToDataTable(processed);

    var options = {
      title: "Housing Tenure",
      pieHole: 0.8,
      pieSliceText: "none"
    };

    var chart = new google.visualization.PieChart(
      document.getElementById("tenure-chart")
    );

    chart.draw(chartData, options);
  }
});
```

As you can see, the script simply hardcodes the names for each piece of data and includes the relevant value. The end result is the donut chart in Figure 15-4.

Housing Tenure

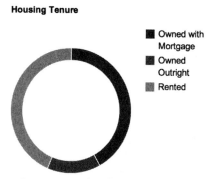

FIGURE 15-4: This chart shows housing tenure data for New York.

You can find this example in the Chapter 15 folder on the companion website. It's named `tenure-chart.html`.

Age by Sex Chart

So far you've been working with small data sets. But now it's time to think a bit larger and display a chart showing how the population is dispersed across different ages and genders. For these purposes, you need to leverage the mammoth P12. Sex By Age data set.

Because you're going to be grabbing a lot more data (46 values to be exact), start by creating a function to generate the keys you need:

```
function build_age_request_string(offset) {
  var out = "";

  for ( var i = 0; i < 23; i++ ) {
    var this_index = ("0" + (i + offset)).slice(-2);

    out += "P01200" + this_index + ",";
  }

  return out;
}

var age_request_keys = build_age_request_string(3) + build_age_request_string(27);

age_request_keys = age_request_keys.slice(0,-1);
```

Don't get too hung up on this script; it's just a quick piece of code to output the 46 keys you need (P0120003 through P0120025 for men and P0120027 through P0120049 for women).

Next, pass these references into an API call:

```
$.ajax({
  url: "http://api.census.gov/data/2010/sf1",
  data: {
    get: age_request_keys,
    for: "state:36",
    key: "[your API key]"
  },
  success: function(data) {
    var male_data   = data[1].slice(0,23),
        female_data = data[1].slice(23,46);
  }
});
```

Here the script uses the `age_request_keys` string you previously generated to pull the data, and then it slices out the male and female data sets from the result. Next, if you look at the Census API reference, notice that these age buckets are not all equal. For the most part, they represent a five-year age range—for example, 5–9 or 10–14—but there are a handful of outliers such as 15–17 and 18–19. In order to build a relevant visualization, it's important to rectify these differences and create useful comparisons.

Fortunately, the unusual age groupings can be merged into the standard five-year buckets:

```
function combine_vals(arr, start, end) {
  var total = 0;

  for ( var i = start; i <= end; i++ ) {
    total += arr[i];
  }

  arr[start] = total;

  arr.splice( start + 1, end - start);

  return arr;
}

function clean_age_range( age_data ) {
  // convert all the values to numeric
  for ( var i in age_data ) {
    age_data[i] = ~~age_data[i];
  }

  // merge values starting with highest (to preserve array keys)

  // merge 65-66 && 67-69
  age_data = combine_vals( age_data, 17, 18 );

  // merge 60-61 & 62-64
  age_data = combine_vals( age_data, 15, 16 );

  // merge 20, 21 & 22-24
  age_data = combine_vals( age_data, 5, 7 );
```

```
    // merge 15-17 & 18-19
    age_data = combine_vals( age_data, 3, 4 );

    return age_data;
}

male_data = clean_age_range(male_data);
female_data = clean_age_range(female_data);
```

Here the script first defines the function `combine_vals()` for merging array values and then leverages that in the `clean_age_range()` function, which manually groups the unusual values. Next you can further refine this data to use with Google Charts:

```
var processed = [
  ["Age", "Male", "Female"]
];

for ( var i = 0, max = male_data.length; i < max; i++ ) {
  var row = [];

  switch(i) {
    case 0:
      row[0] = "Under 5";
    break;

    default:
      row[0] = (i * 5) + "-" + (i * 5 + 4);
    break;

    case max - 1:
      row[0] = (i * 5) + "+";
    break;
  }

  row[1] = male_data[i];
  row[2] = female_data[i];

  processed.push(row);
}
```

Here the code simply loops through the age data and outputs a useful name along with the male and female populations. Finally, pass this information into a Google Charts column chart:

```
var chartData = google.visualization.arrayToDataTable(processed);

var options = {
  title: "Age"
};

var chart = new google.visualization.ColumnChart(
  document.getElementById("age-chart")
);

chart.draw(chartData, options);
```

To wrap things up, let's look at the code all together:

```
function build_age_request_string(offset) {
  var out = "";

  for ( var i = 0; i < 23; i++ ) {
    var this_index = ("0" + (i + offset)).slice(-2);

    out += "P01200" + this_index + ",";
  }

  return out;
}

var age_request_keys = build_age_request_string(3) + build_age_request_string(27);

age_request_keys = age_request_keys.slice(0,-1);

$.ajax({
  url: "http://api.census.gov/data/2010/sf1",
  data: {
    get: age_request_keys,
    for: "state:36",
    key: "[your API key]"
  },
  success: function(data) {
    var male_data   = data[1].slice(0,23),
        female_data = data[1].slice(23,46);

    // merge the dissimilar age ranges

    function combine_vals(arr, start, end) {
      var total = 0;

      for ( var i = start; i <= end; i++ ) {
        total += arr[i];
      }

      arr[start] = total;

      arr.splice( start + 1, end - start);

      return arr;
    }

    function clean_age_range( age_data ) {
      // convert all the values to numeric
      for ( var i in age_data ) {
        age_data[i] = ~~age_data[i];
      }

      // merge values starting with highest (to preserve array keys)

      // merge 65-66 && 67-69
      age_data = combine_vals( age_data, 17, 18 );
```

```javascript
      // merge 60-61 & 62-64
      age_data = combine_vals( age_data, 15, 16 );

      // merge 20, 21 & 22-24
      age_data = combine_vals( age_data, 5, 7 );

      // merge 15-17 & 18-19
      age_data = combine_vals( age_data, 3, 4 );

      return age_data;
    }

    male_data = clean_age_range(male_data);
    female_data = clean_age_range(female_data);

    var processed = [
      ["Age", "Male", "Female"]
    ];

    for ( var i = 0, max = male_data.length; i < max; i++ ) {
      var row = [];

      switch(i) {
        case 0:
          row[0] = "Under 5";
        break;

        default:
          row[0] = (i * 5) + "-" + (i * 5 + 4);
        break;

        case max - 1:
          row[0] = (i * 5) + "+";
        break;
      }

      row[1] = male_data[i];
      row[2] = female_data[i];

      processed.push(row);
    }

    var chartData = google.visualization.arrayToDataTable(processed);

    var options = {
      title: "Age"
    };

    var chart = new google.visualization.ColumnChart(
      document.getElementById("age-chart")
    );

    chart.draw(chartData, options);
  }
});
```

After this script reformats the data, it creates the column chart in Figure 15-5.

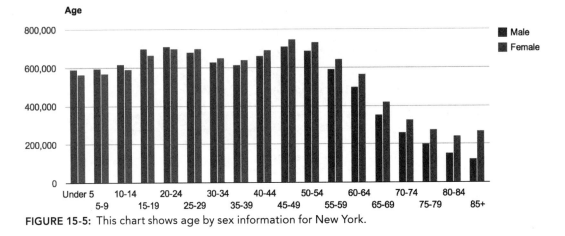

FIGURE 15-5: This chart shows age by sex information for New York.

You can find this example in the Chapter 15 folder on the companion website. It's named `age-chart.html`.

Population History Chart

At this point, you've built a number of charts showing various demographic breakdowns. Next, you can take things in a different direction to display population growth over time. However, to access this data you're going to need a different API: the Total Population and Components of Change API you can read about at

```
http://www.census.gov/data/developers/data-sets/population-estimates-and-
projections.html
```

The workflow for this API is largely the same:

1. Create the API call for the data you need.

2. Request that data with Ajax and reformat.

3. Display the data in a Google Chart.

Fortunately (or unfortunately), the data set for this API is significantly smaller than that of the Decennial Census Data, as you can see here: `http://api.census.gov/data/2013/pep/natstprc/variables.html`. That makes it much easier to build the API call. For example, to grab population change data for New York, you can call:

```
http://api.census.gov/data/2013/pep/natstprc?get=POP,DATE
    &for=state:36&key=your_api_key
```

You can use the same API key you used for decennial data, which returns the following:

```
[["POP","DATE","state"],
["19378102","1","36"],
["19378105","2","36"],
["19398228","3","36"],
["19502728","4","36"],
["19576125","5","36"],
["19651127","6","36"]]
```

Each row represents another year of population data, from July 1, 2008 (DATE:1) through July 1, 2013 (DATE:6). Next, access this data from your JS and build a chart:

```
$.ajax({
  url: "http://api.census.gov/data/2013/pep/natstprc",
  data: {
    get: "POP,DATE",
    for: "state:36",
    key: "[your API key]"
  },
  success: function(data) {
    var processed = [
      ["Year", "Population"]
    ];

    for ( i in data ) {
      if ( i == 0 ) continue;
      processed[i] = [ ~~data[i][1] + 2007, ~~data[i][0] ];
    }

    var chartData = google.visualization.arrayToDataTable(processed);

    var options = {
      title: "Population Growth",
      legend: "none"
    };

    var chart = new google.visualization.LineChart(
      document.getElementById("population-chart")
    );
    chart.draw(chartData, options);
  }
});
```

This script loops through the data the API returns, creating a year string from the DATE values and inserting the population count. It then passes the processed data into Google Charts to render the line chart in Figure 15-6.

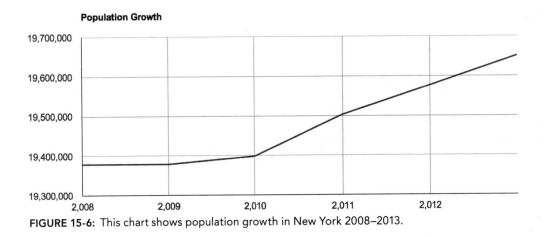

FIGURE 15-6: This chart shows population growth in New York 2008–2013.

You can find this example in the Chapter 15 folder on the companion website. It's named `popula-tion-chart.html`.

CREATING THE DASHBOARD

Now that you've rendered charts for a variety of data sets, you can combine them in a dashboard. For now, you still hardcode the dashboard for New York's data, but it makes an excellent jumping off point for the interactive app.

You can find this example in the Chapter 15 folder on the companion website. It's named `respon-sive-dashboard.html`.

Basic Markup and Styling

First, combine the wrappers for each chart in some basic markup:

```
<div class="census">
  <div class="charts">
    <h1>
    Census Data - New York
    </h1>

    <section class="population">
      <h2>
      Population
      </h2>

      <div id="population-chart" class="chart"></div>
      <div id="age-chart" class="chart"></div>
    </section>
```

```
<section class="demographics">
  <h2>
  Demographics
  </h2>

  <div id="race-chart" class="chart"></div>
  <div id="sex-chart" class="chart"></div>
</section>

<section class="housing">
  <h2>
  Housing
  </h2>

  <div id="household-chart" class="chart"></div>
  <div id="tenure-chart" class="chart"></div>
</section>
</div>
</div>
```

Next, apply some basic CSS:

```
body {
  font-family: "Gill Sans", "Gill Sans MT", Calibri, sans-serif;
}

h1, h2 {
  font-weight: normal;
}

h2 {
  padding: .5em 1em;
  background: #DDD;
}

.census {
  position: relative;
  overflow: hidden;
}

/* charts */

section {
  overflow: hidden;
}

.chart {
  height: 350px;
}

.demographics .chart, .housing .chart {
  width: 50%;
  float: left;
}
```

That renders the charts in the dashboard shown in Figure 15-7.

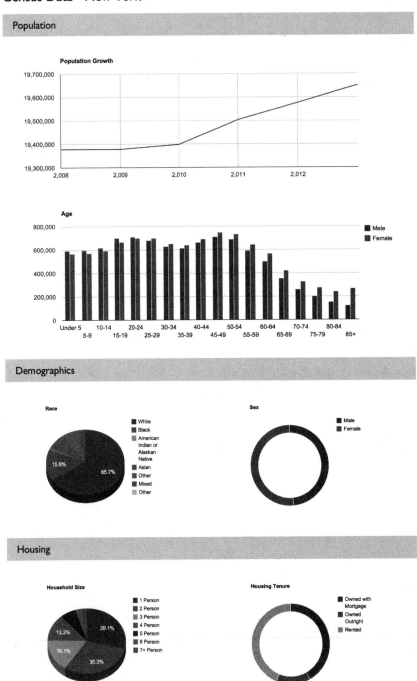

FIGURE 15-7: At this point the script renders the initial dashboard.

You can find this stylesheet in the Chapter 15 folder on the companion website. It's named `css/census-charts.css`.

Responsive Layer

So far, the dashboard is looking decent on medium-sized devices. Next, you should add a responsive layer to maximize the screen real estate for both tiny mobile devices and large desktop monitors. To do so, add some simple media queries to the CSS:

```
@media all and (min-width: 700px) and (max-width: 1000px) {
  .demographics .chart, .housing .chart {
    width: 50%;
    float: left;
  }
}

@media all and (min-width: 1001px) {
  .population:not(.single) {
    width: 66.6666%;
    float: left;
  }

  .demographics {
    width: 33.3333%;
    float: right;
  }

  .housing {
    clear: both;
  }

  .housing .chart {
    width: 50%;
    float: left;
  }
}
```

Here, the styles for `.demographics .chart, .housing .chart {}` have been moved into a block that displays only on windows between 700 and 1000 pixels. That ensures that smaller windows, such as those on phones, don't get the columned layout for these charts and instead display each line by line.

Additionally, some styles have been added for windows larger than 1000px wide. These new rules reposition the demographics column next to the population data, with the two housing charts floated underneath. That gives a much more integrated dashboard feel for larger monitors, which you can see in Figure 15-8 and in the color insert.

You can find this stylesheet in the Chapter 15 folder on the companion website. It's named `css/census-charts.css`.

Census Data - New York

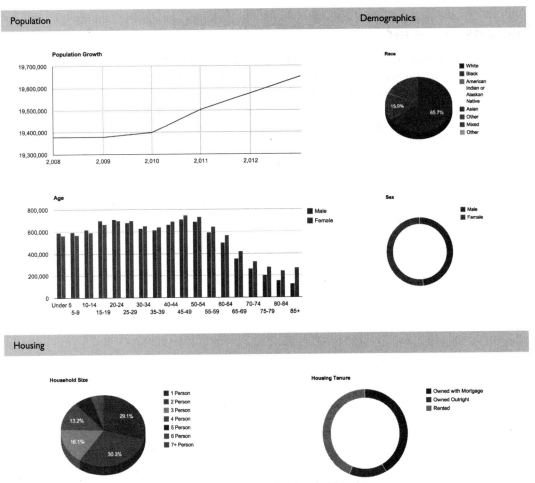

FIGURE 15-8: This screenshot shows the larger layout for the dashboard.

CONNECTING COMPONENTS WITH BACKBONE

Now that you've built all the necessary components, it's time to integrate them into an application. To provide some structure for this app, you build it on top of Backbone. The Backbone implementation is fairly lightweight because the app is relatively simple.

The script has to handle three tasks:

1. Render charts of national data for the app's home screen.

2. Create a drop-down menu of states.

3. Use that drop-down menu to render the charts for a given state using its FIPS code.

You can find this example in the Chapter 15 folder on the companion website. It's named `css/census-charts.html`.

Establishing Models and Collections

To get started, you create some models and collections to work with. First, add a model for general app settings and variables:

```
var Census = Backbone.Model.extend({
  defaults: {
    loc: "00",
    loc_str: "United States"
  },

  validate: function( options ) {
    if ( ! options.api_key ) {
      return "You must enter your API key from www.census.gov/developers/";
    }
  },

  initialize: function() {
    this.on("invalid", function(e, error) {
      console.log(error);
    });
  }
});
```

As you can see, the script first defines some defaults for the location FIPS code (`loc`) and the associated display name (`loc_str`). Next, it creates a validation function that checks for an API key when the model initializes. The idea is to pass in your API key when you instantiate the model:

```
var census = new Census({
  api_key: "[your API key]"
});
```

Next, add a model for state data, such as the state name and FIPS code:

```
var States = Backbone.Collection.extend();

var states = new States([
  { name: "United States", fips: "00" },
  { name: "Alabama", fips: "01" },
  { name: "Alaska", fips: "02" },
  { name: "Arizona", fips: "04" },
  { name: "Arkansas", fips: "05" },
  { name: "California", fips: "06" },
  { name: "Colorado", fips: "08" },
  { name: "Connecticut", fips: "09" },
  { name: "Delaware", fips: "10" },
  { name: "District of Columbia", fips: "11" },
  { name: "Florida", fips: "12" },
  { name: "Georgia", fips: "13" },
  { name: "Hawaii", fips: "15" },
  { name: "Idaho", fips: "16" },
  { name: "Illinois", fips: "17" },
```

```
  { name: "Indiana", fips: "18" },
  { name: "Iowa", fips: "19" },
  { name: "Kansas", fips: "20" },
  { name: "Kentucky", fips: "21" },
  { name: "Louisiana", fips: "22" },
  { name: "Maine", fips: "23" },
  { name: "Maryland", fips: "24" },
  { name: "Massachusetts", fips: "25" },
  { name: "Michigan", fips: "26" },
  { name: "Minnesota", fips: "27" },
  { name: "Mississippi", fips: "28" },
  { name: "Missouri", fips: "29" },
  { name: "Montana", fips: "30" },
  { name: "Nebraska", fips: "31" },
  { name: "Nevada", fips: "32" },
  { name: "New Hampshire", fips: "33" },
  { name: "New Jersey", fips: "34" },
  { name: "New Mexico", fips: "35" },
  { name: "New York", fips: "36" },
  { name: "North Carolina", fips: "37" },
  { name: "North Dakota", fips: "38" },
  { name: "Ohio", fips: "39" },
  { name: "Oklahoma", fips: "40" },
  { name: "Oregon", fips: "41" },
  { name: "Pennsylvania", fips: "42" },
  { name: "Rhode Island", fips: "44" },
  { name: "South Carolina", fips: "45" },
  { name: "South Dakota", fips: "46" },
  { name: "Tennessee", fips: "47" },
  { name: "Texas", fips: "48" },
  { name: "Utah", fips: "49" },
  { name: "Vermont", fips: "50" },
  { name: "Virginia", fips: "51" },
  { name: "Washington", fips: "53" },
  { name: "West Virginia", fips: "54" },
  { name: "Wisconsin", fips: "55" },
  { name: "Wyoming", fips: "56" }
]);
```

You'll use this model for a variety of purposes, such as cross-referencing FIPS codes and display names.

You can find the JavaScript for this example in the Chapter 15 folder on the companion website. It's named `js/census-charts.js`.

Converting the Chart Markup to a JavaScript Template

Next, convert the chart markup to a JavaScript template:

```
<script type="template" class="census-tpl">
  <h1>
  Census Data - <%= loc_str %>
  </h1>
```

```html
<section class="population">
  <h2>
  Population
  </h2>

  <div id="population-chart" class="chart"></div>

  <div id="age-chart" class="chart"></div>
</section>

<section class="demographics">
  <h2>
  Demographics
  </h2>

  <div id="race-chart" class="chart"></div>

  <div id="sex-chart" class="chart"></div>
</section>

<section class="housing">
  <h2>
  Housing
  </h2>

  <div id="household-chart" class="chart"></div>

  <div id="tenure-chart" class="chart"></div>
</section>
</script>
```

As you can see, the template is mostly static at this point, except for adding the location string to the <h1>. That's because Google Charts handles the majority of the visual heavy lifting.

Next, create the initial view for this template in Backbone:

```javascript
var CensusView = Backbone.View.extend({
  el: ".charts",
  template: _.template( $(".census-tpl").text() ),

  initialize: function() {
    this.model.on("change", this.render, this);

    google.load("visualization", "1", {packages:["corechart"]});

    google.setOnLoadCallback($.proxy(this.render, this));
  },

  // render the new charts based on this location
  render: function() {
    // render the main template
    var compiled = this.template( this.model.toJSON() );
    this.$el.html(compiled);

    renderCharts();
```

```
      return this;
    }
  });

  var censusView = new CensusView({
    model: census,
    collection: states
  });
```

There are a few things going on in this script:

➤ The view first binds itself to the `.charts` node in the Document Object Model (DOM) and builds an Underscore template from the markup you created earlier.

➤ When the view initializes, it establishes a change handler to rerender the charts whenever the model changes. This will come in handy when you want to switch between states.

➤ The Google Chart loaders have been moved into this view because they only affect rendering.

➤ The render function regenerates the markup from the template, inserts it into the DOM, and then calls the `renderCharts()` script you wrote earlier. Eventually, you'll move the calls from that script into your Backbone implementation, but leave it out for now.

➤ When instantiating the view, the script passes in both the census model as well as the states collection you created earlier.

Creating the State Drop-down Menu

Next, in order to make the app dynamic, you're going to need form controls, in particular a drop-down menu for states. First create a template for the drop-down menu:

```
<script type="template" class="state-dropdown-tpl">
  <select name="state" class="state-select">
  <% _.each(states, function(state) {
    %> <option value="<%- state.fips %>"><%- state.name %></option>
  <% }); %>
  </select>
</script>
```

This template accepts an array of state name–FIPS pairs and displays them as markup. Next, add the functionality for the drop-down menu to the view:

```
var CensusView = Backbone.View.extend({
  el: ".charts",
  template: _.template( $(".census-tpl").text() ),

  initialize: function() {
    this.model.on("change", this.render, this);

    this.buildDropdown();

    google.load("visualization", "1", {packages:["corechart"]});

    google.setOnLoadCallback($.proxy(this.render, this));
```

```
    },

    // builds the state dropdown with change listener
    buildDropdown: function() {
      // compile the state dropdown template
      var tpl = _.template( $(".state-dropdown-tpl").text() ),
          compiled = tpl({
            states: this.collection.toJSON()
          });

      // append to the DOM
      var $dropdown = $(compiled).appendTo( this.$el.parent() );

      $dropdown.on("change", $.proxy(function(e) {
        this.model.set({
          loc: $dropdown.val(),
          loc_str: $dropdown.find("option:selected").text()
        });
      }, this));
    },

    // render the new charts based on this location
    render: function() {
      // render the main template
      var compiled = this.template( this.model.toJSON() );
      this.$el.html(compiled);

      renderCharts();

      return this;
    },
  });
```

In this code, the `buildDropdown()` function first compiles the drop-down menu template using the hard-coded States collection. Next, it binds a change listener to the drop-down menu, which modifies the Census model with an updated state name and FIPS code. That automatically rerenders the view because it in turn triggers the change handler on the model.

Finally, add some simple styling for the drop-down menu in your CSS:

```
.state-select {
  position: absolute;
  top: .8em;
  right: 0;
  font-size: 2em;
}
```

As you can see in Figure 15-9, the drop-down menu is now rendering at the top of your charts. However, it still isn't changing the charts for each state because you haven't added those hooks to your `renderChart()` function.

Census Data - New York

FIGURE 15-9: The state drop-down menu.

Rendering State Changes

The next step is integrating the code from `renderCharts()` into the Backbone application. You can add them one at a time to the view, starting with the population growth chart.

Population Growth Chart

First, create a function in the view to render the population growth chart:

```
var CensusView = Backbone.View.extend({
  el: ".charts",
  template: _.template( $(".census-tpl").text() ),

  ...

  render: function() {
    // render the main template
    var compiled = this.template( this.model.toJSON() );
    this.$el.html(compiled);

    // create the charts from this markup
    this.renderPopulation();

    return this;
  },

  renderPopulation: function() {
    $.ajax({
      url: "http://api.census.gov/data/2013/pep/natstprc",
      data: {
        get: "POP,DATE",
        for: this.model.get("loc_query"),
        key: this.model.get("api_key")
      },
      success: function(data) {
        var processed = [
          ["Year", "Population"]
        ];

        for ( i in data ) {
          if ( i == 0 ) continue;
          processed[i] = [ ~~data[i][1] + 2007, ~~data[i][0] ];
        }

        var chartData = google.visualization.arrayToDataTable(processed);

        var options = {
          title: "Population Growth",
          legend: "none"
        };

        var chart = new google.visualization.LineChart(
          document.getElementById("population-chart")
        );
```

```
      chart.draw(chartData, options);
    }
  });
  }
});
```

Here the script is largely the same as before, with one key difference: You've added dynamic references to the model's api_key and loc_query values. You should already have the api_key from when you instantiated the census model, but you still need to do a bit of work to generate the loc_query string, which helps drive the APIs. Add a bit of code to the model that creates this loc_query whenever the loc value is modified:

```
var Census = Backbone.Model.extend({
  defaults: {
    loc: "00",
    loc_str: "United States"
  },

  validate: function( options ) {
    if ( ! options.api_key ) {
      return "You must enter your API key from www.census.gov/developers/";
    }
  },

  // creates new location string for API
  buildLocQuery: function() {
    var loc = this.get("loc");
    if ( loc === "00" ) {
      this.set("loc_query", "us");
    }
    else {
      this.set("loc_query", "state:" + loc);
    }
  },

  initialize: function() {
    this.on("invalid", function(e, error) {
      console.log(error);
    });

    this.on("change:loc", this.buildLocQuery, this);

    this.buildLocQuery();
  }
});
```

This code adds a buildLocQuery() function to the Census model, which creates a query string from this data, switching between national and state-specific data. This function is called both when the model initializes and also any time the loc value in the model changes. That ensures that loc_query stays fresh.

Now if you load the script in your browser, you should see the first bit of dynamic behavior. It's only rendering the population growth chart so far, but that chart is changing dynamically as you switch states in the drop-down menu.

National Versus State Data

Next, you can follow the patterns in the population growth chart to establish the other charts. However, pulling national data for these other charts is a bit more complicated because the Census API doesn't aggregate much data nationally. For now, just disable these in the national view by making some changes to the template:

```
<script type="template" class="census-tpl">
  <h1>
  Census Data - <%= loc_str %>
  </h1>

  <section class="population<%- (loc === "00" ? " single" : "" ) %>">
    <h2>
    Population
    </h2>

    <div id="population-chart" class="chart"></div>

    <%
    if ( loc !== "00" ) {
    %>
    <div id="age-chart" class="chart"></div>
    <%
    }
    %>
  </section>

  <%
  if ( loc !== "00" ) {
  %>
  <section class="demographics">
    <h2>
    Demographics
    </h2>

    <div id="race-chart" class="chart"></div>

    <div id="sex-chart" class="chart"></div>
  </section>

  <section class="housing">
    <h2>
    Housing
    </h2>

    <div id="household-chart" class="chart"></div>

    <div id="tenure-chart" class="chart"></div>
  </section>
  <%
  }
  %>
</script>
```

As you can see, a few hooks have been added to remove the markup for certain charts at the national level (whenever `loc === "00"`). Additionally, as you build the other charts, you can add these hooks to your render function.

Age by Sex Chart

Now add the age by sex chart into your view object:

```
renderAge: function() {
  // get sex by age

  // build age request string
  function build_age_request_string(offset) {
    var out = "";

    for ( var i = 0; i < 23; i++ ) {
      var this_index = ("0" + (i + offset)).slice(-2);

      out += "P01200" + this_index + ",";
    }

    return out;
  }

  var age_request_keys = build_age_request_string(3) +
    build_age_request_string(27);

  age_request_keys = age_request_keys.slice(0,-1);

  $.ajax({
    url: "http://api.census.gov/data/2010/sf1",
    data: {
      get: age_request_keys,
      for: this.model.get("loc_query"),
      key: this.model.get("api_key")
    },
    success: function(data) {
      var male_data   = data[1].slice(0,23),
          female_data = data[1].slice(23,46);

      // merge the dissimilar age ranges

      function combine_vals(arr, start, end) {
        var total = 0;

        for ( var i = start; i <= end; i++ ) {
          total += arr[i];
        }

        arr[start] = total;

        arr.splice( start + 1, end - start);

        return arr;
```

```
    }

    function clean_age_range( age_data ) {
      // convert all the values to numeric
      for ( var i in age_data ) {
        age_data[i] = ~~age_data[i];
      }

      // merge values starting with highest (to preserve array keys)

      // merge 65-66 && 67-69
      age_data = combine_vals( age_data, 17, 18 );

      // merge 60-61 & 62-64
      age_data = combine_vals( age_data, 15, 16 );

      // merge 20, 21 & 22-24
      age_data = combine_vals( age_data, 5, 7 );

      // merge 15-17 & 18-19
      age_data = combine_vals( age_data, 3, 4 );

      return age_data;
    }

    male_data = clean_age_range(male_data);
    female_data = clean_age_range(female_data);

    var processed = [
      ["Age", "Male", "Female"]
    ];

    for ( var i = 0, max = male_data.length; i < max; i++ ) {
      var row = [];

      switch(i) {
        case 0:
          row[0] = "Under 5";
        break;

        default:
          row[0] = (i * 5) + "-" + (i * 5 + 4);
        break;

        case max - 1:
          row[0] = (i * 5) + "+";
        break;
      }

      row[1] = male_data[i];
      row[2] = female_data[i];

      processed.push(row);
    }
```

```
        var chartData = google.visualization.arrayToDataTable(processed);

        var options = {
          title: "Age"
        };

        var chart = new google.visualization.ColumnChart(
          document.getElementById("age-chart")
        );

        chart.draw(chartData, options);
      }
    });
  },
```

Again, the only differences between this script and the one previous are the dynamic references to the model's `loc_query` and `api_key` values. Next, add this call to the view's `render()` function, making sure to disable it at the national level:

```
render: function() {
  // render the main template
  var compiled = this.template( this.model.toJSON() );
  this.$el.html(compiled);

  // create the charts from this markup
  this.renderPopulation();

  // render the other charts if not the national data
  if ( this.model.get("loc") !== "00" ) {
    this.renderAge();
  }

  return this;
},
```

Other Charts

As you can see, integrating the chart modules into the Backbone app is pretty straightforward—simply set up the dynamic `loc_query` and `api_key` values in the Ajax calls. Rather than walk through each of these individually, take a look at the script all together in Listing 15-1.

LISTING 15-1

```
var Census = Backbone.Model.extend({
  defaults: {
    loc: "00",
    loc_str: "United States"
  },
```

continues

LISTING 15-1 *(continued)*

```javascript
    validate: function( options ) {
      if ( ! options.api_key ) {
        return "You must enter your API key from www.census.gov/developers/";
      }
    },

    // creates new location string for API
    buildLocQuery: function() {
      var loc = this.get("loc");
      if ( loc === "00" ) {
        this.set("loc_query", "us");
      }
      else {
        this.set("loc_query", "state:" + loc);
      }
    },

    initialize: function() {
      this.on("invalid", function(e, error) {
        console.log(error);
      });

      this.on("change:loc", this.buildLocQuery, this);

      this.buildLocQuery();
    }
});

var States = Backbone.Collection.extend();

var states = new States([
  { name: "United States", fips: "00" },
  { name: "Alabama", fips: "01" },
  { name: "Alaska", fips: "02" },
  { name: "Arizona", fips: "04" },
  { name: "Arkansas", fips: "05" },
  { name: "California", fips: "06" },
  { name: "Colorado", fips: "08" },
  { name: "Connecticut", fips: "09" },
  { name: "Delaware", fips: "10" },
  { name: "District of Columbia", fips: "11" },
  { name: "Florida", fips: "12" },
  { name: "Georgia", fips: "13" },
  { name: "Hawaii", fips: "15" },
  { name: "Idaho", fips: "16" },
  { name: "Illinois", fips: "17" },
  { name: "Indiana", fips: "18" },
  { name: "Iowa", fips: "19" },
  { name: "Kansas", fips: "20" },
  { name: "Kentucky", fips: "21" },
  { name: "Louisiana", fips: "22" },
  { name: "Maine", fips: "23" },
```

```
    { name: "Maryland", fips: "24" },
    { name: "Massachusetts", fips: "25" },
    { name: "Michigan", fips: "26" },
    { name: "Minnesota", fips: "27" },
    { name: "Mississippi", fips: "28" },
    { name: "Missouri", fips: "29" },
    { name: "Montana", fips: "30" },
    { name: "Nebraska", fips: "31" },
    { name: "Nevada", fips: "32" },
    { name: "New Hampshire", fips: "33" },
    { name: "New Jersey", fips: "34" },
    { name: "New Mexico", fips: "35" },
    { name: "New York", fips: "36" },
    { name: "North Carolina", fips: "37" },
    { name: "North Dakota", fips: "38" },
    { name: "Ohio", fips: "39" },
    { name: "Oklahoma", fips: "40" },
    { name: "Oregon", fips: "41" },
    { name: "Pennsylvania", fips: "42" },
    { name: "Rhode Island", fips: "44" },
    { name: "South Carolina", fips: "45" },
    { name: "South Dakota", fips: "46" },
    { name: "Tennessee", fips: "47" },
    { name: "Texas", fips: "48" },
    { name: "Utah", fips: "49" },
    { name: "Vermont", fips: "50" },
    { name: "Virginia", fips: "51" },
    { name: "Washington", fips: "53" },
    { name: "West Virginia", fips: "54" },
    { name: "Wisconsin", fips: "55" },
    { name: "Wyoming", fips: "56" }
]);

var CensusView = Backbone.View.extend({
  el: ".charts",
  template: _.template( $(".census-tpl").text() ),

  initialize: function() {
    this.model.on("change", this.render, this);

    this.buildDropdown();

    google.load("visualization", "1", {packages:["corechart"]});

    google.setOnLoadCallback($.proxy(this.render, this));

  },

  // builds the state dropdown with change listener
  buildDropdown: function() {
    // compile the state dropdown template
    var tpl = _.template( $(".state-dropdown-tpl").text() ),
        compiled = tpl({
          states: this.collection.toJSON()
        });
```

continues

LISTING 15-1 *(continued)*

```javascript
    // append to the DOM
    var $dropdown = $(compiled).appendTo( this.$el.parent() );

    $dropdown.on("change", $.proxy(function(e) {
      this.model.set({
        loc: $dropdown.val(),
        loc_str: $dropdown.find("option:selected").text()
      });
    }, this));
  },

  // render the new charts based on this location
  render: function() {
    // render the main template
    var compiled = this.template( this.model.toJSON() );
    this.$el.html(compiled);

    // create the charts from this markup
    this.renderPopulation();

    // render the other charts if not the national data
    if ( this.model.get("loc") !== "00" ) {
      this.renderAge();
      this.renderRace();
      this.renderSex();
      this.renderHousing();
      this.renderTenure();
    }

    return this;
  },

  renderPopulation: function() {
    $.ajax({
      url: "http://api.census.gov/data/2013/pep/natstprc",
      data: {
        get: "POP,DATE",
        for: this.model.get("loc_query"),
        key: this.model.get("api_key")
      },
      success: function(data) {
        var processed = [
          ["Year", "Population"]
        ];

        for ( i in data ) {
          if ( i == 0 ) continue;
          processed[i] = [ ~~data[i][1] + 2007, ~~data[i][0] ];
        }

        var chartData = google.visualization.arrayToDataTable(processed);
```

```javascript
        var options = {
          title: "Population Growth",
          legend: "none"
        };

        var chart = new google.visualization.LineChart(
          document.getElementById("population-chart")
        );
        chart.draw(chartData, options);
      }
    });
  },

  renderAge: function() {
    // get sex by age

    // build age request string
    function build_age_request_string(offset) {
      var out = "";

      for ( var i = 0; i < 23; i++ ) {
        var this_index = ("0" + (i + offset)).slice(-2);

        out += "P01200" + this_index + ",";
      }

      return out;
    }

    var age_request_keys = build_age_request_string(3) +
      build_age_request_string(27);

    age_request_keys = age_request_keys.slice(0,-1);

    $.ajax({
      url: "http://api.census.gov/data/2010/sf1",
      data: {
        get: age_request_keys,
        for: this.model.get("loc_query"),
        key: this.model.get("api_key")
      },
      success: function(data) {
        var male_data   = data[1].slice(0,23),
            female_data = data[1].slice(23,46);

        // merge the dissimilar age ranges

        function combine_vals(arr, start, end) {
          var total = 0;

          for ( var i = start; i <= end; i++ ) {
            total += arr[i];
          }
```

continues

LISTING 15-1 *(continued)*

```
      arr[start] = total;

      arr.splice( start + 1, end - start);

      return arr;
   }

   function clean_age_range( age_data ) {
     // convert all the values to numeric
     for ( var i in age_data ) {
       age_data[i] = ~~age_data[i];
     }

     // merge values starting with highest (to preserve array keys)

     // merge 65-66 && 67-69
     age_data = combine_vals( age_data, 17, 18 );

     // merge 60-61 & 62-64
     age_data = combine_vals( age_data, 15, 16 );

     // merge 20, 21 & 22-24
     age_data = combine_vals( age_data, 5, 7 );

     // merge 15-17 & 18-19
     age_data = combine_vals( age_data, 3, 4 );

     return age_data;
   }

   male_data = clean_age_range(male_data);
   female_data = clean_age_range(female_data);

   var processed = [
     ["Age", "Male", "Female"]
   ];

   for ( var i = 0, max = male_data.length; i < max; i++ ) {
     var row = [];

     switch(i) {
       case 0:
         row[0] = "Under 5";
       break;

       default:
         row[0] = (i * 5) + "-" + (i * 5 + 4);
       break;

       case max - 1:
         row[0] = (i * 5) + "+";
       break;
```

```
        }

        row[1] = male_data[i];
        row[2] = female_data[i];

        processed.push(row);
      }

      var chartData = google.visualization.arrayToDataTable(processed);

      var options = {
        title: "Age"
      };

      var chart = new google.visualization.ColumnChart(
        document.getElementById("age-chart")
      );

      chart.draw(chartData, options);
    }
  });
},

renderRace: function() {
  // get race data
  $.ajax({
    url: "http://api.census.gov/data/2010/sf1",
    data: {
      get: "P0080003,P0080004,P0080005,P0080006,P0080007,P0080008,P0080009",
      for: this.model.get("loc_query"),
      key: this.model.get("api_key")
    },
    success: function(data) {
      var races = [
        "White",
        "Black",
        "American Indian or Alaskan Native",
        "Asian",
        "Native Hawaiian or Pacific Islander",
        "Other",
        "Mixed"
      ],
      processed = [
        ["Race", "Population"]
      ];

      // lose the last value (state ID)
      data[1].pop();

      for ( i in data[1] ) {
        processed.push([
          races[i],
          ~~data[1][i]
        ]);
      }
```

continues

LISTING 15-1 *(continued)*

```
        var chartData = google.visualization.arrayToDataTable(processed);

        var options = {
          title: "Race",
          is3D: true
        };

        var chart = new google.visualization.PieChart(
          document.getElementById("race-chart")
        );

        chart.draw(chartData, options);
      }
    });
  },

  renderSex: function() {
    // get basic sex data
    $.ajax({
      url: "http://api.census.gov/data/2010/sf1",
      data: {
        get: "P0120002,P0120026",
        for: this.model.get("loc_query"),
        key: this.model.get("api_key")
      },
      success: function(data) {
        var processed = [
          ["Sex", "Population"],
          ["Male", ~~data[1][0]],
          ["Female", ~~data[1][1]]
        ];

        var chartData = google.visualization.arrayToDataTable(processed);

        var options = {
          title: "Sex",
          pieHole: 0.8,
          pieSliceText: "none"
        };

        var chart = new google.visualization.PieChart(
          document.getElementById("sex-chart")
        );

        chart.draw(chartData, options);
      }
    });
  },

  renderHousing: function() {
    // get household size
```

```
      $.ajax({
        url: "http://api.census.gov/data/2010/sf1",
        data: {
          get: "H0130002,H0130003,H0130004,H0130005,H0130006,H0130007,H0130008",
          for: this.model.get("loc_query"),
          key: this.model.get("api_key")
        },
        success: function(data) {
          var processed = [
            ["Household Size", "Households"]
          ];

          // lose the last value (state ID)
          data[1].pop();

          for ( i in data[1] ) {
            processed.push([
              (~~i+1) + ( i == 6 ? "+" : "" ) + " Person",
              ~~data[1][i]
            ]);
          }

          var chartData = google.visualization.arrayToDataTable(processed);

          var options = {
            title: "Household Size",
            is3D: true
          };

          var chart = new google.visualization.PieChart(
            document.getElementById("household-chart")
          );

          chart.draw(chartData, options);
        }
      });
    },

    renderTenure: function() {
      // get housing tenure
      $.ajax({
        url: "http://api.census.gov/data/2010/sf1",
        data: {
          get: "H0110002,H0110003,H0110004",
          for: this.model.get("loc_query"),
          key: this.model.get("api_key")
        },
        success: function(data) {
          var processed = [
            ["Tenure", "Housing Units"],
            ["Owned with Mortgage", ~~data[1][0]],
            ["Owned Outright", ~~data[1][1]],
            ["Rented", ~~data[1][2]]
          ];
```

continues

LISTING 15-1 *(continued)*

```
        var chartData = google.visualization.arrayToDataTable(processed);

        var options = {
          title: "Housing Tenure",
          pieHole: 0.8,
          pieSliceText: "none"
        };

        var chart = new google.visualization.PieChart(
          document.getElementById("tenure-chart")
        );

        chart.draw(chartData, options);
      }
    });
  }
});

var census = new Census({
  api_key: "ddda45df6ccb8e1e722aca5f142d7db2a032c330"
});

var censusView = new CensusView({
  model: census,
  collection: states
});
```

Here's a recap of what happens:

1. The script creates a Census model to store settings and global variables. This model validates against the api_key and also creates a dynamic loc_query string that adjusts to match the loc value.

2. It then builds a States collection with state names and FIPS codes.

3. The view initializes, binding a change listener to rerender the templates for any change to the model, building the drop-down menu, and loading the Google Charts API.

4. In the render() function, the script recompiles the template and also makes calls to render the individual charts, depending on whether it is at the national level.

NEXT STEPS

Now the script is dynamically rendering charts for various states. But that's really just the bare bones for this application, and there are a number of additional features you can add to the code.

Rerendering on Resize

For instance, you may have noticed that Google doesn't refresh the charts as you resize the window. That's mostly fine, but it can cause some visual issues with the responsive layout. Fortunately it's easy to add a handler to redraw the charts on resize. Simply add the following to the view's `initialize()` function:

```
// redraw charts on window resize
var debouncedRender = _.debounce($.proxy(this.render, this), 1000);
$(window).resize(debouncedRender);
```

While you could have just applied the `render()` function directly in the `resize()` callback, it's important to use the debounced approach here. The script leverages Underscore's `debounce()` utility function to prevent the `render()` function from firing repeatedly as the user resizes her window. Instead, it fires the resize only after a full second of resizing.

> **TIP** *The debounced approach is always useful for window.resize() handlers but is especially so when calling a resource-heavy render such as our Google Charts implementation.*

Other Improvements

Additionally, there are a variety of improvements you can add to this script:

➤ Aggregate the state data to show all the charts at the national level.

➤ Cache previously visited states in `localStorage` to avoid unnecessary API calls.

➤ Enable routing and history using either `hashchange` or `pushState` and Backbone's History API.

SUMMARY

In this chapter, you created an interactive dashboard of U.S. Census data. You learned how to work through the headaches of the Census API in order to access a wealth of demographic data. You then massaged this data and displayed it in Google Charts using a responsive layout for the dashboard.

Next you integrated these components into a Backbone app, which dynamically updates the charts based on user input. Finally, you explored some new directions to take the script.

In the next chapter, you follow another practical charting example, this time leveraging D3 to create another set of interactive visualizations.

16

D3 in Practice

WHAT'S IN THIS CHAPTER

- ➤ Styling D3 charts
- ➤ Rendering axes in D3
- ➤ Working with Voronoi maps
- ➤ Creating reusable visualizations

> **CODE DOWNLOAD** *The wrox.com code downloads for this chapter are found at* www.wrox.com/go/javascriptandjqueryanalysis *on the Download Code tab. The code is in the chapter 16 download and individually named according to the names throughout the chapter.*

If you choose to incorporate D3-based charts into your application, you will have to deal with challenges inherent in general web design:

- ➤ Will the person implementing the visualization also be styling it? If not, you have to be mindful of the separation of styles and visual logic. You also need to create some standards around what class names you use.

- ➤ Will visualizations be one-off or will they be reused in many places? Making visualizations reusable requires more care than making one-off examples. This chapter explores an example of how to make a reusable visualization.

- ➤ How much control do you have over the data that will be displayed?

Unless you are making a visualization on top of a specific data set, you need to make sure your code works with extreme values.

MAKING D3 LOOK PERFECT

This section covers some techniques that come in very handy when working with D3.

Inline Styles Versus CSS

An SVG (or HTML) element's appearance can be set in two ways: using a `.style()` operator that modifies the element's own style or using a CSS selector to assign styles to the element.

It can be tempting to use the `.style()` operator to declare all the styles—especially because in D3 it is so easy to operate on entire selections of elements—but this method is not ideal. You should use the `.style()` operator when the element's style is data-driven. Non-data-driven styles are best placed in a style sheet. Putting data-independent styles into style sheets forces you to assign meaningful classes to elements and allows non-D3-savvy people to change the styles.

A drawback of placing styles into a style sheet used to be the inability to offer a user an SVG download of the visualization; this can now be overcome using the SVG Crowbar tool (`https://nytimes.github.io/svg-crowbar/`) developed to work with D3. SVG Crowbar collects all the relevant styles from the style sheet and bundles them up for a self-contained SVG.

Margin

Any content rendered outside of the area of the SVG element will not be shown onscreen. This is problematic if you want to have labels or axes that are positioned outside of the area dedicated to the visualization itself. To solve this common problem, Mike Bostock introduced the Margin Convention (`http://bl.ocks.org/mbostock/3019563`), which is employed in almost every D3 example.

```
var margin = {top: 20, right: 20, bottom: 20, left: 20}

var width = outerWidth - margin.left - margin.right
var height = outerHeight - margin.top - margin.bottom

var mainContainer = d3.select("body").append("svg")
  .attr("width", outerWidth)
  .attr("height", outerHeight)
  .append("g")
    .attr("transform", "translate(" + margin.left + "," + margin.top + ")")
```

The margins are declared as an object. You calculate the effective `width` and `height` by subtracting the margins from the outer dimensions. A `<g>` element is added to the `<svg>` and offset by (`margin.left`, `margin.top`); every subsequent element is then appended to this container.

```
var xScale = d3.scale.linear()
  .range([0, width])

var yScale = d3.scale.linear()
  .range([height, 0])
```

Any scales can be created using the `width` and `height` of the `mainContainer`.

> **NOTE** *The* `mainContainer` *variable is commonly given the name* `svg` *despite being a selection of a* `<g>` *element.*
>
> `g` *elements do not need to be sized with* `.attr("width", width)`, *and so on as they have no meaningful boundary; they only perform a coordinate transformation.*

Ordering

In SVG, the order of the elements within their parent container determines the order in which they will be rendered onto the screen. Unlike HTML there is no `z-index` (or equivalent) style to control the ordering. This can lead to some problems.

Consider the following code to render a bar chart with a label over each bar:

```
var svg = d3.select("body").append("svg")

function render(barData) {
  // Create the bars
  var rectSelection = svg.selectAll('rect').data(barData)
  rectSelection.enter().append('rect')

  rectSelection
    .attr('x', ...) // Define the rectangles

  rectSelection.exit().remove()

  // Create the labels (on top)
  var textSelection = svg.selectAll('text').data(barData)
  textSelection.enter().append('text')

  textSelection
    .attr('x', ...) // Define the labels

  textSelection.exit().remove()
}
```

This code seems to work at first, but if `render` is called again with more data, the new bars will be on top of the existing labels. This glitch is only seen if the labels ever overlap with bars other than their own.

The solution is to create separate `<g>` elements for each logical layer of the visualization:

```
var svg = d3.select("body").append("svg")

var rectContainer = svg.append('g').attr('class', 'bars')
var labelContainer = svg.append('g').attr('class', 'labels')

function render(barData) {
  // Create the bars
  var rectSelection = rectContainer.selectAll('rect').data(barData)
```

```
rectSelection.enter().append('rect')

rectSelection
  .attr('x', ...) // Define the rectangles

rectSelection.exit().remove()

// Create the labels on a higher 'layer'
var textSelection = labelContainer.selectAll('text').data(barData)
textSelection.enter().append('text')

textSelection
  .attr('x', ...) // Define the labels

textSelection.exit().remove()
}
```

Now all labels are always on top of the bars.

One issue that might occur with such a layering approach is that the overlapping labels block mouse events from reaching the bars. This could prevent a detail-on-demand hover from appearing on a bar if the cursor is placed on top of a label that is obscuring the bar. This can be solved using the `pointer-events` style deceleration examined in the next section.

Pointer Events

An advantage of making visualizations in SVG (or HTML) over Canvas is that each visual element can receive its own mouse and touch (collectively known as *pointer*) events.

By default, the top element at a given pointer location receives pointer events. This occasionally leads to undesired effects as detailed in the previous section.

Thankfully, elements can be told to ignore all pointer events by setting the `pointer-events` style to none (see https://developer.mozilla.org/en-US/docs/Web/CSS/pointer-events for more information about the other values this style can have). This also speeds up the visualization by simplifying the internal pointer event resolution process of the renderer.

It is recommended that you turn off pointer events for all elements that do not need them.

Crisp Edges

The following is another style that deserves a special mention:

```
line, rect {
  shape-rendering: crispEdges;
}
```

This declaration tells the SVG renderer to turn off anti-aliasing for that element, which is useful if you are creating axes-aligned shapes such as vertical/horizontal lines and rectangles. Anti-aliasing can cause your elements to have blurry edges. If you are dealing with an axis-aligned element then try setting `shape-rendering` to `crispEdges`. You can read more about it here:

https://developer.mozilla.org/en-US/docs/Web/SVG/Attribute/shape-rendering

WORKING WITH AXES

An informative visualization must have axes that describe the scales used to plot the data on the screen. Because rendering axes is such a common operation, D3 actually provides a convenient helper for rendering axes.

Chapter 12 examines two types of helper functions. Simple helpers such as `d3.scale.linear()` and `d3.svg.line()` generate functions that help you render the data. Layout helpers such as `d3.layout.treemap` operate on the data and add metadata to it to allow you to render it in novel ways. The `d3.svg.axis()` helper does not fall into either of those categories; instead, it draws an entire visualization for you in the container of your choosing.

Using the axis helper, you can quickly create a scatterplot visualization complete with axis.

For this example, we used a data set of car miles-per-gallon (MPG) ratings. This dataset contains a subset of the fuel economy data that the EPA makes available on `http://fueleconomy.gov`. It contains only models that had a new release every year between 1999 and 2008; this was used as a proxy for the popularity of the car. The data look like so:

```
var mpg = [
  {
    "manufacturer": "Audi",
    "model": "a4",
    "displ": 1.8,
    "year": 1999,
    "cyl": 4,
    "city": 18.2,
    "highway": 28.6,
    "drive": "f"
  },
  // ... 233 data points omitted ...
]
```

You can find the full file of the preceding code on the companion website in the `examples` `/scatterplot-axis/mpg.js` file.

Examine the relationship between highway and city MPG:

```
var margin = {top: 20, right: 20, bottom: 30, left: 40}
var width = 700 - margin.left - margin.right
var height = 600 - margin.top - margin.bottom

var xScale = d3.scale.linear()
  .range([0, width])

var yScale = d3.scale.linear()
  .range([height, 0])

var xAxis = d3.svg.axis()
  .orient('bottom')
  .scale(xScale)

var yAxis = d3.svg.axis()
```

```
  .orient('left')
  .scale(yScale)

var mainContainer = d3.select('body').append('svg')
  .attr('width', width + margin.left + margin.right)
  .attr('height', height + margin.top + margin.bottom)
  .append('g')
    .attr('transform', 'translate(' + margin.left + ',' + margin.top + ')')

var xAxisContainer = mainContainer.append('g')
  .attr('class', 'x axis')
  .attr('transform', 'translate(0,' + height + ')')

xAxisContainer.append('text')
  .attr('class', 'label')
  .attr('x', width)
  .attr('y', -6)
  .style('text-anchor', 'end')

var yAxisContainer = mainContainer.append('g')
  .attr('class', 'y axis')

yAxisContainer.append('text')
  .attr('class', 'label')
  .attr('transform', 'rotate(-90)')
  .attr('dy', '1.2em')
  .style('text-anchor', 'end')

var pointContainer = mainContainer.append('g')
  .attr('class', 'points')

function renderScatterplot(data, xMetric, yMetric) {
  xScale
    .domain(d3.extent(data, function(d) { return d[xMetric] }))
    .nice()

  yScale
    .domain(d3.extent(data, function(d) { return d[yMetric] }))
    .nice()

  xAxisContainer.call(xAxis)
  xAxisContainer.select('.label').text(xMetric)

  yAxisContainer.call(yAxis)
  yAxisContainer.select('.label').text(yMetric)

  var pointSelection = pointContainer.selectAll('.point').data(data)

  pointSelection.enter().append('circle')
    .attr('class', 'point')
    .attr('r', 2.5)

  pointSelection
    .attr('cx', function(d) { return xScale(d[xMetric]) })
    .attr('cy', function(d) { return yScale(d[yMetric]) })
```

```
    pointSelection.exit().remove()
}

renderScatterplot(mpg, 'highway', 'city')
```

The preceding code is on the companion website in the `examples/scatterplot-axis/script` `.js` file.

At the core, the scatterplot visualization consists of a single data binding to create the `.points`. The x and y axes on the chart, however, require a few visual elements to render. The scale ticks—the human-friendly marks such as 10, 15, 20, and so on—need to be represented using text labels and little lines. All this is done by the axis helper:

```
var xScale = d3.scale.linear()
    .range([0, width])

var yScale = d3.scale.linear()
    .range([height, 0])
```

First you create two scales for the x and y axes. The scales' range is set to the visualization size and their domains (the data extent) will be configured later.

```
var xAxis = d3.svg.axis()   .orient('bottom')
    .scale(xScale)

var yAxis = d3.svg.axis()
    .orient('left')
    .scale(yScale)
```

You create two corresponding axis helpers, which are configured with the intended orientation and the scale that they will be operating on. The axis helper draws all the size and tick information from the scale itself.

```
var xAxisContainer = mainContainer.append('g')
    .attr('class', 'x axis')
    .attr('transform', 'translate(0,' + height + ')')

xAxisContainer.append('text')
    .attr('class', 'label')
    .attr('x', width)
    .attr('y', -6)
    .style('text-anchor', 'end')
```

You need to explicitly create and position the `<g>` element that will contain the scale. A class of `.x.axis` is applied, which enables you to apply styles from a style sheet. You also append a `text`. `label` to the container to hold the name of the metric projected onto this axis.

```
xAxisContainer.call(xAxis)
xAxisContainer.select('.label').text(xMetric)

yAxisContainer.call(yAxis)
yAxisContainer.select('.label').text(yMetric)
```

Later, when you want to render the axis, all you have to do is `.call()` the axis function. The D3 `.call` operator is a convenience method to call the given function with the selection as the argument and the `this` object. It is equivalent to `xAxis.call(xAxisContainer, xAxisContainer)`.

```
.axis path,
.axis line {
  fill: none;
  stroke: black;
  shape-rendering: crispEdges;
}
```

You can customize the look and feel of the axis by manipulating the style sheet. In this example, I set the style of `<line>`s (the tick markers) and the `<path>` (the margin) to be black and precisely aligned on the pixels.

The axes-enabled scatterplot is in Figure 16-1.

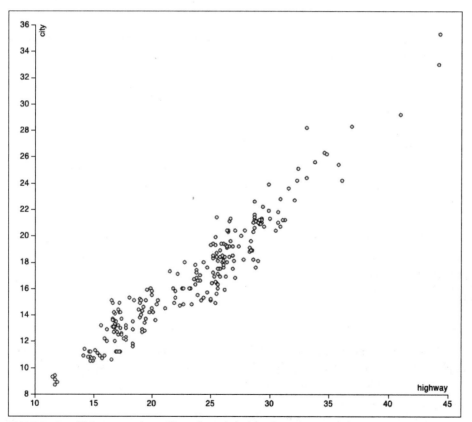

FIGURE 16-1: This scatterplot utilizes the axis helper function.

In effect, the axis helper is a subvisualization, and this section showed you how D3 has neatly packaged it. Later, you will see how to build on top of this concept and package your own visualizations in a similar way.

WORKING WITH THE VORONOI MAP

The Voronoi tessellation, named after Georgy Voronoi, is a method to subdivide a space around a number of centers. The space is divided into polygons, one for each center, such that each point in the polygon is closest to that polygons' center.

D3 is very amenable to extension with beautiful algorithms. Helpfully, D3 comes with a Voronoi tessellation algorithm, which is used for this section to create a pretty picture and a powerful selection user interface (UI). This section also describes how best to package D3 helper functions if you decide to write one.

A Basic Voronoi Map

This example shows how to contract a basic Voronoi map. (See the `examples/voronoi-basic/data.js` file on the companion website.) Given a list of centers in the following format:

```
var centers = [
  { x: 0.17059, y: 0.51567 },
  { x: 0.89967, y: 0.59811 },
  // ... 54 data points omitted ...
  { x: 0.74111, y: 0.30413 },
  { x: 0.44484, y: 0.63658 }
]
```

generate a Voronoi map from these centers and also mark the centers themselves for clarity:

```
var width = 700
var height = 500

var voronoi = d3.geom.voronoi()
  .x(function(d) { return d.x * width })
  .y(function(d) { return d.y * height })
  .clipExtent([[0, 0], [width, height]])

var svg = d3.select('body').append('svg')
  .attr('width', width)
  .attr('height', height)

var polygonContainer = svg.append('g')

var centerContainer = svg.append('g')

var colors =  d3.scale.category20b()

function polygonToString(d) {
  if (!d) return 'M0,0Z' // In case of duplicates
  return 'M' + d.join('L') + 'Z'
}

function render() {
  // Polygons
  var pathSelection = polygonContainer.selectAll('path')
    .data(voronoi(centers))
```

```
pathSelection.enter().append('path')
  .style('stroke', 'white')
  .style('fill', function(d, i) { return colors(i) })

pathSelection
  .attr('d', polygonToString)

pathSelection.exit().remove()

// Centers
var center Selection = centerContainer.selectAll('circle')
  .data(centers)

center Selection.enter().append('circle')
  .attr('r', 1.5)

center Selection
  .attr('cx', function(d) { return d.x * width })
  .attr('cy', function(d) { return d.y * height })

center Selection.exit().remove()
}

render()
```

You can find the preceding code in the `examples/voronoi-basic/script.js` file on the companion website.

As you can see, the code to generate the beautiful visual in Figure 16-2 is hardly more complex than the code used previously to generate a bar chart. All the hard space division is neatly encapsulated in the `d3.geom.voronoi()` helper function.

```
var voronoi = d3.geom.voronoi()
  .x(function(d) { return d.x * width })
  .y(function(d) { return d.y * height })
  .clipExtent([[0, 0], [width, height]])
```

As is standard for D3 helper functions, calling `d3.geom.voronoi()` returns a function that takes an array of centers and computes the polygons that represent the Voronoi tessellation. In accordance to the informal D3 standard, the `voronoi` function can be configured using setter/getter methods. Calling `.x(function(d) { return d.x * width })` on voronoi tells the algorithm what function to use to compute the x coordinate of the center; the return value is the `voronoi` function itself so you can keep chaining these setters. Calling `voronoi.x()` would, conversely, return the current x coordinate function.

```
var svg = d3.select('body').append('svg')
  .attr('width', width)
  .attr('height', height)

var polygonContainer = svg.append('g')

var centerContainer = svg.append('g')

var colors =  d3.scale.category20b()
```

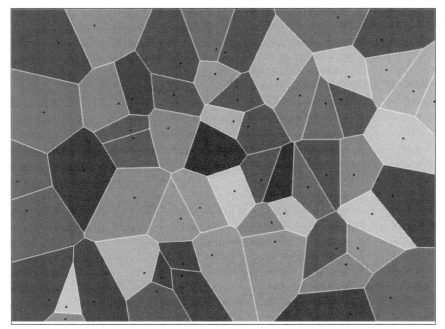

FIGURE 16-2: This Voronoi tessellation shows the centers.

You create an `<svg>` element and two containers: one for the polygons and one for the center dots. Finally, you create a categorical color scale. The scale created by `d3.scale.category20b()` does not need to be given an explicit domain (although it could). Instead, it just allocates a new color every time it is given a new value.

```
function polygonToString(d) {
   if (!d) return 'M0,0Z' // In case of duplicates
   return 'M' + d.join('L') + 'Z'
}
```

You define `polygonToString` to convert the arrays of points returned from the `voronoi` function into SVG drawing strings. Each polygon is represented as an array of points where a point is an array of two elements `[x,y]`. Because arrays are natively converted to strings by comma concatenation, the expression `d.join('L')` neatly produces an SVG drawing command. Note that the Voronoi shape is undefined for duplicate centers; you account for that by returning a drawing string that produces no output in that case.

```
polygonToString([[1,1], [2,2], [3,0]])
   // =>"M1,1L2,2L3,0Z"
```

If given duplicate centers, the `voronoi` function produces an `undefined` result for all but the first of the duplicates. You guard against that by adding a fallback to the `'M0,0Z'` no-op path.

Finally, you make two selections to create the visual elements: one for the polygons and one for the center points. The data for the polygons comes from the `voronoi` function and the data for the center points are the centers themselves.

Voronoi Point Picking

The simplest (and arguably the most useful) interaction that a visualization can offer is the ability for the user to hover over a visual element and get some extra details about the underlying data.

This example covers the ways a hover label could be added to the MGP scatterplot that was built previously. As with most things in software development, there are several different approaches that you can take. Several are offered here so you can compare their differences.

Naive Hover

First, consider the naive solution. The simplest way to add a hover behavior is to instrument the elements with `mouseenter` and `mouseenter` handlers to detect the start and end of the hover action.

You can extend the previous scatterplot example to see how it is done. The code is not printed in full due to its similarity to the previous example. The full listing can be found in the `examples /scatterplot-voronoi/script.js` file on the companion website.

```
var hoverContainer = mainContainer.append('g')
  .attr('class', 'hover')

hoverContainer.append('text')
  .style('display', 'none')
  .attr('dx', '0.5em')
  .attr('dy', '0.2em')
```

You start by adding a container and a text label that will be used to display the hover information. The label is hidden by default. The actual positioning of the text relative to the origin of the label is fine-tuned using the `dy` and `dx` attributes.

```
function setHover(hover, i) {
  hoverContainer.select('text')
    .style('display', null)    .attr('x', xScale(hover[xMetric]))
    .attr('y', yScale(hover[yMetric]))
    .text(hover.manufacturer + ' ' + hover.model + ' (' + hover.year + ')')
}

function dropHover() {
  hoverContainer.select('text')
    .style('display', 'none')
}
```

The hover can be triggered on any datum. You position the text label using the same scales as you use for the data, ensuring that it is positioned in the correct place. Alternatively, you could have extracted the position attributes from the element itself or from the mouse position.

```
pointSelection.enter().append('circle')
  .attr('class', 'point')
  .attr('r', 2.5)
  .on('mouseenter', setHover)
  .on('mouseleave', dropHover)
```

Finally, you add two event handlers to every point during creation. The handlers will make the hover text appear and disappear as the user's mouse moves in and out of the element boundary.

The hover label, as it would appear when the user hovers over a data point, is shown in Figure 16-3. Please check out `examples/scatterplot-voronoi/index.html` on the companion website and play with the hover behavior. It should become apparent that this hover technique, although very easy to implement, possesses a critical flaw: the scatterplot points are too small to be adequate hover targets. This issue is addressed in the next section.

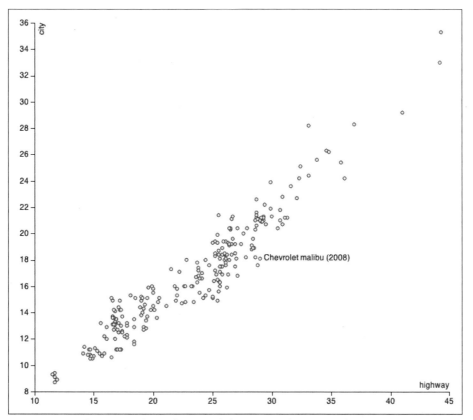

FIGURE 16-3: The scatterplot is shown with hover on a data point.

Voronoi Hover

To address the problem of having a small hover target, you could divide the space into (invisible) bounded Voronoi sections and have those serve as hover targets. In a sense, you are creating a little Voronoi halo around each point and assigning the mouse events to it.

You can find the full code in the `examples/scatterplot-voronoi` folder on the companion website. Following are the additions needed to create the Voronoi halos:

```
var voronoi = d3.geom.voronoi()
  .clipExtent([[0, 0], [width, height]])
```

Create a Voronoi helper:

```
var haloClipContainer = mainContainer.append('g')
  .attr('class', 'halo-clip')

var haloContainer = mainContainer.append('g')
  .attr('class', 'halo')
```

Two new containers are required: one to contain the clip paths that prevent the Voronoi polygons from taking over the entire screen and one for the Voronoi polygons themselves.

```
var haloClipSelection = haloClipContainer.selectAll('clipPath').data(data)

haloClipSelection.enter().append('clipPath')
  .attr('id', function(d, i) { return 'clip-' + i })
  .append('circle')
    .attr('r', 16)

haloClipSelection.select('circle')
  .attr('cx', function(d) { return xScale(d[xMetric]) })
  .attr('cy', function(d) { return yScale(d[yMetric]) })

haloClipSelection.exit().remove()
```

For every data point, a `<clipPath>` element is created with a `<circle>` positioned on the data point inside of it. The contents of a `<clipPath>` element act as a mask for any element with a reference to its id; a unique id is assigned to each `<clipPath>` element.

```
voronoi
  .x(function(d) { return xScale(d[xMetric]) })
  .y(function(d) { return yScale(d[yMetric]) })

haloSelection = haloContainer.selectAll('path').data(voronoi(data))

haloSelection.enter().append('path')
  .attr('clip-path', function(d, i) { return 'url(#clip-' + i +')' })
  .on("mouseover", setHover)
  .on("mouseout", dropHover)

haloSelection
  .attr('d', polygonToString)

haloSelection.exit().remove()
```

The `<path>` elements that represent the Voronoi segments are created. Each element is assigned a corresponding clip path id via the function `function(d, i) { return 'url(#clip-' + i +')' }` to constrain them within the clip circle. Finally the `setHover` and `dropHover` event handlers are attached to the halo.

The result of a hover is shown in Figure 16-4. Normally, when using this technique you would not assign a fill or stroke to the hover targets, leaving them invisible so as not to distract from the data. With some style-sheet tweaks, the hover targets can be made visible. The hover behavior is now greatly improved. Please try out the example yourself at: `examples/scatterplot-voronoi /index.html`.

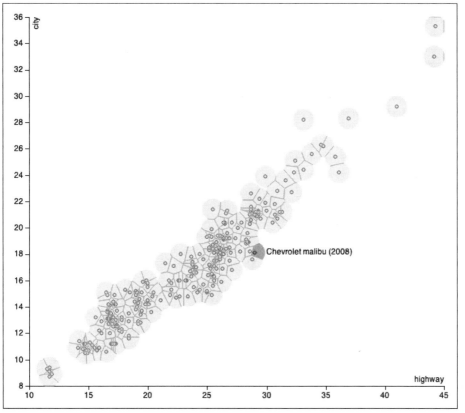

FIGURE 16-4: The Voronoi map is used as a hover aid.

MAKING REUSABLE VISUALIZATIONS

So far, none of the D3 examples in this chapter and Chapter 11 have been reusable. Every example starts with a `d3.select('body')`, which implicitly assumes that the visualization needs to be created directly on the `<body>` element. This is not practical for actual visualizations that need to live within a larger application such as a dashboard.

This section examines the best practices for creating reusable D3 visualizations by packaging up the scatterplot example used in previous chapters.

The best strategy for packaging a charting function in D3 is to have it work similarly to the helper function such as `d3.scale.linear` and `d3.svg.axis`. Mike Bostock, the creator of D3, wrote up a short article explaining the merits of this approach; you can find it at `http://bost.ocks.org /mike/chart/`.

In this example you call the scatterplot chart like so:

```
// Create and configure the charts
var highwayCityChart = scatterplot()
  .width(300)
  .height(300)
  .x(function(d) { return d.highway })
  .xLabel('Highway / mpg')
  .y(function(d) { return d.city })
  .yLabel('City / mpg')

var displacementCityChart = scatterplot()
  .width(300)
  .height(300)
  .x(function(d) { return d.displ })
  .xLabel('Displacement / L')
  .y(function(d) { return d.city })
  .yLabel('City / mpg')

// Attach the data to the element that will hold the chart and 'call' it.
d3.select('#chart1').datum(mpg)
  .call(highwayCityChart)

d3.select('#chart2').datum(mpg)
  .call(displacementCityChart)
```

This code, which you can find in the examples/scatterplot-reuse/script.js file on the companion website, creates two scatterplots depicting the relationship between two different pairs of variables, as shown in Figure 16-5.

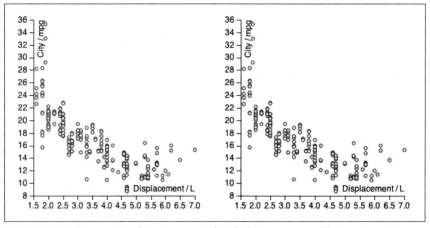

FIGURE 16-5: Two scatterplots are created with the same reusable component.

The advantages of following this method include

➤ A chart can be easily configured and reconfigured using the setter/getter operators.

➤ No chart state needs to be maintained by the caller.

➤ The instance of a chart is a template that can be applied to any data-bound selection and can be applied over a selection containing multiple elements filling each of them individually.

➤ It follows the conventions set by native D3 methods such as `d3.svg.axis`.

The following code, which is in the `examples/scatterplot-reuse/scatterplot.js` file on the companion website, shows you how it might actually be implemented:

```
function scatterplot() {
  var options = {
    width: 700,
    height: 600,
    margin: {top: 20, right: 20, bottom: 30, left: 40},
    xLabel: null,
    yLabel: null,
    x: function(d) { return d[0] },
    y: function(d) { return d[1] }
  }

  var xScale = d3.scale.linear()
  var yScale = d3.scale.linear()

  var xAxis = d3.svg.axis()
    .orient('bottom')
    .scale(xScale)

  var yAxis = d3.svg.axis()
    .orient('left')
    .scale(yScale)

  function render(selection) {
    var margin = options.margin
    var innerWidth = options.width - margin.left - margin.right
    var innerHeight = options.height - margin.top - margin.bottom

    xScale.range([0, innerWidth])
    yScale.range([innerHeight, 0])

    selection.each(function(data) {
      xScale.domain(d3.extent(data, options.x)).nice()
      yScale.domain(d3.extent(data, options.y)).nice()

      // -------------
      var svgContainer = d3.select(this).selectAll('svg.scatterplot').data([data])
      svgContainer.enter().append('svg').attr('class', 'scatterplot')

      svgContainer
        .attr('width', options.width)
        .attr('height', options.height)

      // -------------
      var mainContainer = svgContainer.selectAll('g.main').data([data])
      mainContainer.enter().append('g').attr('class', 'main')
```

```
    mainContainer
      .attr('transform', 'translate(' + margin.left + ',' + margin.top + ')')

    // -------------
    var xAxisContainer = mainContainer.selectAll('g.x.axis').data([data])
    xAxisContainer.enter().append('g').attr('class', 'x axis')

    xAxisContainer
      .attr('transform', 'translate(0,' + innerHeight + ')')
      .call(xAxis)

    // -------------
    var xLabelSelection = xAxisContainer.selectAll('text.label').data([data])
    xLabelSelection.enter().append('text').attr('class', 'label')
      .attr('y', -6)
      .style('text-anchor', 'end')

    xLabelSelection
      .attr('x', innerWidth)
      .text(options.xLabel)

    // -------------
    var yAxisContainer = mainContainer.selectAll('g.y.axis').data([data])
    yAxisContainer.enter().append('g').attr('class', 'y axis')

    yAxisContainer
      .call(yAxis)

    // -------------
    var yLabelSelection = yAxisContainer.selectAll('text.label').data([data])
    yLabelSelection.enter().append('text').attr('class', 'label')
      .attr('transform', 'rotate(-90)')
      .attr('dy', '1.2em')

      .style('text-anchor', 'end')

    yLabelSelection
      .text(options.yLabel)

    // -------------
    var pointContainer = mainContainer.selectAll('g.points').data([data])
    pointContainer.enter().append('g').attr('class', 'points')

    // -------------
    var pointSelection = pointContainer.selectAll('.point').data(data)
    pointSelection.enter().append('circle').attr('class', 'point')
      .attr('r', 2.5)

    pointSelection
      .attr('cx', function(d) { return xScale(options.x(d)) })
      .attr('cy', function(d) { return yScale(options.y(d)) })

    pointSelection.exit().remove()
  })
}
```

```
    // Make options configurable
    Object.keys(options).forEach(function(optionName) {
      render[optionName] = function(value) {
        if (!arguments.length) return options[optionName]
        options[optionName] = value
        return render
      }
    })

    return render
}
```

Let's break this code down step by step:

```
var options = {
  width: 700,
  height: 600,
  margin: {top: 20, right: 20, bottom: 30, left: 40},
  xLabel: null,
  yLabel: null,
  x: function(d) { return d[0] },
  y: function(d) { return d[1] }
}
```

Define all the configurable options and give each a meaningful default. The D3 standard is to express data points as [x, y] pairs; hence function(d) { return d[0] } and function(d) { return d[1] } are a good default choice for the x and y options.

```
var xScale = d3.scale.linear()
var yScale = d3.scale.linear()

var xAxis = d3.svg.axis()
  .orient('bottom')
  .scale(xScale)

var yAxis = d3.svg.axis()
  .orient('left')
  .scale(yScale)
```

Set up the scales and axes that will be used in the rendering:

```
function render(selection) {
  var margin = options.margin
  var innerWidth = options.width - margin.left - margin.right
  var innerHeight = options.height - margin.top - margin.bottom

  xScale.range([0, innerWidth])
  yScale.range([innerHeight, 0])

  ...
}
```

Create the `render` function that will be returned. You expect this function to be used in a `selection.call(...)` so the first argument is assumed to be the selection within which to create or update the scatterplot. At this point, you can inspect the `options` object to determine the physical size of the visualization.

```
selection.each(function(data) {
  xScale.domain(d3.extent(data, options.x)).nice()
  yScale.domain(d3.extent(data, options.y)).nice()

  ...
})
```

The `render` function receives a selection that you assume to be bound to the chart's data. Because you want your chart to work in the event of a selection containing multiple elements, filling each with its own scatterplot, you need to use the `.each` method that executes the code for each element of the selection, setting `data` accordingly each time.

```
var svgContainer = d3.select(this).selectAll('svg.scatterplot').data([data])
svgContainer.enter().append('svg').attr('class', 'scatterplot')

svgContainer
  .attr('width', options.width)
  .attr('height', options.height)
```

One constraint that you have not encountered before is that there is no way to know whether there already is a chart within this element. You can leverage the D3 selection mechanism to take care of that. By performing a data bind with an array of one element `[data]` you guarantee that you will create at most one `<svg>` within each selection element. This pattern is followed throughout to create or update every part of the visualization.

```
var pointSelection = pointContainer.selectAll('.point').data(data)
pointSelection.enter().append('circle').attr('class', 'point')
  .attr('r', 2.5)

pointSelection
  .attr('cx', function(d) { return xScale(options.x(d)) })
  .attr('cy', function(d) { return yScale(options.y(d)) })

pointSelection.exit().remove()
```

The points are created or updated as before. You use the x and y getters within `options` to extract the x and y dimensions of the data.

```
Object.keys(options).forEach(function(optionName) {
  render[optionName] = function(value) {
    if (!arguments.length) return options[optionName]
    options[optionName] = value
    return render
  }
})
```

You take the `options` and create getter/setter functions for every key in it. When called without a parameter `!arguments.length` evaluates to true and the option value is returned. Otherwise, the parameter is set as the value of the option `options[optionName] = value` and the `render` function is returned, which allows for method chaining. This creates an application programming interface (API) that is consistent with the built-in D3 helper functions.

```
return render
```

The `render` function is returned to the caller. The `render` function forms a closure over the `options` variable, which allows the render function to refer to the options whenever the function is called. The chart can now maintain its own parameterization.

```css
svg.scatterplot {
  font: 12px sans-serif;
}

svg.scatterplot .axis path,
svg.scatterplot .axis line {
  fill: none;
  stroke: black;
  shape-rendering: crispEdges;
}

svg.scatterplot .point {
  fill: #F3F3F3;
  stroke: #333333;
}
```

You can find the preceding code in the `examples/scatterplot-reuse/scatterplot.css` file on the companion website.

Finally, you should define some default style sheet for the cart. You could have placed all the styles inline, but that would have made the chart much less amenable to styling by the end user.

This example is purposefully made very simple. In practice, you might want to extend the capabilities of the scatterplot with the following:

➤ Ability for the user to define the point size

➤ An option to color the dots by a categorical dimension

➤ An option to use different symbols to express a categorical dimension (look up the `d3.svg.symbol()` helper function)

➤ Ability to add transitions to the chart; note that a key function needs to be supplied (See the "Key Functions" section in Chapter 11)

All of the preceding possibilities are great exercises to hone and test your D3 skills.

SUMMARY

This chapter built on the information in Chapter 11 and showed you some more advanced techniques for creating great visualizations:

➤ You learned the considerations of separating style from visualization logic.

➤ You learned about the D3 margin convention that enables you to leave room for other necessities, such as axes and legends.

➤ You learned how groups (`<g>`) can be used to enforce render ordering in a complex, multi-element visualization.

➤ You learned about some useful yet lesser known CSS properties, such as `pointer-events` and `crisp-edges`, that allow your visualization to look and function at its best.

➤ You learned about the D3 helper functions for creating complete axes.

➤ You saw how easy it is to build a basic scatterplot chart by utilizing built-in helper functions.

➤ You saw how the Voronoi layout can be used to divide the space between a given number of points.

➤ You learned about SVG's `<clipPath>` element.

➤ You learned how to implement an advanced hover behavior by utilizing the Voronoi layout.

➤ You have seen how to convert one-off visualizations into reusable, modular, data-schema-agnostic components.

INDEX